Illusions of Wealth

Doug Eberhardt

ISBN 978-0982586167

Dedicated to Weenter

I would like to thank the many people who have helped form my opinions about the markets over the years, from my parents who have continually provided me with materials on investments from a young age to the bulletin board group at Richard Russell's Dow Theory Letters and Richard Russell himself where I learned there is more to investing than what you learn in textbooks or even in the financial services industry, and to the many I have engaged in conversations with over the years who opened my eyes to points of view I hadn't considered allowing me to formulate the concepts for this book.

I would like to especially thank Chris Furman for his support and dedication in allowing me the time to finish this book. A Godsend indeed.

DISCLAIMER

EVERY EFFORT HAS BEEN MADE TO ACCURATELY REPRESENT THIS PRODUCT AND SERVICES OFFERED, AND ITS POTENTIAL. THERE IS NO GUARANTEE THAT YOU WILL EARN ANY MONEY USING THE TECHNIQUES AND IDEAS IN THIS BOOK. EXAMPLES IN THE BOOK ARE NOT TO BE INTERPRETED AS A PROMISE OR GUARANTEE OF EARNINGS. EARNING POTENTIAL IS ENTIRELY DEPENDENT ON THE PERSON USING THE INFORMATION INCLUDED TO THE BOOK AND THE IDEAS AND THE TECHNIQUES. WE DO NOT PURPORT THIS AS A GET RICH SCHEME. YOUR LEVEL OF SUCCESS IN ATTAINING THE RESULTS IN THIS BOOK DEPENDS ON THE TIME YOU DEVOTE TO THE IDEAS AND TECHNIQUES MENTIONED, YOUR FINANCES, KNOWLEDGE AND VARIOUS SKILLS. SINCE THESE FACTORS DIFFER ACCORDING TO INDIVIDUALS, WE CANNOT GUARANTEE YOUR SUCCESS OR PROFIT LEVEL. NOR ARE WE RESPONSIBLE FOR ANY OF YOUR ACTIONS. MATERIALS IN THIS BOOK MAY CONTAIN INFORMATION THAT INCLUDES FORWARD-LOOKING STATEMENTS THAT GIVE OUR EXPECTATIONS OR FORECASTS OF FUTURE EVENTS. YOU CAN IDENTIFY THESE STATEMENTS BY THE FACT THAT THEY DO NOT RELATE STRICTLY TO HISTORICAL OR CURRENT FACTS. THEY USE WORDS SUCH AS ANTICIPATE, ESTIMATE, EXPECT, PROJECT, INTEND, PLAN, BELIEVE, AND OTHER WORDS AND TERMS OF SIMILAR MEANING IN CONNECTION WITH A DESCRIPTION OF POTENTIAL EARNINGS OR FINANCIAL PERFORMANCE. ANY AND ALL FORWARD LOOKING STATEMENTS IN THIS BOOK ARE INTENDED TO EXPRESS OUR OPINION OF EARNINGS POTENTIAL OR PROFIT POTENTIAL. MANY FACTORS WILL BE IMPORTANT IN DETERMINING YOUR ACTUAL RESULTS AND NO GUARANTEES ARE MADE THAT YOU WILL ACHIEVE RESULTS SIMILAR TO OURS OR ANYBODY ELSE'S, IN FACT NO GUARANTEES ARE MADE THAT YOU WILL ACHIEVE ANY RESULTS FROM OUR IDEAS AND TECHNIQUES IN OUR MATERIALS AT ALL.

Table of Contents

Introduction

"All wealth derives from knowledge." George Gilder, author, *Knowledge and Power*

There are basically three types of wealth: income from employment, assets (real estate, stocks, bonds, mutual funds, CDs, annuities, and the interest these provide), and inherited, which can be most any asset and can include business interests. Whether it is wealth you have accumulated over the years, or newly found wealth from a loved one passing away, your goal is the same: to hold on to it, but also to invest wisely and have it grow.

The one thing the 2007–2009 financial crisis taught us is that stocks, bonds, mutual funds, hedge funds, real estate, and commodities like oil and gold are all illusions of wealth until you do one thing: lock in profit. Most financial advisors, economists, and those at the Federal Reserve didn't see the last crisis coming. The lesson to be learned by investors is that until they convert their wealth to cash or another asset, locking in profit, the value of each asset can and will swing wildly, depending on where it is in its investment cycle. Even the U.S. dollar's value swings wildly. Can you predict any future black swan event that could erase much of the wealth you've accumulated? This book will help you forecast what's to come, good or bad.

What are the economic conditions on the horizon that can affect your wealth? Why do you invest the way you do? Is it because someone told you to invest that way? Who do you trust for investment advice, and why? Are they any good? How much do they make from their recommendations to you? Did they protect your portfolio during the last financial crisis? Is another financial crisis around the corner? How have you structured your portfolio differently to protect your wealth if we were to experience another economic downturn?

This book will address many weaknesses we have as investors, one of the most important being that our educational system simply doesn't instruct us on how to invest, let alone keep and grow wealth. So we either count on financial advisors, insurance agents, and money managers or we're left to our own devices—if we are lucky enough to have the time to do the necessary research.

What you'll gain after reading this book is an awareness that fills the void in our education, and the means to develop insight into how to best manage your wealth without worry, giving you more control of the decision making, rather than leaving it in the hands of someone you may trust, but who may not really understand the big picture. It will help you choose the right advisors to manage your wealth, or measure how equipped you are to manage your own wealth by going it alone—and saving the fees and commissions.

To obtain a full understanding of investing, we first must look at a history of our monetary system that is never taught in schools or discussed publicly. We'll next get into an economic discussion that will give you the basic data you need to know to predict what those who run our financial system have in store, so you can arrange your assets accordingly.

Then we'll take a look at the banking system in the U.S., explaining how we got to where we are and, what to expect next. We've seen *The Big Short*, but are we in the process of a *Big Short Part II*? Will banks once again need to be bailed out? Was the Dodd-Frank Wall Street Reform and Consumer Protection Act *really* about safeguarding consumers?

An analysis of the Federal Reserve System is included in this book, as it seems financial media outlets such as CNBC have advised investors to follow the Fed, from analyzing the size of Alan Greenspan's briefcase since 1998, or speculating on whether or not the Fed will raise interest rates through December 2015—when that finally happened, leading to the worst stock market open ever, in 2016. CNBC said the Fed chickened out in September 2015 by not raising rates and when they finally did raise rates, which I had predicted was a one-and-done "credibility" increase, look what happened. Be careful what you wish for without fully understanding the consequences.

Is this really what investment advice has come to in this day and age, relying on what the Fed may or may not do with interest rates, rather than studying valuations or applying accounting ratios to a company's balance sheet?

We'll then dive into the main reason investors bought this book and that's advice on what to do with your wealth. Investing has become more and more difficult, with so many choices available today, and the Investment chapter provides you with a complete analysis of how conservative investors can turn a maze of options into a straightforward path to keeping and growing their wealth. But in order to keep this wealth from being an illusion, you must possess the ability to adjust your portfolio as the economic climate changes. Buy and hold can work with some assets, but it should not be the way forward for all of them. Applying the common sense of this book can grant you control of your future and your wealth.

Some of you may wish to skip over the history, economic, Fed and banking sections and I understand this. It's not for everyone. But I feel this foundation is important to your investment success.

When you've gained the necessary knowledge about investing after reading this book, I hope to see success story after success story. I want to see fees and commissions go to *your* investment account, not your advisor's—although I do recommend a good advisor for those who can't or don't want to take the time to go it alone. There is nothing wrong with doing what you love and leaving the management of your wealth to professionals. You'll be able to interview many advisors and choose the right one for you with the criteria I have set forth.

Why should I trust you, Doug Eberhardt, to advise me on what to do with my investments?

My background: I have 30 years' experience in the investment business. I started out after college in the insurance industry, and learned it well. I got a taste of investments when the insurance business expanded into investments in the 1980s, and decided I wanted to be there instead. I learned from my years in these industries that people buy from me, the individual, not the company I work for, and went out on my own early, as it gave me more flexibility in providing solutions for investors. I became a Certified Specialist in Planned Giving because I wanted to help clients with giving away their wealth, and decided I also wanted to become a Certified Financial Planner (CFP).

It was in 2002 that I started reading Richard Russell, writer of *Dow Theory Letters*, which had a forum where I could communicate with people from all over the world. It was through that forum, and reading Russell's thoughts on the markets and his understanding of gold as an investment, that I began to get my real education on money and investing. I discovered Austrian economics, which was different theory from what our schools teach, and started to think outside the box more as to why we as investors invest the way we do. I spent three years diving into all I could learn about the economy, and how it fits with what I had learned the previous 15 years in the financial services industry.

I bought all the CFP books to rush through and get my designation quickly—as I knew having credentials was expected in the financial services industry—because I wanted to find my own niche in selling gold as an asset that investors needed to buoy their portfolio. I wanted to be the go-to gold guy.

I started my CFP studies with the investment book in 2005. In reading through it, I got to the section on gold, and since I had my own understanding from my research into gold, I knew a lot about the precious metal... but was extremely disappointed by what the author of this book had to say about precious metals. I turned that discouragement into a passion. I wanted to set the investment world straight on gold, but I needed to have a book under my belt to do so. I decided in 2006 to learn even more about the precious metals industry, and worked for a gold dealer to get insider information, as eventually I wanted to start my own company. I did that for six months, learned how the industry worked, and decided it was time to write my book.

When I set out to write a book in mid-2006, I had accumulated a lot of reading material, as I had not yet discovered Google. I decided to take on the bigger picture by not only writing a book about gold—I became obsessed with changing America for the better, as a result of the red flags I kept seeing pop up with our government. This was just before the 2007–2009 financial crisis. I spent the next three years researching this book and a political book called *We the Serfs!*, but when I saw the price of gold begin to creep higher, I knew I had to get a precious metals book out to the public to help them invest.

I wrote the book *Buy Gold and Silver Safely* in 2010, and started my precious metals company the same year. Congress actually wanted me to testify at the September 2010 gold hearings, as I'd exposed most of the industry as a high-commission scam in Chapter 8 of that book. I was in touch with Rep. Anthony Weiner's office—they liked my book, said that "everyone needs to read it," and sent it off to the Energy and Commerce Department for review to see if they could use my testimony for an upcoming September hearing on the industry. The department, Weiner's office told me, decided against my testimony and the main reason was… a well-deserved critique of Congress included in the book.

From 2010 on, I continued working on *We the Serfs!*, as the red flags I originally saw were still there—and getting worse. But during this time, I also decided I needed to get a book out to the 99% of America that really doesn't know anything about investing. This is how *Illusions of Wealth* was born. After a few years of work, it is now available for all to see what I see—and if they agree with what I see, to act accordingly to protect and grow their wealth.

Having a background in investments, insurance and now precious metals, as well as starting my own Leveraged ETF Trading Service, has given me the opportunity to now share my years of research and discovery with you. I don't have a hidden agenda, as my businesses offer me self-sufficiency and will grow on their own. I do think you can take what is written here and go it alone if you choose to. The feeling of freedom that taking control of your wealth offers is like no other. But you need the intellectual foundation, which I think this book provides. What you do with your wealth once you feel confident about keeping it is up to you, but it will no longer be an illusion. It will be real, and the only thing I ask is that you give back in following your passion, passing on your wealth to those areas you care about most, and make a difference in this world.

On a side note, I am the only gold dealer in the U.S. the last few years who kept warning investors about buying gold and silver, as I was dollar bullish. I am overall extremely bullish on precious metals and have been recommending a dollar-cost-average approach to investing in them. One thing you will see is that I do my own research, which has helped me call the precious metals market better than anyone. I am trying, as I said, to bring this awareness to you. Just as I publicly provided in my articles the 8 indicators that told me where gold will go next, this book will tell you where your investments will go next—if you apply what you learn here.

As people live longer and longer it is more important today than ever to keep as much of your wealth as possible, and to make the extra effort to understand how to grow it. You can read magazines that all give the same buy-and-hold advice, or tell you about the latest hot investment, only to have that investment reverse course by the time you buy it. Or, you can presuppose what that next hot investment is by putting the pieces of the economic and investment puzzle together yourself. That insight is what this book provides.

Can a single book transform your investment life? I think it can. One way to look at this book is how you look at a cow and milk. The cow is the wealth, as it produces the milk. This book is the wealth, as it produces you—a better investor.

PART 1 – Understanding Money

Chapter 1 - Our Monetary System: How We Got to Where We Are Today

In this chapter, you will learn some things that many aren't aware of. In bringing this information to the forefront of your understanding of money and investments, my intent is not so much to claim we have a faulty monetary system here in America, but to explain that those who have managed it over the years haven't exactly been doing a good job in maintaining its health—some cracks are forming that you need to be aware of. To grasp these issues, we must begin with some history of our monetary system. Some may want to skip this section, but this is the type of information you won't learn in school, no matter how many years you attend.

A Little History of Money

China used paper money in the 10th century, seven centuries before the concept was brought over to the West by Marco Polo.[1] The Chinese government took over the country's monetary system in the 12th century, providing us with the world's first government-issued paper money.[2] The image that follows is the earliest example of paper currency—from 1375 CE during the Ming Dynasty—that survives today.[3]

[1] https://archive.org/stream/bookofsermarcopo01polo#page/n7/mode/2up
[2] http://afe.easia.columbia.edu/song/econ/money.htm
[3] https://archive.org/stream/bookofsermarcopo01polo#page/378/mode/2up/search/xxIV

BANK-NOTE OF THE MING DYNASTY.
(Half the Length and Breadth of the Original)

It was this act of control that allowed the government to confiscate citizens' wealth for the first time, as explained in 1871's *The Book of Marco Polo*:

> *Several times in the year a proclamation is made through the city that anyone who may have gold or silver or gems or pearls, by taking them to the Mint shall get a handsome price for them. And the owners are glad to do this, because they would find no other purchaser give so large a price. Thus the quantity they bring in is marvelous, though these who do not choose to do so may let it alone. Still, in this way, nearly all the valuables in the country come into the Kaan's (Great Kaan of the Mongol Empire 1260– 1294) possession.*[4]

In the 17th century, paper money arrived in Europe. In 1633, we saw the first goldsmith certificates transformed from receipts for individuals who stored gold with the goldsmith to certificates (money) circulated among individuals who viewed them "as good as gold." The recipients knew they could exchange that receipt for gold at any point in time.

It was only when some tried to collect their gold that it was learned the goldsmiths were offering more certificates to people than there was gold in the vault, and the system collapsed.

Fast-Forward to Today's Monetary System

We have indeed flourished under the current U.S. monetary system like no other country before, but at what cost? The purpose of this book is to show how all your investments are based on faith in our monetary system. If there are cracks in the system, you need to know about them. Just like the crack in a dam that starts off small, if it is not patched up to prevent it from becoming bigger, disaster will inevitably follow. But the patch job eventually begins to crack—and you'll be able to decipher after reading this book just where we are with the issues of our monetary system, the patching that's been conducted by the Federal Reserve and our government, and whether or not you should adjust your portfolio according to the evidence presented.

---

[4] https://archive.org/stream/bookofsermarcopo01polo#page/380/mode/2up/search/proclamation

An awareness of these issues is your foundational basis for making good investment decisions.

In describing what's going on today, I want to emphasize that many in the media throw those who speak about our monetary system into some sort of conspiracy camp to discredit them. I would like you to think of this quote while reading the rest of this chapter, to keep things in perspective. It comes straight from Congress, and was written in 1964:

> *The manufacturers of money possess immense power which, if properly used, can work in the public interest. But the same power, if abused, can be greatly detrimental to national welfare. The power has been abused, and reforms are needed to promote the public interest." Aug. 5, 1964 Subcommittee on Domestic Finance – Committee on Banking and Finance, 88th Congress, 2nd Session, Congressman Wright Patman, Chairman: "A Primer On Money.*[5]

It is in this "public interest" that I have begun this chapter.

A Sound Monetary System?

All we want in America is a sound monetary system so we can earn our pay, take care of our families, buy our things, retire, and live happily ever after. What could go wrong? Even with the best intentions, the best advisors, and a conservative portfolio, those who manage our monetary system can take those dreams of being a good provider, getting to the point of retirement, and living your dreams and turn them upside down. Let's analyze this system and see what the government and Federal Reserve have done to our money, and whether there may be cause for concern moving forward.

---

[5] http://www.devvy.com/pdf/2006_October/Patman_Primer_on_Money.pdf

Chapter 2 - What Is a Dollar or Federal Reserve Note, and What Backs Our Money?

If you were to ask 10 people this question, you will get 10 different answers as to what a dollar or Federal Reserve Note really is and what backs it. Some of the hardcore Constitutionalists will say it is a certain weight of silver. But most will agree that a dollar is that piece of paper in your wallet, otherwise known as a Federal Reserve Note. It is one of the most searched-for questions I see via Google search when people come to my website and an article I wrote asking this question a few years back.

The place to find the answer to this question comes directly from the Department of the Treasury website where they provide an answer:

> *Federal Reserve notes are not redeemable in gold, silver or any other commodity, and receive no backing by anything. This has been the case since 1933. The notes have no value for themselves, but for what they will buy. In another sense, because they are legal tender, Federal Reserve notes are "backed" by all the goods and services in the economy.*[6]

What they are essentially saying is that our economy is what backs our money. If this is true, then we need to analyze what's going on in the economy to get an idea of how strong the dollar is, which is what we will do in Part 2, Understanding Economics.

You pull dollar bills out of your wallet, you buy things, you check your accounts and you see you have money and you go about your day with complete trust your money will be there tomorrow. But did you know that your money has changed over time? Did you know what really backs your money a century ago versus now?

---

[6] http://www.treasury.gov/resource-center/faqs/currency/pages/legal-tender.aspx

> *It has been traditional for bankers and other private managers of money to cloak the working of the money system with the mantle of secrecy. And many of our high public officials share this view. Although they are appointed to represent the public interest they seem to feel that it would be somehow dangerous to talk about the monetary system in ways that let the public understand who does what, and why. ("A Primer On Money.")*

Federal Reserve Notes (what we in America refer to as dollars) come in denominations of $1, $2, $5, $10, $20, $50 and $100 bills. In the past we have also had $500, $1,000, $5,000 and the non-circulated $100,000 bill. While you might be able to say you know which president is pictured on each of these notes, the odds of you knowing the text above and below those presidential portraits and how those words have changed over time are probably quite slim. Pull out a bill now and follow along.

Gold Certificates

The $10 bill that was in existence after the Federal Reserve was created in 1913, and through to 1933, was actually called a Gold Certificate, and had the following inscribed:

"This Certificate is a legal tender in the amount thereof in payment of all debts and dues public and private" and "This certifies that there have been deposited in the treasury of the United States of America Ten Dollars in gold coin payable to the bearer on demand."

Legal Tender and Confiscation

What is "legal tender?" Legal tender is money that the U.S. government declares usable for payment of taxes and debt, both public and private.

By the time 1933 rolled around, there had been a run on the banks and people were rushing to either exchange their paper money for real gold or simply withdraw it, as they didn't trust the banks. President Franklin D. Roosevelt had to do something to stop the bank depositors from exchanging their bills for gold and declared a bank holiday, as over 10,000 banks had failed. He then passed Executive Order 6102 to have the citizens turn in their gold coins in exchange for equivalent bills, mostly $10 and $20 to correlate to the most popular $10 Eagle and $20 Double Eagle gold coins in existence at that time. It is of note that Roosevelt did this without authorization from Congress, and the money used to buy all the gold was created through the Federal Reserve and the U.S. Mint out of thin air.

In 1934, upon getting all the gold from the fine citizens of the United States—who simply did what their government told them to do and turned it in—FDR raised the value of gold from $20.67 an ounce to $35 an ounce. By default, everyone who received those newly printed Federal Reserve Notes saw their purchasing power compared to gold decrease by 75%, a huge windfall for the U.S. government.

At the same time, what was printed below the portrait of the president on the 1934 Federal Reserve Note changed, too.

The new notes now said this:

> *"This note is legal tender for all debts, public and private, and is redeemable in lawful money at the United States Treasury, or at any Federal Reserve Bank"*
>
> and
>
> *"Will pay to the bearer on demand ten dollars."*

The note was still legal tender, yet was no longer redeemable in gold coin,[7] but instead "lawful money," which most citizens presumed of course to be gold, even though they couldn't exchange the bills for gold. But governments still traded currency for gold amongst themselves.

---

[7] http://www.federalreserve.gov/faqs/currency_12770.htm

Current **FAQs**

Informing the public about the Federal Reserve

Is U.S. currency still backed by gold?

Federal Reserve notes are not redeemable in gold, silver, or any other commodity. Federal Reserve notes have not been redeemable in gold since January 30, 1934, when the Congress amended Section 16 of the Federal Reserve Act to read: "The said [Federal Reserve] notes shall be obligations of the United States.... They shall be redeemed **in lawful money** on demand at the Treasury Department of the United States, in the city of Washington, District of Columbia, or at any Federal Reserve bank." Federal Reserve notes have not been redeemable in silver since the 1960s.

The Congress has specified that Federal Reserve Banks must hold collateral equal in value to the Federal Reserve notes that the Federal Reserve Bank puts in to circulation. This collateral is chiefly held in the form of U.S. Treasury, federal agency, and government-sponsored enterprise securities.

The Federal Reserve Notes didn't change again until President Richard M. Nixon, due to demands by foreign countries to exchange Federal Reserve Notes for U.S. gold, saw that some countries were trying to redeem their notes for physical gold. There were simply too many dollars floating around and the chickens were coming home to roost back here in America. Nixon had a choice: Give away all our gold, or just say no to redemption. Nixon closed the gold exchange window completely in 1971.

The Federal Reserve Notes you hold in your wallet since 1971 were changed to now simply say:

> *"This note is legal tender for all debts, public and private"* and *"Ten Dollars."*

These new notes didn't even say they were redeemable in *dollars* any longer!

This Is What a Dollar Is

In addition to all the issues mentioned in this chapter, there is one more aspect to the dollar that most in the investment world don't understand… but you need to. This is also not taught in schools, and the majority of people in the financial world are clueless about it. The following is what the dollar represents when you hear the media talk about the dollar. It is a representation of 6 currencies.

US Dollar Index (USD)

Delayed 30 minutes

The U.S. Dollar Index® is computed using a trade-weighted geometric average of six currencies. The six currencies and their trade weights are:

Euro	57.6 %
Japan/yen	13.6 %
UK/pound	11.9 %
Canada/dollar	9.1 %
Sweden/krona	4.2 %
Switzerland/franc	3.6 %

Whatever these currencies do, the dollar will do the opposite. The Dollar Index is heavily weighted towards the Euro (57.6%). Whatever the Euro does, the dollar will more than likely do the reverse.

Next up is a long-term chart of the Dollar Index. You will see a number that coordinates with the index. Presently it is 99.01. This is the number that represents that basket of currencies in the preceding table, and shows you the overall strength or weakness the dollar has when priced in these other currencies. We hear terms like "strong" and "weak" dollar, but many don't know how volatile the dollar really is over time. It's really not the steady investment many think it is, because at times it buys more and other times less, as the following chart shows.[8] In and of itself, the dollar loses purchasing power over time.

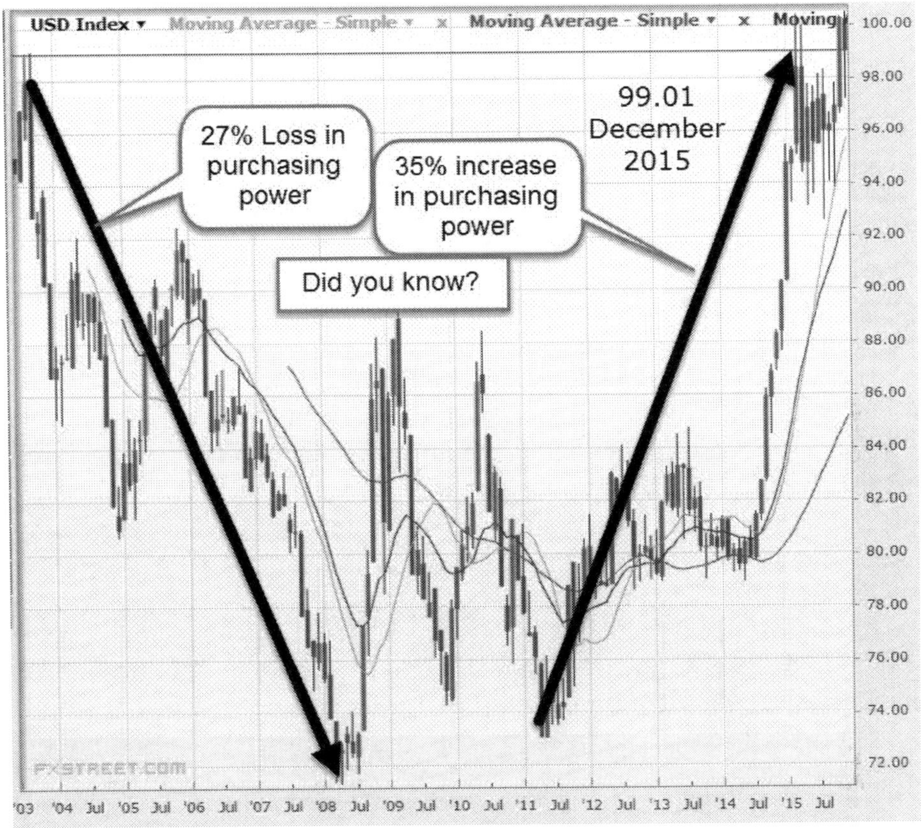

[8] **http://www.fxstreet.com/rates-charts/usdollar-index/**

What's ironic is that you never see this figure on CNBC, Bloomberg or Fox Business Channel. You only see the euro/dollar, yen/dollar, and pound/dollar figures that most investors watching these shows—let alone the public in general—don't even understand the meaning of.

For example, CNBC will show the euro/dollar figure (1 euro=x dollars) and the pound/dollar figure (1 pound=x dollars) but in quoting prices for the Japanese currency, they reverse the equation to dollar/yen (1 yen=x dollars).

Don't you find it rather peculiar that the financial media don't tell Americans daily how the one asset our entire financial system is based on is doing overall, but just show its relationship to a few other currencies—even though most people have no idea what it really means?

We can clearly see from the chart that at times our dollar has been weak versus these six currencies, but presently it is stronger, despite all the issues I cover in the forthcoming Economics section. There is a reason for this, as you'll discover.

As an investor, you need to know this, as it helps you position your portfolio to protect it against any potential dollar decline. But the real illusion isn't in hiding dollar weakness from people. It's the fact that all currencies being priced in each other actually means something, because it takes more of every currency each year to buy things than it did 5, 10 or 20 years ago.

If you have the dollar on one side of a ship, and all these other currencies on the other side, and they run from one side of the ship to the opposite when priced in each other, what difference does that make when the entire currency ship is sinking? That's what inflation is, and it destroys a currency over time.

How do these currencies maintain purchasing power over time? This is what most economists, gurus, financial planners and Congress don't understand. It's the dirty little secret that no one wants anyone to discuss, and it's not conspiracy. Economist John Maynard Keynes spelled it out for all to see in 1919 in his book, *The Economic Consequences of the Peace*, just six years after the Federal Reserve was created:

Lenin is said to have declared that the best way to destroy the Capitalist System was to debauch the currency. By a continuing process of inflation, governments can confiscate, secretly and unobserved, an important part of the wealth of their citizens. By this method they not only confiscate, but they confiscate arbitrarily; and, while the process impoverishes many, it actually enriches some... Lenin was certainly right. There is no subtler, no surer means of overturning the existing basis of society than to debauch the currency. The process engages all the hidden forces of economic law on the side of destruction, and does it in a manner which not one man in a million is able to diagnose. [9]

You never hear the regular media talk about the dollar either, as they bombard you with the latest Hollywood gossip, news stories on racial divide or some murder case (and of course lately anything to do with ISIS and terrorism). You'll hear a few-second clip on what stocks or bonds did that day and maybe a story about a company that did something wrong—and that's the extent of nightly national coverage of investing. This leaves the few—and I truly mean few—of you, meaning the ones who actually bought this book, research the internet, buy books and magazines, and watch documentaries to find the truth.

This isn't even discussed in the Certified Financial Planners (CFP) books and it certainly isn't taught in the training an advisor sits through to get their licenses from the SEC and NASD.

---

[9] http://www.econlib.org/library/YPDBooks/Keynes/kynsCP6.html #Chapter 6

The three questions I propose you ponder at this point:

1. How much lower can the purchasing power of the dollar and other currencies get?

2. Who will tell me whether this can possibly get worse?

3. What can I do to protect the purchasing power of my portfolio?

These questions will be answered in this book, but first let's look at a brief history of coins in America, and further reveal what the government has done to our money.

U.S. Coinage

While Federal Reserve Notes have changed over time, so too has the coinage of America. We already know that gold coins were used until 1934, but silver, copper and nickel were also used as money. Pennies were made of 95% copper; nickels of copper and 25% nickel. And dimes and quarters were 90% silver.

This all changed in 1964, when they stopped minting 90% silver dimes and quarters and replaced them with coins made up of 91.67% copper and 8.33% nickel.

The mostly copper pennies were replaced with 97.5% zinc and now contain only 2.5% copper (Pennies made prior to 1982 are worth 2.7 cents each today.)

Money should have the characteristic of possessing a store of value.

Investopedia explains store of value:

> *Possessing a store of value is an underlying basis for any economic system, as some medium is necessary for a store of value in order for individuals to engage in the exchange of goods and services. As long as a currency is relatively stable in*

> *its value, money (such as a dollar bill) is the most common and efficient store of value found in an economy.*[10]

But does Investopedia have it correct? Are coins a good store of value?

In 2016, the same 1964 quarter with 90% silver mentioned earlier, exchanged for the scrip of the day (dollars), can buy you a gallon of gas. Guess what a 1965 quarter can buy you? You're right, 25 cents worth of gas. And that's what the government has done to our money.

While it is illegal to melt U.S. coins, it seems that some are doing this—upsetting U.S. Mint director Ed Moy, who said this could lead to shortages: "The nation needs its coinage for commerce," he said in a statement. "We don't want to see our pennies and nickels melted down so a few individuals can take advantage of the American taxpayer."[11]

> *Thy silver is become dross, thy wine mixed with water*—Isaiah 1:22

I find amusing claims that citizens taking current U.S. coins and melting them down would be taking advantage of American taxpayers, but hasn't the government been taking advantage of taxpayers by debasing the coins to begin with? Isn't it funny how the tables have turned on the government, just by playing their own game? But even the government's own Bureau of Engraving knew what the key ingredient in the monetary system was and still is today: "the public's willingness to accept it."

> *The Bureau prints approximately sixteen million notes each day. The Bureau has the power to create money and almost any amount of it. The only limiting factors are the speed of the presses, and the public's willingness to accept it*—Government Securities, U.S. Bureau of Engraving

---

[10] *http://www.investopedia.com/terms/s/storeofvalue.asp*

[11] http://usatoday30.usatoday.com/money/2006-12-14-melting-ban-usat_x.htm

What really puts this government action of debasement into perspective is the fact that our government still values the gold we possess in Fort Knox at $42.22 an ounce.[12]

Why in the world would they do that? In 1985, the U.S. government passed the Gold Bullion Coin Act, which for the first time authorized the U.S. Mint to create a gold coin called the American Eagle. What was the dollar amount they stamped on the one-ounce gold coin? The answer is $50. They did so knowing full well that the actual spot price of gold at the time was $322.25 per ounce.

These geniuses did one other peculiar thing in pricing the gold Eagle coins. They also came out with a ½-ounce coin with a face value of $25; a ¼-ounce coin with a face value of $10; and a 1/10-ounce coin with a face value of $5. Anyone notice what's wrong with the math here? Four of the ¼ ounce coins total $40 in value according to the government's math. They should have $12.50 stamped on them, not $10. You simply can't make this stuff up.

Does a Coinless Society Make Sense?

Since the government continually debases the value of coins, this leads to the question, "Are coins even needed now?" Please note that I am not advocating a cashless society here, but coins aren't silver or gold any longer, and thus have no real intrinsic value.

It may be hard to imagine doing away with coins, but the truth is that coins should be outlawed in the U.S. The days of getting Bazooka Joe gum for a penny or a candy bar for under $1 are long gone. The days are also gone taking your collected coins to Vegas and throwing them in a slot machine.

What do you do with your change when you accumulate so much of it? Do you wrap it up in sleeves and take it to the bank? How much time does it take to count, wrap and transport them? How much is your

---

[12] https://www.usmint.gov/about_the_mint/fun_facts/?action=fun_facts13

time worth per hour? Or are you one of those who are strapped for time, and just head to the grocery store's coin-counting machines and pay 5% to 10% to cash in? Do you *like* losing 10% on your money?

There's just no real use for coinage anymore, because it doesn't represent what it did when coins held their value. Whether it's pennies, nickels, dimes, or quarters, they all don't buy what they used to, so why bother with them? Why hold on to something when the government keeps changing its true value?

Money Today Is Simply Debt

One thing you should understand about money in general is that it's debt. In a sense, it is a promissory note that someone else has to eventually accept for you to acquire what you need. At some point, they may decide to no longer accept that note. While the U.S. is far from such a situation, we have seen these notes (or money) rejected throughout the history of mankind from the German mark of WWI (which had lasted 53 years), the Argentine peso of 1983, 1985 and 1992, the Zimbabwe dollar of 2006 (pictured), the Peruvian sol of 1985 that had endured for 122 years, and the 170-year-old Mexico silver peso.

Zimbabwe 100 trillion-dollar note

I bought 300 of the 100 trillion Zimbabwe notes on eBay when I heard they stopped printing them after becoming worthless in Zimbabwe, because I figured they might become a collector's item. I paid $1 each for them and sold them a few years later for $10 each. They are worth much more now. But you should know this is the exception to the rule on worthless money—we had never seen a 100 trillion note before. You will find them today on eBay though for over $35 each.

The amazing aspect to all currencies is the average lifespan is 37 years. Let that sink in for a second. Most people reading this book will have lived through half the world's currencies going under at one point or another.

The U.S. dollar in its current form was first created in 1913, but since Nixon took us off the gold standard in 1971, this new version of the Federal Reserve Note only does one thing: accumulate more debt to back it. What does more debt eventually do to a currency? It erodes the trust in it. This is why you want some protection or insurance for your portfolio, whether or not the currency fails. Whether it be paper money, plastic money like credit cards or digital money, it's all faith based and there is a matter of trust involved.[13]

Are We Moving to a Cashless Society?

In 1934, just after the government had confiscated the gold and handed out Federal Reserve Notes that they immediately devalued, the board game Monopoly from Parker Brothers (now Hasbro) came out. What most don't know about this game is one of the rules actually states; *The Bank never "goes broke." If the Bank runs out of money, the Banker may issue as much more as may be needed by writing on any ordinary paper.*[14]

This is what the Federal Reserve does, through the U.S. Mint and with the blessing of congress.

It is no secret that gold has been the enemy of the fiat printers of money and they have done a good job of eliminating gold's connection

---

[13] http://www.rapidtrends.com/history-of-fiat-and-paper-money-failures/

[14] http://www.hasbro.com/common/instruct/monins.pdf

as money over the years. Now it seems that some want to do away with some of our cash that we carry around like the $100 bill.

Former treasury secretary and Harvard professor Lawrence H. Summers wants to do away with high-denomination bills completely[15]—in the best interests of ordinary citizens, he tells us—because of their links to crime, primarily drugs (and of course terrorism). Perhaps the government should stay out of funding drug running[16] and terrorism,[17] themselves as a start.

As a child you may have got used to the game Monopoly and using your Monopoly money, which many have compared to Federal Reserve Notes, as your way to buy real estate like Boardwalk or Park Place. Did you know that they have come out with a version of the Monopoly game that is cashless? It is called the Ultimate Banking edition and it does all the arithmetic for the players. But Monopoly is behind the times as many countries around the world are already becoming cashless.

These are the leaders in cashless consumer spending, and their percentage of financial transactions. We're already getting there in the U.S. and most don't even know it.

Belgium 93%
France 92%
Canada 90%
United Kingdom 89%
Sweden 89%
Australia 86%
Netherlands 85%
United States 80%

---

15 https://www.washingtonpost.com/news/wonk/wp/2016/02/16/its-time-to-kill-the-100-bill/
16 https://en.wikipedia.org/wiki/Allegations_of_CIA_drug_trafficking
17 https://en.wikipedia.org/wiki/State-sponsored_terrorism#United_States

New World Currency

There is always talk of a new currency that may surface to replace the dollar. For example, some think the U.S., Canada and Mexico will band together and create a currency that would compete better with the euro, called the Amero. This is just a silly rumor. You will find out later in this book that the euro is having problems with some countries (like Greece, Spain and Italy) threatening its strength. It doesn't make sense for Canada or the U.S. to take on a country with a history of monetary failure and corruption, like Mexico. This simply won't happen.

As for anyone else replacing U.S. dollar as reserve currency… if they could, they would. China, for instance, has no credible bond infrastructure, lacks transparency, refuses to join the free-float foreign exchange market, and has the most overleveraged banking system in the world. The yuan does not have the capacity or credibility to become a reserve currency. At least not yet, but it is now included in the IMF's Strategic Drawing Rights basket (SDRs).

There are also rumors that at some point we may have a one-world currency. The speculation is that it would be run by the IMF via their SDRs, or possibly be a basket of the well-known producing economies of the world. Some say a new world currency might be backed by gold and come from China. Mike Maloney, of *Rich Dad, Poor Dad* fame, says that the "change to a new monetary system is inevitable."[18]

I disagree. A new world currency makes no sense, as it would automatically put countries that have weak economies at par with countries that have strong economies. If one country wanted to go to war with another, it would need to somehow fund the war and get permission from the printers of the currency to do so. Who would give up their sovereignty to another entity or group of individuals that control the monetary system, especially when they are already a world power?

---

[18] http://hiddensecretsofmoney.com/videos/episode-3

For any global currency to come to fruition, the U.S. dollar would have to fail. With the dollar still used by 60% to 70% of the world, this won't be happening anytime soon, especially when you also have the world's strongest military.

Lastly, it is true that all fiat currencies have indeed failed from a historical perspective, but we in the U.S. have shown that the world's largest economy can afford to have some major debt while at the same time deflecting attention away from calculating how serious of a problem this debt can become when interest rates rise. Even those in Congress don't think ahead more than a few years, as you'll see when we talk about debts and deficits—another foundational requisite to managing, growing and preserving your wealth—in the Economics section.

Cryptocurrency

Cryptocurrency, according to Investopedia, is a "digital or virtual currency that uses cryptography for security. A cryptocurrency is difficult to counterfeit because of this security feature. A defining feature of a cryptocurrency is that it is not issued by any central authority, rendering it theoretically immune to government interference or manipulation."[19]

Bitcoin is an example of one of these cryptocurrencies. Bitcoin has a limited supply—unlike Federal Reserve Notes—which make it attractive for many. It can be used for purchases of goods and services where accepted, just like cash or credit cards.

---

[19] http://www.investopedia.com/terms/c/cryptocurrency.asp

Coinbase[20]

The price of Bitcoin has fluctuated from the teens just a few years ago to over $1,100 in 2013. It has been known to swing wildly, with a range sometimes reaching over $300 in a day from high to low.[21]

---

[20] https://www.coinbase.com/charts

[21] http://ftalphaville.ft.com/tag/bitcoinmania/

This is Jean-Paul Rodrigue's stages of a bubble chart:

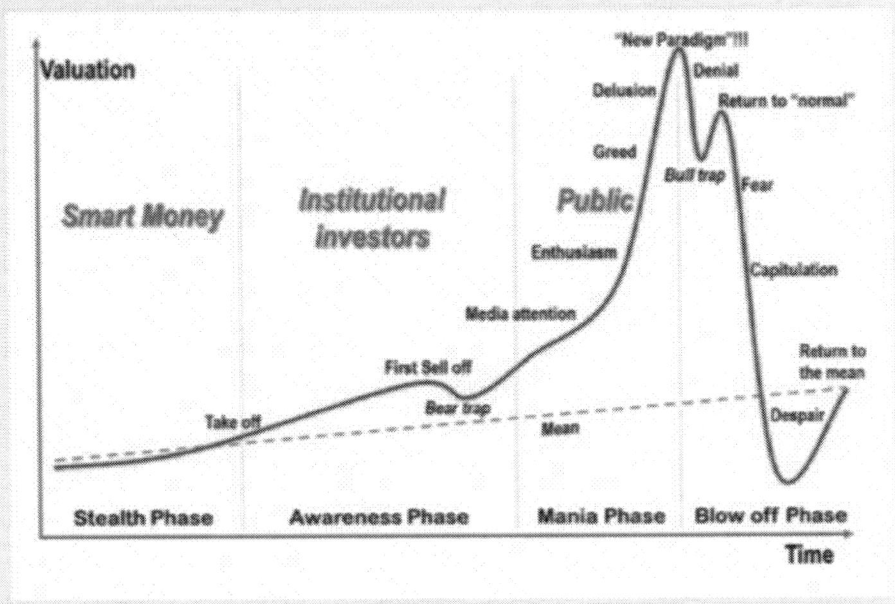

This is a chart of the price of Bitcoin from the BoE:

Chart 2 The price of bitcoins (linear scale)

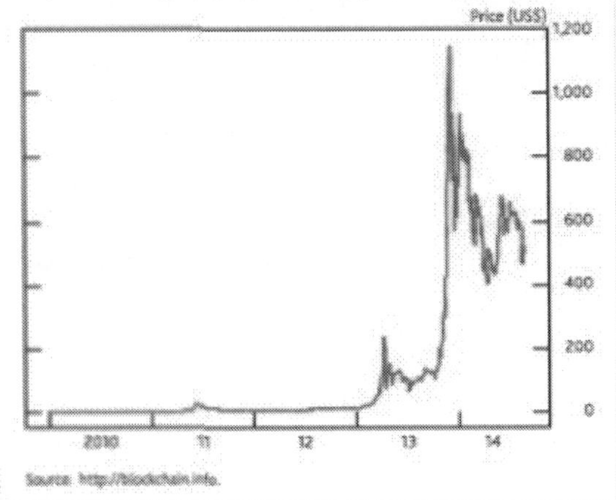

See any resemblance?

One can create an account and obtain Bitcoin on the open market through an exchange like Coinbase Bitcoin Exchange.[22] Businesses can also begin accepting payment in Bitcoin through this type of exchange.

The U.S. Department of the Treasury claims that digital currencies have real value, but we are still in the infancy stage, so naturally you can expect more legislation to come.

There are competitors to Bitcoin, such as Litecoin or Zerocoin, and rumor has it that J.P. Morgan and several other banks are partnering with financial tech firm R3 on verifying cryptocurrency transactions. "This partnership signals a significant commitment by the banks to collaboratively evaluate and apply this emerging technology to the global financial system," said R3 CEO David Rutter.[23] Why not? If you can get people to buy something you create out of basically nothing, then you have indeed sold them some magic beans!

Personally, I don't have a problem with competing currency, and I think all currencies should be taxed the same. Let the people choose what they want to use as money. But I don't see individuals getting paid salaries in Bitcoin anytime soon.

Sweden says they would give Bitcoin "the same tax treatment it would an antique Persian rug or a painting by Andy Warhol."[24]

The IRS taxes Bitcoin as property, not currency.[25] The U.S. already taxes gold at a higher rate, and that used to *be* money. The last thing the U.S. government wants is competition to Federal Reserve Notes.

---

22 https://exchange.coinbase.com/

23 http://www.idigitaltimes.com/bitcoin-exchange-jp-morgan-barclays-and-bbva-adopt-virtual-technology-477511

24 http://business.time.com/2014/01/22/here-comes-the-bitcoin-taxman/#ixzz2rAA2cVuz

25 http://time.com/37428/bitcoin-irs-property-virtual-currency/

The Russian government wants nothing to do with Bitcoin, and according to Coindesk.com, "the Ministry is working on a draft law that would seek to punish those converting cryptocurrncies like Bitcoin into the ruble, with up to four years in prison."[26]

Naturally, one of the reasons governments will want to ban Bitcoin is their claim that they can connect it to terrorist-funding activities. Perhaps they should ban the U.S. dollars Congress doles out too, but that's a story for another book.

Bitcoin is too new for anyone conservative to acquire, as our government has issues with its use thus far— $28 million worth of Bitcoin was seized by U.S. authorities after raiding an alleged criminal enterprise thought to be accepting Bitcoin in exchange for drugs.[27]

Regulators are also eyeing Bitcoin. In March of 2013, the U.S. Treasury declared that all firms that exchange or transfer virtual currencies will be considered "money service businesses" and be required to provide anti-money laundering policies.[28]

At the bottom of each article on *ftalphaville.ft.com/tag/bitcoinmania*, you'll see a section called BITCOINMANIA SERIES, which is a good place to do your homework and see what the latest scoop is on Bitcoin. There is also a book by Jeffrey Robinson called *BitCon: The Naked Truth About Bitcoin,* which I recommend reading before converting dollars to this type of currency.

Bitgold

I was going to write something about a company called Bitgold, which is intriguing to me, but evidently not yet ready for prime time as they

---

26 http://www.coindesk.com/russia-ban-bitcoin-not-blockchain/

27 http://techcrunch.com/2013/06/27/the-dea-seized-bitcoins-in-a-silk-road-drug-raid/

28 http://www.ft.com/intl/cms/s/0/b810157c-b651-11e2-93ba-00144feabdc0.html

didn't return my calls or emails. The concept is paying for transactions with a digital gold account, but just like we citizens don't know if the gold is in Fort Knox, it's difficult to trust the gold will be there for you—or at what cost—when you need it most.

The bottom line is that you need to do your due diligence, as with any investment.

It seems our government does want to transition to digital money through debit and credit cards, and it seems to be the wave of the future. It just may be finalized once we remove coinage from the system. Libertarian types may not like it, but it they haven't liked the fact that paper money took over for gold, either. The more control government has over the monetary system, the more control they have over most everything else. The question will become "How will they screw it up?"

Now you know what the government and Federal Reserve have done to your money. ***Your dollars aren't redeemable in gold, lawful money or even dollars any longer, but you can exchange them for other dollars. Your coins are cheap metal with a value stamped on them rather than a metal that clearly holds its purchasing power.***

Chapter 3 - Mocking Money

The Barackazillion

In trying to get an understanding about what people know about money in the U.S., I decided to create my own currency called the Barackazillion.[29] I approached members of the public and tried to convince them that a new currency had just been introduced in America. I explained to people that the Barackazillion was "as good as gold," since it had a picture of Fort Knox on it. The print on my bill read, "This note is for all debts where accepted," but of course did not say it was legal tender. It did say that Barackazillions were redeemable in more Barackazillions. Lastly I told them it was the world's strongest currency. Then handed it to them and challenged them to rip it in half. They couldn't, because it was made of Yupo[30] paper, which can't be torn.

Here's the Barackazillion:

29 http://barackazillion.com

30 http://yupousa.com/what-is-yupo/

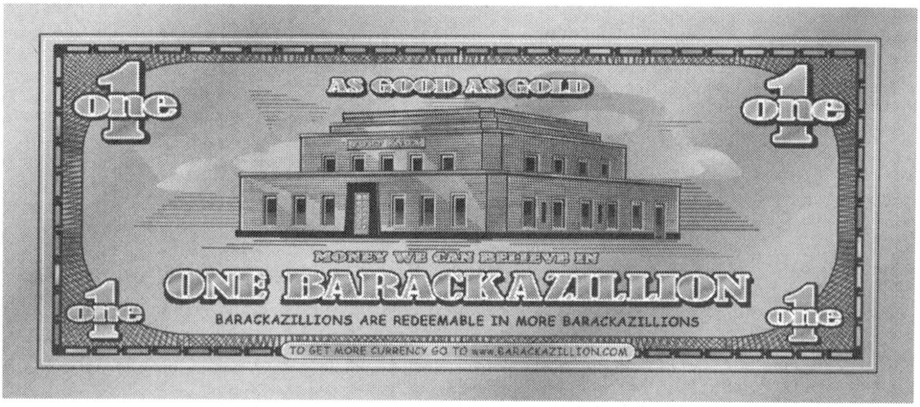

Naturally I was mocking our own Federal Reserve Notes, and for good reason, as you have seen how the Fed changes them over time. I did take it one step further and tried to pay for my taxi ride, and when I handed the driver a Barackazillion for an $8 fare, he asked, "What's this?" I explained that it was a new currency, and it was worth $10—so he could keep the change. He was actually going to do so, until unable to keep a straight face any longer, I told him I was just joking (I wouldn't do that to someone trying to earn an honest living).

My little experiment proved what I already predicted: People don't really know much about money. But it's not their fault. We could put any future or past president since the creation of the Federal Reserve in 1913 on a currency such as this except for Harding and Coolidge, who were the only presidents to give us a surplus rather than add to the national debt (not to be confused with reducing deficits). This will be true of any future president (left or right) as well, and I could use their name and add zillion to it, unless things are done to stop the spending madness of these leaders—and that includes making some hard decisions on what to cut that many won't be happy with, but will be cut one way or another with the path we are on. This is why I mock our currency with the Barackazillion and will continue to mock with each president who doesn't reverse this course.[31]

---

[31] http://useconomy.about.com/od/usdebtanddeficit/p/US-Debt-by-President.htm

PART 2 – Understanding Economics - Do Not Be Afraid

Chapter 4 - Keynesian vs. Austrian Economics

When you first took an economics class in high school or college, you were probably intimidated by what it all entails. The word "economics" alone might scare people away, or cause them to lose interest if the subject is brought up in discussion. But have our government schools taught us all we need to know to have a good, functioning and prosperous economy? If so, how the heck did we end up trillions in debt? It seems all the brightest economists in the U.S. can't guide Congress to balance a budget instead of simply kicking the can of debt down to the next generation. Before we get into what you should do with your money, it is important to know why you should invest the way this book recommends. An awareness of economics is the foundation of your investment success.

In this chapter, I'll do my best to make it less boring than your professors did. If you're new to economics, you'll find yourself light years ahead of the family members or friends at your next get-together. What I learned in college is nothing compared to what I learned through my own research *after* college. And even armed with this research, you probably won't find one economist who will agree on the best way to move forward.

For the most part, what we all learned in school was the theory of 1930s-era British economist John Maynard Keynes. What we *didn't* learn about was Austrian economics.

Rather than debate whose school of thought is superior, I propose that you look at the data, and let it tell you what's going to occur in the future. I don't need a fancy, drawn-out formula to do this, only common-sense thinking, something formulas don't offer.

John Maynard Keynes - Hero of Our Textbooks, the Fed, and Government

As we saw in the previous chapter, we Americans don't know much about our monetary system, and the same goes for economics. Our schools teach us mostly the Keynesian point of view. Keynesian economics is simply a philosophy dictating that if the economy is not producing, to stimulate it through government expenditures (congressional borrowing) that will make up the lag time until the economy is booming again.

This is exactly what we are seeing, with high budget deficits and increased national debt to the tune of trillions of dollars, along with quantitative easing (aka QE—central bank creating money by buying mortgage-backed securities and government treasury bonds) by the Federal Reserve. In a nutshell, the more money in the system, the more it will flow to those who will spend it, thus stimulating the economy.

What the Fed is fighting, even though they don't like mentioning the word, is deflation.

Former Fed chairman Ben Bernanke told us in his 2002 speech "Deflation: Making Sure 'It' Doesn't Happen Here" that the biggest mistake of the Great Depression was the government not doing enough to stimulate the economy, and the "depression" was a result of this lack of action by the Fed.[32] Bernanke used Milton Friedman's example of simply throwing money out of helicopters to get the economy going, and that's what the increased budget deficits, increasing national debt, and quantitative easing have tried to do.

In and of itself, this is actually true. If I gave you $10,000, your temptation would probably be to go out and spend this "found money" and live a little. This was and remains the hope of the Fed.

---

[32] http://www.federalreserve.gov/boarddocs/Speeches/2002/20021121/default.htm

But what happens when you don't spend the money, but instead hoard it?

Keynes' theory essentially is that "excessive saving, i.e. saving beyond planned investment, was a serious problem, encouraging recession or even depression. Excessive saving results if investment falls, perhaps due to falling consumer demand, over-investment in earlier years, or pessimistic business expectations, and if saving does not immediately fall in step, the economy would decline."[33]

The government and Fed naturally don't want this.

If money is not moving, the economy is not growing. How can the Fed reach a goal of 2% inflation when they can't get money moving in the economy? The answer is by adding more money to the economy, albeit covertly through quantitative easing, hoping for lower rates and more loan activity. Sounds pretty simple so far, right?

This is what the Fed had been doing since after the crisis with quantitative easing, in providing liquidity to the economy and lowering of interest rates. But their mistake was handing some of this money over to the banks and assuming the banks would loan more with the lower rates that resulted. Instead, the banks have shored up their own balance sheets and are happy with the small return they get on the money they hold with the Fed.

Wouldn't you love to be given a loan where you pay 1% interest, but can earn 2-3% with no risk?

This is exactly the favor the Fed granted to most of the financial industry and Wall Street in general during the last financial crisis. You'll see shortly that the trillions doled out to their favorite sons was not by accident. Michael Douglas' character Gordon Gekko had this to say in the movie *Wall Street: Money Never Sleeps*: "I tell you, the

---

[33] https://en.wikipedia.org/wiki/Keynesian_economics - Excessive_saving

government's worse than a wife. They got all the power, they got half the money. Now they're working on getting the other half."[34]

Well, Gordon, giving money to bankrupt corporations to shore up their balance sheets is Ponzi financing at its worst. Eventually more problems will arise (moral hazard) and these corporations will have their hands out begging for money again. Worse yet, the Fed will see that all the QE they have put into the economy isn't working, and add even more deficit spending as a solution.

In the 1930s, this resulted in the Great Depression. What our government should do is cut spending, taxes and unnecessary regulation; eliminate subsidies and tariffs; let housing do what it does naturally; stop interfering in the stock market; lower the tax on profits (capital gains) so more money can seep out into the economy; let prices and wages go where the markets take them; and put restrictions on what Congress can spend. If there is a recession, let it work itself out, hit bottom, and the cream will rise to the top. Don't interfere, like the Fed continually does with the blessing of the Congress that created it.

But this book isn't written to solve all the problems that we have today… it is about keeping and growing your wealth. My next book, *We the Serfs!* (which I have been working on for almost 10 years), will address those issues—I don't want to detract from the investment focus of this book. You can sign up to receive notice of the release of this book at www.wetheserfs.com/book.

It's not just quantitative easing that was implemented. Other industries fared well from government intervention as well: Cash for Clunkers helped the auto industry and incentives to buy real estate helped the real estate industry. In fact, the Economic Stimulus Act of 2008 that was supposed to give the economy a booster shot and give each taxpayer a $600 rebate to the tune of $120 billion did nothing to boost the economy and the financial crisis came anyway. Unfortunately it's deja vu all over again.[35]

---

[34] http://www.imdb.com/title/tt1027718/quotes

Liquidity Trap, Velocity of Money, Pushing on a String

All of the quantitative easing and other stimulus made the Fed believe that all was well. The unemployment rate was falling, and because the Fed thought the economy was on the right track, they began to taper and cut back on quantitative easing. But the banks still were hoarding, and the economy did not rebound.

Keynes described this action of stimulation as a "liquidity trap," where central bank injections into the private banking system fail to stimulate economic growth. All is not well with the economy, and you can see it in one simple chart that shows money velocity.

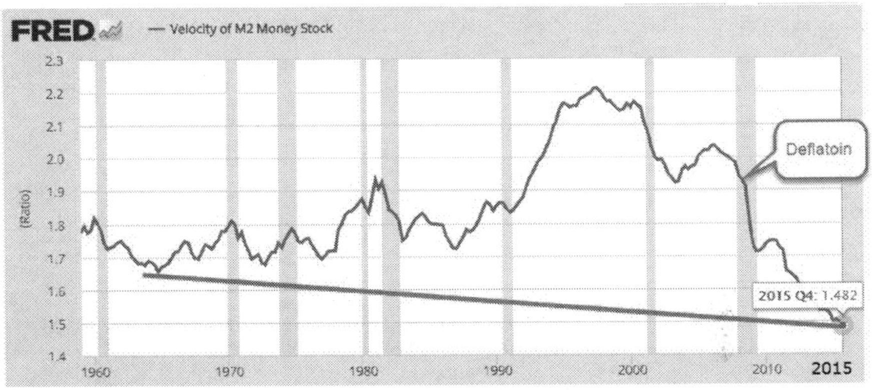

From the Fed:

> ***Declining Velocity***
>
> *The issue has to do with the velocity of money, which has never been constant, as can be seen in the figure above. If for some reason the money velocity declines rapidly during an expansionary monetary policy period, it can offset the increase in money supply and even lead to deflation instead of inflation.*[36]

---

[35] http://money.cnn.com/news/storysupplement/economy/bailouttracker/

As you can see, the attempts by the Federal Reserve, and Bernanke's solutions for fighting deflation, have failed miserably. It is in economic terms the equivalent of "pushing on a string," another phrase associated with Keynes. Monetary policy can't induce spending by consumers. If you simply produce things, it doesn't mean the consumer will buy, and it does not increase money velocity. The consumer may have more important things to do with their money, like be frugal for once, or save for a rainy day or retirement. Many consumers who lost money in the last financial crisis aren't the spenders they used to be, even if the money is sent to them by the government.

The original intent of "pushing on a string": Under present circumstances, there is very little, if anything, that can be done.[37] That's where the Fed and Congress are, and they don't like it.

It should be noted that money velocity is at a standstill, despite out-of-control growth in M2 and the monetary base.

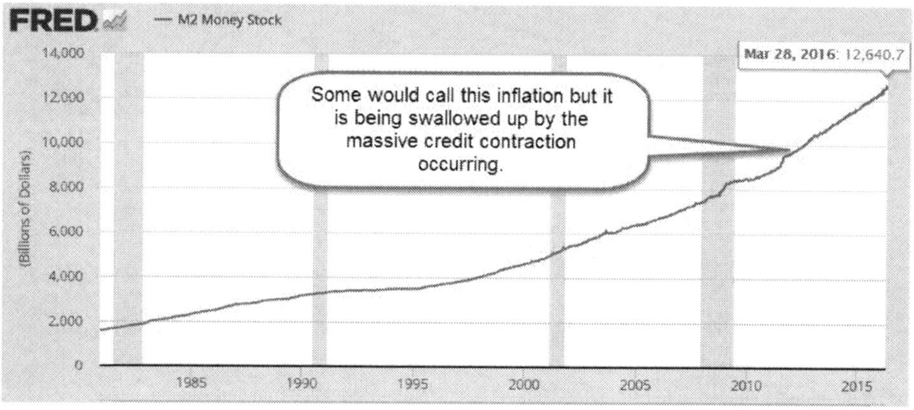

---

[36] https://www.stlouisfed.org/on-the-economy/2014/september/what-does-money-velocity-tell-us-about-low-inflation-in-the-us
[37] https://en.wikipedia.org/wiki/Pushing_on_a_string

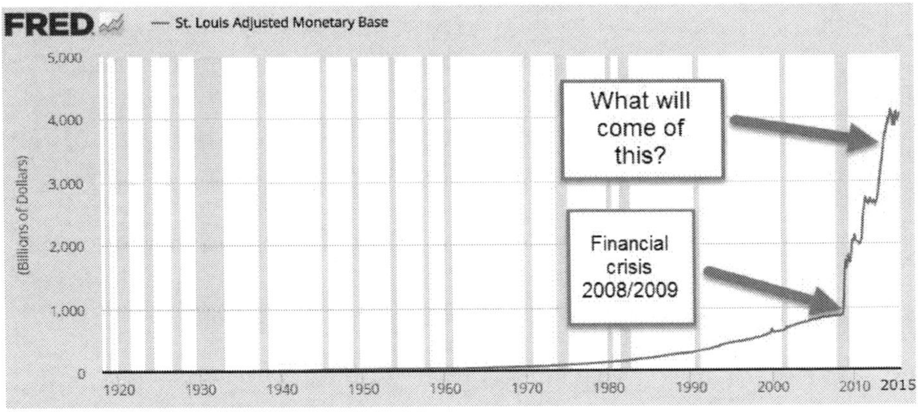

So far so good, but you'll have to bear with me for this next section.

The Monetary Base and the Fed

We'll go into more detail on the Fed later, but for now it's important to see how their policy fits in with what you have learned so far.

The monetary base[38] consists of credit from the bank that is converted to base money on demand (withdrawals, transfers, etc.). Bank reserves which have grown because of quantitative easing, also part of the monetary base, were supposed to result in keeping the bank credit system functioning as interest rates fall and loans to consumers and businesses increase, but it's just not happening. The banks are happy just receiving their interest payments from the Fed as we said. If you owned a bank, wouldn't you prefer to lock in a low-interest loan for the next 10, 20, 30 years—when we are at historic lows?

This is what most don't understand about what's going on today, and the frustrating part is that the Federal Reserve doesn't understand the failure of their own policy. The banks aren't lending, but hoarding! Bernanke wrote in 2002 that he thinks the Fed can drop money from helicopters to stimulate demand anytime they want to. The problems they face, however, stem from a lower demand for credit. Boomers

---

[38] http://wfhummel.cnchost.com/monetarybase.html

and others are choosing to pay down debt and save any money that comes their way. The Fed may resort to negative interest rates to try and spark money velocity and stroke inflation higher, but will it work? This is *deflation* that the Fed is fighting, and they will pull out all stops to do so.

If the Fed were to lower the rate (known as the Fed funds rate) it pays banks, this would resolve some of the issues, as money would flow to where it can earn the best rate. But so far, they have not.

To show you how clueless the Fed has been, consider that they talked about raising rates during almost all of 2015. They were simply looking at the economy through rose-colored glasses and ignoring money velocity. In December 2015, they finally did raise rates. The result? The first week of trading in January 2016 was the worst week ever. Let me repeat that: worst week ever! Yet the Fed members and those at Goldman Sachs and CNBC (like Steve Liesman) called for Fed interest rate hikes three or four more times in 2016. They ignored the fact that production is not improving, which we'll get to in a moment. And with the subsequent Fed meeting in March, the Fed cut back on their four rate increases to two and this was the case for the April meeting. Odds favor zero rate increases and the Fed is exposed as not really knowing what's going on.

The Fed rate increase was them trying to either save face with a token rate hike, or just making plans to cut rates again in the future when they finally start reading the economic data the way it should have been—or both.

Herein lies the problem that even Keynes himself would acknowledge. The Fed will implement more quantitative easing (or call it by some other name) because they simply cannot have deflation. Their entire existence depends on inflation and they will stop at nothing to get it, even if that means destroying their own balance sheet, which we will discuss in Part 6 on the Federal Reserve.

Some would even go so far as to say that what the Fed did was not just unprecedented, but illegal, based on what purchases are allowed under section 14.2 of the Federal Reserve Act.[39]

What happens next is not a guess. The Fed only knows one direction, and that is full-speed quantitative easing ahead. Their next moves to fight deflation will be the death of the Fed if implemented. But it won't be just the Federal Reserve who will be stimulating; it will be all central banks of the world. Even Keynes believed that spending should be temporary in nature and cut back in times of recovery and expansion. But what extreme measures these central banks are taking is heretofore unseen, and so will be the consequences. We are taking this chapter one thought at a time to give you the background first, and allow you to come to your own conclusions based on the facts presented. I don't have an agenda except to bring awareness, and help you decide the best way to protect your wealth moving forward.

We have spoken much about Keynesian economics, but we haven't touched on an economic school of thought that lends a lot of credibility to how things should work, yet at times is also a little bit utopian: Austrian economics.

Austrian Economics - What Our Textbooks, Fed and Government Should Practice More

What I like about Austrian economic thinking is their understanding of free markets and the business cycle. What they say about the dollar is that it will crash due to the amount of the debt load, and they view gold as the ultimate currency… but they miss out on what some debt has been able to accomplish in this world. At times, the dollar is king, but at other times it is not. They for the most part don't see the illusion of what the dollar really is—a representation of other currencies, as we discussed—and if that currency were to crash, by default the other currencies that make up the dollar index, mainly the euro, yen, pound or 83.1% of the dollar, would have to skyrocket. That's just not going

[39] http://www.federalreserve.gov/aboutthefed/section14.htm

to happen. The truth of the matter is that all currencies are subject to failure, because if you were to lose faith in the entire system, there would be a mad dash to gold—which the Austrians understand. But under a gold standard, the economy would be restricted in allowing growth to occur, like during the Reagan boom years. There is also the fact that a gold standard would be cast aside with any onset of war. Governments need debt to fund their wars.

We saw just a taste of potential future issues during the 2007-2009 financial crisis. This next crisis will be different, because we haven't learned any lessons. The government's solution is not reining in spending and living within our means, but to keep spending because that's all they know. If a heroin addict wants to keep getting the same level of "high" as their first one, they take more heroin, because that's all they know. But if they can't afford the heroin, they will do anything to get it. If they can't get it, they go into withdrawal. Our congress people have access to a money-printing press, and so far never have had to experience the withdrawal symptoms. They need to go into withdrawal, as painful as it is, or else we all suffer the consequences. The questions we must ask are if we're too late to solve our problems, and if the Fed and Congress will dig the hole even deeper with that unlimited heroin supply.

Eventually the Austrians will be proven right, and Ludwig von Mises' "crack-up boom" will put in a bottom for the business cycle. Artificially low interest rates have caused an artificial growth in credit, resulting in lenders overextending themselves. First a deflationary episode occurs, followed by inflation, super-inflation, and the crack-up (flight to real goods) boom as a result of hyperinflation. It is at that time that the masses will have lost faith in the money masters (the Fed) and Congress will be up the proverbial creek without a paddle, twiddling their thumbs and wondering what the heck happened.

The economics lesson is not over, though. We have to dig deeper into the numbers if you are going to possess the awareness needed to take control of your investing.

Chapter 5 - GDP Growth is the Key Issue

Every successful economy needs one thing: GDP growth.

What is GDP?

GDP[40] is defined as the monetary value of all finished goods and services within a country's borders in a specific time period. It includes all private and public consumption, government outlays, investments and exports less imports that occur within a defined territory. In short, it is all those things that make an economy grow. The Fed needs growth for their inflation targets to be met.

To break it down: GDP = C + I + NX + G

Where:
"C" is equal to all private consumption, or consumer spending, in a nation's economy.
"I" is the sum of all the country's businesses spending on capital.
"NX" is the nation's total net exports, calculated as total exports minus total imports
(NX = Exports – Imports).
"G" is the sum of government spending

To understand GDP better we need to break these categories down and distinguish fact from fiction.

First we will look at the consumer, where spending is said and generally understood to make up 70% of GDP growth. Without the consumer, you don't have growth in GDP, period. Then we will analyze business spending and trade deficits, and finally, we'll address government spending.

---

40 http://financial-dictionary.thefreedictionary.com/Per+capita+GDP

Consumer Spending

U.S consumer spending has been flat of late,[41] and this is noteworthy because gas prices have fallen so much—and you would think that with having more money in one's pockets, this excess would be put back into the economy.

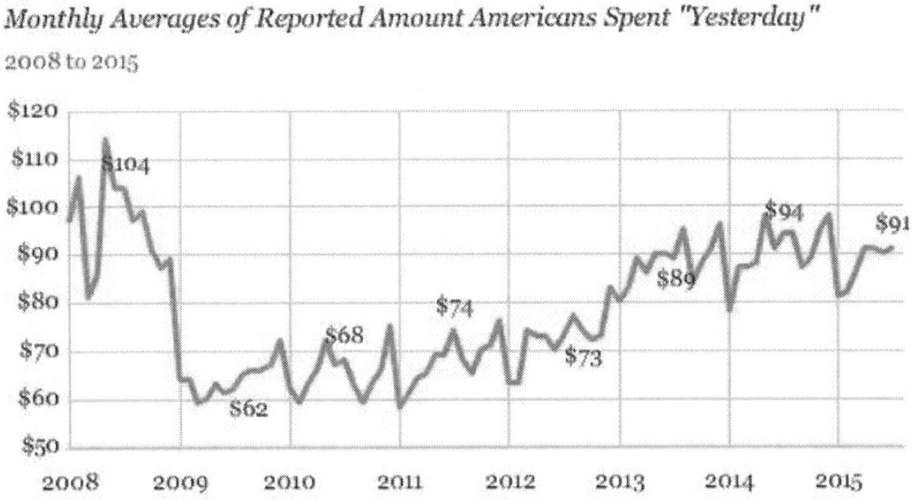

You can see from the preceding chart that just before the financial crisis, the consumer was spending like crazy. This was because of the newfound wealth from the rapid rise in home prices, and consumers tapping into that vein through home equity loans or personal loans from more-than-willing banks. Refinancing and subprime lending ruled the roost, and "home prices could never fall" was the theme of that booming era.

Then of course the crisis came, and consumers were the last to see it coming. Most financial advisors, financial magazines and yes, the Fed didn't see it coming either.

---

[41] http://www.gallup.com/poll/184433/july-consumer-spending-flat.aspx

We've had a nice steady rise in GDP since the crisis, but things are beginning to crack and retail sales, a leading indicator, have been declining.[42]

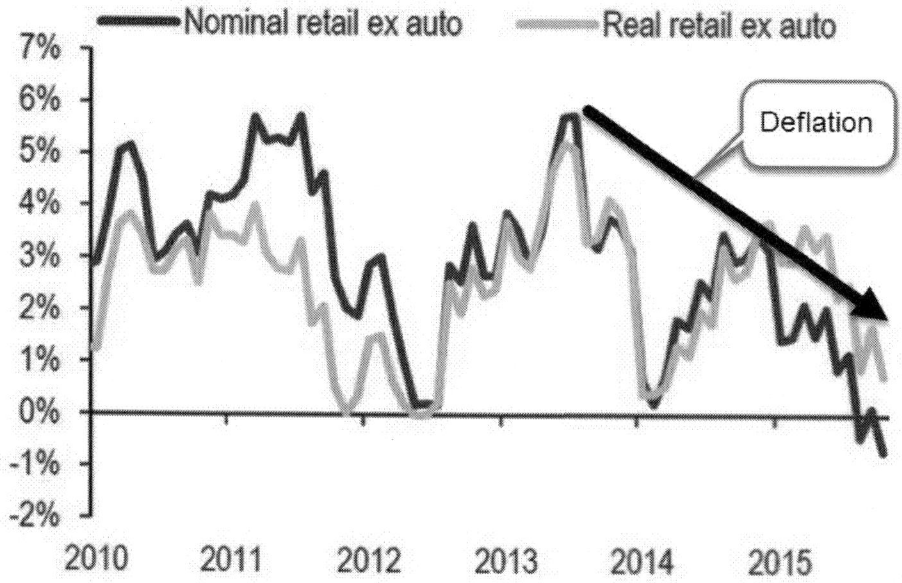

Source: BAC internal data, Bureau of Labor Statistics

There may be some blips higher in spending because of government programs to induce consumption, or more subprime lending like we had in 2015 for the auto industry to help those who otherwise wouldn't qualify for purchases. But again, this is not the right medicine for sustained growth.

The government, in an effort to make GDP look better, has decided that the way they have been calculating GDP is wrong, and have changed it to include more growth naturally.

---

[42] http://www.cnbc.com/2016/03/15/us-retail-sales-dip-in-february-prior=month-weak.html

> *From now on, government statisticians will take into account money earned from creative works including movies, television shows, books, theater and music. Money spent on research and development, which has, until now, been considered a cost of doing business will also be included. Lewis Alexander, chief U.S. economist for Nomura, says the new additions are meant to reflect a shift in what's important in a twenty-first century economy. "You can think of it as the growing importance of the IT industry, but obviously the entertainment industry as well," Alexander said.*[43]

If you think about it, most of the additions are what consumers who have discretionary income spend money on. In other words, anything they can do to make the economy look better, our governments brightest will try to include in their data. If everyone "feels" like the economy is doing well, they won't hoard, but spend the way MasterCard tells you to spend: "There are some things money can't buy. For everything else, there's MasterCard"[44] was their famous advertising slogan.

Consumer Debt

To determine where consumers stand in all this, we must analyze consumer debt. We need to scrutinize their spending habits and extrapolate from that if the 70% of GDP growth will come from consumers parting with their income and savings, or if it will have to come from the other 30% that makes up GDP where Keynes government spending picks up the slack.

As you can see from the following table, total outstanding consumer credit has increased every year since 2010, a 33% increase, to help improve GDP.[45] Credit card (or revolving) credit use is a big part of this

[43] http://www.marketplace.org/topics/economy/us-economy-grow-3-under-new-gdp-calculation

[44] http://www.textart.ru/database/slogan/credit-card-advertising-slogans.html

[45] http://www.federalreserve.gov/releases/g19/current/

increase, and has been growing at an annual rate of 12%. This can be attributed to a recovering economy—or the fact that consumers needed access to funds to pay current bills because they had no other choice. Is this really a recovery? What do you think? I hardly doubt this increase is from those who are jetting around the world, living the dream.

Consumer Credit Outstanding [1]
Seasonally adjusted. Billions of dollars except as noted.

	Year					Quarter					Month		
						2014		2015					
	2010	2011	2012	2013	2014	Q3	Q4	Q1	Q2	Q3[r]	Sep[r]	Oct[r]	Nov[p]
Total outstanding	2,646.9	2,755.4	2,922.9	3,098.8	3,317.2	3,267.5	3,317.2	3,363.4	3,434.9	3,496.4	3,496.4	3,512.1	3,526.0
Revolving	839.5	841.2	845.9	858.2	890.0	883.4	890.0	890.8	910.2	923.4	923.4	923.5	929.1
Nonrevolving [2]	1,807.4	1,914.2	2,077.0	2,240.6	2,427.2	2,384.0	2,427.2	2,472.6	2,524.6	2,573.0	2,573.0	2,588.6	2,596.9

Consumer loans jumped 11.2% in 2016, more than double the growth of 2015, the highest since 2000 and most of this is consumers using credit cards.[46]

Visa: "It's Everywhere You Want To Be." Are they inferring that where consumers want to be is in debt? Or are the issuers of these cards simply enslaving consumers for years to come? The point here is to understand what is really pushing GDP higher, and increased credit card debt is part of it. This is not real growth.

Student Loan Debt

Another type of debt wreaking havoc on the economy is student loan debt, to the tune of $1.7 trillion.[47] How are these 10 million loans going to contribute to growth if these consumers are straddled in debt for years to come? Suze Orman calls it "the most dangerous threat to our economy."[48]

---

46 http://www.cnbc.com/2016/03/31/us-consumers-whipping-out-the-credit-cards-again.html

47 http://www.newyorkfed.org/newsevents/news/research/2015/rp150217.html

48 http://www.usatoday.com/story/money/personalfinance/2014/10/25/student-loan-debt/17773131/

And only 4 in 10 borrowers with direct federal student loans are paying them back, according to a report by the Consumer Financial Protection Bureau,[49] and $125 billion worth is in default. One Houston resident was arrested at his house by marshals in full combat gear over an unpaid $1,500 student loan debt from 1987, all according to the law, as attorneys and debt collectors obtain judgments in federal court.[50]

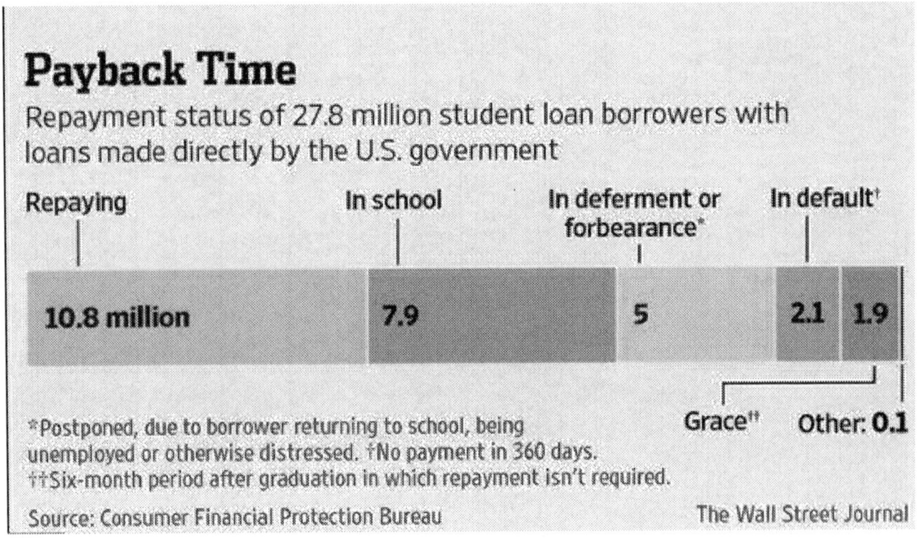

Don't you find it odd, though, that most of the student debt in existence today came *after* the last financial crisis? The following chart from Doug Short of Advisor Perspectives shows the 665% increase in loans since Q4 2007.[51]

---

49 http://online.wsj.com/news/articles/SB10001424127887323420604 57865042016 6447266

50 http://www.fox26houston.com/news/local-news/92232732-story

51 http://www.advisorperspectives.com/dshort/commentaries/Federal-Government-Assets-and-Student-Loans.php

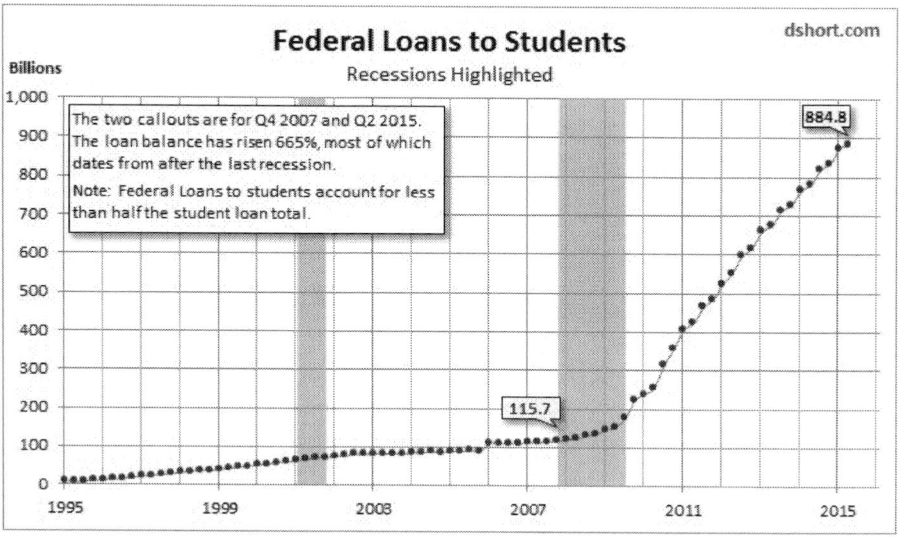

On one hand, you have consumers saddled with debt or accumulating more debt. On the other hand, you have millions saving for retirement or hoarding their wealth as they struggle to meet their retirement goals. This leaves a small segment of the population contributing to GDP with discretionary income, and I highly doubt this small percentage of consumers will account for the 70% of GDP needed to stimulate the kind of growth our economists and the Fed are looking for.

If you want to analyze consumer spending honestly, you must look at consumer debt for a complete picture, and not just assume that spending derives from discretionary income.

Before going further, I want to touch on one of the Federal Reserve's mandate, unemployment, as it fits in with consumer spending and consumer debt and is the glue that holds the economy together. If it is high, the economy is weak. And if it is low, the economy is supposed to be strong. What is it really showing us today?

Unemployment

The Federal Reserve has a dual mandate of stable prices and maximum employment, with a target inflation rate of 2%. The Fed is failing on inflation and presently dealing with deflation. We'll get to deflation later in the book, but how is the Fed doing with maximum unemployment?

The unemployment rate you hear in the financial news media, and the Federal Reserve throws around, is the U-3 rate—which is presently 5%. It is indeed a great improvement, considering the unemployment rate was twice that in October of 2009. But this 5% rate is of course just another illusion.

The International Monetary Fund (IMF), in its assessment of the U.S. economy,[52] also speaks of falling unemployment in the U.S. and uses this U-3 data as a means to claim that the U.S. economy is strengthening.

What you never hear from the mainstream media, the Fed, and the IMF is the real unemployment rate, which is the U-6 rate that includes those who the Department of Labor and Statistics claim are "marginally attached" to the labor force, as well as those forced to work part time for economic reasons. If there are no jobs to be had, and the unemployed have been looking for a job for the last 12 months but can't find one, they are not counted in the U-3 statistics—and naturally this makes the unemployment data the Fed and IMF analyze look much better than it really is.

The U-6 rate, however, is presently 9.9%—almost double the U-3 rate.[53] Do you see what a farce of a statistic the U-3 rate is?

---

[52] https://www.imf.org/external/pubs/ft/survey/so/2015/car070715b.htm
[53] http://www.bls.gov/news.release/empsit.t15.htm

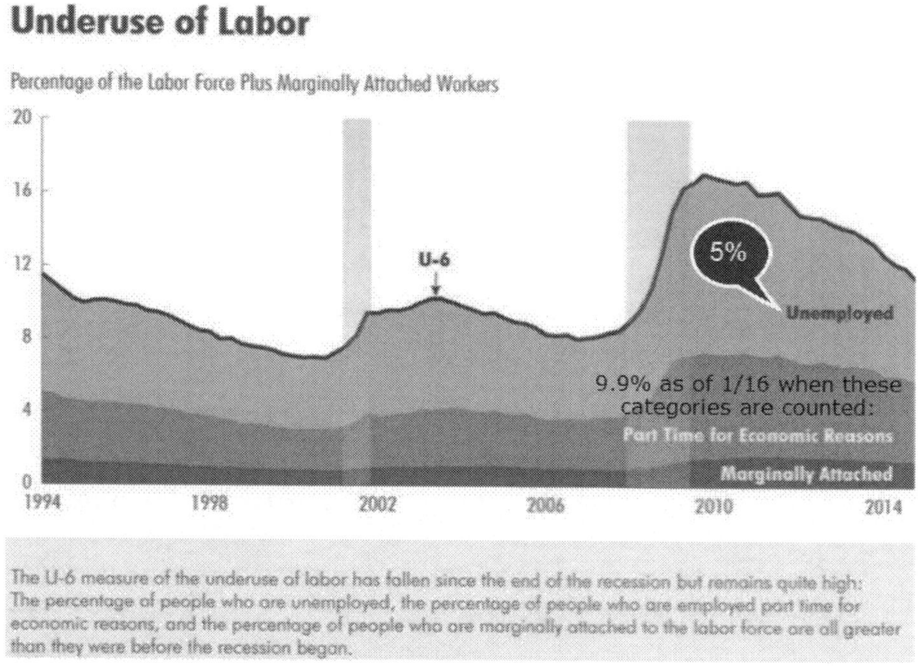

Congressional Budget Office[54]

One area contributing to the problem is civilians aged 25-54 who can't find jobs, as seen in their labor participation rate below. For this group, we are very close to the same rate of participation as 1984.[55]

[54] https://www.cbo.gov/sites/default/files/114th-congress-2015-2016/presentation/ 50796-presentation.pdf
[55] https://research.stlouisfed.org/fred2/graph/?id=LNS11300060

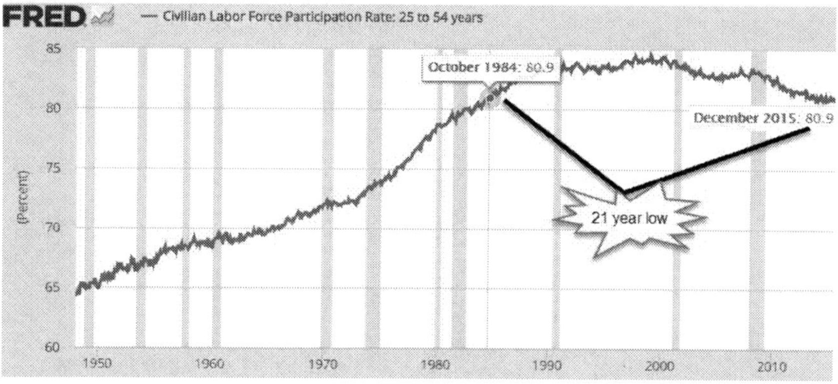

The unemployment rate for teens is even worse, sitting at 16.1%.[56]

Not only is the unemployment picture still bleak overall, but wages are declining and projected to continue to decline for manufacturing and production workers in America. As these wages decrease, what will be the economic impact for these communities, and the families of the wage earners? Wages are not keeping up with inflation, and that's while inflation is low. What happens when inflation rears its ugly head?

[56] http://www.bls.gov/web/empsit/cpseea10.htm

Measures of Compensation Paid to Employees

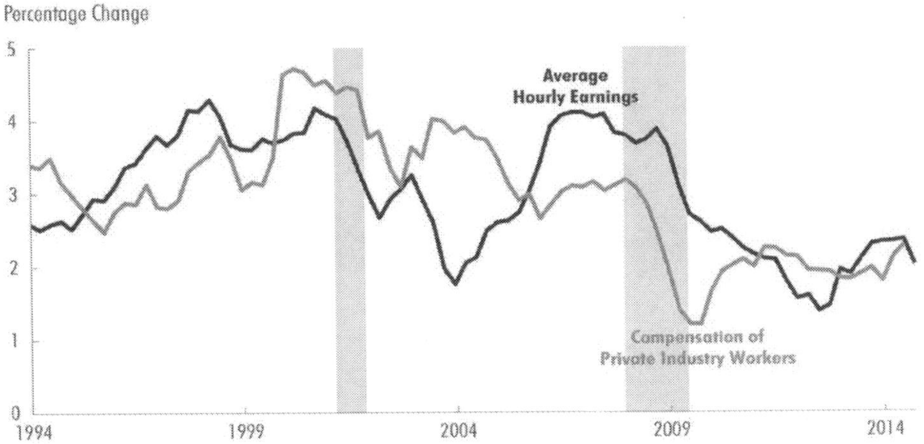

When labor is underused—as is currently the case—firms can hire from a relatively large pool of underemployed workers and thus have less incentive to increase compensation to attract workers. Accordingly, compensation has been growing considerably more slowly than it did before the recession.

Figure 1. Relative Wages of Manufacturing Workers to All Workers

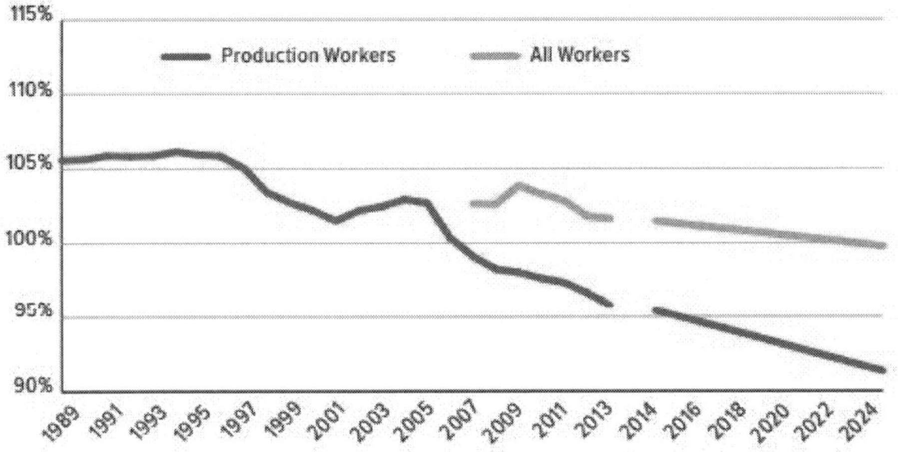

Source: U.S. Census Bureau, Current Population Survey.

National Employment Law Project [57]

Many of these manufacturing jobs seeing a decline in wages come from the auto industry, where jobs have been outsourced to low-paying countries, or replaced by robotics (see graph in Robotics chapter in investment section). The staffing of temporary employees has also grown, as employers look to cut the costs of providing benefits. Unions are finding themselves powerless to stop this trend, and simply give in to the changes or risk being eliminated entirely. Fifty years ago, nearly a third of U.S. workers belonged to a union. Today it's 1 in 10.[58]

---

[57] http://www.nelp.org/content/uploads/2015/03/Manufacturing-Low-Pay-Declining-Wages-Jobs-Built-Middle-Class.pdf

[58] http://www.npr.org/sections/money/2015/02/23/385843576/50-years-of-shrinking-union-membership-in-one-map

Percentage of Workers In Unions

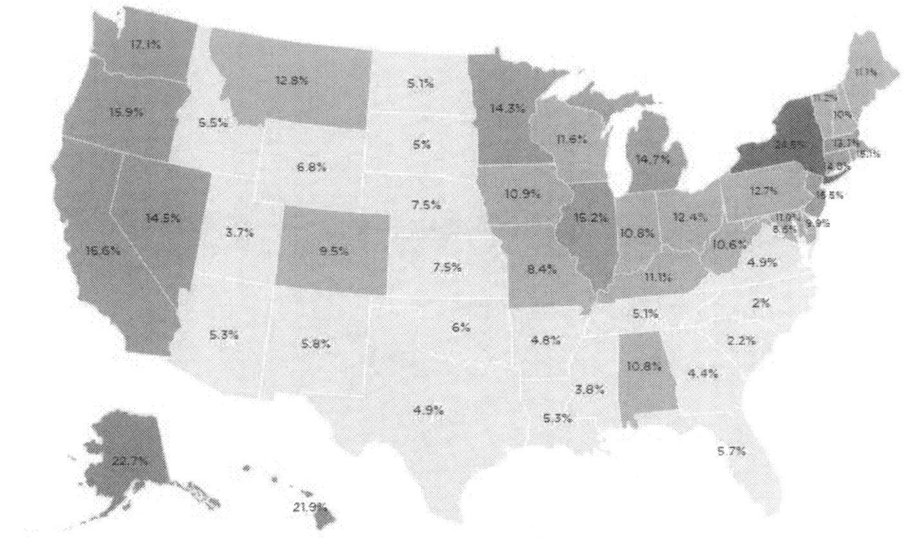

2014

Even wages for college grads are lower than they were 15 years ago.[59]

What we are really seeing here is the illusion of the middle class. Many may not realize this, but the U.S. middle class not only lags behind the rest of the world, but is just below Greece.[60]

---

[59] http://www.huffingtonpost.com/2015/06/02/low-college-grads-salary_n_7484204.html

[60] http://economics.uwo.ca/people/davies_docs/credit-suisse-global-wealth-report-2014.pdf

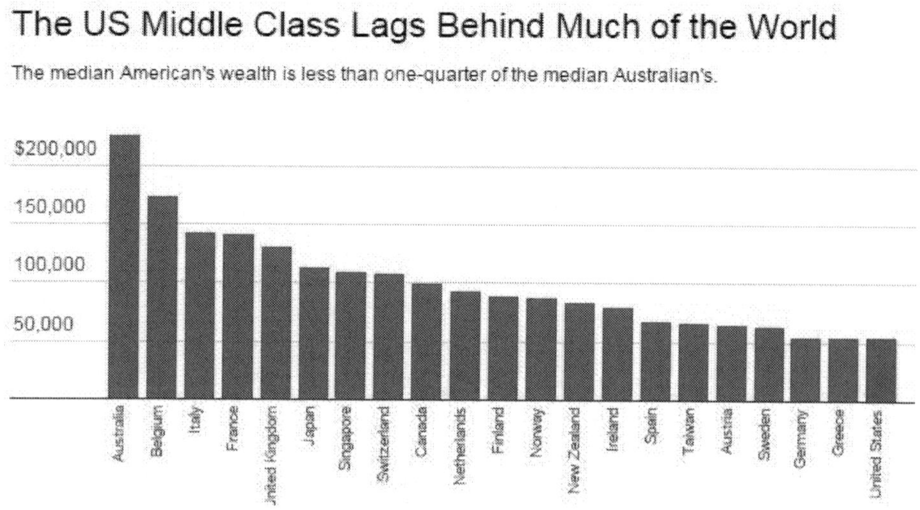

Does this employment picture look like the makings of a sound economic recovery, or is it just an illusion of prosperity for many who are slowly becoming serfs in America?

In fact, 80% of Democrats and Republicans responding to exit polls in Michigan and Mississippi said that the economy is their number-one concern in voting for their favorite candidate for president. The numbers were 70% for Republicans in Illinois and North Carolina and 81% for Democrats in Missouri, while 75% of Democrats were worried about the economy in Ohio. Why the concern if everything is so great in America? Perhaps the real employment data plays into this worry because many are out of work and the economy is on the verge of something worse than most think.[61,62]

If you look at those with a net worth of $50 million or more, you can see that the U.S. by far exceeds any other country as the next chart shows.[63]

---

61 http://www.cnbc.com/2016/03/15/us-retail-sales-dip-in-february-prior-month-weak.html
62 http://www.cnn.com/2016/03/15/politics/super-tuesday-exit-polls/index.html

Ultra high net worth individuals 2014: Selected countries

Source: James Davies, Rodrigo Lluberas and Anthony Shorrocks, Credit Suisse Global Wealth Databook 2014

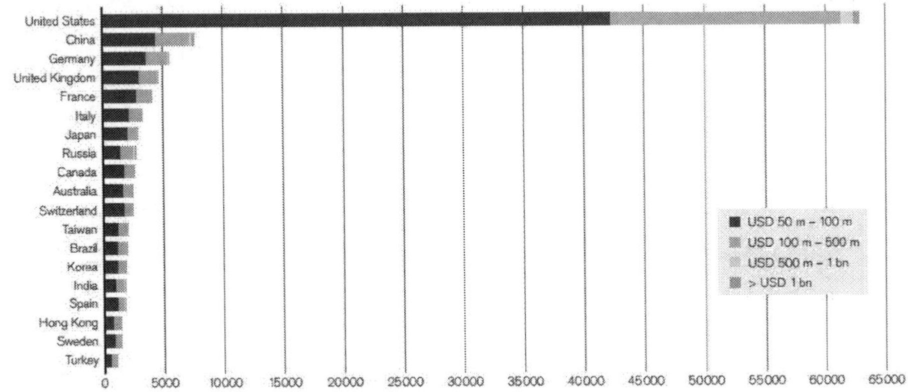

The richest 1% will surpass the other 99% in terms of wealth in 2016, according to Oxfam, an international organization dedicated to fighting poverty.[64]

We will have our own issues here in the United States fighting poverty unless we can turn around the middle class and make them productive members of society again, so their wages keep pace with inflation at a minimum. If this doesn't happen, then retirement is just an illusion for this group. While I cover this in more depth (and provide solutions) in my upcoming book *We the Serfs!* all is not hopeless if you take control of your wealth. You do have to educate yourself the same way the top 1% does, but it's not necessarily a formal education. The top 1% didn't get wealthy by being any smarter than you. They made good decisions with the wealth they had, and then kept making good decisions. That wealth can also be achieved by you, if you don't have it yet, or grown if you do.

---

63 http://economics.uwo.ca/people/davies_docs/credit-suisse-global-wealth-report-2014.pdf

64 http://www.oxfam.org.uk/blogs/2015/01/richest-1-per-cent-will-own-more-than-all-the-rest-by-2016

Whether you are employed, unemployed, or underemployed, use your spare time wisely by stepping away from the TV and reading as much as you can on investing. If you have access to a computer, or can get access at a local library or a friend's house, take what you have learned from this book and keep digging to gain an awareness of how to make real money.

One other aspect to jobs that needs addressing is the number of government jobs our nation has. Government jobs are paid for by the taxes collected. If there are not enough taxpayers to support the growth of government, then cuts have to be made.

Roughly 56% of all government employees work for three departments: Defense (33%), Veterans Affairs (14%), and Homeland Security (8%). The average wages were higher for all federal employees who had less than a doctorate or professional degree, and the benefits were better for all levels of education if you worked for the government versus the private sector.[65]

In other words, if you are not a doctor or lawyer, it pays to work for the government!

Immigrants who come to America love getting military or postal jobs, as they know their incomes are secure.

Naturally there is a case to be made for government to protect us (military and police), incarcerate us (something the U.S. leads the world in), and provide for those in need (health and food).

While jobs have been cut on a federal level,[66] local governments have boomed from the mid-50s' 4 million employees to over 14 million today.

---

[65] http://www.cbo.gov/sites/default/files/cbofiles/attachments/01-30-FedPay.pdf

[66] http://blogs.wsj.com/economics/2014/11/07/the-federal-government-now-employs-the-fewest-people-since-1966/

Government Growth

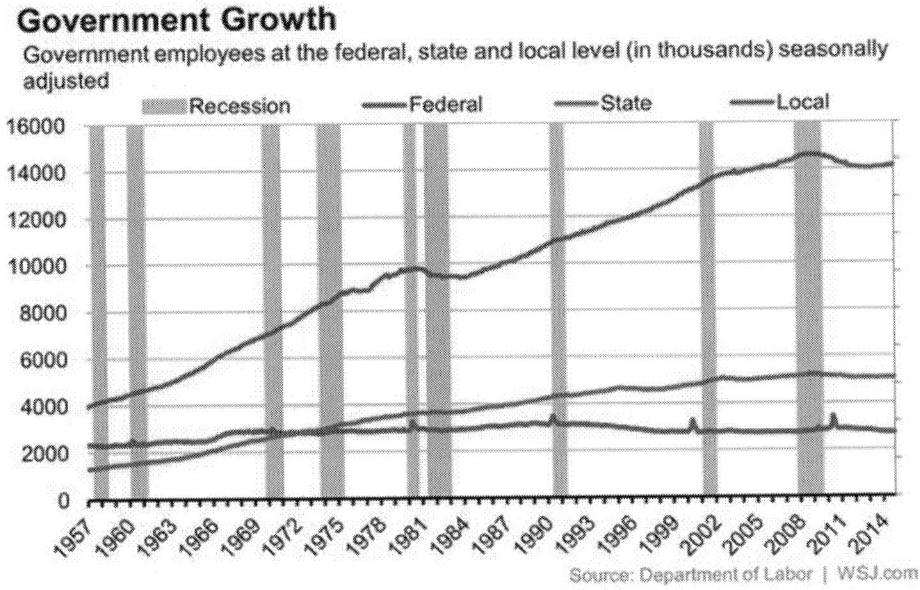

Total expenditures, however, are increasing despite the overall decrease in those employed by government, as they now amount to 34% of GDP. This is because government contractors are not counted as federal employees.

The problem here, though, is that as the economy contracts (see section on deflation), there will have to be more cuts to government jobs. While there is no indication this is an issue today, because Congress can't see beyond their outstretched hands asking for campaign contributions, it will become an issue in the future. Leviathan can only grow so large, and while government has reduced its size on a federal level, if you work for local government, having a plan B in place may make sense.

Politicians don't get elected by raising taxes, and this means that further cuts will at some point have to be made. The only other choice is to keep government as large as it is to inflate away its debt issues.

This of course would be disastrous for the economy, and is not presently a viable option.

It's important to understand the significance of the unemployment figures, as without jobs and consumer spending, the economy grinds to a halt. What one needs to consider, however, is of those who are currently employed, what is the likelihood they will spend some of their income and wealth to keep the economy growing? Sure, the top 1% will spend in good times and bad, but as you'll see in the Retirement section in Part 9, many are just trying to get by, and those who are retired are just determined to make sure their money lasts a bit longer than they do.

When saving for retirement, as long as you have a job, everything is fine and you can plan for your future accordingly. But just in case a wrench is thrown into your plans, it pays to have a backup plan with a side business of your own. This can be a company you start and get your children or other family members involved in, something you have expertise in, or something fulfilling a local niche currently not being addressed. There is always something you can do—that is, if you can pull yourself up off the couch (for some of you!). And it doesn't hurt if this second job is also a passion; something you enjoy doing.

Taxes

To make matters worse for consumers, tax revenues topped a record in 2015,[67] an 8% growth over those collected in 2014. Individuals paid five times more taxes than corporations. This is all due to the change in the tax code during the Obama administration. Don't worry, taxpayer, your government knows how to spend your money for you. They have your best interests at heart, right?

---

[67] http://www.forbes.com/sites/kellyphillipserb/2015/08/13/tax-collections-hit-record-highs-with-no-dip-in-spending/

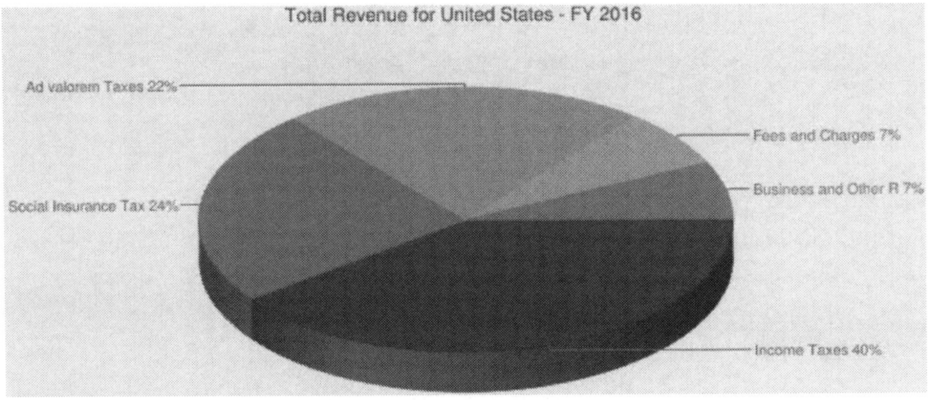

Business Spending

If an economy is growing, business spending has to be contributing to GDP. We are lucky to have a chart from the Fed on durable goods orders that can give us some insight.[68]

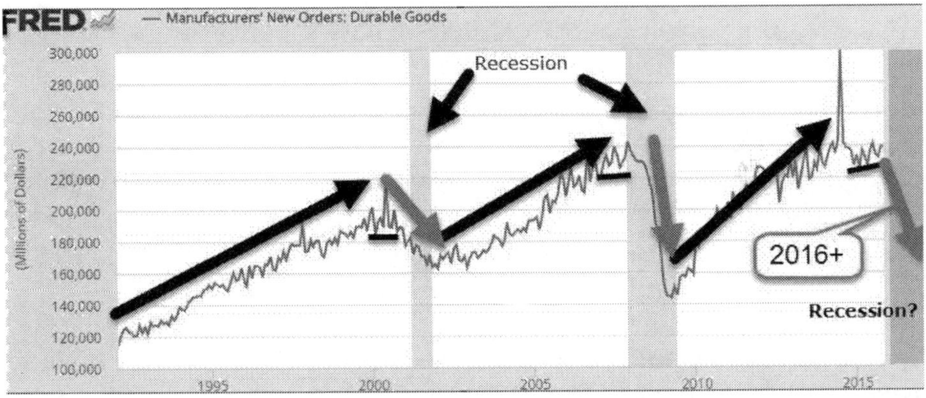

We can see from the chart some flattening out of the trend that had been higher since the end of the financial crisis. But we can also see another grey shaded area coming, which would signify another recession is on the way. The data of late has been flat for quite some

[68] https://research.stlouisfed.org/fred2/series/DGORDER/

time. This is NOT growth, but setting up something worse, and most of the data you'll see next backs up this prediction.

Construction Spending

Construction spending saw its biggest drop in a year[69] and global capital spending (Capex), led by the worldwide commodities crash, looks mediocre[70] as companies hoard cash, according to analysts.

Productivity

When a recovery begins, there is a drastic improvement in productivity and productive capacity utilization. These developments positively impact profits and the willingness of firms to invest.

When we analyzed the unemployment data, the conclusion was that middle-class workers, who have been the backbone of the country for 50 years, are coming to the conclusion that they have to change their goals regarding wealth or be replaced by either a lower wage earner in another country, or robotics. Either these people have to accept a significantly lower standard of living or find a way to reframe their thinking and reinvent themselves. We, as a nation of workers, are not producing like we used to. This was confirmed prior to 2012 with the Fed conclusions in a paper written by Board of Governors members Justin Pierce and Peter K. Schott, entitled "The Surprisingly Swift Decline of U.S. Manufacturing Employment."[71]

The mistakes that these Fed members and Yale scholars continue to make is that they are Monday-morning quarterbacks (and the same can be said for many economic and investment books). They analyze what has happened, then write about why it happened. They are not forward

---

[69] http://www.businessinsider.com/r-us-construction-spending-gain-smallest-in-five-months-2015-8
[70] http://blogs.wsj.com/cfo/2015/08/03/commodity-companies-dragging-down-global-capex-sp/
[71] http://economics.yale.edu/sites/default/files/schott-09-oct-2013.pdf

thinking whatsoever. If they were forward thinking, don't you think that one of these "experts" would have seen the 2009 financial crisis coming? None of them did. While this book does analyze the past, it is also predicting the future, and you'll see in the investment section just how you can prepare.

In 1982, I read a book by John Naisbitt called *Megatrends*.[72] The author wrote about 10 new directions transforming our lives. One of these transformations was from a predominantly national economy to one in the global marketplace.

Since that time, Democrats and Republicans alike have handed over our country's production to China and other low-cost labor countries with the passing of WTO, NAFTA and other international treaties, setting us up to be less competitive and transforming us from a country of producers to a country of consumers. If you add the fact that our major corporations set up shop in these countries to take advantage of not only cheap labor, but less intensive regulations (or none at all), tax advantages and less government intervention in their business affairs, can you honestly blame them? That's what capitalism is. Corporations were pushed out by these treaties and increased regulations, and the reason you pay lower prices is because these companies reduced their labor costs.

China produced 2 million cars a year in 2000. Today, in joint ventures with companies including Volkswagen, General Motors, Hyundai, Nissan, Honda, Toyota and Mitsubishi, they produce more than any other country at 23 million cars a year, and have since 2008.

In 2003 China had no billionaires. Today they rank number 2, behind only the U.S. with 130 billionaires.[73]

---

[72] http://www.amazon.com/Megatrends-Ten-Directions-Transforming-Lives/dp/0446356816

[73] http://www.cnn.com/2009/BUSINESS/10/24/intl.china.billionaires/index.html? eref=rss_latest

These dealings with China have made many stock investors much wealthier. We can blame corporations and their greed for this wealth if you want to hold someone accountable, or we can blame Congress for selling us out to low-cost foreign labor. We can also adjust and take advantage of change. Those who can't adjust have unfortunately found themselves out of business or standing in unemployment lines. But again, it's not too late to reinvent yourself.

This is also an issue that is being addressed by 2016 presidential candidates, but I will save that analysis for the next book, as raising tariffs isn't a real possibility because it will simply increase prices here, but free trade is.

Chapter 6 - Lies and Statistics: What Does the Economic Data Tell Us?

Even with the changing of the guard from a producing country to a service country (80% of our economy is a service economy now), companies are finding that without the consumer consuming, production declines—and so does their profit with it.

Industrial Production

U.S. industrial production posted its third straight drop from the December 2015 report, its worst showing since March 2012. Before that, there were downward revisions to prior reports.[74]

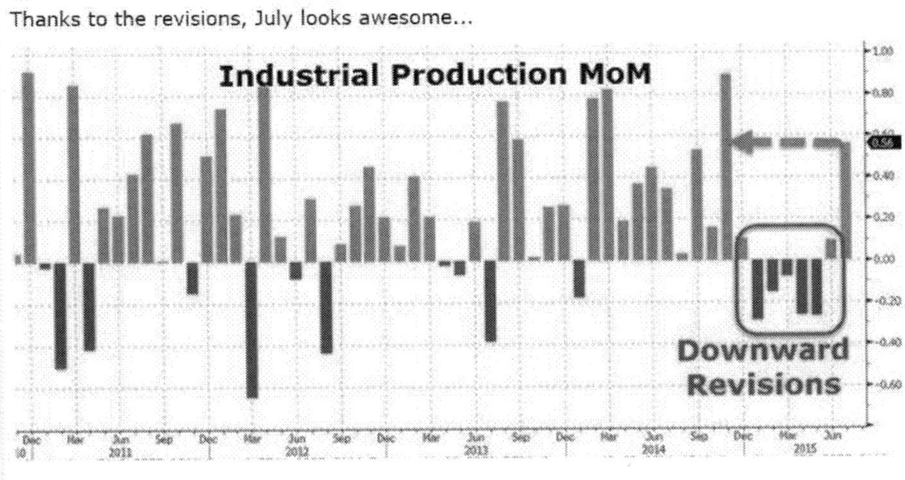

There was a blip up in auto production with increased subprime lending, but there is no denying that overall production has been weak, and the first week of stock market returns being the worst ever show why this data is predictive of what's to come—and something you should keep an eye on as an investor.

---

[74] http://www.zerohedge.com/news/2015-08-14/industrial-production-rises-most-november-after-significant-downward-revisions

Manufacturing Production

Manufacturing production has floundered this year as dollar appreciation and weaker overseas economies lessened demand for U.S.-made goods, and oil producers cut back on new investment.[75]

One must analyze the entire body of data to come to a conclusion. I have compiled this data and you can view it at http://buygoldandsilversafely.com/what-does-this-economic-data-tell-us/

The data didn't look good for most of 2015, but the stock market began 2014 by breaking to new highs. Price action, though, can sometimes trump any negative data, but eventually the chickens will come home to roost—and observing the way 2016 started, we are finally seeing the beginnings of just how fragile this stock market can be and what should be signs of what's to come, even though it rebounded with oil for a time. If we had a multi-year scenario of a declining stock market, this would be one of the worst times to have it, with so many Baby Boomers set to retire. The good news though, as you'll see in the Investment section, is that profit can still be made.

The fact is we are not producing as much as we used to, as a service economy. We push money (wealth) around from person to person, convincing buyers that what our company makes is of value, whether it be a tangible product or service or internet related. For example, if seniors have most of the wealth and a steady stream of income from company pensions and Social Security, your job as a businessperson is to try and get them to part with some of that money. But what do seniors really need that they don't have, outside of the normal food and shelter, healthcare, vitamins, and some leisure time expenses? They are a thriftier generation, as they learned from their parents that a penny saved is a penny earned, and not to be frivolous. They are also concerned about outliving their money should inflation come back

[75] http://www.bloomberg.com/news/articles/2015-12-16/factory-production-in-u-s-stagnates-on-less-output-of-durables

again. They remember the '70s and high inflation and know the stories of the Great Depression. We all could learn from this generation.

Comparing Production Today to the Great Depression Era

In his 1936 book *Crises and Cycles*, German economist Wilhelm Röpke described similar circumstances to our deflationary environment today. It's important to understand this, as it can give us some insights into our own investment choices moving forward. "The saddest and most obvious expression of the world crisis," he wrote, "is to be found in the shrinkage of production throughout the world."[76]

Building activity fell 50% in Germany and the United States. Automobile production fell, along with world trade. But it was the international credit crisis of 1931 and consequent abandonment of the gold standard in most countries that resulted in an almost complete breakdown of the system.

It was during this credit contraction that banks also began to suffer. Wrote Röpke: "The banking statistics are of special interest in this connexion, since they reflect the process of credit contraction (deflation) underlying the more general process of business contraction. Especially significant in this respect are the figures of the decrease of bank credits and advances, of the turnover of bank deposits (velocity of circulation of bank deposits), and of the volume of bank clearings. Bank credits and advances had dropped in 1932 in Germany (Big Berlin Banks) and in Austria to almost one-half compared with 1929, in France and Holland to two-thirds, and in the United States, England and Wales, and Italy to about three-quarters. The velocity of circulation of bank deposits (ratio of bank debits to the average of bank deposits) declined, in the United States, from the peak rate of 3 in October, 1929, down to the rate of about 1 at the end of 1932 and in the first months of 1933."

---

[76] https://mises.org/sites/default/files/Crises%20and%20Cycles%20(1).pdf

Why is this important to us today? Because we are currently repeating this scenario. In the 1929-1933 deflationary era, balance of payments became an issue because France and the United States had most of the gold. Röpke:

> *With the declining volume of world trade and the complete collapse of the prices of raw materials, the burden of this foreign indebtedness became increasingly unbearable for the greater part of debtor countries, especially for the countries producing raw materials. This, in turn, had disastrous effects on the banking systems of the creditor countries. So it was that numerous bank failures in the United States were closely connected up with the South-American failures. In addition to all this, irregular movements of capital, directed by the motive of security rather than by the motive of economic yield, gained an importance unheard of hitherto.*

To substitute for this lack of liquidity, or hoarding, today central banks around the world—including here in the U.S.—have been implementing quantitative easing (QE), which we have already discussed a few times.

The truth of the matter, as Röpke concluded, was that "without the spirit of confidence, optimism, and easiness, all recovery programmes will rest on sandy ground." It's rather cliché of me to say here, that if you ignore history you are doomed to repeat it … but I have to say, many in government, as well as investors, act more like Homer Simpson when he sticks his finger in a light socket, gets shocked and sticks it in again expecting a different result. Remember in the monetary system section, when I spoke about how long the average currency lasts and that most of you will have lived through a currency crisis? It doesn't have to start here in the U.S., but we do have a history of losing confidence, and you can bet your conclusion after finishing this book will be that recovery programs "rest on sandy ground." But again, there are ways to profit.

Baltic Dry Index

According to Investopedia, "changes in the Baltic Dry Index can give investors insight into global supply and demand trends. This change is often considered a leading indicator of future economic growth (index is rising) or contraction (index is falling)."[77]

You can only draw one conclusion from the following chart, and it's not a bullish one for economic growth and higher GDP. In fact, the data shows we recently dipped below where we were when the financial crisis was at its peak.[78]

[77] http://www.investopedia.com/terms/b/baltic_dry_index.asp#ixzz3jPnPXUYE
[78] http://investmenttools.com/futures/bdi_baltic_dry_index.htm

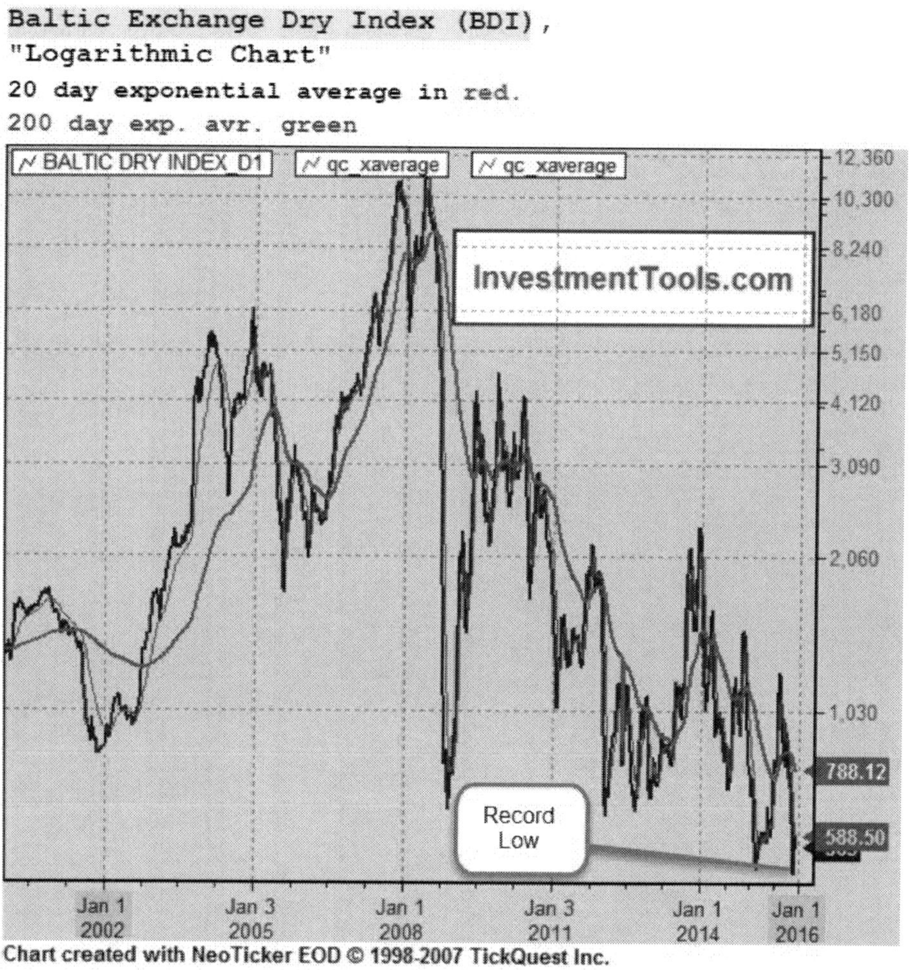

Trade Deficit

Since 2011, the dollar has only moved higher and higher, and this has hurt U.S. companies trying to be competitive in a global market. During this time, the Euro has become weaker and weaker, and as a result, imports from Europe grew to a record. The trade gap between Europe and the U.S. is the largest it's been since 1992.[79]

---

79 http://www.bloomberg.com/news/articles/2015-08-05/trade-gap-

The following chart shows imports vs. exports, where we as a country have been running at a deficit since 1994.[80]

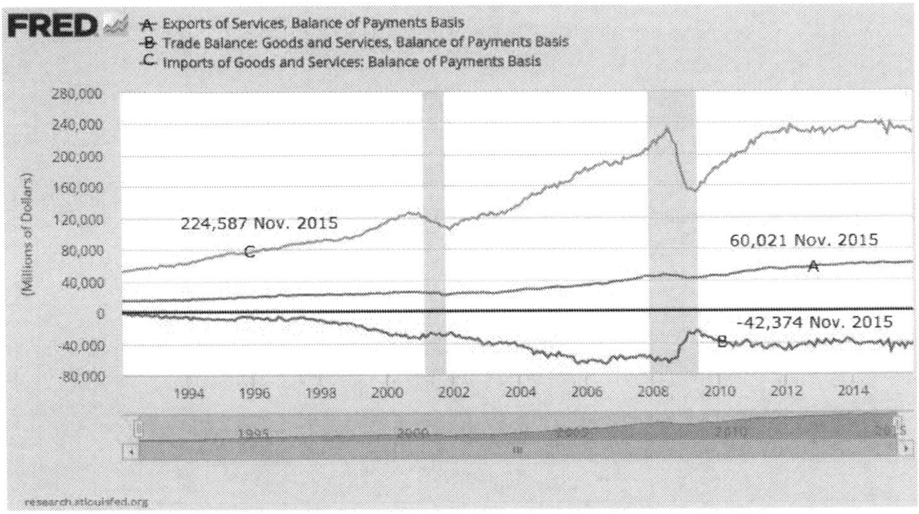

With the rise in the U.S. dollar, exports have fallen to their lowest level since early 2012.[81]

If imports are higher than exports, that does not result in growth and a contribution to GDP. The Chinese economy has grown to number two in the world by exporting more than they import.

U.S. consumers will almost always choose price as their main purchase incentive, and that goes for foreign consumers as well. The owners of Wal-Mart became multi-billionaires by offering lower-cost, mostly Chinese goods. The only ways to reverse the trend of lower exports are to either lower the prices of U.S. goods or have a weaker dollar. One way to lower prices is to pay our workers less. Paying our workers less will lower the standard of living and lead to an

---

widened-in-june-showing-effect-of-strong-u-s-dollar

[80] https://research.stlouisfed.org/fred2/graph/?id=BOPSEXP,#

[81] http://www.marketwatch.com/story/us-exports-fall-to-lowest-level-since-early-2012-2016-01-06

elimination of the middle class. It's hard to weaken the dollar when other countries are weakening their currencies at a faster rate. It will be difficult to find growth in the U.S. when there is so much working against it.

Chapter 7 - Government Spending

The government spending portion of GDP is out of control. Congress never looks past its nose when passing spending bills. Promises by government officials to take care of this and pay for that are made without much deliberation on how it will all be paid for. Much of what you hear from the mouths of those running for office is just enough for the politicians to get elected, but they are never held accountable for their promises. Collectively, without consideration for the future, they continue the failed policies of the past with your tax dollars and future generations' tax dollars. But eventually, after you are fed up with the higher taxes, there is only one way they can pay for their promises—through higher inflation, which we will discuss later. As an investor, you need to think about that as you read through and contemplate the contents of this section.

To get an idea of how government spending has evolved, take a look at this chart from an era when the U.S. government lived within its means.

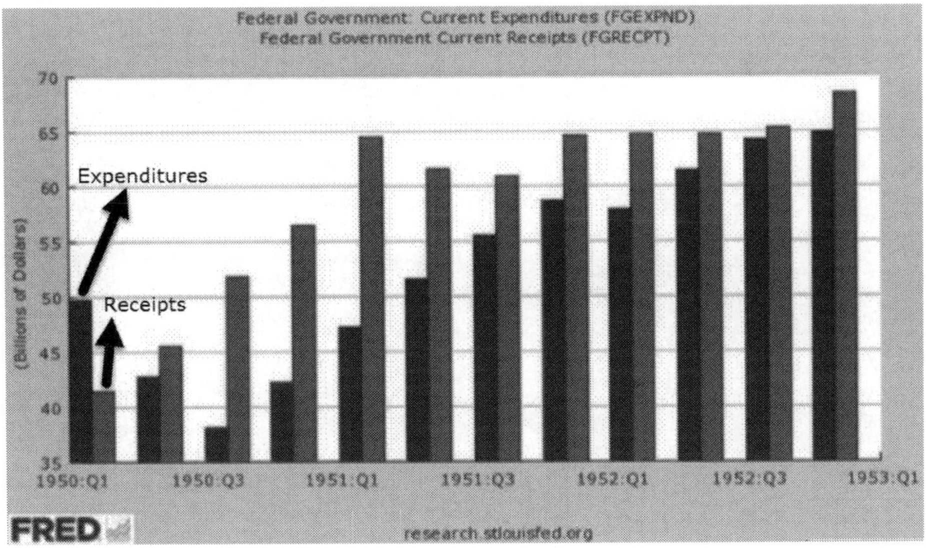

WWII had ended and the U.S. was producing things, while taxes were not funding big government programs. Therefore, the tax receipts were more than enough to cover expenditures for and by government. What we have seen since the 1950s is the growth of government well above the taxable means to support it.

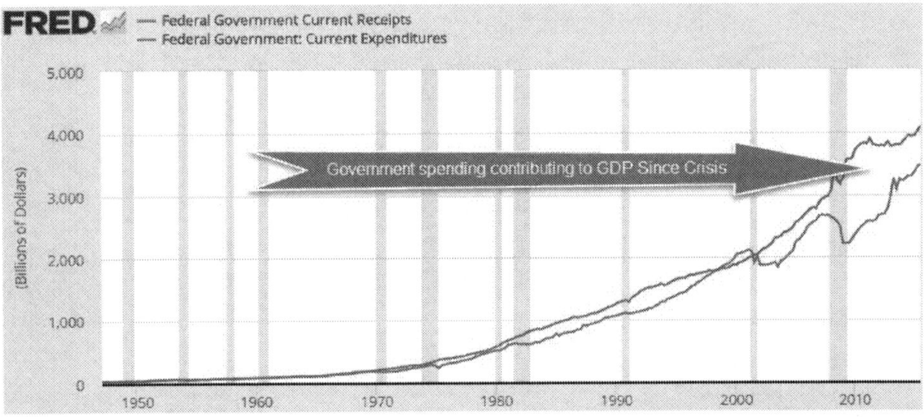

It is true that as long as you are within range, you can pay off debt with a little growth. This is what the Fed is doing their best to accomplish with their monetary policy and manipulation of interest rates in trying to stimulate the economy. But you can see from the chart what happens during a recession.[82] Tax receipts go down, but government expenditures for the most part do not. Are we close to another recession? Is your portfolio prepared for the potential of another recession right now?

Budget Deficit

The difference each year between receipts and expenditures is called a budget deficit.

If your average middle-class family had the ability to run a deficit when times got tough, they would have to find a way to pay off that debt with

[82] https://research.stlouisfed.org/fred2/graph/?id=GRECPT,GEXPND,#

extra income at some point in the future. If they don't pay it off, they are debt slaves to whomever they borrowed from, or they have to default/declare bankruptcy if the debt is eligible to be eliminated.

Our nation is a debt slave to whom? Ourselves. But you and I didn't agree to the debt, we just voted the people into office who are supposed to have our best interests at heart. Instead those in office have the government's best interests at heart. When we elect officials, this government itself becomes a living, breathing, ravenous monster that needs to be fed your tax dollars. When that's not enough to pay for their programs, it demands to still be fed and Congress has to borrow money to feed it(self). In Biblical terms, we can call this monster Leviathan, which the Bible (Job: 41) does a magnificent job of describing.

It is important enough, whether you are Christian or not, for me to post that chapter here.

Job: 41, New International Version (NIV)[83]

1 *"Can you pull in Leviathan with a fishhook*

or tie down its tongue with a rope?

2 *Can you put a cord through its nose*

or pierce its jaw with a hook?

3 *Will it keep begging you for mercy?*

Will it speak to you with gentle words?

4 *Will it make an agreement with you*

for you to take it as your slave for life?

---

83 https://www.biblegateway.com/passage/?search=Job+41#fen-NIV-13890a

5 *Can you make a pet of it like a bird*

or put it on a leash for the young women in your house?

6 *Will traders barter for it?*

Will they divide it up among the merchants?

7 *Can you fill its hide with harpoons*

or its head with fishing spears?

8 I*f you lay a hand on it,*

you will remember the struggle and never do it again!

9 *Any hope of subduing it is false;*

the mere sight of it is overpowering.

10 *No one is fierce enough to rouse it.*

Who then is able to stand against me?

11 *Who has a claim against me that I must pay?*

Everything under heaven belongs to me.

12 *I will not fail to speak of Leviathan's limbs,*

its strength and its graceful form.

13 *Who can strip off its outer coat?*

Who can penetrate its double coat of armor?

14 *Who dares open the doors of its mouth,*

ringed about with fearsome teeth?

15 *Its back has rows of shields*

tightly sealed together;

16 *each is so close to the next*

that no air can pass between.

17 *They are joined fast to one another;*

they cling together and cannot be parted.

18 *Its snorting throws out flashes of light;*

its eyes are like the rays of dawn.

19 *Flames stream from its mouth;*

sparks of fire shoot out.

20 *Smoke pours from its nostrils*

as from a boiling pot over burning reeds.

21 *Its breath sets coals ablaze,*

and flames dart from its mouth.

22 *Strength resides in its neck;*

dismay goes before it.

23 *The folds of its flesh are tightly joined;*

they are firm and immovable.

24 *Its chest is hard as rock,*

hard as a lower millstone.

25 *When it rises up, the mighty are terrified;*

they retreat before its thrashing.

26 *The sword that reaches it has no effect,*

nor does the spear or the dart or the javelin.

27 *Iron it treats like straw*

and bronze like rotten wood.

28 *Arrows do not make it flee;*

slingstones are like chaff to it.

29 *A club seems to it but a piece of straw;*

it laughs at the rattling of the lance.

30 *Its undersides are jagged potsherds,*

leaving a trail in the mud like a threshing sledge.

31 I*t makes the depths churn like a boiling caldron*

and stirs up the sea like a pot of ointment.

32 *It leaves a glistening wake behind it;*

one would think the deep had white hair.

33 *Nothing on earth is its equal—*

a creature without fear.

34 *It looks down on all that are haughty;*

it is king over all that are proud."

While solutions to Leviathan's reach are covered more in my next book *We the Serfs!* an understanding of what government is and does is necessary for you to invest appropriately which this book does. If there is no end in sight to government spending, what are the consequences, and how have you insured your portfolio just in case things don't turn out the way government plans?

Budget Deficits Accumulated Each Year Add to the National Debt

Nobel Prize-winning economist and *New York Times* columnist Paul Krugman wrote an opinion piece in 2015 called "Debt Is Good,"[84] where he concluded "there's a reasonable argument to be made that part of what ails the world economy right now is that governments aren't deep enough in debt."

This is the same Paul Krugman, mind you, who criticized the "gross fiscal irresponsibility" from the Bush administration for 8 years.[85] Now all of a sudden in August 2015 Krugman wrote; Debt is good? The blame game will go on and on but understand both parties gladly contribute to the debt and don't know what it means to be fiscally responsible.

George W. Bush's administration added $5.849 trillion to the national debt and Barack Obama's administration through the end of 2015 will have added approximately $7.16 trillion.[86] We are increasing our national debt by about $1.2 billion a day.[87] This is down from the $1.98 billion a day a few years ago, but future obligations to what has been promised to those on Social Security, disability, SNAP, and our healthcare expenditures are destined to cost us more than what's

[84] http://www.nytimes.com/2015/08/21/opinion/paul-krugman-debt-is-good-for-the-economy.html?ref=topics
[85] http://krugman.blogs.nytimes.com/2009/08/27/a-note-on-the-bush-fiscal-legacy/
[86] http://www.treasurydirect.gov/NP/debt/current
[87]http://www.treasurydirect.gov/NP/debt/search?startMonth=08&startDay=21&startYear=2014&endMonth=08&endDay=20&endYear=2015

available, and any uptick in the interest rate will just exacerbate the problem, as you'll see shortly.

Government or Leviathan only knows how to do one thing: grow larger. Each year they add on more debt, printing money out of thin air to pay for what Congress approves by passing spending bills. In a sense, that's what Congress' job is—to pass spending bills. Have you ever heard of Congress getting together and passing a bill to cut spending? Only in times of crisis or when forced to cut do they stop their spending madness.

This debt that Congress gives us each year, which makes up the budget and is accumulated, is called the national debt. The national debt grows each year, interest is paid on it, and that payment is also part of the budget deficit, paid for by tax receipts or printing more money.

This national debt today is approaching $20 trillion. Your obligation to pay off this debt is $58,397 per person in the U.S. or $157,490 per taxpayer (more on the national debt in a bit). This is money that will be stolen from your retirement or your children's retirement. I used to joke (even though it's not a laughing matter) that there is a reason why our kids' calculators don't compute 1 trillion or more. If they somehow knew the truth about what an unsustainable mess our government got us into, they would just give up their future dreams, drop out of school and try to find a way to start their own society where debt was not out of control.

In the late 1960s, I saw a movie called *Wild in the Streets,*[88] which depicted young people upset with all the lies they had been told by government. They wanted to elect their own leader—a rock star of course—and they slipped LSD (a mind-altering drug) into the water system to get the Supreme Court high enough to lower the voting age from 21 (which it was prior to the passing of the 26th amendment in 1970) to 14. If they could get their chosen rock star elected, naturally life would be much better than it was. Well, by the end of the movie, the 14-21 year-old youth had alienated the under-14 group, who were contemplating their own takeover of the country. Maybe Kanye West

---

[88] http://www.imdb.com/title/tt0063808/

saw that movie too when he announced his run for President for the 2020 term. Maybe by then the Kardashians will all be senators.

As I said earlier, the only way government can pay off all this debt is to tax you more or inflate the currency to make the debt burden smaller. They could also default, but I don't think the Fed would put itself out of business by letting Congress choose that option. Our youth today are not going to be happy with the results of anything our government or Federal Reserve may do, as they can wager it won't be in their best interest. In this sense I do have pity on whomever the next preside is unless they listen to the solutions in my next book We the Serfs! And I mean that with all sincerity as I do have a young daughter and care for hers and all other youth's future.

Future Obligations (Insolvencies of Social Security, Medicare, Medicaid, SSDI)

To make a bleak future even grimmer, forthcoming obligations to fund Social Security, the Affordable Care Act, Medicare and Medicaid are not calculated into this current national debt figure. While we address the problems of funding Social Security in a future section, we already know that government is not in control of healthcare costs, as well as Medicare and Medicaid expenditures that keep rising at a rate higher than inflation every year. More and more are on the government dole receiving Supplemental Nutrition Assistance Program payments, or SNAP (formerly called food stamps), and expenditures are increasing for those on government disability as the numbers grow. A recent *Washington Post* article stated that sometime in 2016 the federal safety-net program for disability could be out of cash.[89]

One major problem that the government also has to deal with is a Medicare system paying out fraudulent claims, perpetrated by doctors and providers to the tune of over a billion dollars. There is a rather sick part

[89] https://www.washingtonpost.com/opinions/a-wise-prescription-for-social-security-disability-insurance/2015/07/27/a8baa402-348a-11e5-8e66-07b4603ec92a_story.html

(pun intended) about fraud and our government. A recent report, "How Initiatives to Reduce Fraud In Federal Health Care Programs Affect the Budget," the government admits that "the Government Accountability Office (GAO) has concluded that 'there currently is no reliable baseline estimate of the amount of healthcare fraud in the United States,' and CBO has not estimated the amount of fraud—either detected or undetected—in Medicare, Medicaid, and CHIP." And here's the kicker: "In fiscal year 2014, spending on dedicated anti-fraud activities through the Health Care Fraud and Abuse Control (HCFAC) program was about $1.4 billion."[90]

Below you can see a projection of how long the disability, Medicare and Social Security programs are set to last.[91] And that's if you believe the government data.

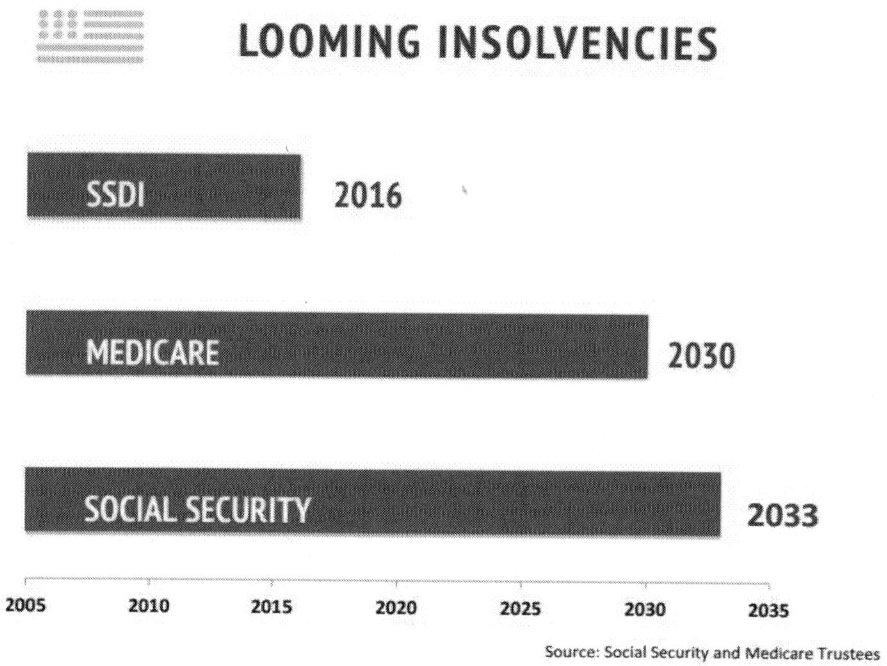

---

[90] https://www.cbo.gov/sites/default/files/113th-congress-2013-2014/reports/49460-ProgramIntegrity.pdf
[91] http://budget.house.gov/uploadedfiles/fy16_charts.pdf

I made my own modifications to the graph below,[92] which is from a website where the House presents its version of the future. The government obviously thinks they will control their future spending, resulting in a debt-free economy and a "path to prosperity." I changed the description to call it what it really is: nonsense.

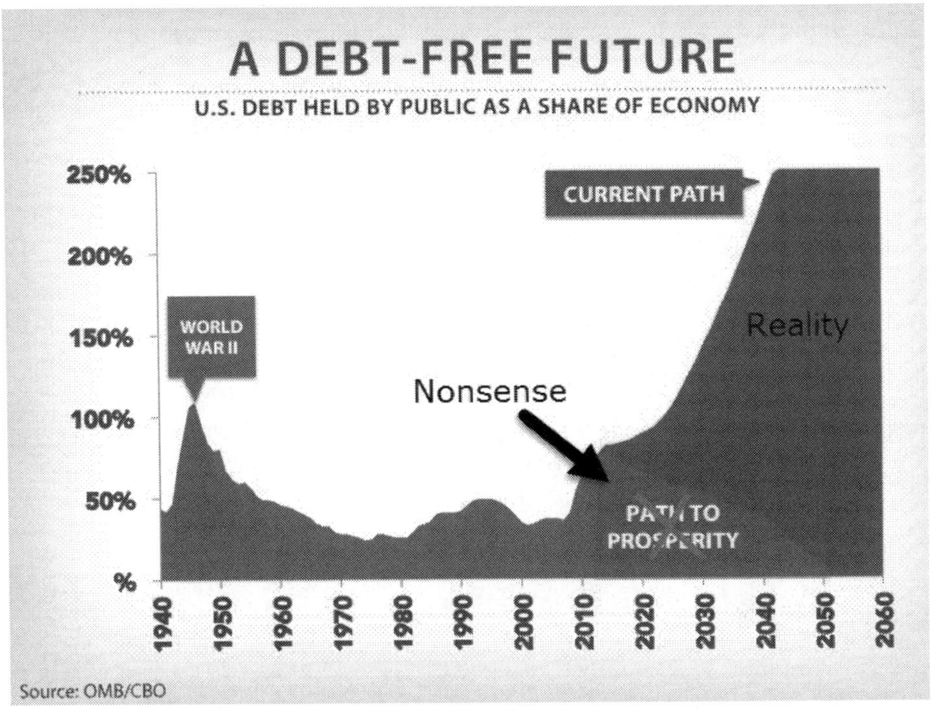

What the government has figured out since the time of Ronald Reagan is that as long as the people have faith in the dollar, the government can go into even more debt to finance projects. This financing of course is negotiated through lobbyists, who write the spending bills for congress people to approve. This is a game that will at some point come to an end, and rather harshly for those who are unprepared. But there are ways to profit from this, as will be revealed in the investment section.

---

92 http://budget.house.gov/uploadedfiles/fy2014_budget_charts.pdf

What is even more comical—at least to those like me, who mock Congress—but actually playing out more like a Shakespearean tragedy, is that our leaders vote each year to increase the debt ceiling to avoid a "terrible accident," as Treasury Secretary Jack Lew wrote in an opinion piece on October 26, 2015.[93] He said that Congress had pushed the U.S. "to the brink of potential economic catastrophe" in 2011 and 2013 by waiting until the last moment to raise the then-debt ceiling. Lew also told CNBC in an interview a week earlier that the government can't prioritize what bills to pay. He said, "We have about 80 million transactions a month. Our system wasn't set up not to pay."[94]

Let that sink in for a moment. We citizens have bills to pay and if we don't pay them, there are consequences. If our government can't pay their bills, they don't have a system in place to pay, so their only option is to raise the debt limit. There is no thought whatsoever as to the consequences, by Lew or anyone else in Congress. But there will be. Remember, this is a tragedy in the making, a tragedy that has been managed to date, but gets worse each and every year. Just look at Senate projections for the next 10 years as a percentage of federal spending and as a percentage of GDP.[95]

---

93 http://www.usatoday.com/story/opinion/2015/10/25/jack-lew-debt-limit-column/74585584/

94 http://www.cnbc.com/2015/10/19/lew-i-worry-there-could-be-a-debt-limit-accident-that-could-be-terrible.html

95 https://www.fas.org/sgp/crs/misc/RL33074.pdf

Figure 2. Components of Mandatory Spending as a Percentage of Federal Spending (FY1970-FY2025)

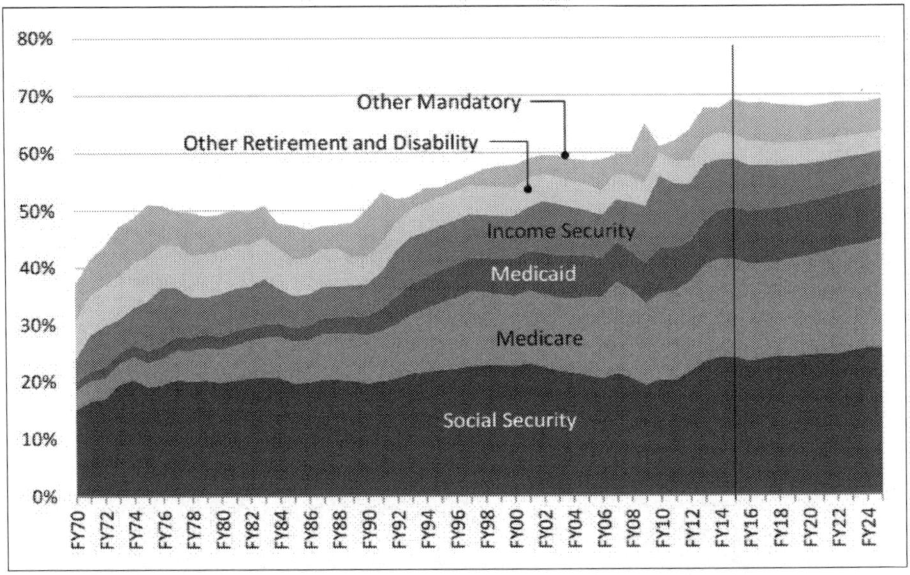

Source: CRS calculations based on data from CBO, Historical Tables and Budget Projections.

Notes: The "Other Mandatory" category includes Health Insurance Subsidies, Exchanges, and Related Spending, MERHCF, CHIP, veterans' programs, agriculture, deposit insurance, Fannie Mae and Freddie Mac, higher education, and other mandatory spending. Offsetting receipts are excluded. CBO baseline projections depicted to the right of the vertical line.

Figure 3. Mandatory Spending Before Offsetting Receipts as a Percentage of GDP (FY1970-FY2025)

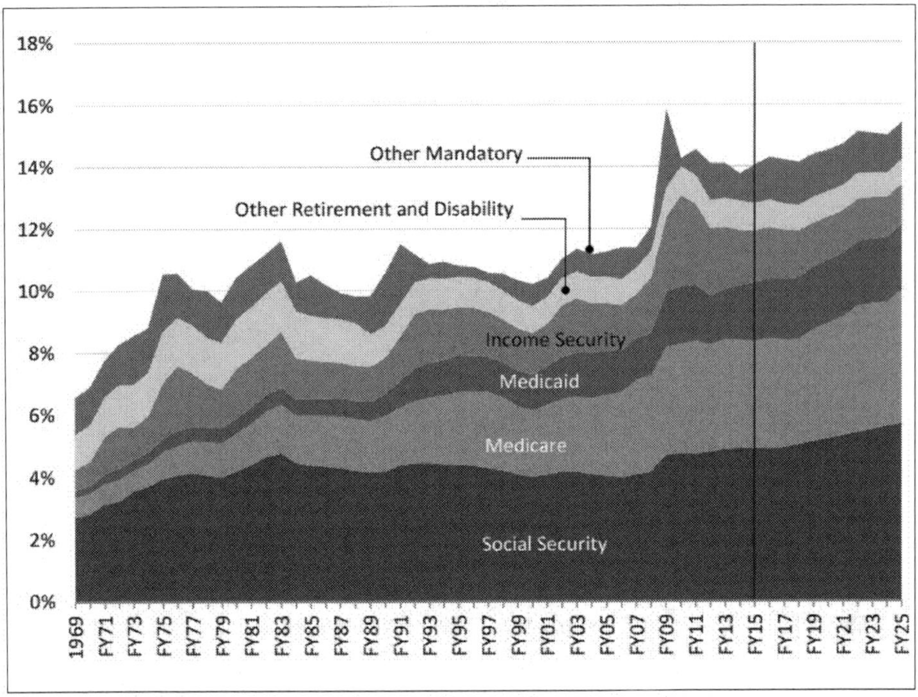

Source: CRS calculations based on data from CBO, *Historical Tables* and *Budget Projections*.

Can the government live on 30% of what's left, and keep America great? (pun intended)

The U.S. government simply cannot afford the high cost of borrowing to service the national debt should interest rates increase. This is the looming disaster. The average cost of servicing U.S. debt has come down from about 6% in 2001 to just over 2% in 2015. Even if we were to only increase to 4%, discretionary spending by Congress will be crowded out by interest payments.[96]

[96] http://bawerk.net/2015/11/15/how-the-fed-gave-away-its-independence-interest-rate-sensitivity-at-zlb/

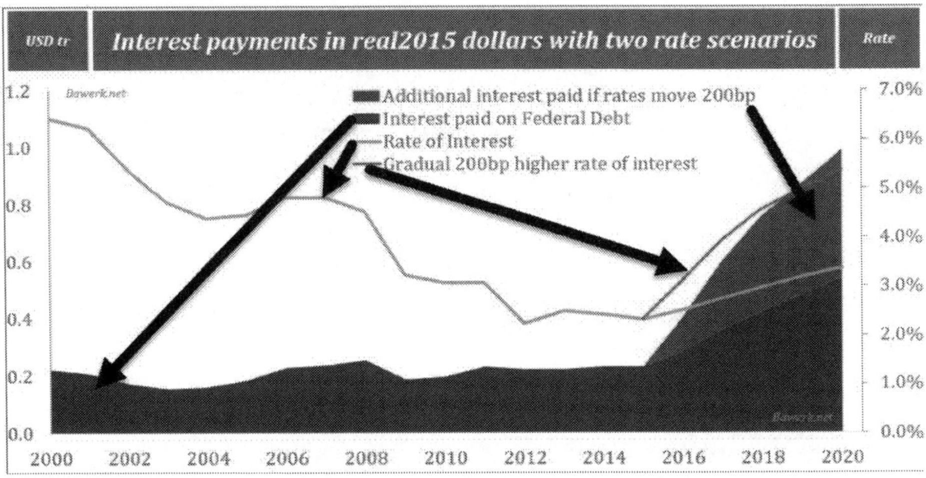

Source: Office of Budget Management, Bureau of Economic Analysis, Bawerk.net

If going into more debt by raising the debt ceiling is eventually prevented by the passing of a bill (I know, I'm dreaming here), then cuts would have to be made or the currency devalued, unless of course Congress taxes you more. But Congress will take the easy way out.

Do you think there are no consequences to this increase in the national debt? Wouldn't it make sense to have some portfolio insurance just in case the projections by Congress don't work out as planned? Just in case the tax receipts can't cover both expenditures and future obligations?

If you want to relate to the massive budget deficit numbers on a personal level, I invite you to watch a video[97] of a gentleman who walks into a bank and asks the loan officer to raise his debt limit. He is a family man, and wants to go on a trip and buy a big screen TV, but the banker doesn't understand how the man can pay for it without increasing his income. It's done with great humor, as the banker mocks his entire approach to handling his debt versus his spending habits and income. Here is the video link: https://www.youtube.com/watch?v=Li0no7O9zmE

---

[97] https://www.youtube.com/watch?v=Li0no7O9zmE

In reality, the numbers the video uses were the actual scaled-down numbers for our country's debt in 2011. I wish they'd update the video with the same actors every year. It shows you how insane our financial situation really is, and the man's solution is naturally passing the debt on to his two-year-old child... who scribbles her name on the loan document. It's funny but also reality. No wonder younger generations are fed up.

Ponzi Scheme

Has our government become a Ponzi scheme?

I'll leave it to the reader to decide based on the definition[98] of Ponzi scheme:

> *The Ponzi scheme generates returns for older investors by acquiring new investors. This scam actually yields the promised returns to earlier investors, as long as there are more new investors. These schemes usually collapse on themselves when the new investments stop.*

What is the only thing that keeps the game going for the government to pay its bills? Artificially low interest rates, to where the debt burden is covered mostly by the current tax receipts coupled with the borrowing of newly printed money (adding to the deficit/national debt). When interest rates rise and the interest paid on the debt becomes too much of a burden for taxpayers and the youth are still paying off their student loans, who's left to pay? We are still a ways off from this but adding more debt isn't a fiscal solution.

How It Ends

Lastly, how can anything the government does be counted as growth when it is an expenditure? If you look at the current debt growth, and

---

[98] http://www.investopedia.com/terms/p/ponzischeme.asp#ixzz3jV5sDz2x

compare that to the current GDP growth, if debt is not producing more in growth, then it is adding to the problem—it's not creating more growth. Printing money to pay for things isn't "growth," its debt, and the U.S. leads the world in that category!

Debt reality check—Congress keeps promising what can't be delivered and confusing more debt for a "balanced budget." What are the odds Congress gets the budget projections right? I say ZERO percent.

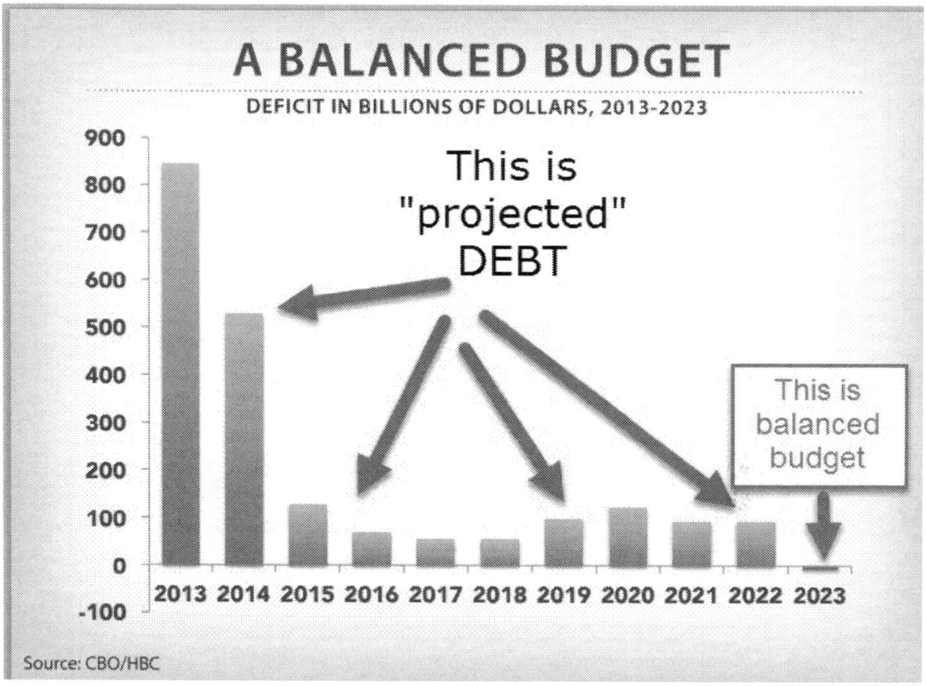

Since the U.S. went off the gold standard, the U.S. government has had a deficit every year but four, when Bill Clinton was president from 1998-2001. Budget deficit in 2005 (Nov.) was $319 billion and 2.6% of GDP.

The 2015 budget deficit was $483 billion and 2.8% of GDP, which was the lowest level since 2007 but what is ignored from 1970 forward is the fact the nation's debt has gone up every single year, including the Clinton years. It should be noted that even though during these Clinton years the budget deficit shrank, the national debt still increased every year. The reduced deficit is still adding debt. Please understand the difference.

President Obama, while running for office in 2008, called President George W. Bush's $4 trillion addition to the national debt "unpatriotic"[99] yet Obama in 7 years has increased the national debt by about $8 trillion, although some can blame the Bush administration for undeclared wars adding to the continued foreign policy expense Obama inherited, or for that matter, a Republican-led Congress. Remember, both parties are to blame. Blaming one party over another is just the distraction of the masses while the elephant (national debt) in the room is ignored and grows ever larger!

The National Debt

A simple comparison of 1980 through 2000 to 2016 can give you an idea of what you owe for this spending that has been allowed to go on unabated for 35+ years.

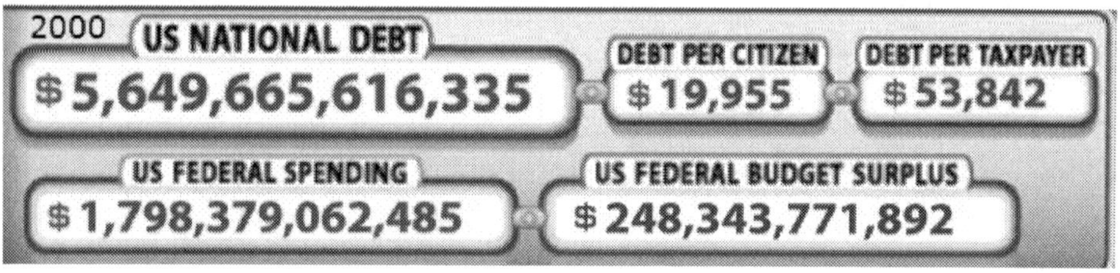

---

99 https://www.youtube.com/watch?v=1kuTG19Cu_Q

For an update on where we stand with the national debt, see www.usdebtclock.org, if you can keep up.

The Congressional Budget Office projected in 2013 the U.S. national debt would be $16.6 trillion by 2020.[100] How are we doing? They only missed the mark by $3 trillion!

The CBO lists unexpected developments[101] that would affect the budget and our national debt:

- A severe economic downturn
- Changes in losses on federal insurance or credit programs
- Catastrophes
- The effects of climate change
- Changes in natural resources

Naturally they exclude the nation's banks or the Fed as a reason for unexpected issues.

IMF to the Rescue?

The International Monetary Fund (IMF) does present solutions for debt reduction, explaining that there are essentially five ways to reduce large debt-to-GDP ratios, and that most historical episodes have involved some combination of these.[102] I've listed them here, with my comments as to where we are with each.

---

100 http://www.cnbc.com/2013/09/25/the-feds-hidden-agenda-behind-money-printing.html

101 https://www.cbo.gov/publication/51023

The Elements of Debt Reduction

1. **Economic growth**: We're just not seeing it come to fruition, as you saw with the GDP data earlier.

2. **Fiscal adjustment/austerity**: Congress doesn't know what this means, although some cuts were forced upon them through sequestration in 2013, when according to Wikipedia, "the Bipartisan Budget Act of 2013 increased the sequestration caps for fiscal years 2014 and 2015 by $45 billion and $18 billion, respectively, in return for extending the imposition of the cuts to mandatory spending into 2022 and 2023, and miscellaneous savings elsewhere in the budget."[103]

In other words, Congress increased spending for two years and kicked the can down the road to make up for it.

3. **Explicit (de jure) default or restructuring**: The U.S. Congress hasn't considered default, as the system as we know it would unravel, exposing the Ponzi scheme. They attempted this once in 1933 with the "abrogation of the gold clause in conjunction with a 40% reduction in the gold content of the U.S. dollar." Then President Roosevelt invoked Executive Order 6102 (which we spoke about in Chapter 2), and instructed anyone with more than $100 in gold coin to turn it in to their local bank and get Federal Reserve Notes in the same amount in return, or face a $10,000 fine and possible prison sentence.[104] Our government would not allow deflation to weed out the excesses and punish the appropriate offenders. Instead, they punished those whose gold they took, and other depositors. Who benefited from this confiscation? Wall Street.

Isn't Wall Street, which benefited from the rounds of QE shoring up the balance sheets of the banks and the Fed artificially keeping rates low, holding debt issues at bay? Problem solved, right? Just ignore the

---

[102] http://www.imf.org/external/pubs/ft/wp/2013/wp13266.pdf

[103] https://en.wikipedia.org/wiki/Bipartisan_Budget_Act_of_2013

[104] https://en.wikipedia.org/wiki/Executive_Order_6102

$20 trillion national debt, deficits and unfunded future obligations the rest of us are responsible for. Believe in the Fed. They are here to help.

This isn't 1933. We're in quite a different predicament today. There was no looming national debt back then. Government was small, our military wasn't involved in policing so many other nations, and our social programs were not an expense in 1933.

4. **Inflation surprise**: Inflation is always a way to make current debt cheaper, but as you will see shortly, despite the Fed implementing three rounds of quantitative easing and one round of operation twist (selling short-term treasury bonds and buying long-term bonds in order to pressure long-term bonds yields lower) to stimulate the economy

and obtain their 2% inflation target, they have failed to generate inflation, as deflation has taken over with a credit contraction that is swallowing up any increase in the money supply explained in Chapter 9 on Exter's Pyramid.

5. **A steady dose of financial repression accompanied by a steady dose of inflation**: This involves "some combination of capital controls, financial repression, inflation, and default." This solution deserves some digging into, as it should scare the heck out of you.

Carmen M. Reinhart, the Minos A. Zombanakis Professor of the International Financial System at Harvard Kennedy School, describes financial repression this way:

Includes directed lending to the government by captive domestic audiences (such as pension funds or domestic banks), explicit or implicit caps on interest rates, regulation of cross-border capital movements, and (generally) a tighter connection between government and banks, either explicitly through public ownership of some of the banks or through heavy "moral suasion." Financial repression is also sometimes associated with relatively high reserve requirements (or liquidity requirements), securities transaction taxes, prohibition of gold purchases (as in the United States from 1933 to 1974), or the placement of significant amounts of government debt that is non-marketable. A large presence of state-owned or state intervened banks is also common in financially "repressed" economies. In the current policy discussion, financial repression issues come under the broad umbrella of "macroprudential regulation."[105]

This is important for investors to understand, because it very well could be the next step that the Fed and our government take. What investors need to think about is whether or not this could be reality, and how to adjust their portfolios if it were to come to fruition.

---

[105] http://www.nber.org/papers/w16893

Reinhart further explains in a 2012 paper, "The Return of Financial Repression":

The surge in public debts that followed during the Great Depression and through World War II only made the case for stable and low interest rates and directed credit more compelling to policymakers. The resurgence of financial repression in the wake of the 2007–2009 financial crises alongside the surge in public debts in advanced economies is documented here. This process of financial 'deglobalization' may have only just begun.

At present, the levels of public debt in many advanced economies are at or near uncharted territory: some of these governments face the prospect of debt restructuring. Furthermore, public and private external debts (which are a relatively volatile source of funding) are at historic highs. It seems probable that policymakers for some time to come will be preoccupied with debt reduction, debt management, and, in general, efforts to keep debt servicing costs manageable. In this setting, financial repression (with its dual aims of keeping interest rates low and creating or maintaining captive domestic audiences) will probably find renewed favor and the measures and developments we have described and discussed in this note are likely to be only the tip of a very large iceberg.[106]

These are the lengths our governments have gone to, and will go to again if necessary. What other choices do they have? The Romans, to solve their debt problems, just conquered another country and used its confiscated gold to pay debts. We're not Romans today (although some may think otherwise), but what real choices are there that won't affect your investments negatively?

Reinhart, in another paper written for the IMF, "The Liquidation of Government Debt," gives us another glimpse of what may come:

---

[106] https://www.banque-france.fr/fileadmin/user_upload/banque_de_france/ publications/Revue_de_la_stabilite_financiere/2012/rsf-avril-2012/FSR16-article-04.pdf

Debt is also reduced through financial repression, a tax on bondholders and savers via negative or below market real interest rates. After WWII, capital controls and regulatory restrictions created a captive audience for government debt, limiting tax-base erosion. Financial repression is most successful in liquidating debt when accompanied by inflation. For the advanced economies, real interest rates were negative ½ of the time during 1945–1980. Average annual interest expense savings for a 12—country sample range from about 1 to 5 percent of GDP for the full 1945–1980 period. We suggest that, once again, financial repression may be part of the toolkit deployed to cope with the most recent surge in public debt in advanced economies.

More:

To deal with the current debt overhang, similar policies have re-emerged in the guise of prudential regulation rather than under the politically incorrect label of financial repression. Moreover, the process where debts are being "placed" at below market interest rates in pension funds and other more captive domestic financial institutions is already under way in several countries in Europe. In addition, some European countries have already imposed capital controls. There are many bankrupt (or nearly so) pension plans at the state level in the United States that bear scrutiny (in addition to the substantive unfunded liabilities at the federal level).

Markets for government bonds are increasingly populated by non-market players, notably central banks of the United States, Europe and many of the largest emerging markets, calling into question what the information content of bond prices are relatively to their underlying risk profile. This decoupling between interest rates and risk is a common feature of financially repressed systems. With public and private external debts at record highs, many advanced economies are increasingly looking inward for public debt placements.

The incentives to reduce the debt overhang are more compelling today than about half a century ago.[107] In October 2015, Congressman Scott

Peters, Representative for California's 52nd congressional district, referred to committee bill H.R. 3775: Pay Down the Debt Act of 2015. The purpose of the bill is "to amend the Congressional Budget Act of 1974 to provide for a debt stabilization process." In a nutshell, the bill is intended to reduce the deficit or debt held by the public. The problem is, according to the government transparency website GovTrack.us, it only has a 1% chance of passing.

Interest Rates and Spending

Now that we see what debt our nation is in, we have to admit what the Fed has done to keep themselves and our government out of trouble—they've kept rates low, just as suggested by Reinhart.

Instead of letting the market decide where rates should be, the Fed has implemented quantitative easing and operation twist[108] to keep rates artificially low with the goal of somehow stimulating the economy. This in turn has kept the interest owed on all that national debt we have to a minimum. Currently that expense is $402.4 billion annualized.[109]

But if these programs fail to do what the Fed expects them to do—get consumers spending, businesses producing and inflation up to their 2% target—then they have a nightmare on their hands. That nightmare is debt deflation.

Debt deflation is a term attributed to Irving Fisher back in 1933, when we last experienced severe deflation. The following is from Fisher's *The Debt-Deflation Theory of Great Depressions*. Pay close attention to the bolded type. This is exactly what the Fed and other central banks are doing around the world, trying to prevent numbers 4-8 from occurring. But it's not working!

---

[107] http://www.europarl.europa.eu/document/activities/cont/201106/20110617ATT 21648/20110617ATT21648EN.pdf

[108] http://www.investopedia.com/terms/o/operation-twist.asp

[109] https://www.treasurydirect.gov/govt/reports/ir/ir_expense.htm

> *(1) Debt liquidation leads to distress setting and to (2) Contraction of deposit currency, as bank loans are paid off, and to a slowing down of velocity of circulation. This contraction of deposits and of their velocity, precipitated by distress selling, causes (3) A fall in the level of prices, in other words, a swelling of the dollar.* ***Assuming, as above stated, that this fall of prices is not interfered with by reflation or otherwise****, there must be (4) A still greater fall in the net worths of business, precipitating bankruptcies and (5) A like fall in profits, which in a "capitalistic," that is, a private-profit society, leads the concerns which are running at a loss to make (6) A reduction in output, in trade and in employment of labor. These losses, bankruptcies, and unemployment, lead to (7) Pessimism and loss of confidence, which in turn lead to (8) Hoarding and slowing down still more the velocity of circulation.*[110]

If a business has a loan at 5% and rates fall to 3%, this difference hits the profit margin of the business. If interest rates fall further, the debt looms larger. This is what's happening. What is the debt situation of the companies *you* invest in?

Also, what happens when interest rates rise? At projected rates, the interest expense is scheduled to more than double by 2025.[111]

---

110 https://fraser.stlouisfed.org/docs/meltzer/fisdeb33.pdf

111 http://budget.house.gov/uploadedfiles/fy16_charts.pdf

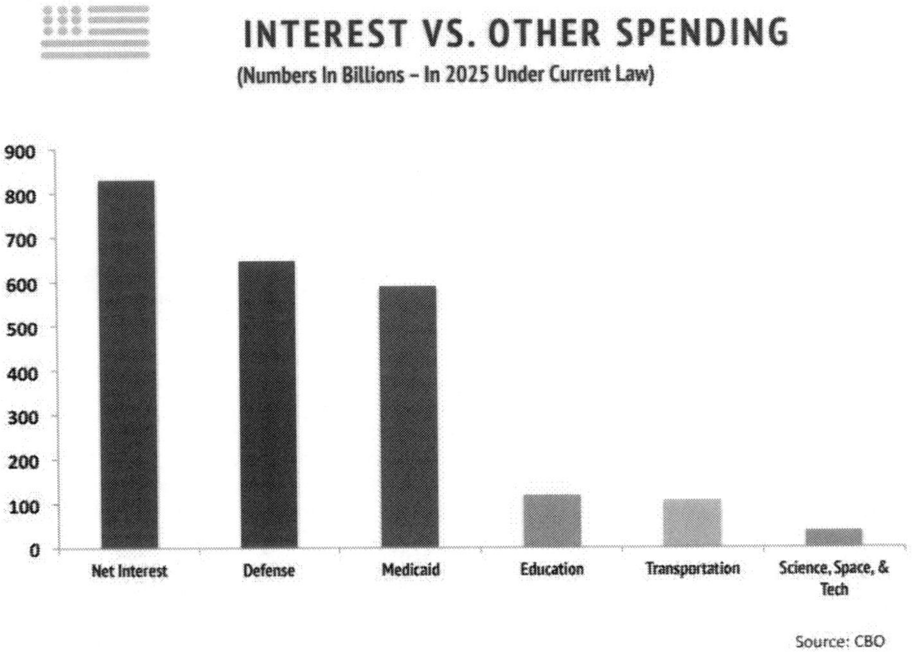

The problem with current CBO projections is that our government seems to think they know where interest rates will be in the future, and they possess the ability to predict exactly the range 5 to 15 years out. That range, according to them, is between 3.4% on the 3-month Treasury bill and 4.6% on the 10-year Treasury note, as seen in the next chart.

The Fed will be powerless to stop inflation when it comes. Look at the "actual" results of interest rates over the years just since 2000 and how volatile they are versus the "projected" rates, and how they look so normalized.[112]

[112] https://www.cbo.gov/sites/default/files/114th-congress-2015-2016/reports/49892-Outlook2015.pdf

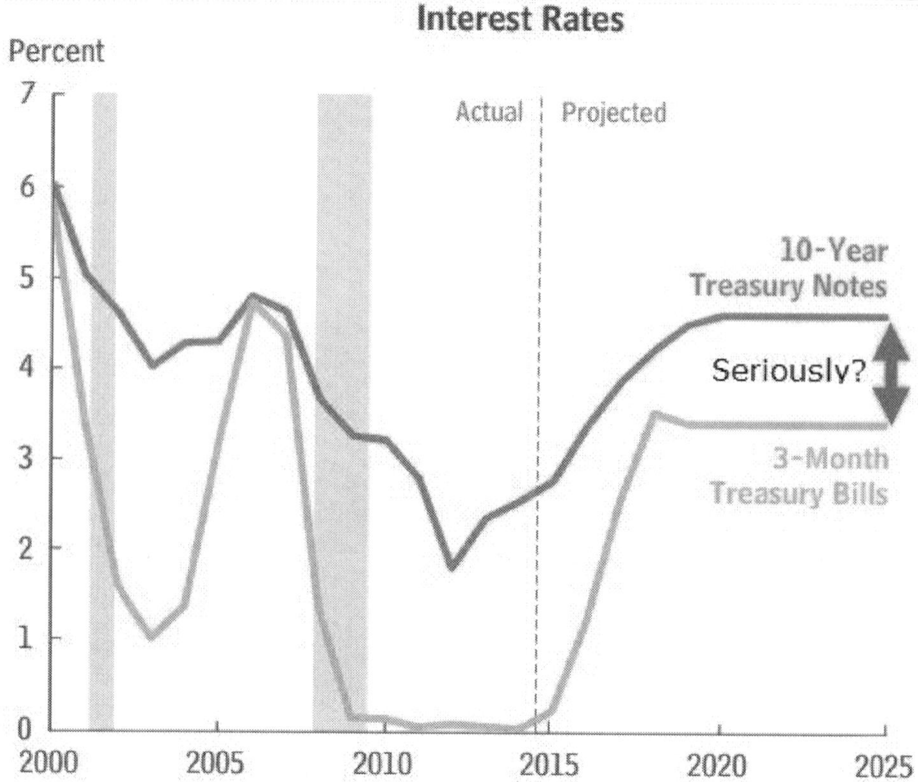

The question that must be answered today is what are the odds of them being right? They readily admit their projections from 2014 were wrong for GDP by .02%. The Fed all of 2015 said they were going to raise rates, but waited till the end of December to finally do so. How does anyone know what the future holds in 5 to 20 years from now?

Here's the kicker. The Fed can't lower rates much more to "save the economy" like Paul Volcker did in 1980. Any further uptick in rates now will be disastrous for business and consumer alike. Higher mortgage rates don't make people go out and buy homes; they *keep people from* buying homes. Businesses don't borrow more when rates are higher, as it is an added expense to their balance sheet (unless of course interest rates are rapidly increasing).

This is a good time to check in with what the International Monetary Fund economists think is coming. We have seen the crash in commodities. We have an example of what the IMF would do with a nation like Greece, which produces virtually nothing but consumes everything. There is no hope for those who have lent Greece money to ever get it back. Even the IMF says the magnitude of the debt today can't be overcome, in a report called "1930s-Style Debt Defaults Likely," written by Harvard economists Carmen Reinhart, who was referenced earlier, and Kenneth Rogoff:

> I*t is clear that governments should be careful in their assumption that growth alone will be able to end the crisis. Instead, today's advanced country governments may have to look increasingly to the approaches that have long been associated with emerging markets, and that advanced countries themselves once practiced not so long ago. In Europe, where the financial crisis transformed into sovereign debt crises in several countries, the current phase of the denial cycle is marked by an official policy approach predicated on the assumption that normal growth can be restored through a mix of austerity, forbearance, and growth. In light of the historic public and private debt levels ... it is difficult to envision a resolution to the current five-year-old crisis that does not involve a greater role for explicit restructuring.*[113]

The suggestion that restructuring is needed is not one the Fed and other central banks will agree with. Not until it's too late. You'll read more about what steps the Fed will take to keep the game going in Part 6 on the Federal Reserve, but first we need to address what the Fed and other central banks are fighting: Deflation.

---

[113] http://www.cnbc.com/2014/01/03/debt-defaults-for-advanced-economies-likely-imf-research.html

PART 3 – DEFLATION

Chapter 8 - Deflation Isn't a Bad Thing, Just Misunderstood

Deflation has to be the most misunderstood word in economics, and is entirely discounted by most economists and journalists because they don't understand what it entails. As a country, we really haven't experienced much deflation. The last deflationary episode for the U.S. was the 1929-1932 era, during the Great Depression.[114]

Chart 12a Deflation episodes are rare

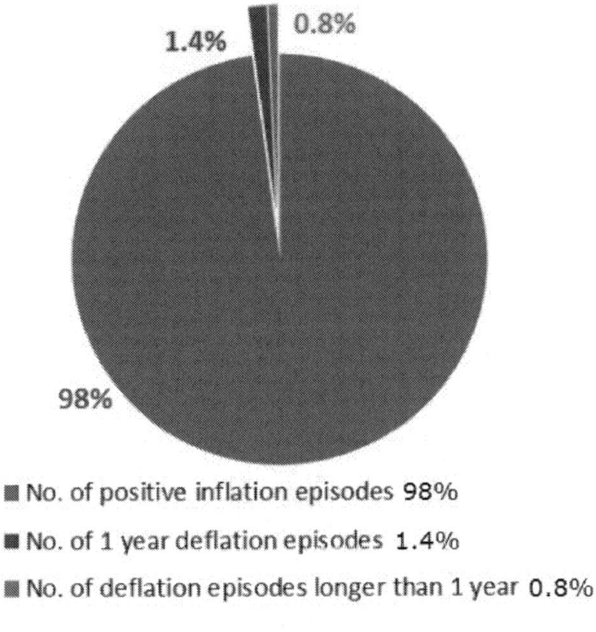

Source: Bordo and Eichengreen, IMF and OECD
Note: Sample 1960-2010; 3300 observations

---

[114] http://www.bankofengland.co.uk/publications/Documents/speeches/ 2015/speech 813.pdf

If you ever have a discussion with anyone about deflation, it helps to first be on the same page regarding what deflation means. I use the definition put forward by Professor Jesús Huerta de Soto, Department of Applied Economics at King Juan Carlos University of Madrid, Spain, in his book *Money, Bank Credit, and Economic Cycles*:

> *Deflation results from the tightening of credit which normally occurs in the crisis and recession stage that follows all credit expansion. Just as credit expansion increases the quantity of money in circulation, the massive repayment of loans and the loss of value on the assets side of banks' balance sheets, both caused by the crisis, trigger an inevitable, cumulative process of credit tightening which reduces the quantity of money in circulation and thus generates deflation. This type of deflation arises when, as the crisis is emerging, not only does credit expansion stop increasing, but there is actually a credit squeeze and thus, deflation, or a drop in the money supply, or quantity of money in circulation.*[115]

Deflation in and of itself is not a bad thing. It is necessary in a free economy to weed out the bad. If we'd weeded out the bad in 2009, there would have been pain for many, especially the financial elite, but we would have recovered quicker and be well on our way to prosperity and economic recovery.

A quote from Tom Osenton's 2004 book The Death of Demand explains well what's also contributing to the deflationary environment:

> *We have more TVs than viewers. More phone numbers than talkers. More homes than households. More cars than drivers. Corporations have pushed for more, and consumers have gorged themselves ... and now they're starting to pull away from the table. Demand is dead. The culprit: the generations of managers at the world's greatest corporations who did their jobs so well they hastened the onset of saturation.*[116]

[115] https://mises.org/library/money-bank-credit-and-economic-cycles

Richard Koo describes this debt deflation as a "balance sheet recession," which is also the title of his 2003 book describing the Japanese deflation.

The problem is that a balance sheet recession is no ordinary recession. In this recession, which is brought about by the fallacy of composition, the economy is weakening because most companies are looking backward as they try to repair their balance sheets. But because the companies are minimizing debt instead of maximizing profits, demand is lost all around the economy. If no one came in to fill the shortfall in demand created by everyone paying down debt, the whole economy could fall into a vicious cycle.

Why are companies looking to minimize debt? Because in deflation, debt becomes more expensive to hold, as illustrated in the following graph:

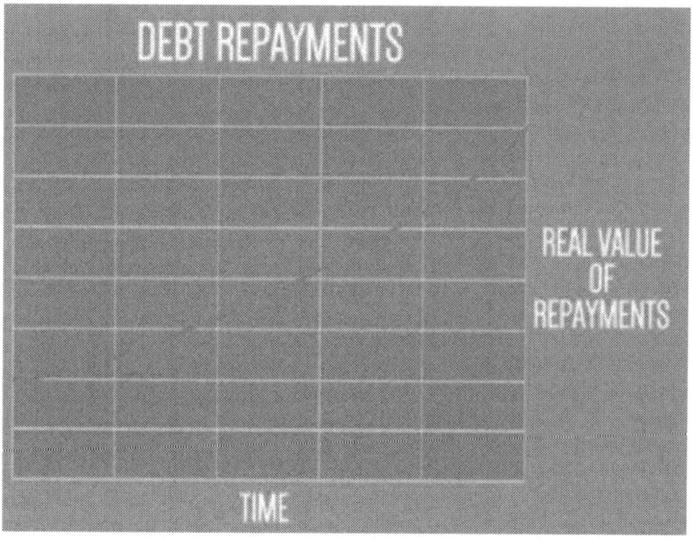

The lack of consumer demand also plagues these companies. If consumers are saturated with multiples of everything, why do they

[116] http://www.amazon.com/The-Death-Demand-Saturated-Financial/dp/0131423312

need more? If there is a saturation level reached, and the next iPhone doesn't offer much more than the last, or an 8k HD resolution display doesn't offer much more depth than 4k, where will the buyers come from when demand dies and business contracts? This is deflationary also.

Once consumers see their wages decrease, their desires or wants also dissipate. Hoarding money becomes more important as consumers spend on necessities only, and hold off on purchasing more of everything. As we already noted, consumer debt is growing and credit card companies are setting themselves up for another round of losses. The lack of credit available by default is deflationary.

Looking at the Commodity Price Index the last 5 years and the Consumer Price Index the last 10 years, though, all we see is deflation, not inflation.[117] Prices have been falling on commodities since 2011 with temporary blips up with short term dollar weakness from time to time. We'll get into why prices are rising in some areas (for those of you I know are saying "I pay more, not less, for things") a bit later but here's a hint: The government is involved.

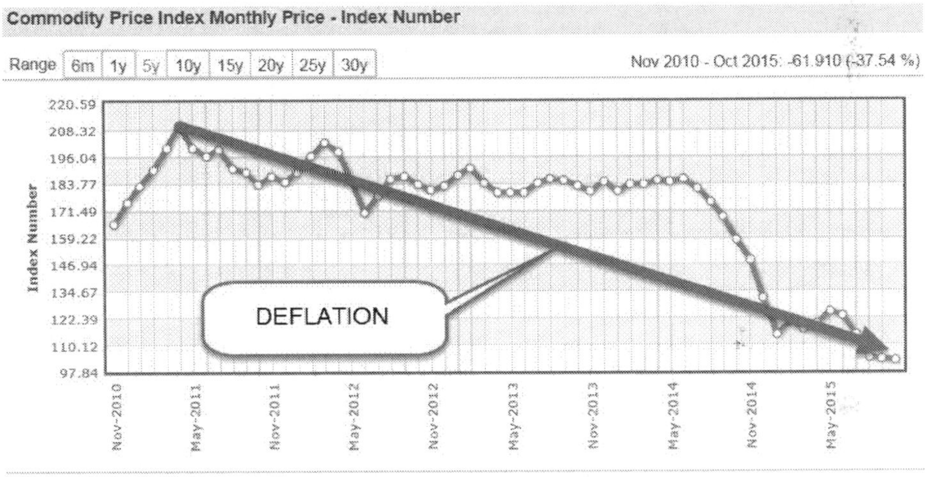

Description: Commodity Price Index, 2005 = 100, includes both Fuel and Non-Fuel Price Indices

---

[117] http://www.bls.gov/cpi/cpid1510.pdf

CPI-U 12-Month Changes, 2005 to Present

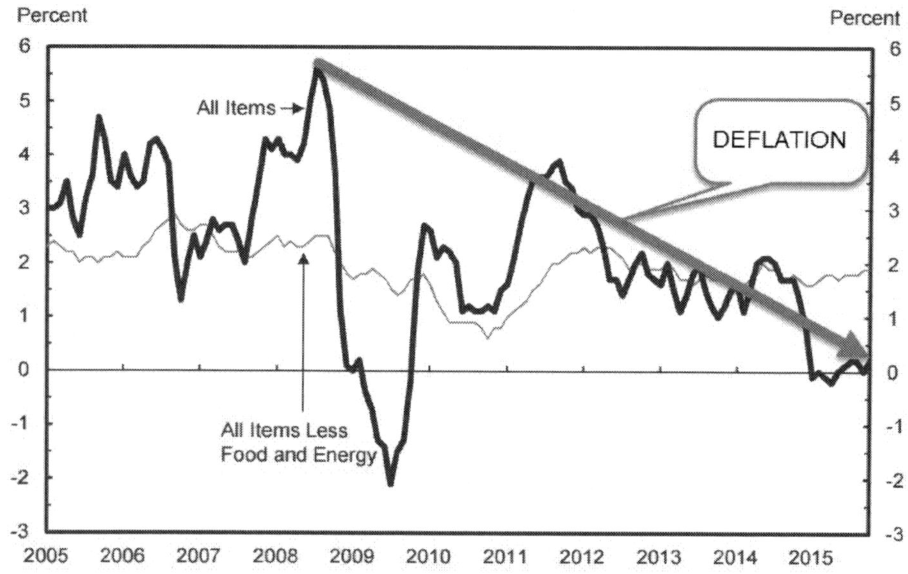

What the Fed is also concerned with regarding deflation is lower wages and thus lower tax receipts, giving the government less money to pay off debt. This is why you are seeing the push for higher minimum wages. To make up for this, the Fed has to step in and stimulate any way they can, all under the theory that the extra money flowing in will improve the economy and spur growth, and higher wages will increase tax receipts. This of course will eventually lead to the desired inflation the Fed is looking for at 2%. Higher wages in and of themselves are inflationary, so look to them as a leading indicator of inflation.

We'll get to inflation a bit later, but first we must understand how much credit we have created since the 1950s, and what happens when this credit can't be paid off or is potentially defaulted on. This is the key to everything. To take this analysis to the point of further enlightenment, I want to introduce you to the term "credit contraction" and in a bit the work of economist John Exter.

Credit Contraction - Understanding Credit Contraction, Liquidity and How Money Flows During Deflationary Episodes

If we are right about a deflationary episode, then you need to understand how a contraction of the excesses (credit) for the last several decades would have to be unwound, and where money will flow in the process. Then it will become clearer to you where you want to put some of your investment capital.

Credit

When I wrote my book *Buy Gold and Silver Safely* in 2010, I included a chart of total credit market debt as a percentage of GDP. It showed the great expansion of credit since the beginning days of the Reagan administration in 1980. Total credit market debt as a percentage of GDP then was 362.6%. Today that figure has been reduced to 349.4%, but it still shows there is a lot of credit outstanding as a nation.

To put this chart into perspective, while total credit market debt today is 349.4% of GDP, it was 260% of GDP in the year 1929, just before the Great Depression. You can see from the chart the last deflationary episode beginning in 1933.

While we have mended many of the bank balance sheets here in the U.S. with unprecedented Fed quantitative easing stimulus since 2009 and eliminated some of this outstanding debt, we are a long way from reining in the loose credit since 1980. While credit has been beneficial for many during this "boom" period, the last financial crisis showed us that trouble can come quickly, and since we have simply kicked the can down the road, one might expect trouble to come quickly again.

The question becomes, will this be an issue moving forward? The answer is a resounding yes which will be explained more shortly through the work of John Exter and his Inverse Pyramid.

One of the problems for those in the U.S. is that since countries are all interconnected, the financial problems in other developed and undeveloped nations could spill over onto our shores. What is happening in these other nations then becomes an area we need to watch. Have countries like the PIIGS (Portugal, Ireland, Italy, Greece and Spain) overcome their problems since the crisis and shored up their balance sheets? The short answer is no. The next section takes a look at the rest of the world's issues.

Europe, China, Japan and the Rest - It's Not Just the U.S. That Matters

No analysis on the economy and investment climate for the U.S. can be complete unless we take into account what's going on in the rest of the world. Primarily we want to look at those countries that are part of the Dollar Index we spoke about earlier, which are the largest economies that make up the euro, UK (part of the European Union but not the euro), Japan, and separately the second largest economy in the world—China.

The main reason we want to analyze the economic conditions and financial climate of these countries is because they're all interconnected these days. The central bank for each country—the European Central Bank (ECB), Bank of Japan (BofJ), and People's Bank of China—set policy based on what is needed in their respective countries. This competes with Fed policy, as all countries strive to grow their economies through improving GDP. If these governments through central bank policy can lower the value of their currency, though, it makes their exports more desirable abroad, and this is what some of these countries are doing—causing the dollar to appreciate, and putting U.S. companies at a disadvantage.

Europe is fighting deflation and has been for some time as seen in the next graph. They have been slow to implement quantitative easing and now are struggling with the effects of negative interest rates.

Inflation in the euro area (annual percentage changes, non-seasonally adjusted)

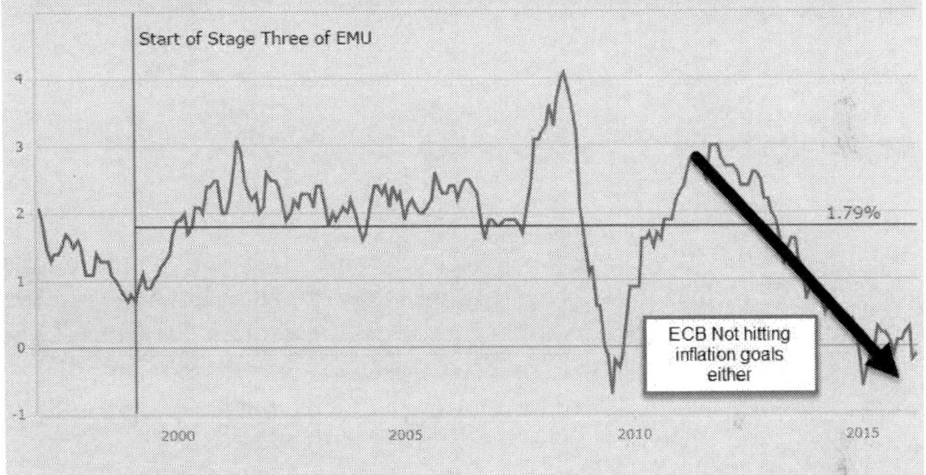

Source: Eurostat. Data prior to 1996 are estimated on the basis of non-harmonised national Consumer Price Indices (CPIs). Average inflation since 1999.

The U.S. dollar has been strengthening since 2011, simply because of the quantitative easing coming from ECB president Mario Draghi and the ECB, and Japanese prime minister Shinzō Abe's weakening the yen in Japan. This has caused a mad dash to perceived safety in the dollar, weakening U.S. exports. If you couple this with negative interest rates these central banks and national leaders are pulling out all stops. Are they desperate?

Japan is our best example of how to survive deflation. They have been experiencing deflation since 1989, after a credit-expansion episode of epic proportions. The Japanese stock market, the Nikkei, reached a high of 38,957.44 December 1989, and 20 years later in March 2009, it had fallen to 7,054—almost 82% below its peak. Residential real estate in Japan fell 64% from 1991 to 2005.[118]

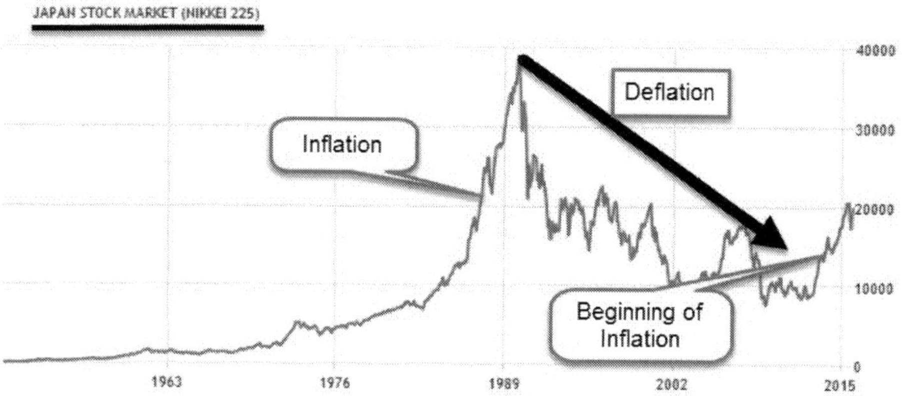

Japan has survived deflation primarily because they had a few things going for them that most other countries don't. They have been a net exporter, and they have owned about a trillion dollars' worth of U.S. Treasuries, while most of their own debt (98%) is owned internally. Conversely, the U.S. is a net importer, and the world's largest debtor nation.

118 http://www.nytimes.com/2005/12/25/business/yourmoney/take-it-from-japan-bubbles-hurt.html?_r=0

By analyzing Japan we can get an idea of what to expect from our own central bank, the Federal Reserve, as well as an idea of how Fed policy decisions may affect your future investment decisions. Investing is easier if you have a roadmap from a country that has experienced or is currently experiencing what your country may be going through soon.

With an aging population and a debt-to-GDP ratio that leads the world, Japan has only one choice, and that is to inflate. Longtime writer of the *Dow Theory Letters*, Richard Russell, used to say "inflate or die" when talking about solutions here in the U.S. This is true for Japan and eventually will be for the U.S. also.

Debt-to-GDP ratio by country and sector

Ranked by decreasing real economy debt-to-GDP ratio, 2Q14[1]

Advanced economy | Developing economy | 1st quartile | 2nd quartile | 3rd quartile | 4th quartile

Rank	Country	Debt-to-GDP ratio[1] %	Real economy debt-to-GDP ratio by sector % Government	Corporate	Household	Financial-sector debt-to-GDP ratio
1	Japan	400	234	101	65	117
2	Ireland	390	115	189	85	291
3	Singapore	382	105	201	76	246
4	Portugal	358	148	127	83	81
5	Belgium	327	135	136	56	75
6	Netherlands	325	83	127	115	362
7	Greece	317	183	68	65	5
8	Spain	313	132	108	73	89
9	Denmark	302	60	114	129	235
10	Sweden	290	42	165	82	125
11	France	280	104	121	56	93
12	Italy	259	139	77	43	76
13	United Kingdom	252	92	74	86	183
14	Norway	244	34	86	124	93
15	Finland	238	65	108	64	59
16	United States	233	89	67	77	36
17	South Korea	231	44	105	81	56
18	Hungary	225	83	114	29	51
19	Austria	225	87	88	50	90
20	Malaysia	222	55	91	76	42
21	Canada	221	70	60	92	25
22	China	217	55	125	38	65
23	Australia	213	31	69	113	61
24	Germany	188	80	54	54	70
25	Thailand	187	46	65	76	64
26	Israel	178	67	73	38	12
27	Slovakia	151	67	52	32	9
28	Vietnam	146	50	76	19	6
29	Morocco	136	62	51	23	15
30	Chile	136	15	86	36	40
31	Poland	134	57	42	35	20
32	South Africa	133	45	49	39	21
33	Czech Republic	128	47	49	33	23
34	Brazil	128	65	38	25	32
35	India	120	66	45	9	15
36	Philippines	116	40	71	6	12
37	Egypt	106	77	23	6	2
38	Turkey	104	35	47	22	29
39	Romania	104	38	47	19	7
40	Indonesia	88	22	46	20	21
41	Colombia	76	32	30	15	6
42	Mexico	73	44	22	7	20
43	Russia	65	9	40	16	23
44	Peru	62	19	29	15	8
45	Saudi Arabia	59	3	43	13	6
46	Nigeria	46	20	22	4	3
47	Argentina	33	19	9	5	7

1 Includes debt of households, non-financial corporations, and government; 2Q14 data for advanced economies and China; 2013 data for other developing economies.

SOURCE: *World economic outlook*, IMF; BIS; Haver Analytics; national central banks; McKinsey Global Institute analysis

You'll note that 10 out of the top 12 countries are part of the European Union and use the euro as their currency (which we'll talk about next), and Japan is number one, with the UK 13th and the U.S. 16th. In other words, from a Debt to GDP ratio analysis, the U.S. is the best of a bad bunch.

Japan also has an aging population problem. Without younger working taxpayers to chip in to keep the payments promised to the elderly going, and a debt burden on top of it, it's so much easier to simply cheapen your currency to keep the promises made to seniors.[119]

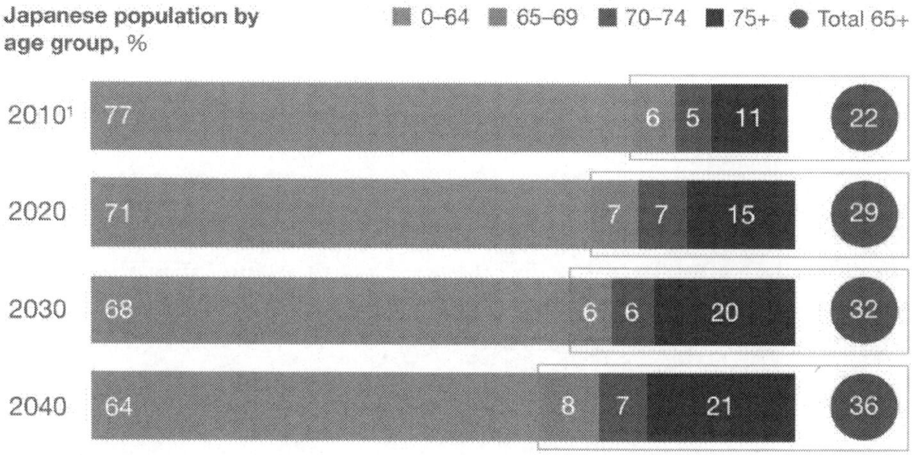

By 2040, estimates suggest, more than a third of Japan's population will be 65 or over.

¹Figures do not sum to 100%, because of rounding.

Source: e-Stat (Japan's portal for government statistics); IHS Global Insight World Market Monitor

And what is the result of all of these central bank policies to fight deflation and increase debt in light of an aging population? It can be seen in the chart of the weakening yen. If your economy isn't growing, then this is your only choice. Take note, all other countries.

---

[119] http://www.mckinsey.com/insights/asia-pacific/japan_lessons_from_a_hyperaging_society

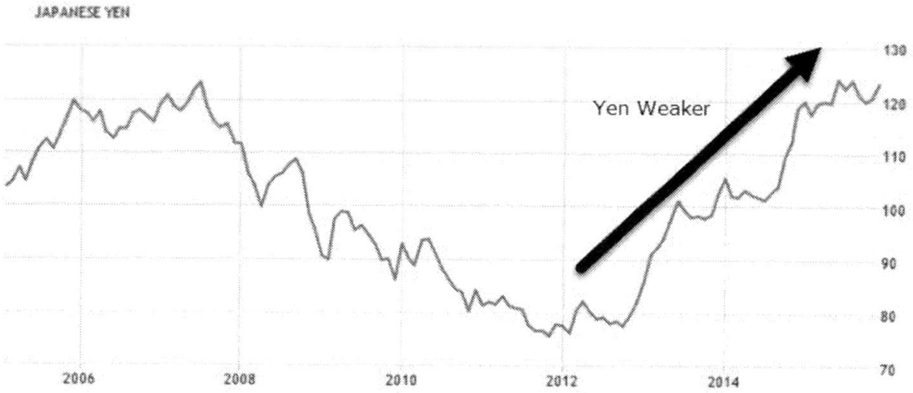

While Japan is trying to weaken their currency and will fight any appreciation that comes, Europe has been going down the same path with no other choice, since individual countries can't print their own currency to solve their own debt issues. It's actually quite the quagmire, and I don't see an easy way out without putting the euro itself in jeopardy.

Germany can't support the euro all by itself, and has their own issues with their auto industry and refugee situation, as do other European countries. In my opinion, the euro is in deep trouble and this by default will be dollar bullish because the Dollar Index is heavily weighted with euros.

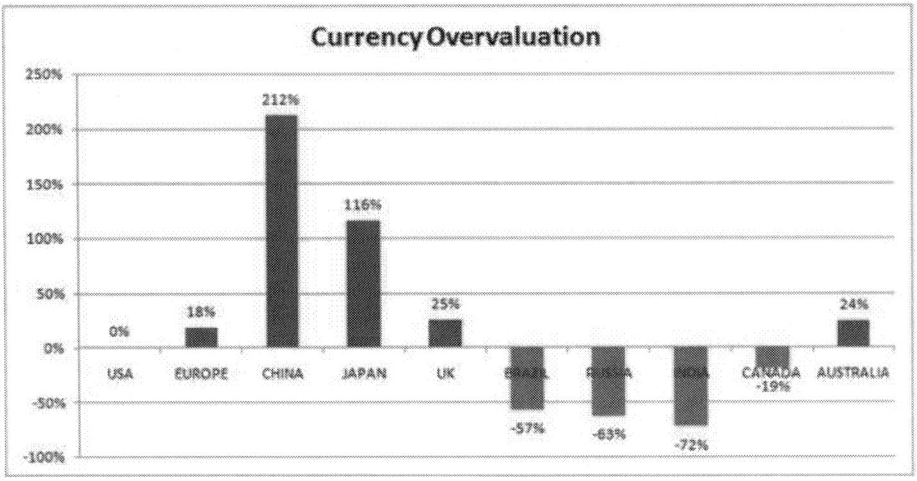

Source: TradingEconomics.com, Currency Rates from CNBC.com

Yes, I keep a close eye on what is going on with the euro, and for good reason. If things unravel there, as I have said, it will spill over to the UK and U.S. shores. If it becomes too much for the central banks of the world to handle, then your portfolio had better have some protection against this.

Europe has a deflation problem, as the ECB. Headed by their President, Mario Draghi, implements quantitative easing to help stave off deflation.

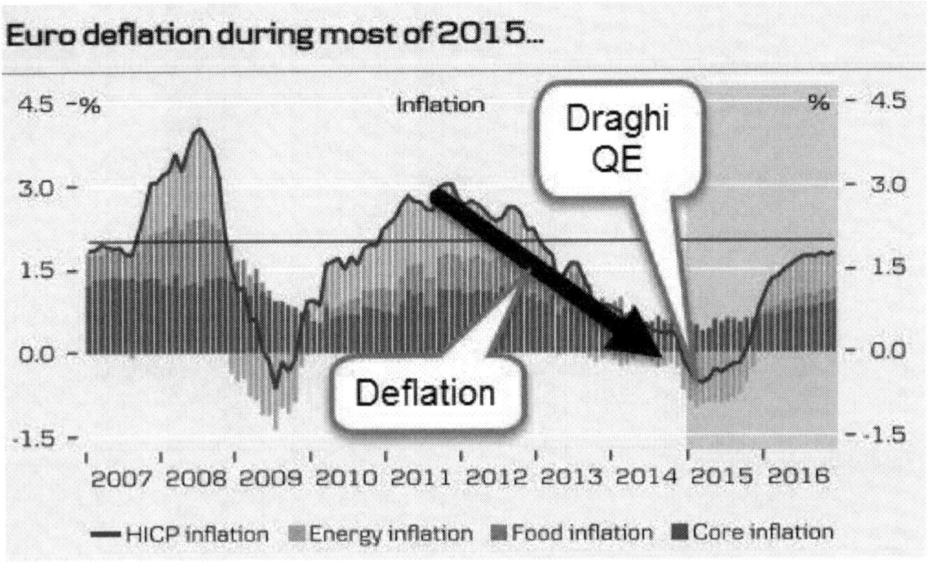

Source: Eurostat, Danske Bank Markets

This is all central banks know how to do: artificially stimulate, instead of letting the bad get weeded out of the economy, including overindulgence by governments. The alternative is letting rates go negative, and that would be troublesome for central banks.

> *Negative inflation rates make servicing existing debt more difficult for leveraged companies and financial institutions (Irving Fisher's debt-deflation argument), because they cannot rewrite debt contracts to lower the impact of falling prices on their balance sheets. This could increase banks' efforts to raise reserves-to-deposit ratios and result in higher risk premia on corporate debt with increased financial fragmentation.*[120]

What is fascinating to me about this report from Europe is military action seems to be their solution to create inflation:

---

[120] http://ec.europa.eu/economy_finance/publications/european_economy/2015/pdf/ee1_en.pdf

> *Risks to the inflation outlook stem from a further depreciation of the euro or from a faster-than-expected recovery, which could add positive price pressures. Also, upward pressures on oil prices, for instance originating from reduced exploration or* ***continued unrest or military actions in oil-exporting countries****, could push inflation higher than expected.*

Let's summarize Europe's position in getting to inflation:

1. Depreciate the euro (they have been doing this, with the euro falling from the 130s to the low 100s through 2016, but they falsely think it will be from a recovery.
2. Upward pressure on oil prices, mostly from a choice of "unrest" or "military actions in oil-exporting countries."

That second option is basically "start a war." How about businesses producing? Innovation in technology? Entrepreneurship? Has Europe so devolved as a society that they have to stoop to currency depreciation and war to bring about inflation? I'm afraid so, and come the investment chapter, you'll learn how to keep and grow your wealth so inflation doesn't eat it away. But first we must deal with the deflation that the ECB and other central banks are fighting.

Europe has another issue that many don't talk about, and that is their pension obligations. Just like you'll see in the Retirement section, Europe has many pensioners who have been promised a pension upon retirement. If these promises to citizens become underfunded because tax revenue decreases (as Europeans possibly lose jobs or see their incomes reduced), where does the money come from to pay these retirees?

The decision making by European Union leaders isn't necessarily the best either. They didn't see the Greece fiasco coming. They let Croatia, who had a large number of government employees and high number of unemployed teens as well as a large deficit, into the union. They also didn't see deflation coming.

They now have a migrant issue, with Syrian refugees putting a burden on each country's borders and economies and a higher expense because of counterterrorism activities and controlling the behavior of the refugees.

Germany and France hold the debt of many countries and are trying to keep the union alive, but now Germany has issues with Volkswagen and the auto industry, the engines (literally) that have kept the country going since WWII.

If the problems of Greece can wreak havoc on world markets, it can happen anywhere else in Europe too. These countries, unlike the U.S., Japan, China, and other large countries with their own central banks, cannot print their own currency and resolve their issues independently as they could prior to the union's formation. They now rely on one central bank that has its hands tied behind its back but they do have a Draghi, "whatever it takes" mentality. You can expect this to be policy and it will be just more cracks in the damn, waiting for the bursting to occur.

In the UK, which is part of the European Union but still uses its own currency the pound, the rate of inflation has been at or around 0% for most of 2015, and they have been deflating since 2011.[121]

---

[121] **http://www.ons.gov.uk/ons/dcp171778_419255.pdf**

Figure B: CPI 12-month inflation rate for the last 10 years: September 2005 to September 2015

United Kingdom

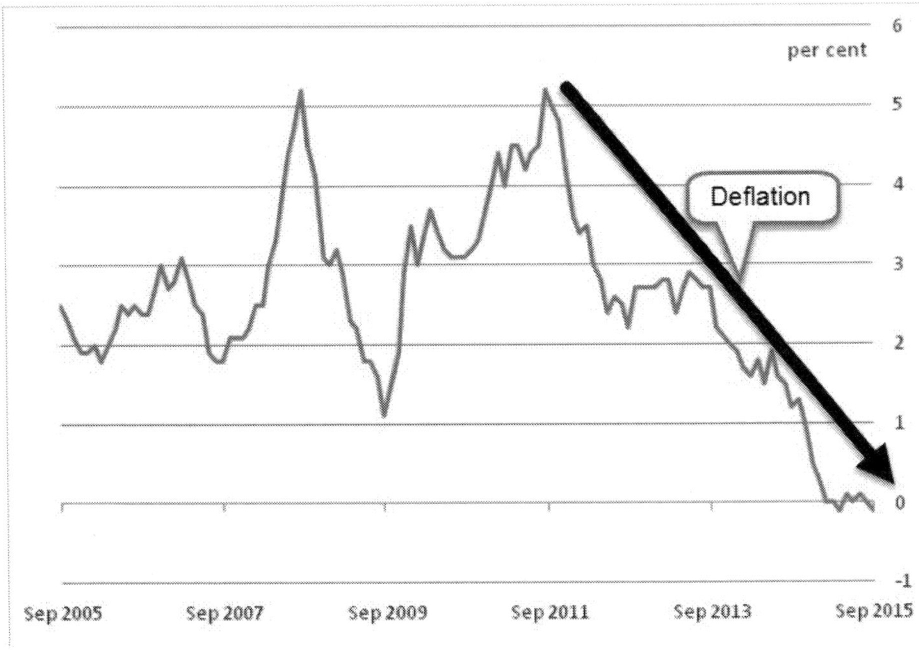

Source: Office for National Statistics

The UK has now left the European Union in a surprising Brexit and the Pound lost 10% to it's lowest levels since 1985. This is dollar bullish as the pound makes up 11.9% of the dollar which jumped 2.75% on the news. Which country is next to leave the European Union? All of this type of activity will continue to be dollar bullish for the short term and central banks of the world will be scrambling to keep the Humpty Dumpty monetary systems together. Gold has reacted favorably in all currencies because of this.

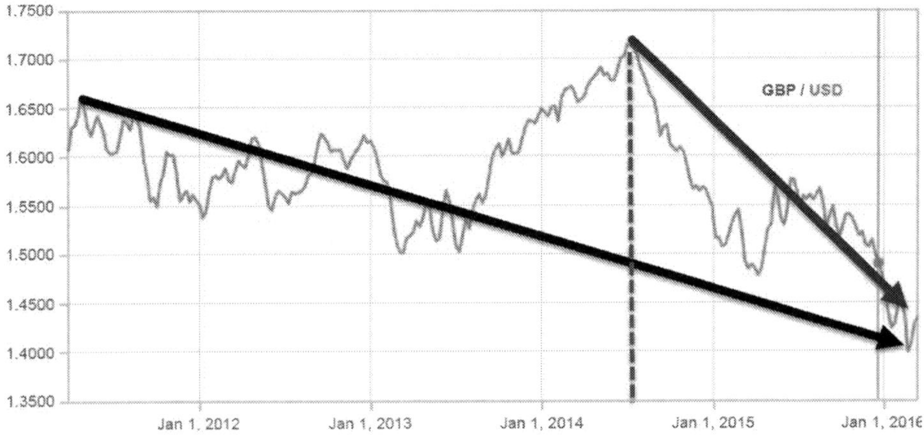

China Fighting Contraction and Deflation

At present, the levels of public debt in many advanced economies are at or near uncharted territory: some of these governments face the prospect of debt restructuring. Furthermore, public and private external debts (which are a relatively volatile source of funding) are at historic highs. It seems probable that policymakers for some time to come will be preoccupied with debt reduction, debt management, and, in general, efforts to keep debt servicing costs manageable. In this setting, financial repression (with its dual aims of keeping interest rates low and creating or maintaining captive domestic audiences) will probably find renewed favor and the measures and developments we have described and discussed in this note are likely to be only the tip of a very large iceberg.

Next we'll take a look at China, the new kid on the block when it comes to being a financial and now a monetary powerhouse. Naturally it has taken time for China to get to this level, but just like any country that experiences growth, there are cracks in the system that need to be considered.

You'll recall from the opening chapter that China originally invented paper money in the 10th century. Since that time, every currency in the world has failed, and the reason is quite simple: Governments print too much of it and citizens lose faith in it.

China achieved its strength by exporting lower-cost products to the world, which produced the great wealth of the Walton family and Wal-Mart, as well as the value of many other businesses that left the U.S. after trade agreements were created, some because loopholes in the regulatory climate prohibited their U.S. operations from flourishing. We discuss China in more detail as to the investment opportunities in the Investment section, but it is important we discuss the consequences of their growth and what issues may be forthcoming that investors need to consider.

China's debt-to-GDP is rising, and while the Chinese government is trying hard to curtail growth and bring the system into a reduced-risk environment, it may be too little, too late.

> *The amount of loans, bonds and shadow finance arranged to cover interest payments will probably rise 5 percent this year to a record 7.6 trillion yuan ($1.2 trillion), according to Beijing-based Hua Chuang Securities Co., whose lead fixed-income analyst Qu Qing was top-ranked by China's New Fortune magazine in 2012 and 2013. Dubbed "Ponzi finance" by Hyman Minsky, the use of borrowed funds to repay interest was seen by the late U.S. economist as an unsustainable form of credit growth that could precipitate financial crises.*[122]

[122] http://www.bloomberg.com/news/articles/2015-11-19/china-has-a-1-2-trillion-ponzi-finance-problem-as-debt-piles-up

Chinese Firms Are Issuing More Debt Just to Pay Interest

Amount of new total social financing used to pay interest on existing debt

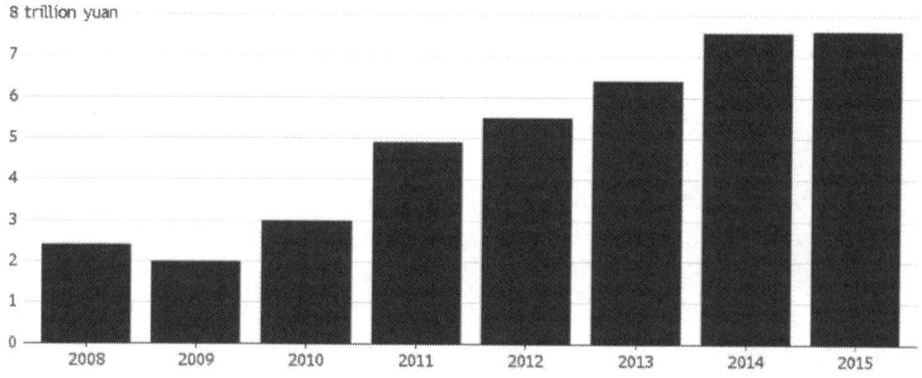

Huachuang Securities Co.

2015 figure is forecast. Total social financing includes bank loans, shadow banking credit and corporate bonds.

One of the companies buying up properties at what many believe is exactly the wrong time is Evergrande Real Estate, which has snatched up $6.4 billion in the last six months buying properties from other developers. But as a recent *Wall Street Journal* article pointed out, "That is a magnificent feat for a company with around $16 billion, or roughly half of its total debts coming due in the next 12 months." The *WSJ* goes on to say that "Evergrande's reported net debt to equity ratio was 86% but when you count perpetual bonds as debt instead of equity, that level is actually 230%. The industry average is 80%."[123] It doesn't take much understanding of accounting to know that this type of balance sheet is prone to problems moving forward.

While China still sees more defaults ahead, their growth is still going quite well. But how much of that growth is reality based? There is the official growth listed by those who run communist China, and then there are other estimates that show a smaller number. If you couple

---

123 http://www.wsj.com/articles/beware-this-debt-fueled-chinese-property-buying-spree-1449132663

this data with the debt issues we discussed, there could be some trouble ahead for China.

We already saw in 2015 just how serious a situation China can cause for the rest of the world. The Chinese stock market lost 40% of its value within two months beginning in June, culminating in its own "Black Monday and Tuesday," where the Shanghai main share index lost 8.49% and 7% on August 24 and 25. The Dow Jones Industrial Average (DJIA) proceeded to suffer its largest one-day drop ever, with a loss of 1,000 points when it opened on Monday, August 24.[124]

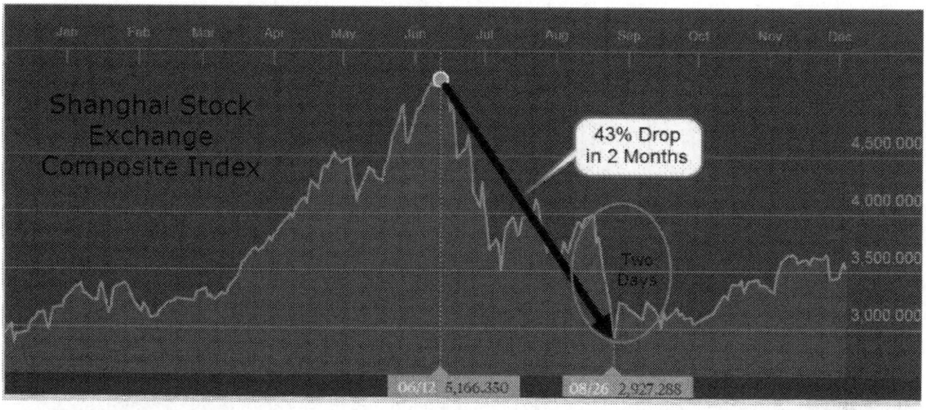

We saw it in Japan. We saw it in the U.S. We have only seen a small taste of it so far in China. There has been much wasteful spending on projects that do little to enhance future economic growth, such as the building of empty cities where mayors are compensated for building with no consequences if no one came to live or do business there—the complete opposite of the voice in the Kevin Costner movie *Field of Dreams*: "If you build it, he will come." For these empty Chinese cities—well documented on the CBS show *60 Minutes* in a segment by Lesley Stahl ("Nobody's home: The ghost cities of China")—no one came.[125]

---

[124] https://en.wikipedia.org/wiki/2015_Chinese_stock_market_crash#Black_Monday_and_Tuesday

[125] http://www.cbsnews.com/news/china-real-estate-bubble-lesley-

But there is still a growth story in China as even their largest mall, once empty just a couple years ago, sees signs of life returning.[126]

Other malls are doing well, like SM Malls from SM Group, a Philippines-based business chain that has opened 56 successful malls in that country.[127] Having set its eyes on China in the past few years, SM has opened five malls in second- and third-tier cities like Xiamen,[128] with four more under construction. The company's niche is understanding that the Chinese are brand conscious and are looking for good brands. SM is adapting to that demand, but also making the malls a lifestyle destination, "with numerous attractions, such as a Science Discovery Center, an ice-skating rink, aquarium, game center, and a 5-star cinema and gym to fulfill its vision as an 'entertainment and relaxation paradise.'"[129]

But those at SM are preparing for eventual higher rates and reducing risk by incorporating fixed loans.[130]

Remember, though, that the Asian financial crisis of the late 1990s was the result of a devaluation in China and a weakening yen, and the same thing is happening today with the Chinese devaluing the yuan in August 2015,[131] and the yen depreciating since 2013.[132]

---

stahl-60-minutes/

126 http://edition.cnn.com/2015/04/28/asia/china-ghost-mall-return-to-life/

127 http://www.financeasia.com/News/374666,sm-plans-future-listing-of-china-malls.aspx

128 http://www.abs-cbnnews.com/business/04/24/15/how-sm-malls-are-faring-china

129 http://www.rappler.com/business/industries/175-real-estate/90462-sm-china-aspirational-lifestyle

130 http://www.bloomberg.com/news/articles/2014-10-16/debt-spree-exposes-philippine-companies-as-world-outlook-dims

131 http://www.wsj.com/articles/china-moves-to-devalue-the-yuan-1439258401

The China Producer Price Index, much like the U.S. Index, has been in a decline,[133] giving us an indication of this slowdown and the eventual deflation that may be coming. According to Investopedia:

> *The Producer Price Index (PPI), the most accurate indicator of future CPI (inflation), is a weighted index of prices measured at the wholesale, or producer level. A monthly release from the Bureau of Labor Statistics (BLS), the PPI shows trends within the wholesale markets (the PPI was once called the Wholesale Price Index), manufacturing industries and commodities markets. All of the physical goods-producing industries that make up the economy are included, but imports are not.*[134]

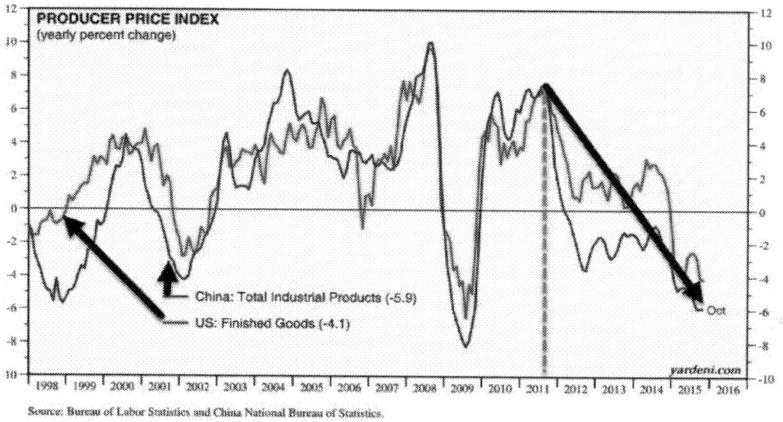

Unlike U.S. investors, when the Chinese invest they expect to make money or get bailed out. This is such a young market that government has so far not really allowed investments to fail. There needs to be some failure and many who invest in the Chinese story are not going

---

[132] http://globalriskinsights.com/2013/08/japans-currency-devaluation-causes-concern/

[133] http://www.yardeni.com/pub/chinainfl.pdf

[134] http://www.investopedia.com/university/releases/ppi.asp#ixzz3tVZZSPM2

to like the outcome. Naturally, just like with the U.S. in 2007-2009, it will be the banking system that may start cracking.

China has a tough road ahead of them: their loan issues could be deceiving the markets. As they reduce their reliance on credit, they also seek a sustainable growth path in line with a central bank that can get them through any rough patches, similar to how the Fed rescued the U.S. banking system after the subprime crisis. Just know that not all banking systems are the same and China is still new at this game. But we are seeing the wealthy Chinese buy up anything and everything to the tune of $106 billion abroad in 2015 and $102 billion in the first 3 months of 2016. We'll discuss this more in the investment section.

The Rest

It's not just the U.S., Europe, Japan and China that are slowing down, but the entire global marketplace, as can be seen in the following charts. Will this evolve into a deflationary collapse? And if so, what will the central banks of the world be able to do to stop it?

The optimistic 2014 forecasts from the IMF have been lowered considerably across the globe,[135] and consensus GDP forecasts continue to come up short.[136]

---

[135] https://sobata416.wordpress.com/

[136] https://dailybrief.oxan.com/Analysis/DB206329/Prospects-for-the-global-economy-in-2016

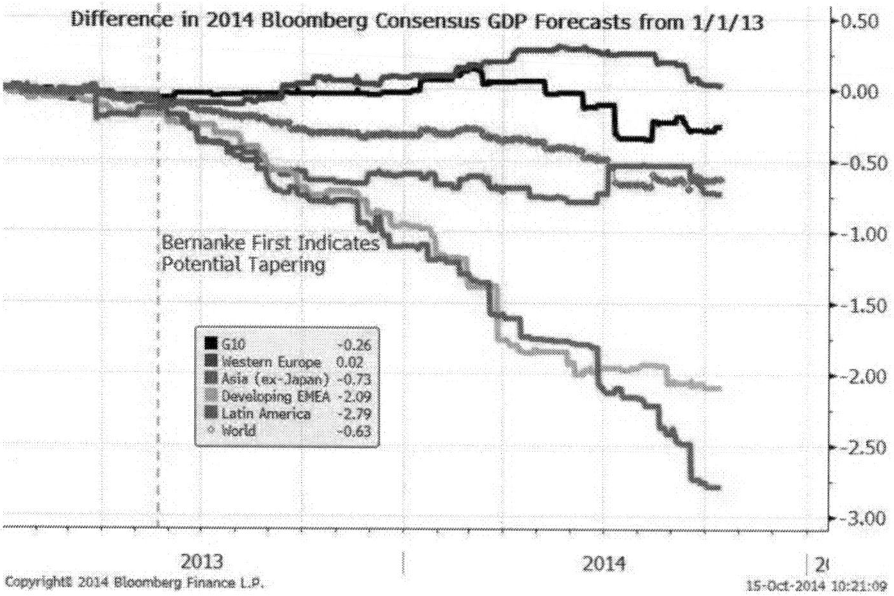

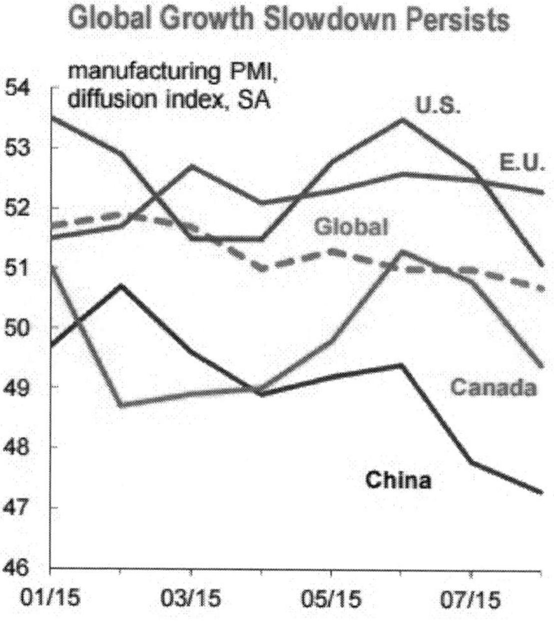

Source: Markit, ISM, Scotiabank Economics.

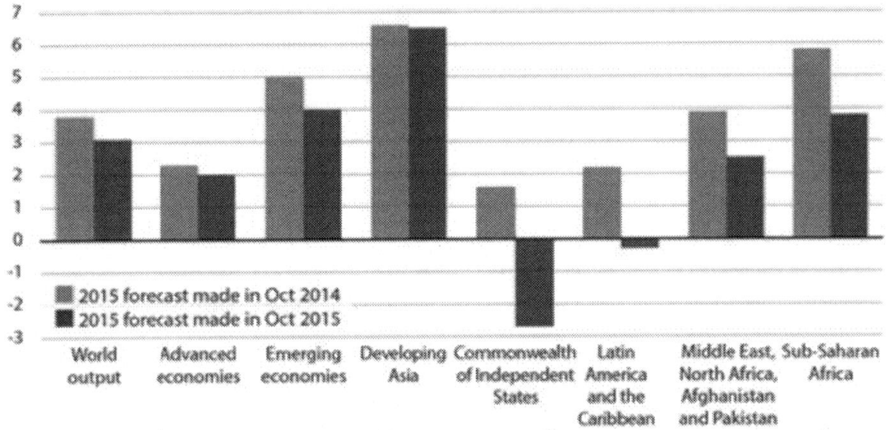

Developing countries' recessions have worsened in the second half of 2015 and they will struggle to stabilise, let alone improve, their growth prospects in early 2016.

Putting It All Together

By 2050, the proportion of the world's population over 65 will double and the number of people aged 80 and older will quadruple to 400 million.

> *Aging will place massive strains on governments (due to budgets involving welfare policies for the aged). Global government debt will exceed world GDP by 2030.—Dominic Barton, global managing director of McKinsey & Company*[137]

But alas, governments and central banks only know how to do one thing when they see deflation as a threat: inflate with quantitative easing to pick up the slack in the world's economies.

[137] http://www.koreatimes.co.kr/www/news/biz/2015/11/488_189737.html

One last note on China;

China, while lower than the U.S., Europe and Japan at 22nd on the list, is in a similar situation to that of the U.S. during 2005-2008, before the financial crisis. The increase in debt for China since 2007 is more than all but four developed countries, three of which are the some of the worst of Europe: Greece, Ireland and Portugal, with the fourth being Singapore.

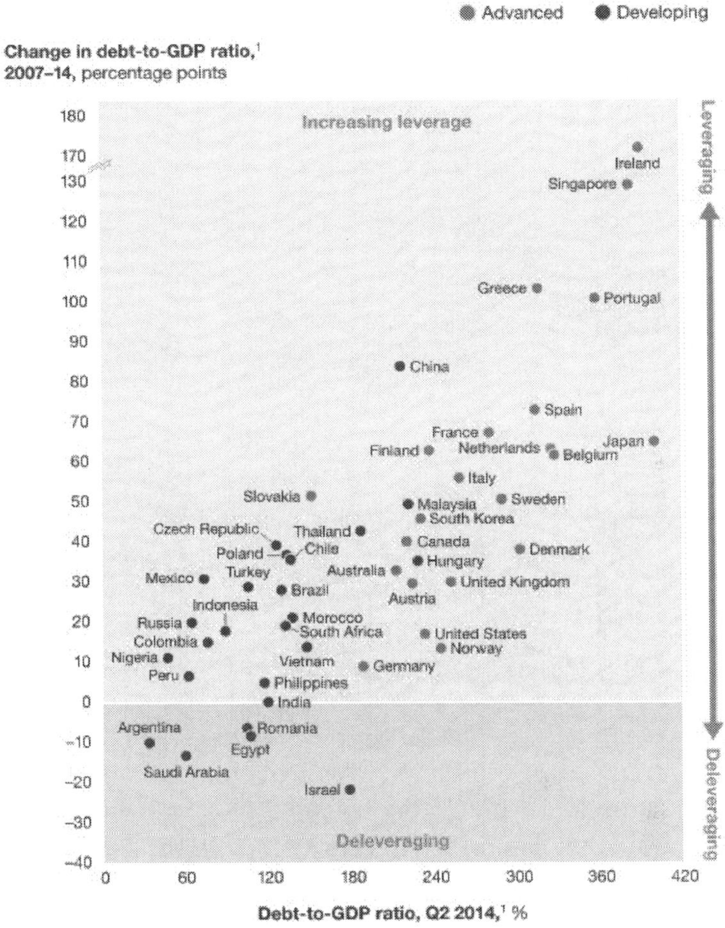

[1]Debt owed by households, nonfinancial corporations, and governments: Q2 2014 data for advanced economies and China; Q4 2013 data for other developing countries.

Source: Haver Analytics; national sources; McKinsey Global Institute analysis

Does anyone think that China, with their empty cities built for the future, won't experience a setback—especially with their own shadow banking situation? China has 4.3 trillion RMB ($692 billion U.S.) on balance exposure to their banks that will take 100% of the losses if borrowers default, and are exposed to another potential 3.1 trillion RMB ($500 billion U.S.).[138]

Shadow banking exposures of eight major banks

	On-balance sheet quasi-credit exposures	Off-balance sheet wealth management products	Off-balance sheet contingent liabilities
Estimated size	**RMB 4.3 trillion**	**RMB 3.1 trillion**	**RMG 8.4 trillion**
Exposure profile	Investment with trust related underlying: e.g. Direct investment in Trust beneficiary rights (TBRs), Third party trust exposures, Resale agreements backed by TBRs	Non-principal guaranteed wealth management products (WMPs) with non-standard credit assets (e.g. trust loans) as investment targets	Mainly bank acceptances bills which are used by corporate for payment and short-term financing purposes
Bank linkage	On bank balance sheet but under inter-bank / investments / receivables	WMPs sold by banks as agents and not consolidated onto balance sheet	Contingent liabilities off bank balance sheet until the bills are discounted
Underlying risk profile	**HIGH** Typically trust loans extended to high risk borrowers such as real estate developers, local government financing vehicle (LGFVs) and manufacturing firms	**HIGH** Also typically high risk corporates or LGFVs, which cannot obtain loans through traditional bank lending directly	**LOW** With short-duration (typically 3-6 months), acceptance bills are mostly used in working capital management by corporates and are low risk compared to standard corporate loans
Estimated cumulative NPL formation (2014-'18)	8-10% *(similar to on-balance sheet high risk sectors total NPL formation through the cycle)*	10-15% *(about 1.5-2x that of on-balance sheet high risk sectors total NPL formation during the same period)*	0-0.5% *(Historically very low NPL formation rate in discounted bills, at 0-10bps per year)*
Loss contingency	As these are on-balance sheet exposures, banks will have to **take 100% of losses** if borrowers default	Contractually no obligation for banks to take part in the losses However, **'implicit guarantees'** for investors persist in the market, which put banks at risk of being forced to share some of the losses during the work-out process	**100% losses** will be absorbed by the bank as the product consolidated onto balance sheet once discounted
Bank treatment	Under-provisioning for these exposure by classifying them as interbank / investment assets	No provisioning for these exposures as they are off balance sheet	Counted towards risk assets and thus capital calculation but are not provisioned until overdue

Source: Bank reports, Bank IR teams, Sanford Bernstein analysis and research

What I am getting at, in pointing out all of this overhanging debt, is that it doesn't matter which country you live in—there are major issues if you are not experiencing enough growth, as the debt will

[138] http://www.brookings.edu/~/media/research/files/papers/2015/04/01-shadow-banking-china-primer/shadow_banking_china_elliott_kroeber_yu.pdf

eventually overtake any production. When or if this happens, there can be a scramble to exit risky assets leading to defaults, liquidity issues, and a rush to safety. Which leads us to John Exter's Pyramid.

Chapter 9 - Exter's Pyramid

I've tried to make the case that it's not just the U.S. that can be hurt by all the existing and new debt worldwide since the 2007-2009 financial crisis. The trigger for the next crisis can come from multiple sources or even ISIS/ISIL-related issues. I do believe that if there are issues in one of these debt laced countries, the U.S. dollar will be viewed as a safe haven at first, as will U.S. Treasuries.

I also see one other asset that can and will move higher with the dollar, because it has been known the world over as a safe haven for a long enough period of time. In fact, for centuries it has been the place where all fiat currencies devolve to. That asset is gold.

Which brings us to Exter's Pyramid and what I believe is the second most important topic for the entire book with the most important being actionable advice on how to invest your money covered in the Investment section.

I first brought up Exter's Pyramid in Chapter 4 of my book *Buy Gold and Silver Safely*, which had 100 footnotes to explain in more complete detail the economic data that I have discussed in this chapter, but I have updated the pyramid and data in the next section to bring us up to speed.[139]

John Exter was a former member of the board of governors of the Federal Reserve System and become known as the Fed's only honest banker according to his son-in-law Barry Downs who inherited all of Exter's writings.

Exter's Inverse Pyramid

Much of what you have read so far on the economy is leading up to a situation where we will begin to see more problems arise in the future.

---

[139] http://discountgoldandsilvertrading.net/e-newsletter/2013/dgst-enewsletter-20130624.html

I didn't write this book with the intention of using fear to sell it, but rather to offer a sound foundation of understanding that enables you to make investment moves that help maintain and grow your wealth.

But when things really start to unravel and the credit contraction unfolds, the relationship between our banking system and the rest of the world will begin to show cracks. The interconnection of the bond market with insurance companies and municipal/corporate bonds will come into play. Corporations that have taken on debt or are still trying to reduce debt will be hit. Real estate investments that are heavily indebted will be hit.

The flow of money will go down the pyramid you see in the next graphic, from the more risky assets like derivatives and speculative ventures in any industry, stocks, bonds (junk first) to the perceived safety of U.S. Treasuries (why else have Treasuries been so strong since 2011?) and finally to real assets: gold and silver, or what has throughout the history of mankind been viewed as holding value when currencies succumb to government monetary failures.

We will discuss in the investment section how we have already seen some liquidity issues in the junk bond category, with investors being told they can't even redeem their shares with one large mutual fund that has over $670 billion in assets. We saw many of the more risky over-the-counter derivatives implode during the last crisis, and there are still plenty of derivative issues, as many are tied to interest rates that can also implode. Let me remind you that this is not just a U.S. issue, but as the next graphic shows, the world market is contracting and will continue to do so as illusions of wealth move down the pyramid, looking to find a home in real wealth. In other words, all of these liabilities that Exter first wrote about in the 1960s need to find value somehow, or a buyer, otherwise the only option is default.

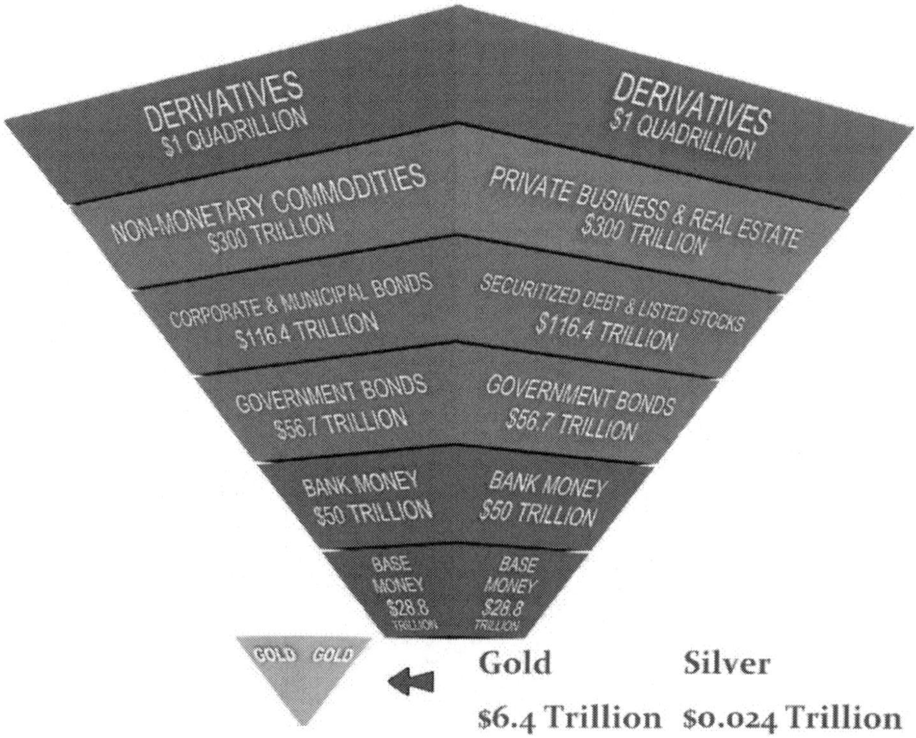

The pyramid flows from least liquid assets to most liquid with gold and silver being the only asset with no counterparty risk and that is why it sits outside the pyramid or at the apex (or base in this case) with all the other illusions of wealth above it. It's technically an illusion until you convert it or lock in that profit or loss after looking at this graphic. It's important to know just how liquid is your portfolio?

Many may not know this, but John Exter was the economist whom Fed chairman Paul Volcker turned to for advice on getting us out of a highly inflationary period when the Fed had a tight monetary policy and the economy was tanking. Interest rates were 17-18% and gold at this time had risen to an all-time high of $850 an ounce by January 1980. After asking Exter for advice, Volcker made the moves as seen in the lowering of the Effective Fed Funds Rate (see next chart) and the loosening of monetary policy.[140] This successfully resolved the situation— rates normalized and the boom years began, with Reagan adding fuel to the boom with increased government spending.

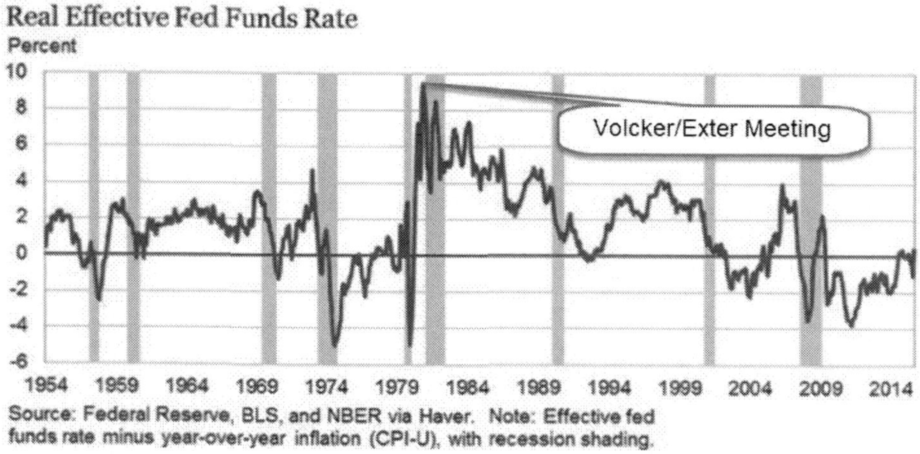

Today, there isn't much wiggle room to lower rates but you can see the effective rate minus inflation has already been low for some time. If the Fed doesn't go negative with rates, government spending along with other Fed intervention is all that is left should some crisis come again. But what choices does the Fed have left with a $4 trillion+ balance sheet outside and negative real interest rates? We'll find out when we get to the section on the Federal Reserve.

According to Barry Downs, John Exter, if he were alive for the 2007-2009, crisis would have analyzed the quantitative easing (monetizing of debt) since the crisis as the first round in stabilizing the world economy, but with greater debt. Downs says that the Fed doesn't have any other tricks up their sleeves other than buying every collapsing debt security and potentially collapsing equities from around the world. There has been broad speculation in the markets when you are allowed to borrow at basically zero. At some point the markets will implode. Then it becomes a matter of who will be a buyer if they do

---

[140] http://www.brookings.edu/blogs/ben-bernanke/posts/2016/03/18-negative-interest-rates

begin to implode. Will the Fed indeed move from lender to buyer of last resort? They already showed this tendency in the 2007-2009 crisis and still carry many of those assets on their books today. If the bids disappear, then at what price will an asset holder be able to sell? This can unravel quickly and catch most by surprise as it did before.

The opposite could potentially occur for some assets where Downs, whose background is in the gold mining industry, sees no offer for gold. In other words, no sellers. Since precious metals is an industry I have expertise in, I can attest that most investors who buy physical metals don't sell them for any reason except for possibly needing liquidity to buy property. It's a certain mindset most metal buyers have, and I expand upon that more in the gold and silver section. There is a reason it sits outside the pyramid.

To analyze what the Fed has done another way, Downs spoke about how when Exter first became involved with the Fed in 1954. The Fed's balance sheet was $28.85 billion which consisted of all short-term Treasury bills. By 1966 it had become $51 billion; by 1980, $180 billion, and he was shocked. Downs said that if Exter was alive today and saw the Fed's balance sheet and what it consists of (standing at $4.5 trillion), he would say to hold 100% of everything in gold because you can't tell when it all goes over the cliff what will hold value. Downs said it could begin at any given time, and when you don't know where to go, you have to go back to the only real money in the world—gold with silver being second best to own. That of course is extreme and I think he was simply saying it's hard to trust some paper assets.

In reality, deflation can be painful—but is necessary to weed out the excesses or bad decisions made to wipe the debt clean and start afresh on another boom cycle. The problem comes from government interfering with the natural weeding-out process of bad banks, bad businesses, etc. and interfering in the free market to bail out, prop up, or take over any business they deem too important to fail. How did this become part of the Fed's mandate? Downs believes John Exter never would have thought the Fed would go as rogue as they have.

Even with all of their interference in the markets with quantitative easing and every other move the Fed has made, they can't dictate how this stimulus is used by the recipients. Instead of succeeding in increasing money velocity, they have had a money flow problem, as they can't direct where it flows.

The Fed will keep fighting any deflation as they cannot tax deflation. What choice do they have? Any potential deflation, though, could be short-lived. The debt we have as a nation can't be defaulted upon, so the only option for the Fed is to inflate—and inflate they will. We will discuss inflation in the next section, but let's close up the deflation conversation by saying the Fed only wants the boom and will never address the bust. They never want the bust to happen, and naturally we don't either. But their moves, as you'll see in the Federal Reserve section soon, are unprecedented and there will be consequences. As long as people perceive the Fed as in control and Federal Reserve Notes as holding value, the system has worked. Unfortunately this kicking the can down the road will eventually have to come to an end, and it won't be pretty. Until that time, they'll just keep kicking. Where your wealth is invested is important to understand, as money flows down Exter's Pyramid and you begin to realize what the true value of your wealth is based on the price at which you are able to liquidate it.

PART 4 – INFLATION

Chapter 10 - Prices Rising Everywhere, but Why?

Government Involvement Skews Inflation Data

If you're living paycheck to paycheck or on a fixed income, you see prices are rising year after year for food, medicine, and many items you need on a weekly or monthly basis. Many look at this and say we have inflation.

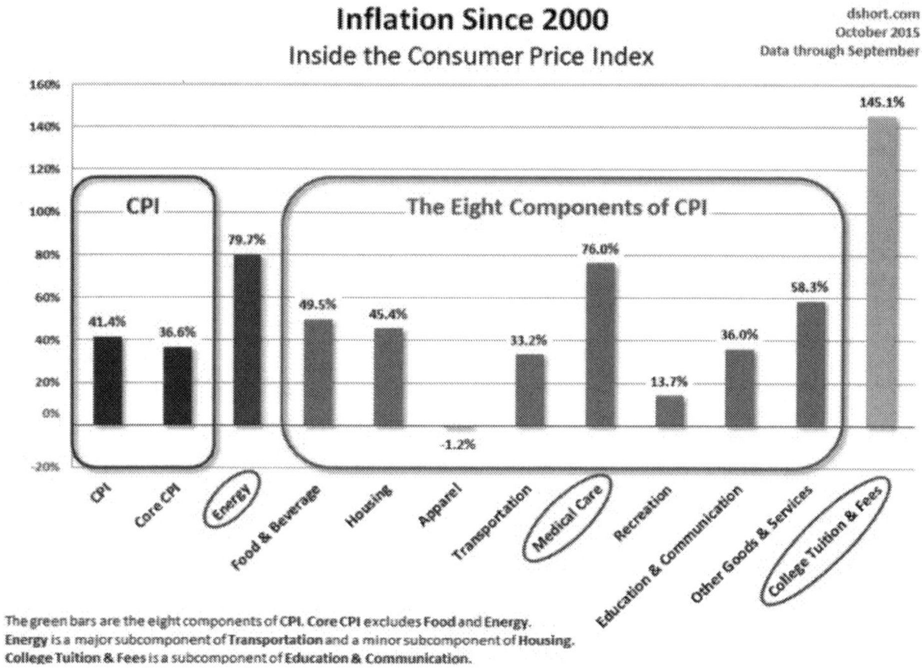

Since 2000:

- College tuition and fees are up 145%
- Medical care is up 76%
- Housing is up 45%

- Energy costs are up 79% but in late 2015 and into 2016, there was a significant drop.[141]

There is a viable explanation for the rise in prices for some areas, and the fall in others.

College tuition hikes are caused by a system where the government is always there to pay the loan. If the loan is guaranteed to the school, what is to stop them from raising tuition?

Many grocery items cost more despite the falling prices in grains the last few years. Some of this rise in price can be attributed to the large increase of U.S. citizens receiving Supplemental Nutrition Assistance Program (SNAP) benefits—formerly called food stamps. We saw the cost of this program rise 130%, or $42 billion, from 2008 to 2015.[142] This is part of the reason why food prices have risen, along with drought conditions in some areas.

The number of people claiming SNAP benefits declined for the first time in 2014, yet usage is still 119% higher than in 2008, despite the better unemployment numbers. Perhaps this is because the real unemployment rate we discussed earlier represented by U-6 was still high at 9.9%, and many of the millions of job seekers no longer counted are using SNAP. If you want to see the real unemployment situation, look at how many are on SNAP. Perhaps that's a better sign of how healthy the economy is.

Healthcare costs have been going up year after year with no end in sight. Even with a system offering more coverage to individuals there are still huge issues as most know. Most states do not limit what the insurance companies charge for healthcare, and they simply raise rates

---

141 http://www.mybudget360.com/two-income-trap-high-wage-myth-median-wage-income/

142 https://en.wikipedia.org/wiki/Supplemental_Nutrition_Assistance_Program#Costs

because now the government mandates all Americans have coverage or be exposed to penalties by the IRS.

Other Reasons for Higher Prices

Higher prices can be attributed to many things: supply and demand, businesses gouging their customers, government involvement in that industry, and Fed policy.

I believe the conversation centered on whether we are experiencing deflation or inflation will be turned on its head at some point. Inflation is coming. In fact, a repeat of '70s-style inflation is coming, but first we have to see how long this deflationary episode will last, and what the Fed will do to fight it.

Government Projections of Inflation

Next is a chart[143] of the projections for inflation, wherein the CBO does what they do best: assume flat-line inflation, ignoring that historical results have been anything but a flat line. Again, I really do find it amusing that the highly educated economists, who create these projections, knowing full well the history of economic turmoil occurring every decade, would expect tame inflation. I say it's not going to be tame, but increase at a good clip once the Fed implements additional quantitative easing to fight deflation.

143 https://www.cbo.gov/publication/49892

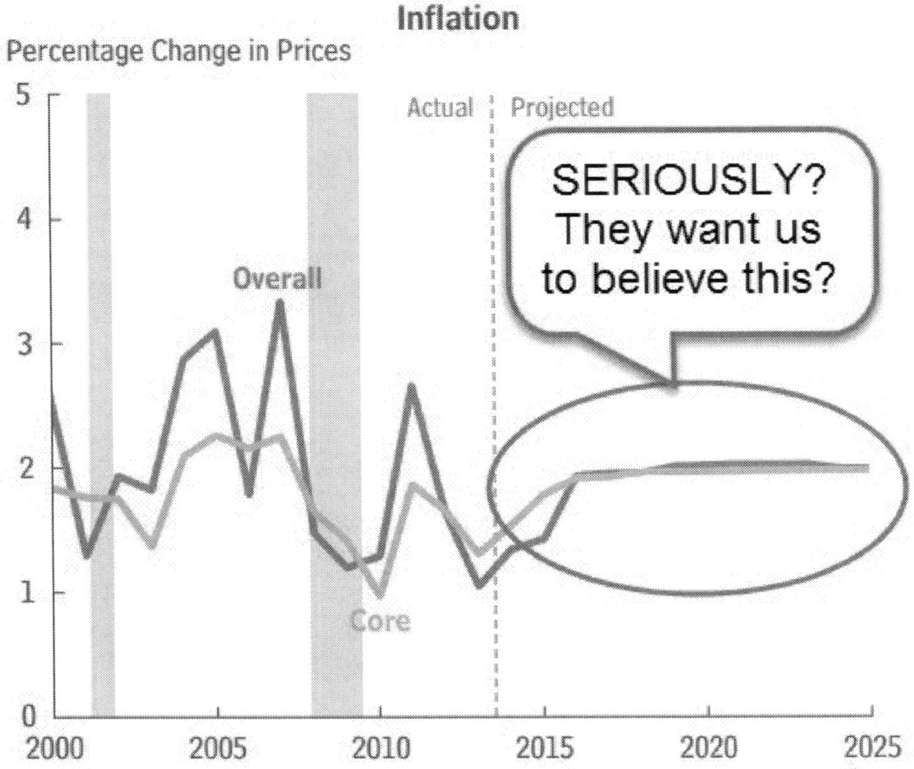

Deflation will eventually end, but it should be allowed to happen naturally, letting the bad get weeded out of the system so we can all prosper. Now our economy is built on a bed of sand instead of a firm foundation, because the government, with the help of the Fed, can't allow deflation to occur.

After inflation arrives, we have to decipher whether we will head to super-inflation with double-digit inflation rates, or if hyperinflation is a possibility, as we sit back and see just how masterful our leaders and Fed economists manage the economy and monetary system, and what tools they have left available to battle this future inflation. May I remind you that our current monetary experiment has only been around since 1971 without a relationship to gold, and during this time we have already had high inflation in the '70s, banking crises in the '80s and 2000s, and stock market crashes in the '70s, '80s and twice in the 2000s. The Asian financial crisis poured over to our shores in the '90s as well. We are in the latter half of the 2010-to-2020 decade. In other words, we are due for another crisis.

Hyperinflation

In general, hyperinflationists (as well as many self-proclaimed Austrians) have ignored and continue to ignore credit, even though credit dwarfs money supply. Those screaming that hyperinflation or strong inflation is at hand missed the boat, and will do so for the foreseeable future. For hyperinflation to occur, you need a loss of confidence in the currency. We don't have that today in the U.S. We do have concerns about the debt burden for today and the future, but other first-tier countries are in worse shape than the U.S. right now. Naturally a loss of confidence in these other countries at first will be bullish for the dollar, but all countries will eventually have to worry about the purchasing power of their currency, and your portfolio needs at least some insurance against any potential future issues.

Another bubble is around the corner, and that bust will be anything but inflationary to begin with—and you can guarantee the Fed, together with a complicit Congress, will use any tool necessary to make sure we get inflation. But they will be slow to act, and there will be much damage prior to their actions. Once they act, they will only be contributing even more to the problem by doing too much and potentially taking us from deflation to super-inflation if we're not careful.

Conclusion - This Time It Really Is Different

There was a nice synopsis of this economics chapter relating to what will transpire in the near future, but it was written a decade too early. The author, Richard Daughty, didn't count on the Fed and Congress throwing $9 trillion at the financial crisis—or the subsequent deflation and further Fed failure of quantitative easing that in the end has simply added fuel to the fire. It addresses how "this time it really is different."

> *This time, consumers don't have an abundance of savings to dip into for a cash flow problem, or an unused credit line available for them to meet additional needs. This time, homeowners don't have a substantial amount of untapped equity built up in their home. This time, the U.S. economy is barely afloat in an endless sea of debt, and would quickly drown under the weight of high real interest rates. This time, there is no base of strong employment to act as a life preserver to ride out the storm. This time, there is no possibility to massively increase the amount we borrow from the rest of the world. This time, we cannot dramatically increase our budget deficit to offset the economic drag caused by high interest rates. This time, there is no political will to be the party responsible for pushing the U.S. economy into depression...this time, it really is different!*[144]

Based on the data presented, what do you see?

What I see is a fast and furious bust that central banks of the world will be hard pressed to do anything to stop. We got a taste of it in 2015 with the Chinese stock market crashing as we mentioned earlier. When the Dow crashed 1000 points Apple stock lost $80 billion of its market cap before recovering. This next bust, when it comes, will be worse than the last crisis because the tools are just not there to counter it like they were in 2007–2009.

To move forward from this bust, it will take production, not monetary stimulus. The pain will hopefully be short in duration. The Fed will try to pull a rabbit out of a hat, but will more than likely prolong the inevitable collapse just as they have been doing all along with episodes

---

[144] http://www.financialsensearchive.com/fsu/editorials/optimist/2005/0404.html

of quantitative easing and other programs at the expense of their own credibility.

It is when we see our floating dollars and Treasuries coming back to the U.S. because no one wants them any longer that we'll realize we need to find some real wealth. Preparing your investments to insure them no matter what happens will be explained more in the Investment chapter. We'll also explain ways to take advantage of any potential turmoil. For now, we have a little time because most other currencies around the world are in awful shape too as we have shown.

There is of course a way out of all this mess. Debt has been managed since the time of Reagan and our economy has expanded. While too much debt will eventually become an issue, the solution lies in getting GDP to 4% again. But I'm just afraid that won't happen until we pay for the sins committed by those who put us in this predicament. Unless we come up with some new technology like free energy, or some advantage no other nation has in some of the areas discussed in the Investment section, we will be hard pressed not to see this business cycle complete its course.

What will happen with deflation is that the wealthy will gobble up hard assets at discounted prices, then just sit back and watch their wealth grow with the coming inflation. What's stopping you from doing this? The only issue is timing, but if you dollar-cost-average your portfolio into the right assets, the timing will be less of an issue.

PART 5 – BANKS

Chapter 11 - Why an Understanding of Banks Matters

> *The people are naturally conservative. They are more conservative than the financiers. Those who believe that the people are so easily led that they would permit the printing presses to run off money like milk tickets do not understand them. It is the innate conservation of the people that has kept our money good in spite of the fantastic tricks which financiers play–and which they cover up with high technical terms. The people are on the side of sound money. They are so unalterably on the side of sound money that it is a serious question how they would regard the system under which they live, if they once knew what the initiate can do with it.*—My Life and Work, *by Henry Ford*[145]

Now that you know a little more about the history of money and the economics involved, it's important to understand the financiers. This section will first provide a historical context of banking, and the extraordinary steps that have been taken time and time again to keep the monetary system from deteriorating. I have done my best to take a mega amount of information that I have gathered and break it down so the reader can comprehend what in my opinion, based on many conversations over 30 years in the industry, is really only understood by very few people.

The goal of this chapter is to make you aware of what has happened within our banking system and what lies ahead. With this additional awareness, which I believe is necessary for all investors, you will conclude for yourself the changes that need to be made to your portfolio, based on the options presented in the Investment section.

---

[145] **http://www.gutenberg.org/cache/epub/7213/pg7213.html**

Why Banks Matter

When it comes to understanding our monetary system, we also need to know what's going on with the bank's finances. Our financial markets are built upon a foundation of trust in banks to keep our funds safe. But how safe is the banking system? Has any protection really been set in place to protect depositors and prevent future banking crises, or are the banks still up to their old tricks, knowing full well that the largest of them are too big to fail, as their friends in Congress and the Federal Reserve will always be there to help bail them out if necessary? What about foreign banks? Can their problems affect the U.S. banking system?

Once we take care of some necessary historical context, we'll take a look at prior banking crises and banking problems here and abroad, the problems leading to the last crisis, what was done to bail the banks out of the crisis, and a current analysis of banks and their relationship to the bankers' bank: The Federal Reserve.

Fractional Reserve Banking

Banks make loans to individuals and businesses, issue credit cards, and collect fees—and that's how they've historically made a profit. You deposit your money in a bank, and they pay you a rate of return for CDs, savings, and checking accounts. They in turn take that money and loan it out at a higher rate for mortgages, car loans, student loans and other types of loans to anyone who qualifies. However, through some magical gift of favoritism only banks enjoy, they get to loan nine times the amount they take in from depositors. For every $1 they take in, they can loan out $9. For every $10,000, they loan out $90,000, and so on. This is the essence of what is called "fractional reserve banking."

Ask your friends and family what fractional reserve banking is, and they'll look at you like you're speaking a foreign language. Those three words alone might get people to skip over this part of the chapter, as they are quite intimidating and might sound too complex to comprehend. But this topic needs to be broken down and understood so you know the risks involved in the banking system, as it is an integral part of our monetary system and foundational in nature to the entire financial community. Depositors need to trust their savings will always be there for them when they need them. Why else would Congress do whatever it took in 2008 to right the quickly sinking banking industry ship during the crisis?

Where Did Fractional Reserve Banking Get Its Start?

In the 1600s we had what were called goldsmith bankers, whom we referenced in Chapter 1, as they brought us the beginning of our present-day monetary system. When these goldsmiths had more receipts (claims on the gold they held for clients) than the amount of gold actually in their possession, they had a "fraction" of the gold on hand needed to cover all the receipts held by clients.

And this is where we are today with banking. The illusion of any depositor at a bank today is that they can walk up to a bank teller and ask for all their money, at any point in time. Well, they can ask for it, but will they get it? That answer depends on how much cash they try to withdraw. While withdrawing over $10,000 can cause a bank to report you to the IRS, who may want to know why you are withdrawing such large amounts (of your own money), it is not illegal to do so, as it's your money, after all. But most banks don't carry around multiple hundreds of thousands of dollars in cash. They don't expect a group of their depositors to come in all at once and demand cash. They may very well tell the people trying to withdraw their funds at the same time to come back in the next day or two, while they get the local Federal Reserve Bank to provide them with more liquidity (cash) to satisfy the demand.

This shouldn't make people panic into withdrawing their cash from banks, and that's not my intent. This system has been this way since 1934—the last time we had a real run on the banks.

The Bank Run Prior to the 1934 Devaluing of the Dollar

While we have done well to keep people from making a run on the banks, it is important to know what led up to the 1934 episode, when thousands of banks failed and the Federal Reserve couldn't stop the people from withdrawing their money or exchanging their Federal Reserve Notes for gold.

You will recall from Chapter 1 that Federal Reserve Notes during this era could be converted to gold. Since too many depositors were trying to withdraw their cash or convert it to gold at one time, President Roosevelt declared a bank holiday, putting an end to the run. No one could get money out of their bank accounts or exchange it for gold. Roosevelt then put an end to the conversion of Federal Reserve Notes into gold, and told all of the citizens to turn in their gold to the Treasury or risk fines and imprisonment. Most everyone in this era did what their government requested of them.

The banking system returned to normal, but those people who received Federal Reserve Notes for their gold weren't too happy about it.

Today the government and Fed aren't worried about a bank run, as you'll see, and they aren't going to knock on your door like census takers asking if you have any gold and take it from you. This is virtually impossible for them to do from a financial perspective, and most that have gold aren't going to tell the government they own it, and aren't going to freely hand it over their gold with the 2nd amendment still in force (the right to bear arms).

Today's banking system isn't what it was in 1934, but neither is the Federal Reserve System, which we'll dive into in the next section. But you do need to be aware of what's going on with banks today, as in one sense they hold the world's monetary and financial system in their hands, and their actions have and can still affect your investments.

Chapter 12 - Banks Today Versus Then

For decades banks made their profits by loaning money you deposited with them, over and over, collecting the interest and hoping a high proportion of depositors don't come in and demand their deposits at once. If that were to happen, the same problems the goldsmiths had when a few of their customers requested their gold at once today: the Federal Reserve has the bankers' backs and banks operate without much fear for the future, which we'll see later in this chapter.

The banking system is the only type of business where they can take what money is deposited with them and use it for their own personal/corporate use. While historically there have been limitations to this and regulations in place to safeguard those who deposit money with banks, decide for yourself after reading the rest of this chapter whether or not you feel comfortable with a lot of your money in a bank. While not all banks are created equal, just one of the largest banks can spoil it for all, just as one goldsmith did back in the 1600s.

Some may call this chapter "fear mongering." However, there may be reason to have some fear when you look at the track record of the banks since the 80s. Since 1980 we have had two banking crises here in the U.S.—the Savings and Loan crisis, and the 2007-2015 era, where hundreds of banks failed.[146] Are all problems solved, or is there a flaw or two in the banking system and those who run and regulate it?

Learning From The Past

It is extremely important to understand the past banking problems to be able to have a high degree of probability of predicting what will happen next. Part of the job of a good prognosticator is to recognize patterns, and some may wonder about my reasoning for bringing up the past, and why it relates to investing. If you can learn from past patterns, then you have a good chance of protecting your wealth and

---

146 http://www.davemanuel.com/history-of-bank-failures-in-the-united-states.php

profiting from it. I'm making the case that the banks, Congress, and the Fed will continue to repeat their actions over and over, as you'll see.

We've already discussed the 1929-1933 banking crisis, where over 10,000 banks failed as depositors lost trust in the banking system. But a more modern example of failure can be found with the S&L crisis of 1980 – 1989, where we saw 563 bank failures (does not include mergers) and a cost of $532 billion.[147] So how did things go wrong?

Table 4.2

S&L Failures, 1980–1988

($Thousands)

Year	Number of Failures	Total Assets	Estimated Cost	Supervisory Mergers	Voluntary Mergers
1980	11	$ 1,348,908	$ 158,193	21	63
1981	34	19,590,802	1,887,709	54	215
1982	73	22,161,187	1,499,584	184	215
1983	51	13,202,823	418,425	34	83
1984	26	5,567,036	886,518	14	31
1985	54	22,573,962	7,420,153	10	47
1986	65	17,566,995	9,130,022	5	45
1987	59	15,045,096	5,666,729	5	74
1988	190	98,082,879	46,688,466	6	25

Sources: FDIC; and Barth, *The Great Savings and Loan Debacle*, 32–33.

> *"The real cause of the disaster is the very financial structure that was fashioned by legislators and guided by regulators; they together created a cartel that, like all other monopolistic concoctions, is playing mischief with its victims."* The Great Banking Scandal," by Hans F. Sennholz, The Freeman, Nov., 1990 p. 405

147 "$532 billion cost" – S&L Industry Rebuilds As Bailout Reaches Final Phase, "Veribanc News Release Veribanc, Ince. (Waskefield, Massachusetts), January 12, 1994. p.2.

Legislation Passed Giving Banks Ability to Take On More Risk

In 1980 we saw the passing of the Depository Institutions Deregulation and Monetary Control Act (DIDMCA), giving the Fed more power over non-member banks and reducing the requirements of net worth in qualifying for loans. It also "removed the power of the Federal Reserve Board of Governors under the Glass–Steagall Act to use Regulation Q to set maximum interest rates for any deposit accounts other than demand deposit accounts (with a six-year phase-out)."[148] [149]

One last thing of importance it did was insure deposits up to $100,000, from the previous $40,000 limit. When the deposit insurance rates are raised, it gives the depositor the illusion that they can put more funds in the bank and not have to worry about losing it, as the government and Federal Reserve have their backs. But put more than $100,000 into that bank, and that insurance no longer applies.

Banks' net income was falling, and they had to do other things to make a profit. With the new deposits brought in by offering higher rates after the passing of DIDMCA, banks only needed $1 of capital for every $33 in deposits. They moved away from the traditional way of making money via mortgage and other loans to more risky business: leveraged buyouts and dabbling in real estate ventures, junk bonds and swaps, as well as futures.

---

[148] http://research.stlouisfed.org/publications/review/86/02/Requiem_Feb1986.pdf

[149] Gilbert, Alton. "Requiem for Regulation Q: What It Did and Why It Passed Away", Federal Reserve Bank of St. Louis: pp. 31-33.

Table 4.1

Selected Statistics, FSLIC-Insured Savings and Loans, 1980–1989

($Billions)

Year	Number of S&Ls	Total Assets	Net Income	Tangible Capital	Tangible Capital/ Total Assets	No. Insolvent S&Ls*	Assets in Insolvent S&Ls*	FSLIC Reserves
1980	3,993	$ 604	$ 0.8	$32	5.3%	43	$ 0.4	$ 6.5
1981	3,751	640	–4.6	25	4.0	112	28.5	6.2
1982	3,287	686	–4.1	4	0.5	415	220.0	6.3
1983	3,146	814	1.9	4	0.4	515	284.6	6.4
1984	3,136	976	1.0	3	0.3	695	360.2	5.6
1985	3,246	1,068	3.7	8	0.8	705	358.3	4.6
1986	3,220	1,162	0.1	14	1.2	672	343.1	–6.3
1987	3,147	1,249	–7.8	9	0.7	672	353.8	–13.7
1988	2,949	1,349	–13.4	22	1.6	508	297.3	–75.0
1989	2,878	1,252	–17.6	10	0.8	516	290.8	NA

* Based on tangible-capital-to-assets ratio.

[1] U.S. League of Savings Institutions, *Savings and Loan Sourcebook*, (1982), 37. It should be noted that during the 1980s, the state-sponsored insurance programs either collapsed or were abandoned.

[2] For a discussion of these issues, see Chapter 6.

Figure 4.1

Percentage of S&L Assets in Mortgage Loans, 1978–1986

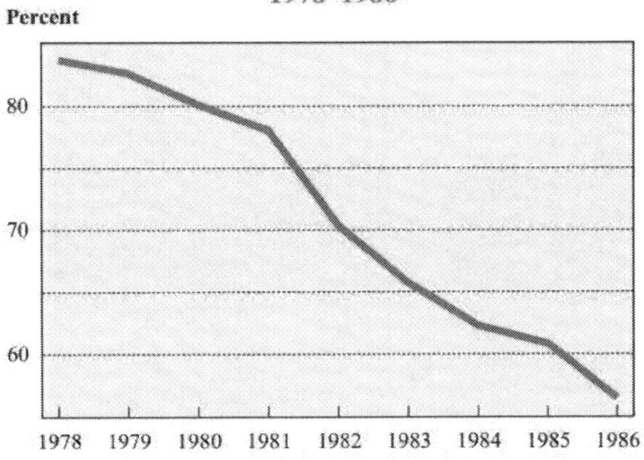

[35] National Commission, *Origins and Causes of the S&L Debacle*, 47.

There was also the passing of the Garn-St. Germain Depository Institutions Act of 1982, which was supposed to "make the thrift industry a stronger, more effective force in financing housing for millions of Americans in the years to come," according to then President Ronald Reagan.[150] A co-sponsor was Charles Schumer. Remember his name, as it will come up again.

The Garn-St. Germain act expanded the scope of securities banks were permitted to invest in. For example, banks used to be limited to traditional home mortgage loans, but could now, with the passing of this act, put up to 40% of assets in commercial real estate loans, 30% in consumer loans, 10% in commercial loans and leases, and another 10% in junk bonds, stocks and real estate.[151]

What banks subsequently did was take on more risk without jeopardizing their depositors' nest eggs, because they were now covered by $100,000 from the FDIC. The primary reason for higher insurance was to prevent the bank runs experienced in the 1929-1933 era. If a depositor knew they would be covered by insurance, they wouldn't care as much what the bank did with their money—if they even knew to begin with, which most didn't and still don't today.

This was the moral hazard bankers were well aware of. If their depositors were "covered" by insurance, then they could take more risks with their depositors' money, knowing the Federal Reserve had their backs. And take risks they did, especially with leverage, as seen in the following chart describing the beginning days of leverage.

---

150 http://www.reagan.utexas.edu/archives/speeches/1982/101582b.htm

151 http://wps.aw.com/wps/media/objects/7529/7710164/appendixes/ch11apx1.pdf

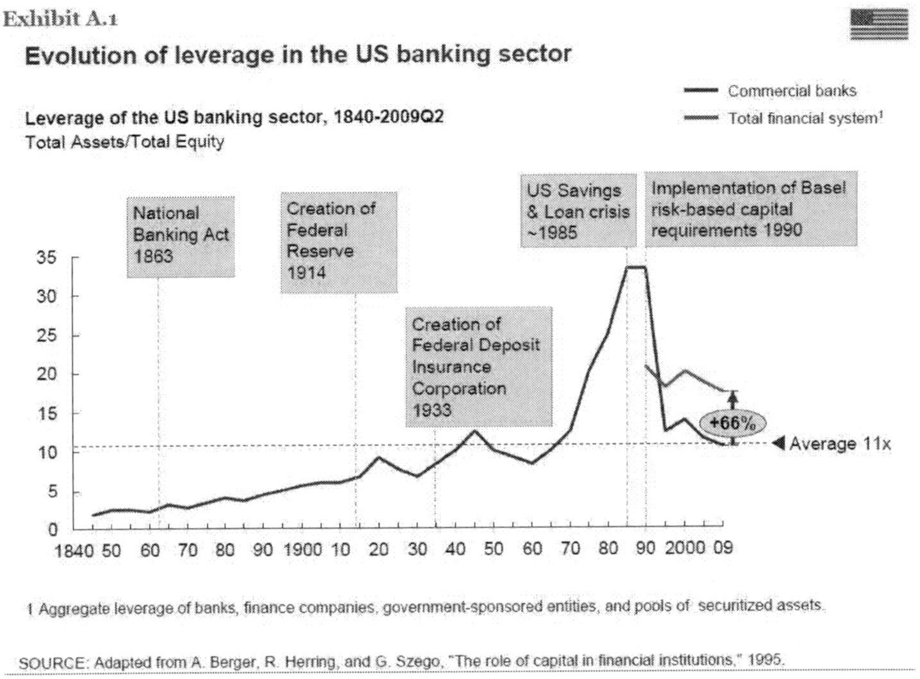

William Black was a former S&L regulator during the crisis, and in his book, *The Best Way to Rob a Bank is to Own One*, he wrote about congressional corruption during the Savings and Loan Crisis. This is one theme you will see throughout this section on banks: It's all about the banks.

Louise Francis, the Consulting Principal and founder of Francis Analytics and Actuarial Data Mining Inc., wrote this about Black's book:

> *William Black describes in detail the complex collusion between bankers, regulators, and legislators that brought about the Savings and Loan crisis of the 1980s and early 1990s. As part of the scheme, leverage was used to purchase bankrupt companies that became the basis for a Ponzi-like speculative bubble that ultimately collapsed. Deceptive accounting rules were used to hide the true state of the banks.*

Litigation and lobbyists were used to delay and frustrate timely enforcement, adding significantly to the taxpayer's bill. Since the bursting of the S&L bubble, a number of additional financial bubbles and debacles have occurred, including Enron, the Internet bubble, the subprime bubble, and the Madoff Ponzi scheme. The details of the S&L crisis—civil and criminal trials and federal agency investigations—have been well documented and will serve as a model for later crises.[152]

Taxpayers to the Rescue

Alas, the FSLIC was underfunded to prevent any type of crisis from all of the excesses of the '80s. Under a fractional reserve system of banking, they or any entity will always be underfunded. The Financial Institutions Reform, Recovery, and Enforcement Act of 1989—paid for by taxpayers of course—established the Resolution Trust Corporation (RTC), which closed hundreds of failed institutions and disposed of their assets, and also made depositors whole.[153]

Fannie Mae and Freddie Mac at that time were given more power to deal with low-and moderate-income families. We'll discuss Fannie and Freddie in more detail in the next section, which will address how banking deregulation and more moral hazard led to the 2007-2009 financial crisis.

What Are Banks in the Business of Today?

Banks historically have been in the business of making loans. They used to be there for the local communities, helping farmers or businessmen get needed capital to expand or grow. While this does still happen, the much larger banks have changed the game, putting the entire banking system at risk. One could categorize these risks that banks take as simply *greed*. Making consistent profit is not enough for many banks. It works for the small farming banks, but when these

---

[152] http://www.casact.org/pubs/forum/10fforumpt2/Francis.pdf
[153] http://www.fdic.gov/bank/analytical/banking/2000dec/brv13n2_2.pdf

banks were allowed to expand their reach into other areas, it was the beginning of the end for the system. Even though the end hasn't arrived yet, the seeds have been planted with failure after failure. To this day banks continue to retreat from mortgage lending as non-bank lenders emerge.[154]

Every Few Years another Crisis Somewhere

You may not realize how often financial crises occur. Just because they don't happen here in the U.S. doesn't mean that the effect of a crisis that begins in another country won't be felt here. Since the Savings and Loan debacle, we have had quite a few instances of economic, monetary and investment dilemmas around the world. Many of these ill-fated episodes were preceded by so-called good times built upon the illusion that all was well, and the good times would last forever. The good times continue for those who realize they are in the bubble, and who manage to escape before the devastation sets in.

There was the Mexican Crisis of 1994, the Asian financial crisis of 1997/1998, the Russian crisis of 1998, the Enron crisis of 2001/2002 and a stock market bubble fueled by then-Fed chairman Alan Greenspan during his tenure in the late '90s. There's also the ongoing Greece crisis, where a country with slightly more residents than Los Angeles threatened the balance sheets of multiple countries that loaned them money. That is still yet to be resolved fully. But nothing compares to the distress and anxiety culminating in the 2007–2009 financial crisis. This will be discussed in detail in the next section.

While reading it, think about how big this last crisis really was, and what extraordinary steps were taken to make sure it didn't get worse. You'll read why we haven't had a crisis here in the U.S. since this last one, where subsequently we saw the book *The Big Short* turned into a dramedy movie of the same name. It was entertaining to watch, but fell

---

[154] http://www.cnbc.com/2016/01/19/big-banks-continue-retreat-from-mortgages.html

short of the actual dollar figures thrown at the crisis, or what it actually cost the taxpayers and Fed to keep the sinking economic ship afloat.

Also keep in mind while reading this section what you think the potential would be for another crisis here or abroad, and pay particular attention to the balance sheets of the Fed and government—who are no better off today than they were before the last crisis, and show no signs of improving. Ask yourselves after reading this section and the Federal Reserve section whether you believe another crisis is on the horizon, based on the evidence presented in this book, and heed the solutions offered in the Investment section if you agree with what is presented.

Chapter 13 - What Led to the 2007–2009 Financial Crisis?

While there are many books and movies that depict what happened, it's easy to describe the mistakes made and hopefully not repeat them again. What sets this book apart is providing you the necessary proof that nothing has really changed when it comes to the banks. The movie *The Big Short* ended with a foreshadowing of banks' involvement in bespoke tranche opportunities being peddled by banks and Goldman Sachs. They are a different term for the same collateralized debt obligations (CDOs) that got us into trouble during the last crisis, as they can't be valued easily and the assets they consist of are leveraged as before. But you'll also see that since the crisis, the one bill that was passed to protect us, The Dodd-Frank Wall Street Reform and Consumer Protection Act of 2010 is tainted by the influence of the banks, and you can thank an inept Congress for that. To this day, they don't even know how to value the banks' derivatives, and yet we see similar products popping up.[155]

Banks Get the Legislation They Need to Begin Wreaking Havoc on the System

Beginning in the late '90s, the banking, insurance and securities industry lobbied Congress hard, as they had been doing for 20 years. With the help of the aforementioned Senator Charles Schumer (D-NY) and a group of paid-for politicians who received tens of millions of dollars from the big three industries, they were able to finally get Congress to pass the Financial Services Modernization Act of 1999.[156]

This is the act that propped the doors wide open for the banks to take on more risk, as it repealed the Glass–Steagall Act of 1933 and allowed all of the big three financial industries to form entities that literally became "too big to fail." This was combined with a change in

---

[155] http://www.bloomberg.com/news/articles/2015-02-04/goldman-sachs-hawks-cdos-tainted-by-credit-crisis-under-new-name

[156] https://www.opensecrets.org/politicians/summary.php?cycle=Career&type=C&cid=N00001093&newMem=N

Fed interest rate policy from inflation targeting to the lowering of rates by Fed chairman Alan Greenspan, as seen in the chart below.

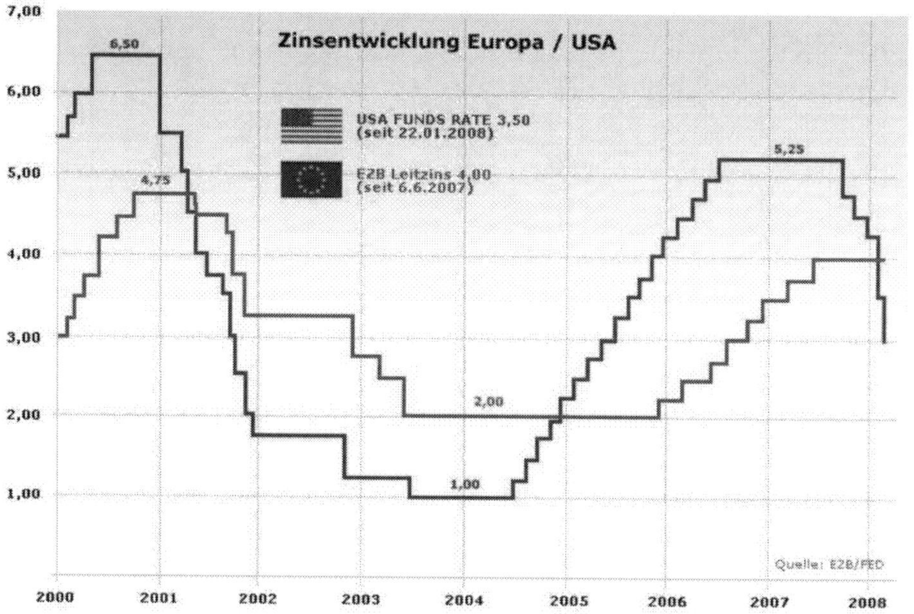

This new interest rate policy, along with the repeal of Glass-Steagall, the introduction of subprime CDOs and other financial market instruments, added to an out-of-control real estate market (fueled by the subprime lending). It set up the situation we now know as the real estate bubble of 2006/2007.

But Congress also did one other thing the banks had no control over. In 1995 the Clinton administration streamlined the loan process under revisions to the original 1977 Community Reinvestment Act (CRA), requiring banks to give loans to people in inner cities, as long as they qualified, of course. In 1999, with the passing of the aforementioned Financial Services Modernization Act, these new banking conglomerates that were all things to all people were also forced to make loans to those in the inner city to be in compliance with the CRA mandates. While the original intent of the CRA was to prevent discrimination against applicants or "redlining" by banks, it evolved into a program with loose lending policies that backfired tremendously.

While things looked good for a while, whether in the inner city or the suburbs, the Greenspan Fed started to raise rates in 2004, as you can see in the preceding chart, and within just a couple of years, the real estate bubble popped—and prices started to come down.

Those who had adjustable rate mortgages or took out home equity loans with the higher real estate prices got hit hard. From 2004 to 2008, many people who should not have qualified to buy a home to begin with found themselves unable to pay the higher payments on their loan, and either stopped paying and squatted until the home was foreclosed upon (some banks in certain areas did not foreclose at all), or simply took everything out of the house, including the kitchen sink, and walked away.

Panic Sets In – TARP or No TARP?

When TARP was first proposed to help homeowners and banks, the House of Representatives voted against it by a narrow vote.[157] Hank Paulson, or Chicken Little, as I like to call him, went to work spreading fear everywhere he could, promises were made to get more Democrats on board, and TARP was passed.

Rolling Stone magazine's Matt Taibbi sums up very well what happened next.

> *What was pitched as a bailout of both banks and homeowners instantly became a bank-only operation – marking the first in a long series of moves in which bailout officials either casually ignored or openly defied their own promises with regard to TARP.*[158]

---

[157] http://www.nytimes.com/2008/09/30/business/30cong.html
[158] http://www.rollingstone.com/politics/news/secret-and-lies-of-the-

Former Wells Fargo president Richard Kovacevich told CNBC years later in 2013:

> *TARP was one of the "worst decisions in the history of the United States,.. but the proposition that Hank put before us was that if we took this money, the confidence in the industry would go up. But I was arguing that day, until I was told to be quiet, the opposite would happen.*
>
> *"Shortly after TARP, the stock market fell by 40%," he continued. "And the banking industry stocks fell by 80%. How can anyone say that TARP increased the confidence level of an industry, when its stock market valuation fell by 80%?*[159]

Much of the TARP funds were simply handed over to the banks, as seen in the next table.

---

bailout-20130104page=2#ixzz2rrvMiPN9

[159] http://www.cnbc.com/id/101032772http://www.cnbc.com/id/101032772

Table 3
Major TARP Fund Recipients through July 16, 2009

Recipient	Amount
AIG*	$40 billion
Other predominately insurance entities Hartford Financial($3.4 billion) Lincoln National ($950 million)	$4.35 billion
Top 10 banking recipients Citigroup, Inc. ($50 billion) Bank of America Corporation ($35 billion) JPMorgan Chase & Co. ($25 billion) Wells Fargo & Company ($25 billion) The PNC Financial Services Group Inc. ($15.2 billion) Morgan Stanley ($10 billion) Goldman Sachs Group ($10 billion) Fifth Third Bancorp ($6.8 billion) U.S. Bancorp ($6.6 billion) Sun Trust Banks, Inc. ($6.2 billion)	$190 billion
Other banking recipients (582 entities)	$55 billion
Auto industry (including suppliers)	$85 billion
Total	$374 billion

*AIG also received a commitment for an additional $29,835,000,000, which has not been drawn as of July 16, 2009.

Source: U.S. Department of Treasury Office of Financial Stability Transactions Report for the Period Ending July 16, 2009.

I remember how desperate the banks were for money just before TARP was passed, as I had an account with Washington Mutual (WAMU). While standing in line one day, I overheard someone from the bank soliciting funds from customers over the phone by offering a 6% rate of return on a CD. At the time, there was no bank savings product on God's green Earth that was paying close to 6%, yet somehow Washington Mutual was offering that rate to their clients. It was during this time that there was a bank run at WAMU, where customers withdrew $16.7 billion in just 9 days. They were simply cash poor. Soon thereafter, WAMU was taken over by the FDIC and eventually sold to Chase for a song.[160]

Keep in mind that the largest portion of the decline in the stock market came after TARP was passed, but Congress had to do something to help save the system, right? In addition to TARP, Congress went to work on the Dodd-Frank Wall Street Reform and Consumer Protection Act.[161]

The long title is "Act to promote the financial stability of the United States by improving accountability and transparency in the financial system, to end 'too big to fail,' to protect the American taxpayer by ending bailouts, to protect consumers from abusive financial services practices, and for other purposes."

What led up to the passing of this Act in 2010 and subsequent discussions on derivatives activity isn't quite discussed too much publicly. Why would the banks want anyone to know what they are up to? It shows to what level the banks, other financial institutions, and our leaders will go to in making sure banks get what they want.

Banks' Assault on Dodd-Frank

The Sunlight Foundation has analyzed the data and it's quite alarming just how involved these financial institutions were in creating Dodd-Frank.

> *Goldman Sachs is the most active organization. It had representatives at 222 meetings, covering 51 topics. JP Morgan participated in 207 meetings, also covering 51 topics. Combined, these two Wall Street giants* alone *participated in 50 percent more meetings (429) than the top 20 most active pro-reform groups* combined *(287).*

---

160 http://www.bloomberg.com/apps/news?pid=newsarchive&sid=aLxCHDTaOaWw&refer=home

161 http://www.sec.gov/about/laws/wallstreetreform-cpa.pdf

Rounding out the top 5 are Morgan Stanley (175 meetings, covering 46 topics), Bank of America (156 meetings, covering 41 topics) and Citigroup (134 meetings, covering 47 topics).

All told, active financial institutions show up in the meetings logs for at least 2,118 meetings during the first three years of implementation. By contrast, active pro-reform groups appeared in only 153 meetings logs – only about one meeting for every 14 regulators held with financial institutions and associations.[162]

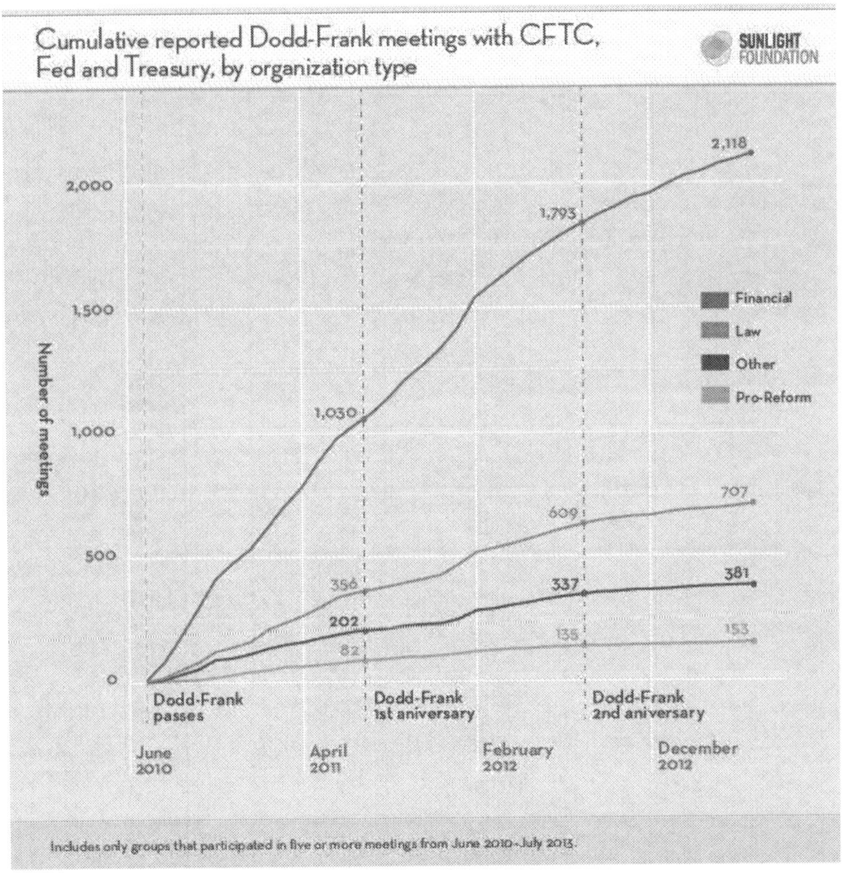

162 http://sunlightfoundation.com/feature/dodd-frank-3-year/

Organization	Total meetings	Total topics	Solo meetings	Top issue
Goldman Sachs	222	51	71	Derivatives Markets And Products
JPMorgan Chase & Co	207	51	67	Volcker Rule
Morgan Stanley	175	46	60	Derivatives Markets And Products
Bank of America	156	41	36	Derivatives Markets And Products
Citigroup Inc	134	47	24	Derivatives Markets And Products

Financial institutions were also involved in the reforming of bankruptcy laws in 2005.

> *as the official report from the US Financial Crisis Inquiry Commission said,*
>
> > *... under a 2005 amendment to the bankruptcy laws, derivatives counterparties were given the advantage over other creditors of being able to immediately terminate their contracts and seize collateral at the time of bankruptcy. (p. 48)*

The conclusion of this legislation is summed up well by Raúl Ilargi Meijer of the Automatic Earth:

So when a bank goes bankrupt, BEFORE even the most senior bond holders, the repo lenders and derivatives traders can remove, or keep, all the assets pledged to them. Because the repo and derivatives traders ran no risk – they could get their money out of a failing bank before anyone else.[163]

---

[163] http://www.theautomaticearth.com/2013/09/derivatives-the-gift-that-keeps-on-taking/

Chris Dodd and Barney Frank's connections to the financial crisis run deep. With this bill they did nothing to prevent future disasters. Dodd was part of the reason we had the 2007-2009 crisis, with his influence (and millions of dollars handed to him by the insurance, securities and banking industries) to repeal Glass-Steagall, along with Senator Jim Leach, whose name was on the Gramm-Leach-Bliley Act, which did away with the 1933 act that kept banks in check.

Frank said in 2009, after the passing of the bill with his name on it, that he agreed there should be "strong, comprehensive and consistent regulation" of the derivatives market, and promised to work toward that end.

The Volcker Rule is supposed to bar banks from speculating with their own money. Yet banks are still allowed to hedge for speculative purposes and can still trade. Dodd-Frank called for transparency, but regulators don't know what they're doing and can't keep track of every move the banks make. Even Frank couldn't keep track of what was going on with Fannie and Freddie, as he said they were "fiscally strong," and even if there were problems, "the federal government doesn't bail them out."[164] Of course the government later did bail Fannie and Freddie out, and in 2013, he said they should be abolished.[165] Guess what? In 2016 Fannie Mae is at risk of needing a bailout.[166]

As we have said, banks used to be in the business of making loans and ensuring the borrowers kept paying their mortgages. When the business model changed from writing loans to packaging loans and getting some sucker to purchase the packages, they found another way to make commissions. Those commissions go to pay lobbyists,

---

164 http://www.boston.com/news/politics/articles/2010/10/14/frank_haunted_by_stance_on_fannie_freddie/
165 http://freebeacon.com/frank-abolish-fannie-mae-freddie-mac/
166 http://www.cnbc.com/2016/02/20/fannie-mae-at-risk-of-needing-a-bailout.html

congress people and of course themselves—in the form of big bonuses or multi-million-dollar salaries.

Congress Passes Anti-Foreclosure Bill

To help homeowners during the financial crisis, the House voted 367-54 to pass the Helping Families Save Their Homes Act. The Senate had voted 91-5 in favor of the bill and approved the final version by unanimous consent in 2009.

The bill also would potentially give banks a break on fees they pay to the Federal Deposit Insurance Corp. to insure customers' deposits. The bill increased FDIC borrowing authority from $30 billion to $100 billion, to allow the agency to reduce the insurance premiums.[167]

The other important part of this bill was the extension of FDIC insurance on deposits held at the bank to remain at $250,000 (you'll read about how it was increased from $100,000 during the crisis in the forthcoming FDIC section). The $250,000 amount became permanent in 2010.[168]

Did Homeowners Deserve to Be Bailed Out?

I am in the camp that homeowners don't need to be bailed out. If I make an investment in an asset and the asset goes against me, why should I be rewarded with a reprieve? It is my choice to invest and hold the asset, and I solely took that risk. I should also take the loss if the investment doesn't go my way.

The Fed and government were simply trying to ride out the storm and buy time until, they "hoped," the real estate market would rebound. In some cities it did, but not to the level it was at the highs in 2006. In other cities—like the Financial District in New York, or where

---

[167] https://www.govtrack.us/congress/bills/111/hr1106/text
[168] https://www.fdic.gov/news/news/press/2010/pr10161.html

politicians live in Washington D.C.—real estate hit record highs after the crisis. Are you surprised?

It's simply not the government's job to give out taxpayer money to help those who made bad investment decisions, period. That's not what investing is all about and bad investments should not be rewarded.

Other industries received money from the government during that time as well.

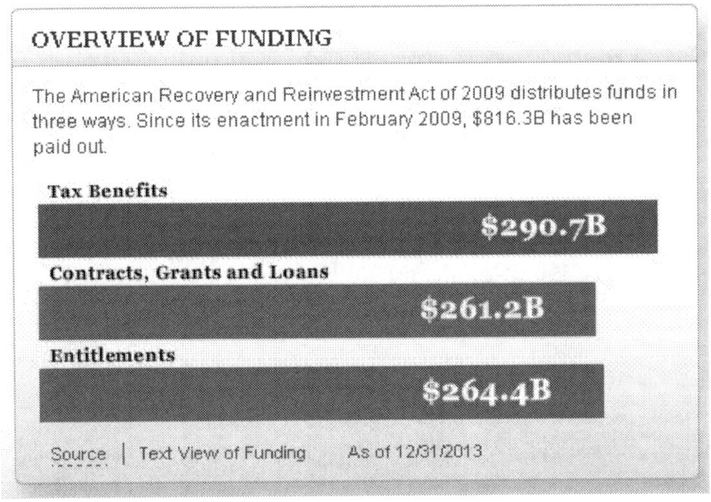

But by the end of 2013, 312 awards were not reported on by prime recipient as required under the American Recovery and Reinvestment Act of 2009, another abuse of taxpayer money. The Recovery Act's mandate for quarterly reporting, including:

- 148 award reports not submitted in the January 2014 reporting cycle
- 86 award reports not submitted in two reporting cycles
- 78 award reports not submitted in three or more cycles since October 2009

The following agencies didn't even submit a non-compliers list to the Recovery Board by that date:

- Department of Housing and Urban Development
- United States Army Corps of Engineers

Q4 2013 was the last time recipients reported on their awards, as the requirement to report was repealed in the Omnibus Spending bill passed in January 2014. Naturally you won't find this information any longer, as the government has already shut down the website.

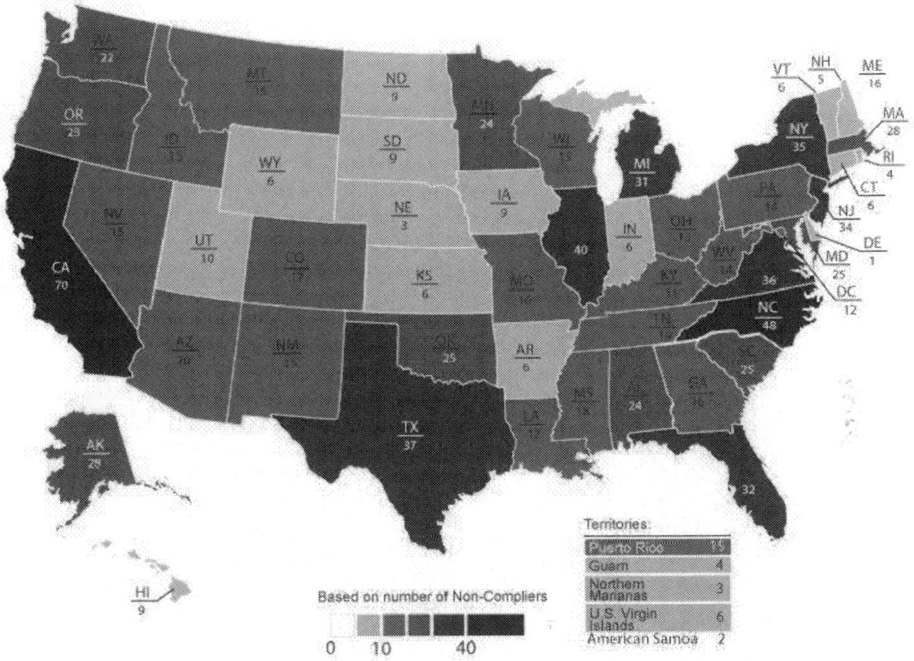

How is it that with all the rules and regulations and tax laws we have to abide by as businesses, if we ignore one, some government overlord is there to penalize us? But a government agency, mandated by Congress to report what they did with the money hard-working taxpayers handed them, can just ignore the request and, the government eventually ends the requirement to report and everyone goes about their business like nothing happened. Is this a government by the People and for the People or a government by the People and for the government? Again, we'll save that conversation for the *We the Serfs!* book, but we have to fully understand the depths that government will go to in making presumptions about what's to come, and what tools they may or may not have left in the toolbox to quell any future crisis. You can see why this information is foundational to your investment success.

What Was the Cost of the 2007–2009 Bailout?

My guess when you ask this question of people they will say the cost of the bailout was something like $700 billion, the amount TARP came to. Then President George W. Bush was even on record two weeks before signing TARP into law saying that "the government would not continue to bail out Wall Street."[169]

Others may say the bailout cost was a few trillion because of the added deficit spending by Congress. Would it be a surprise to anyone reading this that the total cost was almost $10 trillion? That's right: The bailout came to $9,801,818,000,000.[170]

What did $10 trillion get us? Who did it benefit? At what cost, and to whom? I don't even think there is a person in Congress who can actually answer those questions. These next charts paint a clear picture of what lengths Congress and the Fed went to in throwing money—your money or your children's and grandchildren's future earnings—at a system they claim they were saving, but in reality was the biggest power grab in the history of mankind.[171]

---

[169] http://www.today.com/id/26709927/ns/today-today_news/t/wall-street-scrambles-lehman-merrill-falter/#.Uzy8P6hdVEB
[170] http://www.milkeninstitute.org/publications/bailout.taf
[171] http://buygoldandsilversafely.com/just-how-bad-was-the-2008-financial-crisis/

Agency	Bailout Expense in billions
Federal Reserve	$6,048
Congress and White House	$2,466
FDIC	$ 926
Treasury, FDIC, FED	$ 362

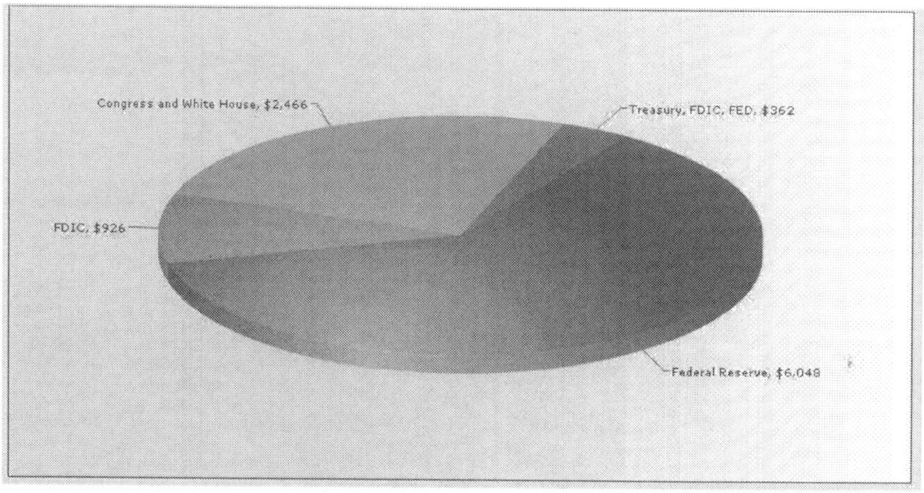

Breakdown of each agency's bailout portion:

Federal Reserve $6,048 trillion

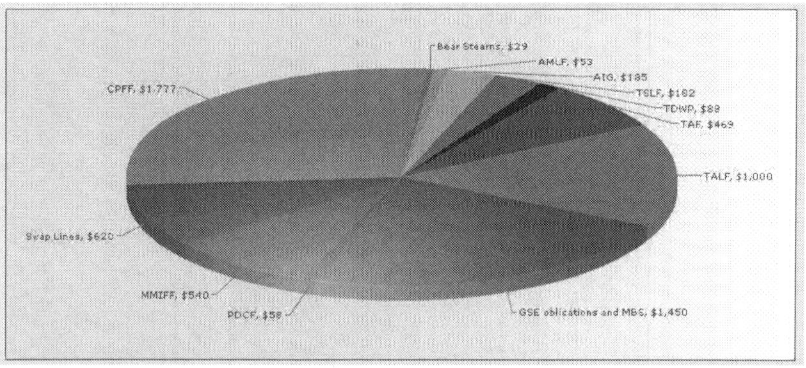

Congress and White House $2,466 trillion

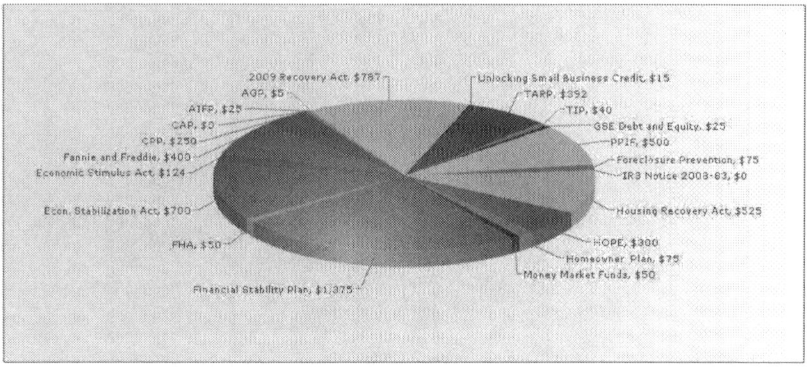

Does this restore your confidence in the economy? Or did they simply pick up the Humpty Dumpty economy and put it back together again with these programs? When the next crisis comes, rest assured that they will throw trillions at it, but sooner or later we have to realize that all the debt we accumulate, as discussed in the section on the national debt, will be exposed for what it really is: a Ponzi scheme on the grandest scale. This action by our government was to save the financial system, and while it did recover, it sits on a shaky foundation. The bailout helped some fix their balance sheets, like our nation's largest banks, but also weakened the bankers' bank (the Federal Reserve), while doing much damage to the biggest balance sheet of all: that of the U.S. government. Where does this madness end?

Chapter 14 - Banks Will Stop at Nothing

What's the Future of Banking for Consumers?

For many of us, banks simply offer what we perceive to be a safe place to put our money. If we need to use it, we go online and pay a bill, or write a check, or go there and withdraw cash. But if for some reason you decide to withdraw more than $10,000 from your account, the bank is required to file a Currency Transaction Report (CTR).

> *For each deposit, withdrawal, exchange of currency, or other payment or transfer, by, through, or to the financial institution which involves a transaction in currency of more than $10,000.*
>
> *Multiple transactions must be treated as a single transaction if the financial institution has knowledge that (1) they are by or on behalf of the same person, and (2) they result in either currency received (Cash In) or currency disbursed (Cash Out) by the financial institution totaling more than $10,000 during any one business day.*[172]

Technically this amount doesn't even have to be $10,000 to raise a red flag on your transaction and report it, as the decision to report is up to the teller.

But there's another interesting thing banks do as it relates to changes in the terms and conditions of your account. Most don't even read them, but there have been cases, because of anti-money laundering laws, where banks want to know what you are doing with that money. While technically it is your money, and it would appear to follow that you can do what you want with it, the bank may dictate otherwise. Naturally they do it for your own protection, but use the excuse of drug or terrorist activities as reasoning.[173]

---

172 http://www.ffiec.gov/bsa_aml_infobase/documents/forms/Form_104.pdf
173 http://www.bbc.co.uk/news/business-25861717

Keeping money at a bank may become similar to the *South Park* episode[174] where the father brings his son to the bank so the child can make his first deposit of his hard-earned savings. The bank teller puts it all into a money market mutual fund and tells the boy within a few seconds that his money is gone. While this may be a cartoon looking to get a laugh out of the audience, 78 money market funds actually had to seek help to keep their share price from falling below $1 from 2007 to 2011. This potential loss prompted a subsequent move by the government to extend FDIC coverage to money market accounts.[175]

Worse yet, we witnessed in 2013 a Greek rescue plan for the banks, where customers' funds were seized if they were over €100,000 ($111,128 U.S.) as well as 30% of deposits over the small sum of €8,000 at one bank.[176]

In the *FRBNY Economic Policy Review* of December 2014, assistant vice president and counsel at the Federal Reserve Bank of New York, Joseph H. Sommer, laid out the situation regarding megabanks in a paper entitled, "Why Bail-In? And How!" [177]

> *Megabanks are highly interconnected. This implies that a weakness in one megabank can become a weakness in all. The mechanism is unimportant. It could be a pure panic attack, with bad news for one bank imputed to all. Or perhaps a markdown of an asset class by one bank triggers markdowns by all. Or an industry-wide hedging model goes south. Or perhaps one megabank's liabilities are others' assets. Or perhaps a clearinghouse goes bad, blocking liquidity. Leverage and liquidity stress seem to be important. To make matters*

---

174 https://en.wikipedia.org/wiki/Margaritaville_(South_Park)

175 https://www.fdic.gov/consumers/consumer/information/fdiciorn.html

176 http://www.ft.com/cms/s/0/9963b74c-219c-11e5-aa5a-398b2169cf79.html# axzz40rYcwGTa

177 https://www.newyorkfed.org/medialibrary/media/research/epr/2014/1412 somm.pdf

> *worse, the asset side also becomes illiquid in times of general stress. (I make no claims of causal direction here.) Therefore, asset liquidity dries up precisely when a megabank most needs this liquidity.*

The solution to these issues, he says, is the bail-in option.

> *A bail-in takes place before a bankruptcy and under current proposals, regulators would have the power to impose losses on bondholders while leaving untouched other creditors of similar stature, such as derivatives counterparties.*

The fact that the Federal Reserve is even talking about this should drive home the point that this is real—and possible.

Beginning in 2016, new regulations for the resolution of banking crises came into force in Europe,[178] as a new countdown for Greece is looming. If you're a bondholder in some of these banks, why?

Circling back to Sommer's paper, I believe that while he gets the interconnectedness of the banking system both nationally and internationally, his conclusions don't consider that if more than one megabank is affected, there is only one bank left to buy the assets and liquidate them piecemeal—and that's the Federal Reserve, which we'll get to shortly. Unfortunately, the Fed will be hard pressed to do so.

Pre and Post Crisis - Banks Unhinged - Moral Hazard

Banks took no moral responsibility for the 2007–2009 financial crisis. They paid their fines and continue to perform more fraudulent activities with no concern for the consequences. In their lust for profit, the largest banks today will do whatever is necessary to obtain the filthy lucre they desire. In the next graphic, you'll see why I use such a harsh term as "filthy lucre."

---

[178] http://www.socialeurope.eu/2015/11/new-countdown-for-greece-a-bank-bail-in-is-looming/

The three largest U.S. banks by assets are JPMorgan Chase, Bank of America, and Citigroup.[179] These companies have been pegged by many as "too big to fail." And from the looks of their actions in paying settlement after settlement, they know it—and don't care. This by definition is known as "moral hazard." The sad part for capitalism as we know it is that they're right. The Fed always has their backs. Congress always works with them, not against them. But let's take a look at just how much these "too big to fail" banks *do* get away with. It might surprise some of you.

U.S. Top Banks by Assets

Rank	Bank name	Total assets (US$ Billion)
1	JPMorgan Chase	$2,600.00
2	Bank of America	$2,100.00
3	Citigroup	$1,890.00

The following is a list of lawsuit settlements made by these three banks since 2009.

JP Morgan: $35.24 billion since 2011[180]

- November 2014 $1.34 Billion - Currency manipulation
- January 2014 $1.7 billion – Bernie Madoff retribution

---

179 **https://en.wikipedia.org/wiki/List_of_largest_banks_in_the_United_States**

180 http://www.dividend.com/dividend-education/a-brief-history-of-jp-morgans-massive-fines-jpm/

- December 2013 $108 million - Libor rigging scandal
- November 2013 $13 billion - The Big One: Misleading "toxic mortgages"
- November 2013 $4.5 billion - Institutional mortgage securities
- September 2013 $5.1 billion - The Fannie and Freddie fines
- September 2013 $920 million - The London Whale
- September 2013 $389 million - Illegal credit card practices
- July 2013 $410 million - Electricity trading scandal
- January 2013 $1.8 billion - Improper foreclosures Pt. 2
- November 2012 $269.9 million - More mortgage misrepresentation
- February 2012 $5.29 billion - Foreclosure abuses and "robo-signing"
- July 2011 228 million - Anticompetitive conduct in municipal bonds
- June 2011 153.6 million - Misleading CDO investments

(Does not include the $6.2 billion trading loss from the London Whale.)[181]

Bank of America: $29 Billion Since 2009[182]

- September 2012 $2.43 billion to shareholders for the acquisition of Merrill Lynch
- February 2012 – $11.8 billion under 50 attorneys general settlement, which included $7.6 billion in payments for borrowers, $1 billion for refinancing, $2.25 billion paid to state and federal governments, and $1 billion to the Federal Housing Authority
- December 2011 – $335 million to settle allegations that Countrywide discriminated against minority borrowers

---

[181] http://fortune.com/2013/01/15/jpmorgans-board-is-unchanged-after-6-billion-trading-loss/

[182] http://blogs.wsj.com/deals/2012/09/28/bank-of-americas-settlements-29-billion-since-2009/

- June 2011 – $8.5 billion for mortgage repurchase demands from bond holders
- May 2011 – $20 million to Department of Justice over allegations Countrywide wrongly foreclosed on active-duty members of the military
- April 2011 – $1.6 billion for Assured Guaranty to settle breaches of representations and warranties on mortgage bonds
- February 2011 – $410 million to checking-account customers who were charged overdraft fees
- January 2011 – $3 billion to Freddie Mac and Fannie Mae to settle demands for mortgage repurchases
- October 2010 – Part of a $67.5 million settlement for former Countrywide CEO Angelo Mozilo was covered by the bank for civil fraud charges
- June 2010 – $108 million to the FTC for claims that Countrywide, before BofA owned it, inflated costs of foreclosure services for customers by up to 400%
- May 2010 – $600 million to pensions that lost money on Countrywide mortgage securities
- February 2010 – $150 million to SEC over the Merrill acquisition, reluctantly approved by judge

Citigroup: $10.6 Billion Since 2014

- August 2015 - $180 million for hedge fund fraud[183]
- August 2015 - $15 million to settle civil charges alleging it failed to enforce policies. designed to prevent and detect insider trading[184]
- July 2015 - $140 million over deficiencies in its anti-money laundering program[185]

---

[183] http://www.marketwatch.com/story/sec-fines-citigroup-affiliates-180-million-for-hedge-fund-fraud-2015-08-17-11911452
[184] http://www.reuters.com/article/us-citigroup-prosiebensat-1-settlement-idUSKCN0QF2A920150810#AeJZAGzhw7yTYP1b.97
[185] http://www.bloomberg.com/news/articles/2015-07-22/citigroup-to-

- July 2015 - $770 million over credit card practices[186]
- June 2015 - $2.5 billion for rigging foreign exchange markets[187]
- July 2014 - $7 billion for packaging bad mortgages

All in all the nation's top 3 banks have had over $113 billion in fines since 2010, but the top 16 global banks incurred fines collectively of over $300 billion, and there are presently 264 investigations involving 46 banks ongoing around the world. What other businesses are you aware of that are investigated and sued, yet still continue to act unscrupulously with no regard for anyone but themselves?[188] They make Al Capone (the early years) and his gang look like angels.[189]

One thing lost, though, when most people analyze banks is the fact that these banks are major owners of government debt. According to truth-out.org, this:

...gives them even greater leverage over the policies and priorities of governments. Exercising this power, they typically demand the same thing: austerity measures and "structural reforms" designed to advance a neoliberal market economy that ultimately benefits those same banks and corporations. The banks in turn create the very crises that require governments to bail them out, racking up large debts that banks turn into further crises, pressuring economic reforms in return for further loans. The cycle of crisis and control continues, and all the while, the big banks and financial institutions engage in criminal conspiracies, fraud, manipulation and money laundering on a massive

---

close-banamex-usa-unit-pay-140-million-civil-fine

186 http://www.reuters.com/article/us-usa-banks-creditcard-idUSKCN0PV1PJ20150721#2QgHzu0PRlgMydwY.97

187 http://www.ibtimes.co.uk/fx-fixing-scandal-citigroup-paid-2-5bn-fines-rigging-currency-rates-bank-made-just-1m-1505515

188 http://www.theguardian.com/commentisfree/2015/feb/15/hsbc-has-form-mexico-laundered-drug-money

189 http://www.rollingstone.com/politics/news/gangster-bankers-too-big-to-jail-20130214?page=4

scale, including acting as the financial services arm of the world's largest drug cartels and terrorist organizations. [190]

This isn't a conspiracy theory, but a well-documented argument that shows banks get away with fraud and manipulation of markets such as the Libor rigging in 2013 by Chase and gold rigging in 2016 by Deutsche Bank.[191] They continually get fined for their actions—more than any other type of business in the world. At least the early days of Capone fulfilled a need with the bootlegging operations of the 1920s Prohibition era (for those who enjoyed a drink now and then). These banks today don't fulfill the needs of even their shareholders, who constantly sue them, or those trapped in their credit card web of usury—like your average American citizen, who carries some credit card debt. It's no wonder those who want to safeguard their money with a sound financial institution are looking for alternatives.

Not only do banks have carte blanche in running their own affairs, but they charge you very high interest rates if you don't pay off your credit card balance each month. The next table shows the average rates charged for credit card balances.[192] Fees can be as high as 24.99% for some cards.[193]

---

[190] http://www.truth-out.org/news/item/33942-bank-crimes-pay-under-the-thumb-of-the-global-financial-mafiocracy

[191] http://www.zerohedge.com/news/2016-04-14/first-silver-now-gold-deutsche-bank-admits-it-also-rigged-gold-prices-legal-settleme

[192] http://www.bankrate.com/calculators/credit-cards/credit-card-minimum-payment.aspx

[193] http://www.bankrate.com/credit-cards/bad-credit-cards.aspx?ic_id=calc_credit%20cards_CreditCardRatesAverages_CreditCards_CardsForBadCredit

CREDIT CARD RATES AVERAGES

Product	Rate	Change	Last week
Balance Transfer Cards	16.37%	▲0.15	16.22%
Cash Back Cards	16.70%	▲0.04	16.66%
Low Interest Cards	11.50%	▲0.02	11.48%

Know Your Limits

Indeed, if push comes to shove during the next financial crisis, and a bank has control of most of your wealth, you would expect to have access to all of it. But will you? One common-sense action is to simply diversify your bank holdings among a few banks, as well as credit unions (which have different protections available to the depositor). Also, there is no reason whatsoever to hold more at one single bank than the amount covered by the FDIC, which is typically $250,000 but can be a million or more for a married couple if set up correctly.[194] You can speak to an FDIC representative for free by calling 1 (877) 275-3342.

[194] http://www.bankrate.com/finance/savings/fdic-insures-bank-deposits-to-250-000-1.aspx

Chapter 15 - Bank Exposures

Rising Rates - Good or Bad for Banks?

One thing we can say for sure is that we are at historically low interest rates in the U.S. But another problem on the horizon is that with an eventual rise in rates, banks are vulnerable to big losses because they carry so many bonds on the books. We saw this in 2013, when long-term bonds rose a full point in anticipation of the Fed's tapering. Collectively the banks lost, on paper, $13 billion, as seen in the next graphic from *The Wall Street Journal*, but didn't have to report the losses on the books because accounting rules allowed banks to keep paper losses on long-term bonds hidden on their balance sheets. In fact, during this time, the four biggest banks gave us the illusion that they were profitable, with $20 billion in net income.[195]

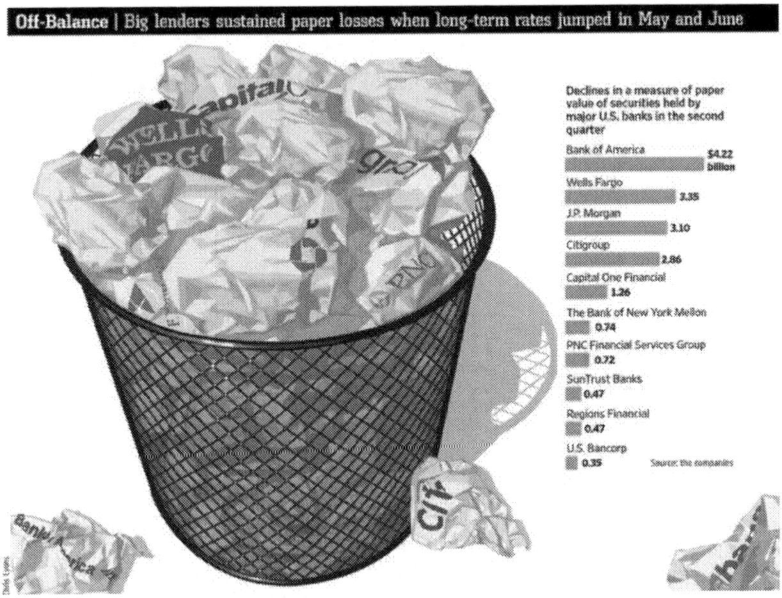

---

[195] http://www.wsj.com/articles/SB10001424127887324170004578636292376029594

Moving forward, as interest rates rise, the banks will again have the same problems, but this time it will be different. It will lead to balance sheets not providing the whole truth. As rates keep going higher and higher, so will losses. Eventually those losses will have to be accounted for, and that's when we'll see what might be the final blow to these big banks, as most undoubtedly deserve what's coming to them. But unfortunately, it will be investors and most others who will feel the pain, because of these covert actions blessed by the Fed, Congress, and bank-influenced Dodd-Frank legislation that allowed it.

One proposal from the Office of the Comptroller of the Currency is to impose on banks with over $50 billion in assets—in addition to annual stress tests—a "survival" stress test to maintain a bank's financial and operational strength during a stressful period. This, in turn, is being viewed by the banks as a detriment to shareholders.[196]

Banks' Exposure to Oil's Slide

Fitch Ratings, at the end of 2014, put out a report about the challenging environment facing banks that had made loans to the shale boom companies when the price of oil was much higher. Many banks since that time have been in trouble as the price of oil has continued to decline, hitting lows not seen since 2003. Oil companies are struggling in Texas and many banks are reporting ever larger impairments. What does the Dallas Fed do? Just like with the bond example above, the Fed has allowed these banks to not have to mark-to-market these loans to these struggling oil companies. The banks' balance sheets are impaired, but who's to know?[197]

---

[196] http://www.wsj.com/articles/banks-would-have-to-show-stress-survival-plans-under-occ-proposal-1450136165

[197] http://www.zerohedge.com/news/2016-01-16/exclusive-dallas-fed-quietly-suspends-energy-mark-market-tells-banks-not-force-shale

Company	Borrowing Base Size Prior	Borrowing Base Size Current	Change (%)	Rating Moody's	Rating S&P
New Source Energy Partners	$49,000,000	$24,000,000	-51.0%	Not Rated	
Emerald Oil	200,000,000	120,000,000	-40.0%	Not Rated	
EXCO Resources	600,000,000	375,000,000	-37.5%	Caa1	B-
Resolute Energy	260,000,000	165,000,000	-36.5%	B3	B-
Penn Virginia Corp	395,000,000	275,000,000	-30.4%	Caa3	B-
W&T Offshore	500,000,000	350,000,000	-30.0%	B3	B
Goodrich Petroleum	105,000,000	75,000,000	-28.6%	Caa3	SD
Berry Petroleum Co.	1,200,000,000	900,000,000	-25.0%	Caa1	B+
Unit Corp.	725,000,000	550,000,000	-24.1%	Ba3	BB-
PetroQuest Energy	70,000,000	55,000,000	-21.4%	B3	B-
SM Energy	2,400,000,000	2,000,000,000	-16.7%	Ba1	BB
NRP Oil and Gas	105,000,000	88,000,000	-16.2%	Not Rated	
Approach Resources	525,000,000	450,000,000	-14.3%	B2	B
Bonanza Creek Energy	550,000,000	475,000,000	-13.6%	B2	B
Denbury Resources	3,000,000,000	2,600,000,000	-13.3%	Ba3	BB-
Energen Corp	1,600,000,000	1,400,000,000	-12.5%	Ba1	BB
Swift Energy	375,000,000	330,000,000	-12.0%	Caa3	D
Whiting Petroleum	4,500,000,000	4,000,000,000	-11.1%	Ba2	BB
LINN Energy	4,050,000,000	3,600,000,000	-11.1%	Caa1	B+
Oasis Petroleum	1,700,000,000	1,525,000,000	-10.3%	B1	BB-
Clayton Williams Energy	500,000,000	450,000,000	-10.0%	B3	B-
Jones Energy	562,500,000	510,000,000	-9.3%	B3	NA
Black Stone Minerals	600,000,000	550,000,000	-8.3%	Not Rated	
Laredo Petroleum	1,250,000,000	1,150,000,000	-8.0%	B1	B+
Black Ridge Oil and Gas	34,000,000	32,000,000	-5.9%	Not Rated	

What does this mean? It means banks don't have to be honest about their losses on the loans they made to these companies. They can keep impaired losses on their books from being discovered until the oil market recovers.

Banks were also given special privilege by the Federal Accounting Standards Board (FASB) when they carried loans on the books much larger than the value of the houses bought during the height of the real estate market. They could mark the value of the home at the original 2006 higher price, even though the true value was tens—if not hundreds—of thousands less. This made their balance sheets look stronger than they really were. It's accounting gimmickry at its finest, all blessed by the Fed and any government oversight accounting agency, like the FASB they can get to help them.[198]

[198] http://www.wsj.com/articles/SB123867739560682309

Bank Ratings

Most investors will, out of convenience, do their banking at a local institution without checking out its rating. But not all banks are the same, and there are rating agencies, like bankrate.com where you can check out a bank's rating.[199]

Here's one example of what ratings can reveal about the health of a bank. Guaranty Bank in Wisconsin has between $1 billion and $5 billion in assets. It receives a 1-star rating out of 5 potential stars from bankrate.com. As you can see, Guaranty is below average in most every category, yet somehow has managed to obtain over $1 billion in assets from depositors. Would you trust your money with this bank after reading the following data?[200]

Key Earnings information and ratios:	Ratio (%)	Assessment
Return on Equity	-22.23	Substantially Below Average
Net Interest Margin	2.98	Below Average
Level of Non-interest Income (1)	6.84	Solid
Overhead (1)	9.82	Significantly Higher Than Average

(1) = As a percentage of average assets
Note: All ratios are based on the latest four quarters of income and expense

Key Asset Quality information and ratios:	Ratio (%)	Assessment
Nonperforming Asset Ratio (2)	98.29	Highly Problematic
Loss Reserve Coverage (3)	46.80	Substantially Below Normal
Loan Yield	4.11	Conservative
Asset Growth Rate	-6.57	Below Normal

2) = Nonperforming Assets/Equity plus Loss Reserves
3) = Loan Loss Reserves/Nonperforming Loans

Key measures of Capital Adequacy:	Ratio (%)	Assessment
Net Worth to Total Assets	2.33	Significantly Below Norm
Regulatory Capital Ratio	4.86	Was Not In Compliance With Requirement

---

199 http://www.bankrate.com/rates/safe-sound/bank-ratings-search.aspx?ic_id=home_smart-spending_bank-rates_globalnav
200 http://www.bankrate.com/rates/safe-sound/memorandums-memos.aspx?fedid=640170

FDIC Is There for You

To prevent bank runs, the Fed increases the amount the FDIC will cover for each bank in which you have money deposited. The most recent was an increase to $250,000 in 2008 as we discussed, during the beginning of the financial crisis (up from $100,000, where it had been since 1980, ironically the same year gold hit an all-time high of $850 an ounce). This increase was due to expire at the end of 2013, but as part of the Dodd-Frank Wall Street Reform and Consumer Protection Act, it became permanent that year.[201]

You can bet that during the next crisis, they'll raise the insurance level to $1 million, just to give you the illusion that your money is safe in the bank. The higher the insurance, the safer you feel, as the FDIC is always there for you, right? But it's also an illusion that your money is kept in a nice pile at the bank, as everything is now handled electronically.

How Is the FDIC Funded?

The FDIC is funded entirely by member banks, which must meet specific liquidity and reserve requirements. The larger the bank, the more it pays into the fund, which is used to help liquidate any foreclosed bank. The fund has reserves of $67.6 billion[202] and the reserve ratio is 1.06% but was supposed to be 1.15%, and raised to 1.35% by December 31, 2015, or assessments would be posed on large banks.[203] This just isn't happening. This $67.6 billion insures approximately $9 trillion of deposits in U.S. banks and thrifts.[204] Please let that sink in for a moment.

---

201 https://firstexchange.com/content/fdic-insurance-coverage-permanently-increased-250000

202 https://www.fdic.gov/news/news/press/2015/pr15071.html

203 https://www.fdic.gov/news/news/financial/2015/fil15053.html

204 https://www.fdic.gov/about/learn/symbol/

A Word About Safety Deposit Boxes

I need to mention safety deposit boxes, as they are another illusion of wealth for many heirs who don't even know their parents have one. Banks don't make it a habit of sending out notices on safety deposit boxes. If the rental payments cease, then after a certain number of years (depending on your state law), and attempts to notify or locate anyone associated with the box, it will be reported as abandoned and the contents given to your state's unclaimed property office and sold. You can go to www.unclaimed.org and still possibly claim the value of the contents. The FDIC, for your information, does not cover contents of a safety deposit box that is stolen or damaged.

Chapter 16 - Foreign Banks and U.S. Bank Exposure

European Banks

European banks have not enjoyed the luxury of recovery that U.S. banks have, with a Fed and Congress so quick to try to resolve the financial crisis. According to Bloomberg, for European banks, "the volume of non-performing loans fell only 1.8 percent to 826 billion euros ($914 billion) since the end of 2013"[205] and continue.

Other problems that face banks in the U.S. and abroad are the lending they do to countries that are having difficulties paying their bills—like Greece, for example.[206]

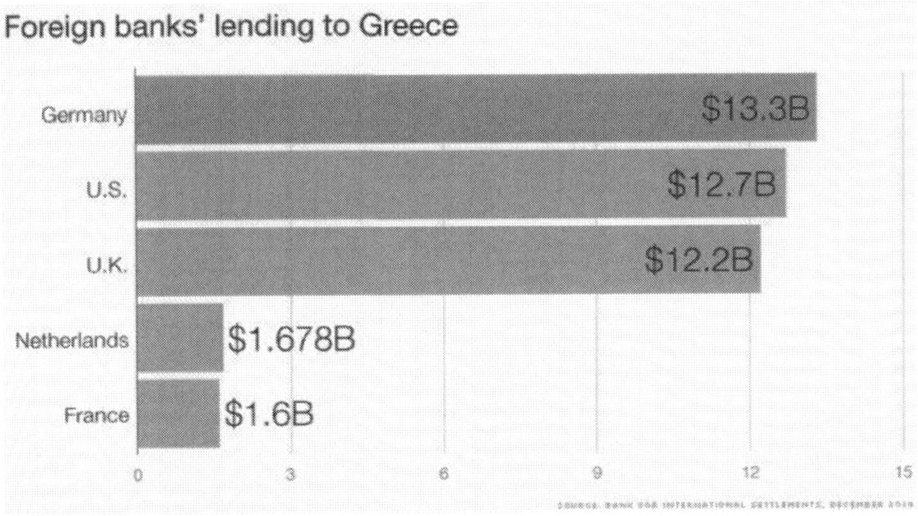

Fitch Ratings' managing director and global head of sovereign ratings says that countries like Africa, Russia and China that rely heavily on the commodity trade are experiencing troubles that could cause their

---

205 http://www.bloomberg.com/news/articles/2015-11-02/euro-banks-barely-cut-bad-debt-levels-under-ecb-linklaters-says

206 **http://money.cnn.com/2015/06/29/news/economy/greece-banks-internation-exposure/**

ratings to be lowered, or in the case of Russia, lowered further.[207] In January 2016 the ruble hit an all-time low against the U.S. dollar.[208]

To prevent banks from getting bailed out by taxpayers again, in Europe they are pushing the burden onto bondholders, shareholders and big depositors in what is being dubbed a "bail-in" which we discussed a bit earlier. This is not set to take place until 2018, which means there still could be trouble ahead for some of the more heavily indebted countries.[209]

Italy, for example had bad loans of 201 billion euros as of November 2015, and as of January 2016, the world's oldest bank, Monte dei Paschi, dropped 34% in January alone. Europe's 46-member Stoxx 600 Banks Index is at the lowest level since 2012.

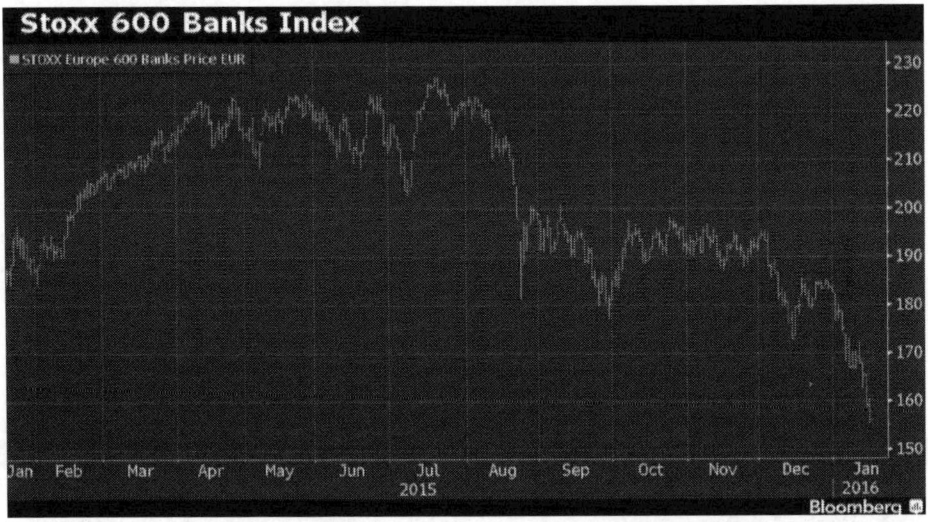

[207] http://www.bloomberg.com/news/videos/2016-01-13/sovereign-risk-why-commodities-are-a-big-concern
[208] http://news.yahoo.com/ruble-close-historic-low-past-key-80-level-095403872.html
[209] http://finance.yahoo.com/news/eu-bank-bailout-roulette-awaits-083551222.html

Chinese Banks

Understanding China and its alleged shadow banking market is essential, if you wish to thoroughly analyze banking.

Hayman Capital Management founder Kyle Bass notes that the banking system in China is $35 trillion against a GDP of $10 trillion, with growth of 400% in the last 8 years and no non-performing loans. So far, so good. But he says a 10% decline in the Chinese banking system would be an equivalent loss of $3.5 trillion, and this could potentially swallow up their foreign exchange reserves. When you lend too much money, there are consequences… eventually. How long this will take to unwind could be a few years, according to CEO Marc Lasry of global investment firm Avenue Capital, which manages $12.7 billion.[210]

The economic slowdown in China isn't helping, but what China has going for it is a lower debt-to-GDP ratio of only 33%.[211] The Chinese are also notorious for government intervention, but the question remains, how long can you hold a band aid over a widening hole of a decline in their banking system? According to *The Financial Times*, lenders in China could require up to $7.7 trillion of new capital funding over the next three years,[212] and that's not a high probability, even if you do have a printing press.

That said, China has established, much to the disliking of the U.S., an Asian Infrastructure Investment Bank (AIIB)[213] and it has been joined by most of the major countries outside of Japan, South Korea and the U.S. It seems to be competition to the U.S. led International Monetary

---

210 http://video.cnbc.com/gallery/?video=3000476898

211 http://www.barrons.com/articles/chinas-shadow-banking-risks-are-overplayed-1449651202

212 http://www.ft.com/intl/cms/s/6d9aa6ce-b860-11e5-bf7e-8a339b6f2164

213 http://euweb.aiib.org/html/aboutus/AIIB/?show=0

Fund (IMF) as a challenge to the existing global economic order. I would pay attention to where this bank puts its funds.

Emerging Markets and Mexican Banks

Agustín Carstens, Mexico's central bank chief, says that emerging markets (EM) could be in for trouble. According to *The Financial Times*, "Many EM companies have filled up on cheap credit over the past decade, after a commodities boom and ultra-loose monetary policies led by the US Federal Reserve resulted in very low borrowing costs. As investors pull out, those costs are set to soar."[214]

Mr. Carstens believes that emerging markets will respond with their own type of operation twist—exchanging high-risk, long-dated assets for less risky, shorter-dated central bank and government liabilities. The problem with this, though, is if the emerging government will stay solvent.

Mexico's largest infrastructure and construction company, Empresas ICA, is on the verge of default and six of Mexico's largest banks have exposure of $12.3 billion pesos ($726 million) in loans. Empresas ICA missed a $6 million interest payment in order to preserve liquidity, and is seeking to restructure.[215]

Closing Thoughts on Banks

> *Every fractional reserve bank depends for its very existence on persuading the public—specifically its clients—that all is well and that it will be able to redeem its notes or deposits whenever the clients demand. Since this is palpably not the case, the continuance of confidence in the banks is something*

214 http://www.ft.com/intl/cms/s/0/968bd686-ba02-11e5-bf7e-8a339b6f2164.html#axzz3xqTCp4Qe
215 http://www.streetinsider.com/Corporate+News/Empresas+ICA+(ICA)+to+Will+Not+Make+$6M+Interest+Payment%3B+Appoints+Financial+Restructuring+Officer/11232059.html

of a psychological marvel—Murray Rothbard, *Man, Economy & State*, Scholar's Edition. (Ludwig von Mises Institute)

Governments will do all they can to help their banking systems stay afloat. We depositors trust banks to act in our best interests, and yet over and over again they keep making bad choices with no concern for the consequences. The U.S. banking system has recovered, thanks to some help from government regulations and the Fed, which we'll discuss further in the next chapter. But the European Union still has a weak banking system and a few years of uncertainty ahead. They are taking the right steps, but as the fall in the euro shows, they are a long way from stabilization. China is an unknown, and being so new to the game, I expect some negative outcomes as things unwind globally.

Banks always seem to have a way of coming out smelling like roses, but it is usually either at taxpayers' expense or the demise of the economy for a period. The nation's top banks were handed billions by TARP, were able to shore up their balance sheets with quantitative easing by the Fed, and receive slaps on the wrist with no accountability for their actions—which included fraud—and still abuse the system to this day. They don't really care about the little guy, as long as they get those bonuses… which account for 38% to 40% of all revenues.

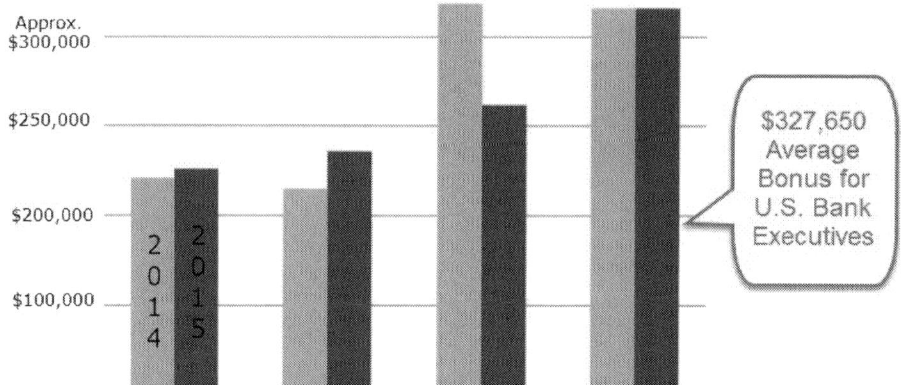

One person to watch in the future when it comes to possibly breaking up the big banks is the President of the Federal Reserve Bank of Minneapolis, Neel Kashkari. He believes that the too big to fail banks pose a risk to the economy and that the Dodd-Frank financial reform passé did not go far enough to solve the problems. He is more than likely to make some proposals once the presidency is decided in 2016.[216]

Until we resolve more of the issues that we have presented in this chapter and those we discuss in the next chapter on the Federal Reserve, investors need to be a little more cautious, especially in light of the run-up in the stock market since the last crisis. Perhaps a little insurance of some sort may be prudent. We'll discuss those options in the Investment section.

---

216 http://www.usatoday.com/story/money/2016/02/23/delamaide-fed-aide-goes-rogue-attack-banks-wall-street-money/80802170/

PART 6 – FEDERAL RESERVE

No thorough analysis of the economy and investment world is complete without a further understanding of the Federal Reserve (the Fed), the central bank of the United States.

When it comes to understanding what the Fed does, most of us are ignorant of the mechanics that make up this banking institution. I do know from looking through grade schoolers' textbooks that not much is taught about our monetary system, let alone about the history of the Federal Reserve System. If you have children or grandchildren in school, I challenge you to look at their Civics/Economics/Social Studies textbooks and see what is written there about the Federal Reserve compared to what this section reveals. At most there may be a paragraph, but never anything about the mechanics.

Wright Patman, Chairman of the Subcommittee on Domestic Finance, had this to say about understanding the Fed in 1964 to the Committee on Banking and Finances, 88th Congress, 2nd Session:

> *Ignorance of what money is and how the Federal Reserve operates prompts many citizens and members of Congress to avoid getting involved in the issue.*

Bring any topic up about our monetary system or the Federal Reserve and you'll typically lose interest, or the one you're conversing with may put you in the conspiracy camp to make you think you're "out there" with your opinions. In understanding a bit more about the Fed, we'll start with a brief history.

Chapter 17 - History of the Federal Reserve

When we look at the Federal Reserve and try to pinpoint who they are and how they fit into investing, we have to give what they say as much credibility as we can, because they move markets.

One has to remember the Fed is still relevant. I got caught up for a while questioning the Fed's very existence. That's what happens when the first book you read on them is Edward G. Griffin's *The Creature from Jekyll Island.* All we really want is a currency we can trust and the Fed, despite some troubled times throughout history, has done a pretty good job overall. The dollar is pretty strong and to consider any potential currency crash, as some who want to end the Fed speculate will occur, one would have to ignore that our economy grows every year, at least for now. We are not Zimbabwe, nor can we be compared to countries that experienced hyperinflation in the past, as the dollar is still used in 70% of the world. We are the "go to" currency, not one that would be disbanded, at least as of this writing. But we'll point out some issues with the Fed that investors should be watching and this should help us adjust our portfolios if need be down the road. Let's start with a little history of the Fed.

From the Federal Reserve's website:

> *Why We Started*
>
> *During the 19th and early 20th century, financial panics and bank runs plagued our nation. The Panic of 1907 prompted Americans to call for a central bank. In response, Congress passed the Federal Reserve Act, which President Woodrow Wilson signed into law on December 23, 1913, to provide our nation with a more stable and secure monetary and financial system. The Fed has three primary responsibilities: conducting monetary policy, supervising and regulating banking institutions, issues currency, and providing payments services to banking institutions. The Fed buys and sells government securities to influence the amount of*

money in the banking system, which affects interest rates throughout the economy.[217]

The Fed's goal is "to promote a healthy financial system."[218]

Before the introduction of the Fed, there was a history of bank failures with the 1st and 2nd banks of the U.S., and the final straw was the Panic of 1907. A group of men got together on Jekyll Island, and by 1913, the Federal Reserve System was created.

Since that time the Fed has weathered WW1, The Great Depression, WWII, the 1970s inflation, the 1987 stock market crash, the Savings and Loan crisis, the Asian financial crisis of 1997, the Long-Term Capital Management fiasco of 1998, the 2000 dot com bust and most recently the 2009 recession. It seems like every 7-10 years on average, there is another crisis. But it wasn't without government collusion at times to help the Fed out. Some may say, though, that it was the Fed that helped government out. Either way, all we want as investors is a sound monetary system, and it has been anything but sound over the years.

I already talked in Chapter 1 about the confiscation of gold in 1933 and 1971 saw President Nixon finally sever the relationship between gold and our monetary system. We then experienced a high-inflation period, only to be saved by lower rates and loose monetary policy implemented by then-Fed chairman Paul Volcker after a meeting with John Exter—witnessed by his son-in-law Barry Downs, whom I interviewed for this book. We also saw unprecedented action by the Fed during the most recent financial crisis. What are the odds another crisis of some sort is lurking? I would say 100%, but the only unknown is when and where it will stem from.

While it's easy to pick on the Fed, they sometimes have their hands tied, and just like with the passing of TARP to help the banks out, it

217 http://www.federalreservehistory.org/Purpose

218 http://www.federalreservehistory.org/Purpose/WhatWeDo/5

seems no matter what the Fed does, it's the banks they support. This relationship does help investors, because if the banks go down, the system falls apart. But not much is done to prevent the banks from continually putting investors at risk with their actions, as we saw in the last section. When there are no repercussions, and only a few fines, why not buck the system and keep on doing what comes naturally? That's what banks are doing and will continue to do. It's the nature of the beast. If your business could do it, then you probably would too, but we all know it doesn't work that way for small businesses in America. If you step out of line, the IRS is auditing you, or some government regulator is knocking on your door collecting fines.

The problem we all should have with the Fed—which, to repeat, is the bankers' bank—is that they can't see the next crisis coming ahead of time. They are always reactive.

The Fed's Dual Mandate

The Federal Reserve is responsible for the banking system. They are known as the "lender of last resort" and are there for banks and other institutions that qualify for their assistance. They have a dual mandate of maximum employment and price stability.[219]

Mandate 1 - Real unemployment is 9.9% as of January 2016, as represented by U-6 data from the Bureau of Labor Statistics, which counts those the U-3 data no longer does because they can't find a job after a certain amount of time and drop off the list, or are part-time employees who would like to work full time, but can't find a job that matches their qualifications.

---

219 https://www.chicagofed.org/publications/speeches/our-dual-mandate-balance-sheet

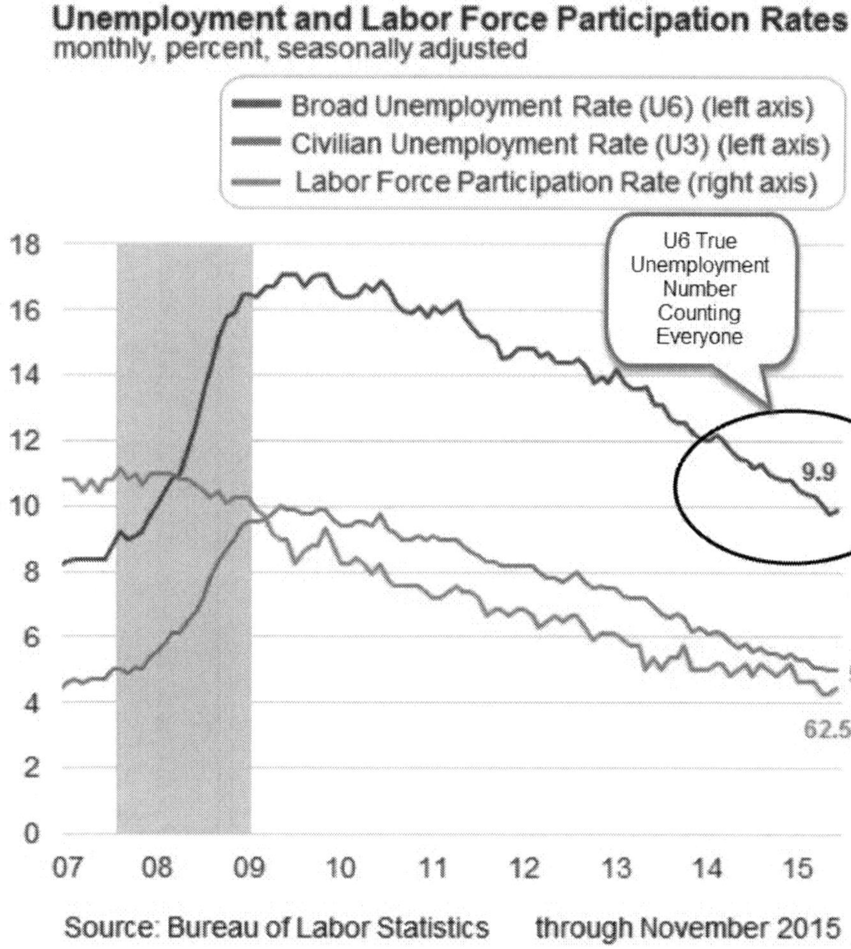

Mandate 2 - The Fed's mandate of price stability is only there for services and durable goods, not for nondurable goods. I personally don't have a problem with falling prices, but the Fed wants 2% inflation. They're only getting it in services.[220]

[220] https://www.frbatlanta.org/economy-matters/economic-and-financial-highlights.aspx

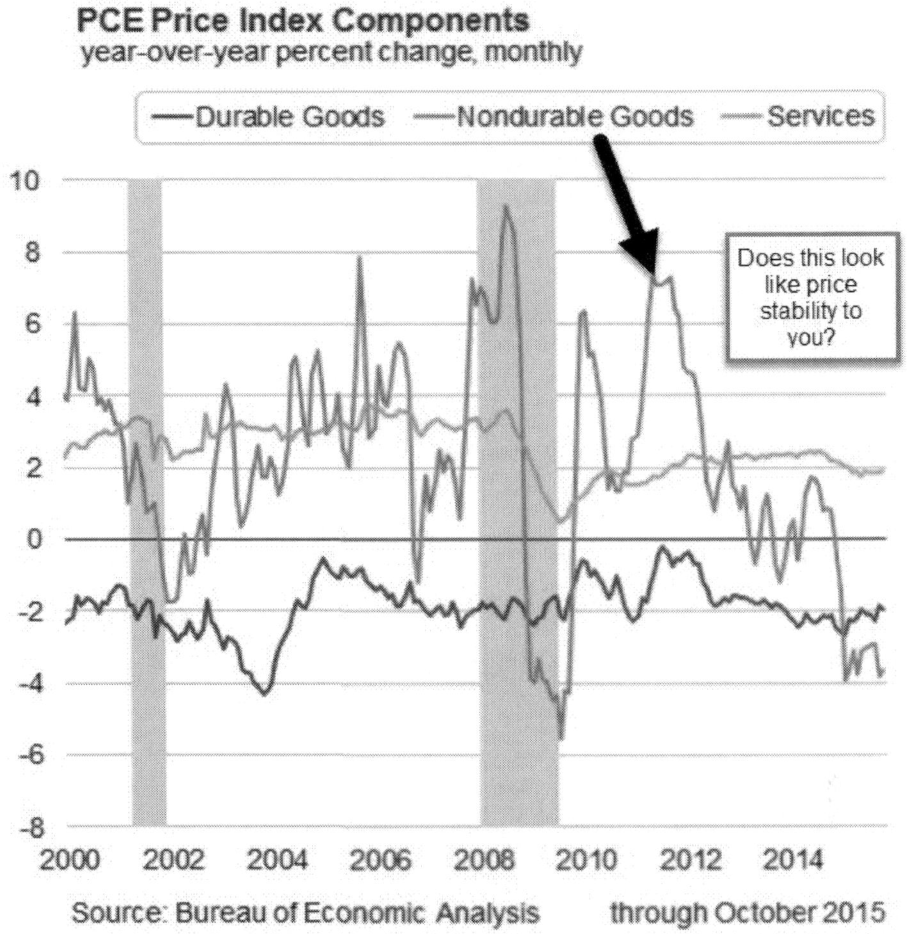

But did you know that at 2% inflation—the Fed's target rate—in just 10 years, it takes $1,218.99 to buy what $1,000 does today? Do you mind paying more for things in the future? Of course you do. Why do we want inflation if we have to pay more for things? It's because this is how our government's bills get paid without taxing us more. Deflation is actually their enemy, as debt becomes more expensive.

The Fed also provides the liquidity necessary to prevent bank runs, and takes action to stave off any financial crisis that may occur. While known as the lender of last resort, some would even go so far as to say they are also the buyer of last resort, which you saw with some of the assets they acquired during the 2007–2009 financial crisis and beyond.

Some say the Fed *caused* the financial crisis, because raising interest rates killed the housing bubble when adjustable-rate mortgages came due at higher rates. This is what the movie *The Big Short* presented as an opportunity for some smart people to capitalize on shorting derivatives. The truth is many of us knew what was going on before it happened especially many who understand Austrian economics. Others look at the Fed and Bernanke as heroes for getting us out of the financial crisis and on the road to prosperity again. Or did they?

Fed Unconventional Policy and Balance Sheet Today

The Fed, as we have pointed out, has been fighting deflation. That's the goal of quantitative easing, and without it, we would have experienced a bigger deflationary spiral in 2007-2009.

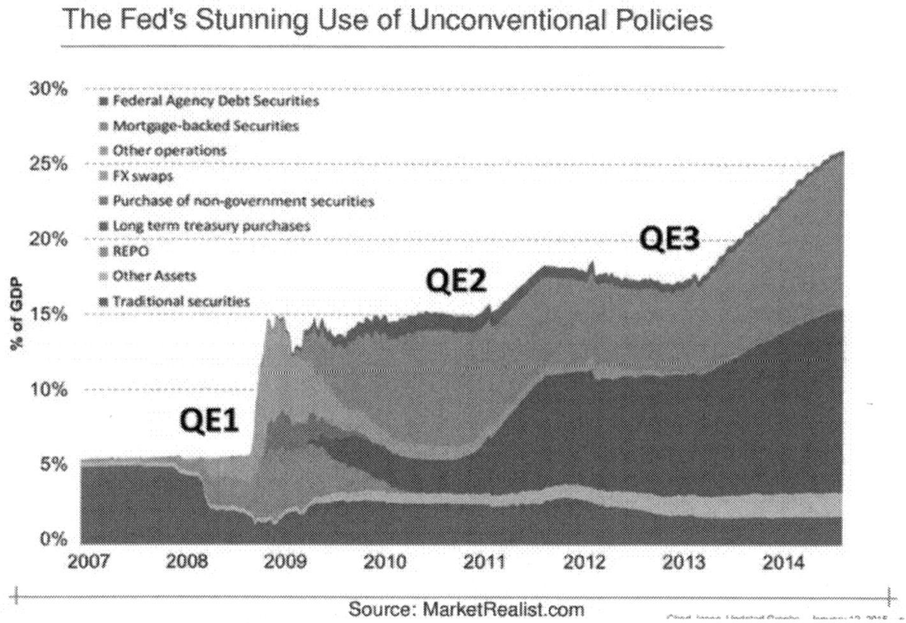

The Fed knows that an economy weighed down by excessive debt needs an inflation cycle so the debt doesn't become too much of a burden. If I have a fixed loan at 4% and deflation drives rates down to 2%, then my loan becomes a bigger burden on my balance sheet. Conversely, if rates rise to 6% because of inflation and growth, my 4% interest becomes more manageable.

The Fed has taken some of the toxic assets of banks and swapped them with an equal amount that becomes bank reserves. While for years the Fed's balance sheet consisted of mostly Treasuries, today it doesn't come close to resembling the past, since the onset of the financial crisis as seen in the following charts.[221] The Fed has no real intention of doing anything with these assets. They can hold until maturity if they have to.

Federal Reserve Balance Sheet

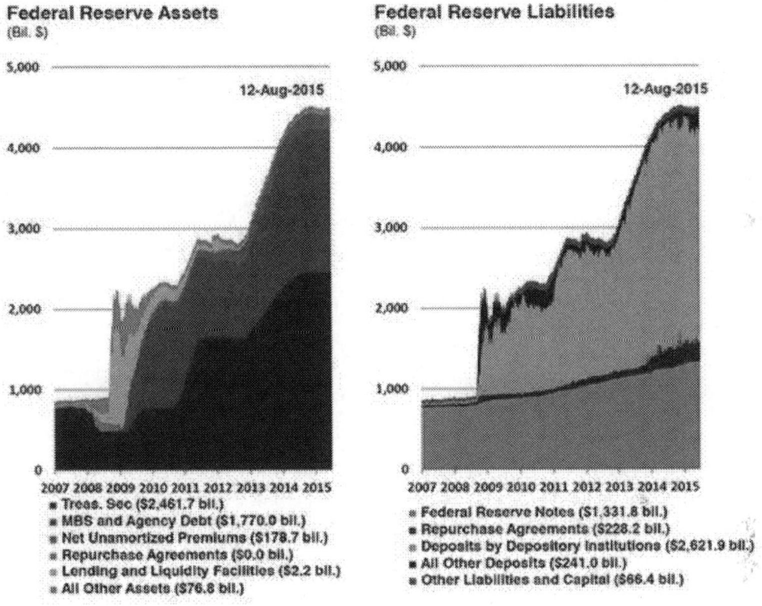

221 https://www.chicagofed.org/publications/speeches/our-dual-mandate-balance-sheet

What exactly does this balance sheet mean to investors? The following data shows the leverage by the Fed of capital to debt is 75:1, as seen in the next chart of liabilities and capital of the Federal Reserve System (in billions).[222] This little factoid goes unchecked by most, but there it is. Some say $4.431 trillion in liabilities with $59 billion in assets doesn't matter. But it sure did when the leverage was an issue in the 2008–2009 financial crisis.

Table liabilities, and capital of the Federal Reserve System

Item	Current October 28, 2015	Change from July 29, 2015	Change from October 29, 2014
Total liabilities	4,431	+4	+*
Selected liabilities			
Federal Reserve notes in circulation	1,350	+22	+95
Reverse repurchase agreements[10]	345	+102	+108
Foreign official and international accounts[10]	189	+33	+87
Others[10]	155	+69	+21
Term deposits held by depository institutions	0	0	−172
Other deposits held by depository institutions	2,668	+35	+41
U.S. Treasury, general account	36	−168	−83
Other deposits[11]	20	+12	+12
Total capital	59	+*	+2

All Central Bank Balance Sheets Are Becoming Skewed

It's not just the Fed either. All the world's central banks are increasing their balance sheets. The next table shows some of the largest central banks' asset growth.[223] The European Central Bank (ECB) was a late bloomer, but looks to be in full swing until 2017, according to ECB president Mario Draghi, who said in 2015, "We'll do whatever it takes"[224] when referencing what the ECB will do to stimulate growth (or help their weak banks, as we saw in the banking section… as that's their real intent).

---

222 http://www.federalreserve.gov/monetarypolicy/files/quarterly_balance_sheet_developments_report_201511.pdf

223 http://www.yardeni.com/pub/peacockfedecbassets.pdf

224 http://www.bloomberg.com/news/videos/2015-12-03/ecb-s-draghi-qe-extended-until-march-2017-or-beyond

Total Assets of Major Central Banks

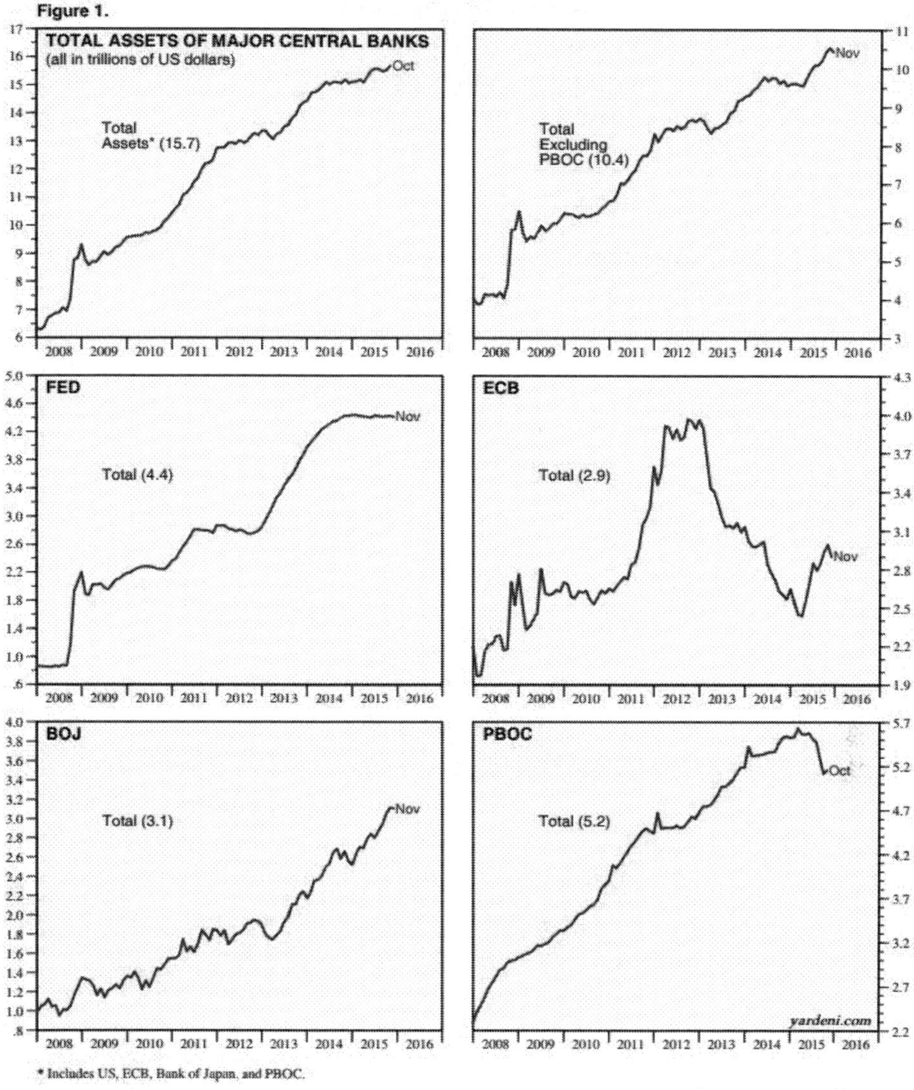

Janet Yellen, who succeeded Bernanke as Fed chairman, has worked closely with him, and approved of the first round of QE, while overall echoing his policies.[225]

The Fed has no choice but to fight deflation, but will do so reactively, not proactively. Justin Wolfers, senior fellow at the Peterson Institute for International Economics and professor of economics and public policy at the University of Michigan, provided some clarity when he said that the Fed is "failing to instill sufficient confidence that it (the Fed) stands ready to fight the drag of very low inflation or outright deflation."[226]

The Fed wants and needs home prices to go up. They can't have another disaster like the last crisis, where multiple banks went under. For that matter, they need oil to go up too, since so many banks are tied to the oil industry in supplying loans. If asset prices are increasing and inflation rolls along at 2%, then everyone's happy they pre-suppose.

The Fed can't force banks to lend out the bailout money they received. They also can't get people to buy homes even though we have interest rates at historic lows. By default, if banks aren't lending and people aren't borrowing, money velocity grinds to a halt. This isn't what the Fed wants, and it's exactly why they can't raise rates. But raise rates they did in December, and Goldman Sachs and others believe the Fed is going to keep on hiking, up to four times in 2016[227]—which started with a thud. At the first Fed meeting in January 2016, some Fed members, like James Bullard, were already regretting their December rate hike and curtailing the talk a bit, blaming the global outlook. Things will begin to unravel now for the Fed.

---

225 http://wallstanalyst.com/WP-WSA-V3/wp-content/uploads/2014/07/Janet-L-Yellen.pdf

226 http://www.nytimes.com/2015/03/08/upshot/derivatives-market-shows-a-rising-fear-of-deflation.html?_r=0&abt=0002&abg=0

227 http://www.businessinsider.in/GOLDMAN-The-Fed-is-going-to-hike-4-times-in-2016/articleshow/49890686.cms

Meanwhile, corporations are using this opportunity to use low rates and automate their businesses, which goes against the Fed mandate of stable employment if the rise of machines takes over human labor.

If the Fed succeeds in their goal of inflation, it's important for you, the investor, to have some insurance against such central bank maneuvers in order to maintain your purchasing power, just like many Japanese investors should be doing as the yen depreciates versus the dollar because of the Bank of Japan's monetary policy.[228] We saw Japan once again surprise everyone in January 2016 with negative interest rates.[229] While this temporarily created a demand for yen, as it's better to have actual yen under your mattress than at the bank, it's a game they are playing that will eventually implode, as at some point proactive prime minister Abe Shinzo will pull a Mario Draghi to get inflation rolling and do whatever it takes to get a weaker yen.

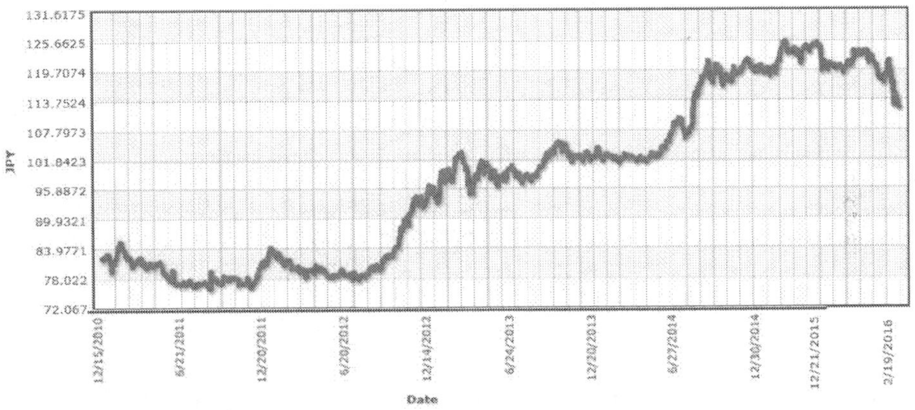

Japan's monetary policy is a prime example of what's to come (and is currently happening) the world over. If you want your exports to increase and thus grow GDP, you need to devalue your currency. This

---

228 http://www.indexmundi.com/xrates/graph.aspx?c1=JPY&c2=USD&days=1825

229 http://www.usatoday.com/story/money/business/2016/01/28/japan-negative-interest/79499096/

is exactly what Japan did through 2015. With a declining birth rate and other issues like the nuclear disaster at Fukushima, it just may be too late for Japan. Europe has their own issues with Greece and the PIIGS (Portugal, Ireland, Italy, Greece, and Spain) and their weak banking sector. The refugee situation in Europe and even the powerhouse Germany with problems in their auto industry because of the Volkswagen's emissions scandal is feeling the pain.[230] Yes, a Black Swan event can come from many places, and you can bank on this (pun intended).

Issues to Consider

Treasury Debt Coming Back to the U.S.

The Fed has seen a steady liquidation of Treasury debt held by foreigners, and this could become a bigger issue in the future.[231] The last thing the Fed wants is all of this debt coming back home to the U.S.

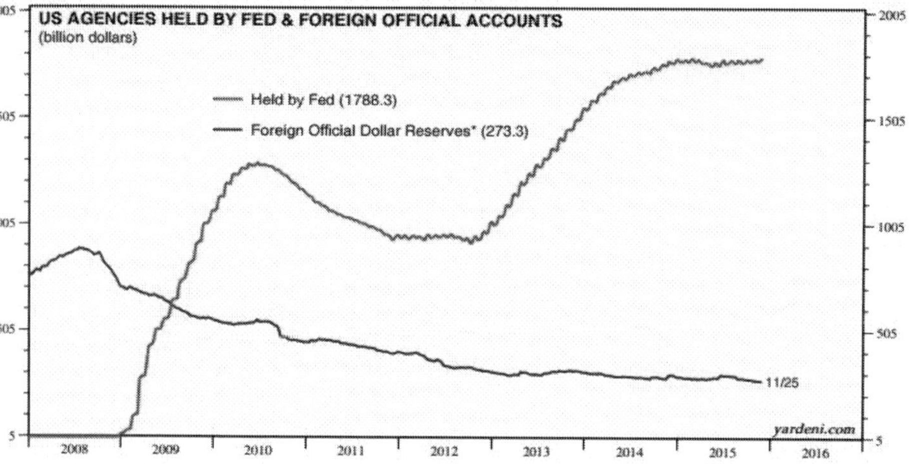

* Held by foreign official institutions at the Fed. Average of week ending Wednesday.
Source: Federal Reserve Board, Table H.4.1.

---

230 http://www.bbc.com/news/business-34324772
231 http://www.yardeni.com/pub/peacockfedecbassets.pdf

The Fed and other central banks can hold on to the assets on their books longer than you can stay solvent by betting against their abilities to do so. This is how they have gotten away with so much for so long without anyone thinking their balance sheet—or for that matter the other elephant in the room, the U.S. balance sheet—in the $20 trillion range will have consequences.

The economic data we showed in the Economics chapter revealed that the economy is not growing, despite all the efforts by the Fed to stimulate. It is the equivalent of "pushing on a string," which simply means Fed policy may make a dent, but snaps right back into the same problem economy we had before the stimulus. They should just let the economy stall out, weed out the bad, and let the good survive. A hard landing is what we need, unfortunately. Kicking the can down the road only lasts so long. Eventually the chickens come home to roost.

What can they do to stimulate? The answer surely is not raise interest rates as the Fed did in December 2015!

Bank lending is picking up, but small businesses are not rushing out to borrow, with so much uncertainty in the economy.

Funding the Military

One thing that people seem to forget is that the U.S. has the world's most powerful armed forces. Right now we are choosing guns over butter, and the reasoning is that we have to. This is a total power grab and the dollar would be the beneficiary. Perpetual debt can live on as long as there is a force behind it. Congress collectively spends more than it can afford on the military and our leaders must change this policy, as it will eventually bankrupt even us.[232]

The alternative of course if we were to get into more wars is higher taxes. The Fed will do whatever it takes to right a sinking ship, and

---

[232] http://www.poynter.org/2014/fact-checking-the-war-comparisons-between-obama-and-bush/272471/

this means possibly helping congress fund some future undeclared war but that analysis we'll save for the next book.

Where We Are Now

We saw 1,000-point drops in the Dow because of Chinese market issues in 2015. We saw the stock market have its worst opening two weeks in its entire history in 2016. Where will the next crisis come from? Will the Fed react quickly enough, or too slowly? Are you prepared with your investments? We'll discuss that important area soon in the Investment section, but keep this graphic in mind while reading it.[233]

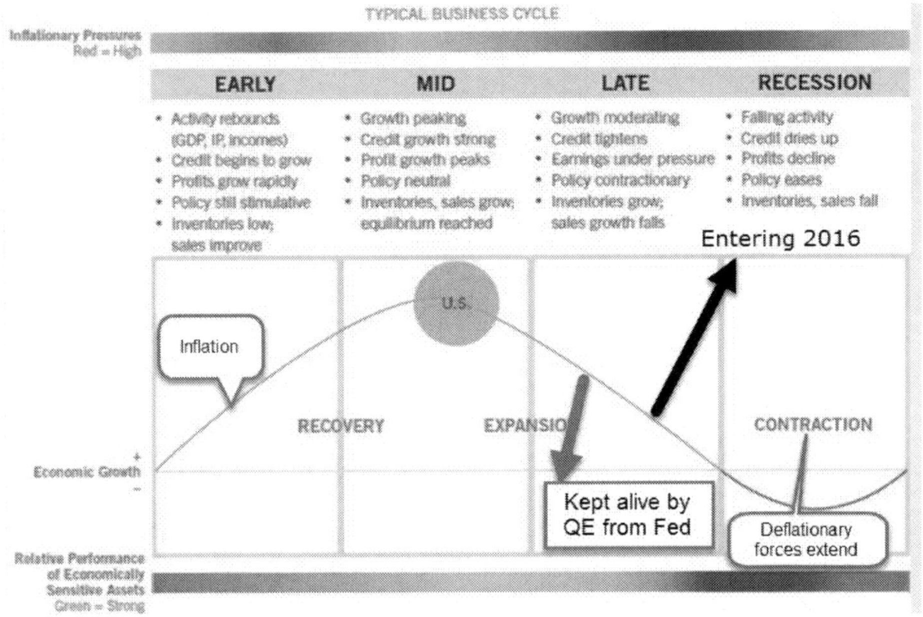

233 https://www.fidelity.com/viewpoints/investing-ideas/business-cycle-investing

PART 7 – KNOWING YOUR ADVISORS: Questions to Ask, Past Performance, Critique and Hidden Agendas

Chapter 18 - Preparing to Interview Your Financial Advisor

Seeking Financial Advice

Investors turn to financial advisors to learn how to best to manage their portfolios; novices inquire about how to plan for future investing. How did you first come by your advisor? Was it a recommendation from a friend or relative, or did you do some due diligence? Or did you simply call someone because you read an ad in a magazine or noticed them in a radio or television spot?

When it comes to picking an advisor, or even making sure your current advisor is up to the task of managing your portfolio in *your* best interest, it is important to ask certain questions to justify either hiring or keeping them as your investment counselor moving forward. Their answers to the questions that follow in the pages ahead will give you the confidence you need to choose or retain the right advisor. Simply put, if they don't know more than you do after you've read this book, then why should they manage your investments?

Even with this scrutiny, it doesn't hurt to get a second or even a third opinion from one or more additional advisors. This is, after all, your money and your wealth—it is your responsibility to choose a competent advisor who'll make sure you can keep and grow it.

In 2015 there was a record number of brokers barred or suspended, according to the Financial Industry Regulatory Authority (Finra), the brokerage industry's personal regulator.[234] This is the highest number since 2001.

---

[234] http://www.usatoday.com/story/money/2016/01/05/record-number-brokers-barred-suspended-2015/78277034/

It also may even make sense to have more than one advisor manage your wealth, dividing up your assets among them. Most advisors will try to manage your entire portfolio because the more they manage, the more they can potentially make, but splitting it up among a few might benefit you, depending on the size of your nest egg.

For some of you, the following questions may not make sense until after you have finished this book. Then you will have the confidence to interview anyone who is advising you, and be able to discern your potential advisors understanding of what's really going on in this investment and economic climate. In fact, I think you'll find that after reading this book, you will know more than many of the advisors you interview. The person you choose to manage your investments may just end up being… you.

Questions You Never Ask Your Financial Advisor, But Should

When seeking investment advice from the advisors you have selected to interview, you need to adopt a fearless mindset. Some advisors may object to you asking these questions, and if they do, they probably aren't suited to managing your money. Simply take control from the beginning and ask if it's ok to ask a few questions before you get started. Write down the answers, or ask if you can record the interview for the protection of both parties. By taking control and doing this first, you will weed out those who are really just there to sell you something, or might be incapable of being your trusted advisor. Remember, it is more than likely illegal to record someone without their permission. Always ask for permission first.

Questions You Need to Answer for Yourself Before Interviewing Your Advisor

1. Do you really know this advisor only on a professional basis, or are they a family friend as well?
2. Are they someone you trust with all your investment planning?
3. Would it hurt to get a second opinion from one or two additional candidates?

4. Do you feel uncomfortable investing in something you don't understand fully?
5. What type of investor are you: short-term trader, swing trader, value investor, conservative, moderate, aggressive? A good advisor will ask before recommending investments.
6. 80% of the mutual fund managers don't beat their related indices. Are you invested in non-indexed mutual funds only, and not the index itself through a mutual fund or ETF, which have minimal management fees and expenses?
7. Do financial advisors add value?
8. Are you afraid to fire your financial advisor?
9. Does your advisor have a verifiable track record?
10. Is your advisor professional in appearance?

General Questions to Ask Your Advisor (Important: Does the advisor ask about your wealth and fully understand the assets you own? If not, then they only want to sell you something, not advise.)

1. Is there a charge for this consultation?
2. Do you work strictly on commissions or a percentage of assets, or both?
3. Will you tell me exactly how much you make from any investment you recommend?
4. Can I get that in writing?
5. Is your fee or commission negotiable?
6. Will you charge me a fee if my investments lose money for the year?
7. Do you only sell stocks, bonds, ETFs, mutual funds and REITs, or are you limited to selling products from the insurance industry, which would include annuities and cash value life insurance (you want to find out if they're really an insurance agent pushing high commission annuities or life products – see insurance chapter)?
8. Will you try and sell me your own company's stock or proprietary products, because you are paid extra bonuses or commissions?

9. How often will we be reviewing my portfolio?
10. Can I ask for three references from clients you have worked with?

Investment Advice Questions for Your Advisor

1. Will you ask me any questions to decipher what kind of investor I am (conservative, moderate, aggressive)?
2. How did you do in advising clients before and after the 2007–2009 financial crisis?
3. How has your financial advice changed to protect clients from any potential future stock or bond market crash?
4. What type of protection does your advice offer against any downturn in stocks?
5. What penalty will there be if after investing with you, I want to liquidate my account the same day I start investing with you?
6. With record-low interest rates and the propensity for rates to move higher, does it make sense to invest in bond mutual funds?
7. Does it make sense to buy or hold on to tax-free bond funds if interest rates move higher, just for the tax benefit?
8. Do you sell Real Estate Investment Trusts (REITs)?
9. How liquid are they?
10. Can I get my money out of a REIT at any time?
11. Do you base your investment recommendations on asset allocation?
12. Will my portfolio maintain its purchasing power over time if the dollar loses value?
13. If so, how does your investment advice provide me with any diversification that counteracts U.S. dollar risk?
14. Are TIPS your only recommendation to counter any potential U.S. dollar decline or inflation?
15. What are your views on diversification into gold? What is the risk investing in precious metals?
16. Where are you primarily invested right now?

Economic and Monetary Quiz

If you want to dig even deeper into what your advisor knows (which you should know now too, after reading this book) and feel comfortable with them managing your money, ask them these economic and monetary questions:

1. What is the current national debt?
2. What is the current interest paid on the debt?
3. When was the last time the national debt decreased?
4. What is the current budget deficit?
5. Does it matter if it's a Republican- or Democratic-controlled Congress as to government spending? (This is not a question meant to turn the conversation political—move quickly on to the next question.)
6. How much are the unfunded liabilities facing Americans in the future?
7. Is the U.S. a net importer or exporter country?
8. What makes up GDP?
9. What percentage of GDP is consumer spending?
10. What backs the U.S. dollar?
11. What is the Federal Reserve?
12. Who is chairman of the Federal Reserve?
13. What is quantitative easing?
14. What is velocity of money?
15. What happens when money velocity increases?
16. What did you used to be able to exchange dollars for at a bank?
17. What is the price of gold right now (approximately)?
18. What is the price of silver right now (approximately)?
19. Do you own gold or silver?
20. If no, why not?

After going through this process, some of you will be able to answer this question: Do financial advisors add value? If professional money managers and hedge fund managers can't beat the indices, then what value does a financial advisor add? For many, advisors are just an added expense, unless they have a proven track record of bringing value. And yes, there are some good advisors out there. You just need to do your homework to find them, and it starts with interviewing them and asking the right questions.

The U.S. Department of Labor, who thinks they know more about investing than all of us, is contemplating implementing rules that would change the way financial advisors are allowed to give advice to their clients.[235] There is a need to know why a broker recommends a certain product and by asking the questions above you can spot the bad ones and don't necessarily need government to help you. They have enough issues to deal with, like balancing their own books.

[235] http://finance.yahoo.com/news/new-dol-fiduciary-financial-advisor-rules-12252 3391.html

Chapter 19 - Performance of Mutual Fund and Hedge Fund Advisors

The Awful Truth about Mutual Fund and Hedge Fund Managers' Performance

Why are you invested in actively managed mutual funds? Many of you were probably told to buy them because some financial advisor recommended you do so. The harsh reality is that those who own 90% of the $15 trillion held in mutual funds didn't beat the market index. The same is true for the rest of the world, which has an additional $15 trillion in mutual funds.

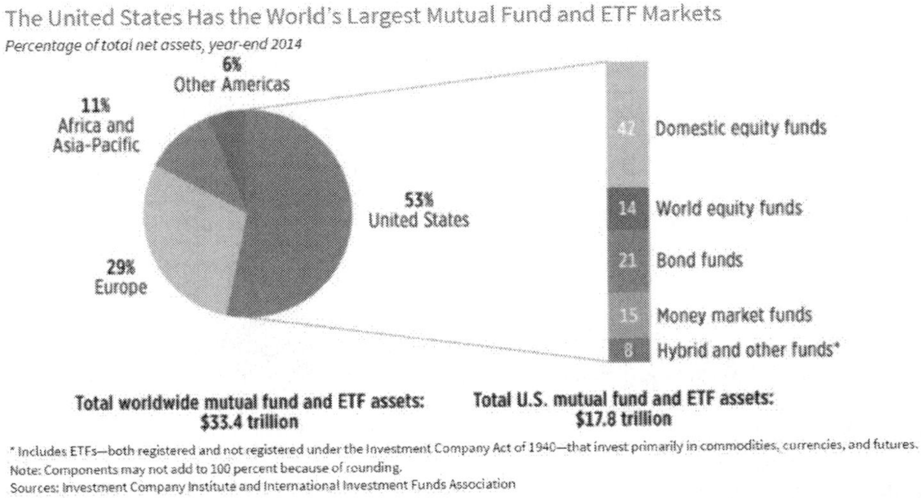

Here is the real truth when it comes to this professional manager performance.

In 2011, 79% of active fund managers didn't beat the S&P 500 stock index.[236]

---

236 http://money.cnn.com/2012/02/23/pf/fund_manager_performance.moneymag

In 2012, 66% of active fund managers didn't beat the S&P 500 stock index.[237]

In 2013 mutual funds fared a little better with 58% underperforming the S&P 500.[238]

In 2014, 86% of active large-cap fund managers failed to beat their benchmarks. Even worse, 89% of those fund managers underperformed the past 5 years and 82% the last decade.[239] For 2015, 75% of large-cap core mutual funds lagged the benchmark.

When you add the fees that mutual fund managers make, it takes even more away from your overall return. Mutual funds have raised their fees from an average of 0.62 % of assets to 1.11%, an increase of 84%.[240]

Interesting point I would like to make here: If you invested $50,000 in a Vanguard index fund with an average expense ratio of 0.19%, in 30 years you would have $65,793 more than someone who invested in a fund with the industry average expense ratio of 1.11%.[241]

The Financial Industry Regulatory Authority (FINRA) has a good calculator you can use to see the fees your mutual fund is charging you. It can be found at http://apps.finra.org/fundanalyzer/1/fa.aspx

Mutual fund sales are big business, and financial advisors make good commissions from selling these actively managed funds to you. But

[237] http://money.msn.com/mutual-fund/fund-managers-fall-short-again
[238] http://www.businessinsider.com/2013-mutual-fund-performance-distribution-2014-2
[239] http://money.cnn.com/2015/03/12/investing/investing-active-versus-passive-funds/
[240] http://www.forbes.com/sites/robertlenzner/2013/05/30/mutual-funds-biting-the-dust-at-an-alarming-rate/
[241] https://personal.vanguard.com/us/insights/article/mutual-fund-costs-122013

are they really working in your best interest in doing so? I don't think so, and the data proves it. What did you pay to get into your current mutual fund? To answer this, you need to know what type of shares you bought: "A," front load; "B," back-end load (charged upon redemption, but reduced typically by 1% a year); "C," annual fees (sometimes called no-load funds); and "H," which is a hybrid of "A" and "B" that includes both a smaller front load and back-end load.[242] On a $10,000 investment in A shares, a 5% front-load fee would be $500. This means you start your investment with $9,500, but there are no back-end fees upon liquidation. When you purchase B shares, you pay fees when you liquidate your investment. You are charged a declining fee that typically starts at 5% and disappears after five to seven years, depending on the fund.

C shares, or no-load funds, typically charge an annual fee—known as a 12b-1—that amounts to 0.25% of the fund's average annual net assets. It is important to note that B back-end load shares most likely also have a 12b-1 fee associated with them. H shares typically have a higher 12b-1 fee.

Below you will find a comparison of three large-cap blend funds with A shares represented by Rydex Funds (RYTTX), B shares represented by Prudential (PTMBX), and a no-load fund represented by Vanguard (VFIAX). The purpose of this analysis is not to say one fund outperforms the other based on how the manager invests, but to show you how fees and commission charged can affect your overall total return. Each fund has an initial investment of $20,000, the same 10-year time frame, and an assumed annual return of 7%.

---

242 http://www.icifactbook.org/pdf/13_fb_table62.pdf

Large Cap Fund	Fees & Commissions 10 Years	Redeemed Fund Value Minus Expenses After 10 Years
Vanguard 500 Index Fund Admiral Class [VFIAX] (No Load)	$142.55	$39,146.82
Rydex Series Trust Dynamic S&P 500 Fund Class A [RYTTX] (Front Load)	$5,301.58	$31,426.95
Prudential Large Cap Core Equity Fund Class B [PTMBX] (Back Load)	$4,314.41	$33,109.84

All things being equal, you can see how lower fees can make a huge difference in your overall return, so you should be aware of what your advisor is selling you and ask about fees.

For Hedge Fund Investors, It's Worse Returns than Mutual Funds

Hedge fund returns have been worse than mutual funds lately. There are over 10,000 hedge funds holding $2.4 trillion in assets, but hedge funds only rose 7.4% on average in 2013, making it the fifth straight year that hedge fund managers have not beat the S&P 500.[243] The simple little S&P 500 Index has outperformed hedge funds for 10 straight years except for 2008, when the S&P lost big, but hedge fund managers edged out mutual fund managers in overall performance.[244]

Let's compare the past few years of hedge fund returns.

The best hedge fund manager of 2013 was David Tepper of Appaloosa Management. His fund was up approximately 38%, or just 9% above the S&P 500 Index. For this performance, Tepper was paid $3 billion.[245]

---

243 http://www.businessweek.com/news/2014-01-07/hedge-funds-rise-7-dot-4-percent-in-2013-to-trail-s-and-p-500-for-fifth-year

244 http://www.economist.com/news/finance-and-economics/21568741-hedge-funds-have-had-another-lousy-year-cap-disappointing-decade-going

245 http://nypost.com/2013/12/29/hedge-fund-titan-to-pocket-3b-for-2013/

Just imagine what the hedge fund managers who are not beating the index are getting paid! According to a recent Citibank study,[246] it's estimated that hedge fund managers need at least $300 million Assets Under Management (AUM) to break even. This would mean that of the $300 million total needed for expenses, an investment manager would receive about 20% of $60 million, or $18 million, even before the fund has invested a dime. The larger the fund, the less the manager makes. But of course that's on a much larger piece of the pie, like in Tepper's case, as he manages approximately $18 billion in assets to have earned his $3 billion in 2013.

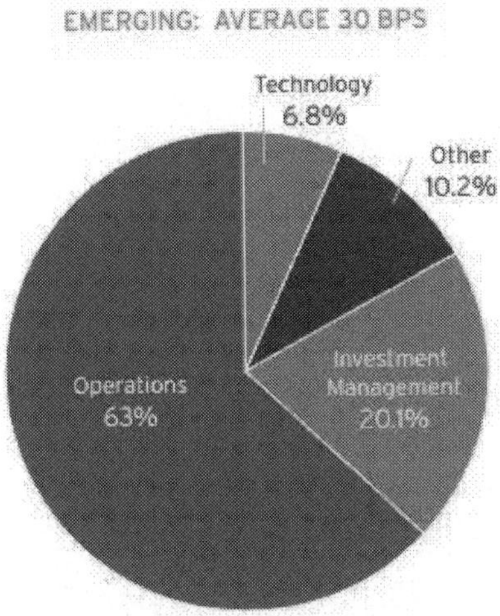

The wealthy in America may impress their friends by saying "I invest in hedge funds," but clearly most that do so are worse off than anyone else. I think you could have thrown darts at a *Wall Street Journal* listing of stocks and done better than the 7.4% average for hedge funds in 2013—plus saved yourself the management fees.

A good theory might be that mutual fund managers did better in 2013 than in past years because pre-2013, mutual fund managers took their

246 http://www.citibank.com/icg/global_markets/prime_finance/docs/2013_Business_Expense_Benchmark_Survey.pdf

horrid record of performance (not beating the indices) to go work for hedge funds to get the higher pay out. The harsh reality, though, is that none of these managers are good at beating the index.

Hedge funds lost 0.6% in 2014, as the S&P 500 gained 14%.[247] They averaged .27% (as of December 16) versus the S&P 500 return of 3.02% in 2015, one of the worst years on record.

So why are you paying someone to manage your money, when it is clear that you have a higher probability of success by simply buying an index fund with lower fees, which will put more money in *your* retirement account instead of your broker's?

Of course it's not as simple as that. Proper asset allocation is needed, along with some built-in protection from unknown forces that can bring a repeat of a financial crisis that took everyone by surprise in 2007–2009, even index funds. You are now informed as to how well "the professionals" are doing with your hard-earned money. And that's not a pretty picture.

Yet investors flock to hedge funds, to the tune of $2.83 trillion.[248]

Breaking Up Is Hard To Do

What you, the investor, also need to know how to do is how to break up with the financial advisor telling you to invest in these mutual funds and hedge funds. Liking someone doesn't mean you need to stay with them if they continually lose you money. You must choose your financial future over friendship.

---

247 http://www.marketwatch.com/story/hedge-funds-produced-vanity-but-no-gains-in-2014-2015-01-09

248 https://www.hedgefundresearch.com/?fuse=products-irglo

Mutual Funds in an Annuity Wrapper

Variable annuities are mutual funds wrapped inside what insurance representatives and other licensed brokers sell, whether they be tax deferred or inside your IRA or 401(k). These variable annuities add another layer of fees, called mortality and expense risk charges, in the range of 1.25% per year on your account value, or $125 per annum on a $10,000 investment. This fee takes care of insurance costs because the annuity is actually an insurance product. It also covers the commission paid to the broker who sold it to you. Variable annuities may show an illustration that doesn't include the commission paid to a broker, but includes it as a percentage of the amount invested, which can vary from 1% to 18%. They may seem no load, but insurance representatives don't work for free.

Another word of caution on variable annuities: The liquidation penalty can run quite high, typically 5% to 10%, if you need your money within the first 5 to 10 years. The higher the liquidation fee, the more the insurance agent makes. There are plenty of annuities out there with very low liquidation fees.

The penalty for withdrawing your money before age 59 1/2 is 10%, but these annuities can be tax-deferred. Unlike investing in mutual funds, however, your growth is not taxed as a capital gain, but rather as ordinary income—at a higher rate.

Variable annuities make zero sense inside of your IRA or 401(k) because of the additional fees, unless you know you're going to live to age 90 or 100, and can take advantage of lifetime income options that beat the mortality tables actuaries draw up.

Are Financial Advisors Needed?

If you're getting up there in age and don't have a family member to help with the management of your portfolio—or you simply don't have the time to pay attention to your investments, a trusted advisor is invaluable and often necessary.

Also, if you're older, you may need some guidance in making investment management decisions. Having a financially competent friend or relative present during the meeting with potential advisors or sitting alongside you during your next meeting with your present advisor makes sense. This may be difficult for those who like to keep financial matters private from family members or friends. But by opening up a little and including a close relative or friend in making investment decisions, you can help protect your wealth and at the same time avoid getting ripped off by some fast-talking, likeable advisor who charms investors into turning over their money.

Most of us don't do the extra homework to manage our own investments. Even those who think they can do well managing their own investments by day trading or timing investments typically learn the hard way that they don't possess the necessary skills to profit, and they lose money—sometimes a lot of money. As you've just seen, even most mutual fund and hedge fund managers can't beat the market. There are of course exceptions, and I believe you can be one of those exceptions after reading and practicing what you learn from this book.

Let's now take a look at some of the so-called experts you see on television, or who are respected in their industry, and how their predictions have done.

Chapter 20 - Critique of Economic Forecasters and Financial Advisors

It is safe to say that most of those who predict the future did not see the 2007–2009 financial crisis coming, and even those who did call for a crisis every year—so they've missed opportunities to profit for their clients since 2009 because they are fear mongers.

Also keep in mind that most have an agenda of some description. Whether it is to get you to invest with them, purchase their newsletter, or sign up for a service, just know what you are getting into first, and look for a track record before shelling out money.

Many of these forecasters use fear tactics that actually work quite well, because fear is a hard emotion to control and people will do whatever it takes to alleviate it. Some may claim that I use fear in this book, but in selling gold, I have never used hyperinflation or a crashing dollar as a reason to do so, like so many others. I was actually dollar bullish and in the deflation camp since 2012.

I am aware of one such marketing company that utilizes these fear tactics: *The Daily Reckoning* (aka Agora Publishing) employs multiple writers whose articles and books make them a ton of money. Fear sells! But markets are not always to be feared. There are ways to profit in up or down markets, as you'll read in the investment chapter, and you have free will to act or not, based on what you learn here. At least you'll be aware of what to act upon, and not just follow advice blindly but instead learn more about the person offering it.

Economist Predictions and Policy Recommendations

Alan Greenspan and Ben Bernanke – Former chairmans of the Federal Reserve

I want to bring up past comments from experts in their field, because it relates to how things will play out in future if we don't learn from our mistakes. The Greenspan Fed kept interest rates low too long and helped fuel the real estate bubble. Greenspan told those taking out a mortgage in 2004 to look at alternatives to fixed-rate mortgages, like the adjustable rate mortgage (ARM) so they could save 1/2% to 1.2% in costs each year. He said in 2004: "American consumers might benefit if lenders provided greater mortgage product alternatives to the traditional fixed-rate mortgage." Interest rates began to shoot up, and soon those who took out an ARM on his advice had to come up with more money every month to pay their mortgage.[249]

What wasn't publicized prior to Ben Bernanke taking over for Greenspan as Fed chairman is that Bernanke had followed Greenspan's advice, and took out an ARM for his own home in 2004—then refinanced in 2009 because his interest rate "exploded."[250]

Bernanke, during his tenure, kept interest rates low the same way Greenspan had done, and bubbles are forming in the stock market and some real estate markets again. In 2006, Bernanke had this to say about the housing bubble popping right before his eyes; "Housing markets are cooling a bit. Our expectation is that the decline in activity or the slowing in activity will be moderate, that house prices will probably continue to rise."[251] He also said in January 2008: "The Federal Reserve is not currently forecasting a recession."[252]

December 2010 projections of the Congressional Budget Office (CBO)

"The Congressional Budget Office (CBO) projects that, under current law, debt held by the public will exceed $16 trillion by 2020, reaching nearly 70 percent of GDP. CBO also projects that interest rates will go up. The combination of rising debt and rising interest rates is projected

---

[249] http://usatoday30.usatoday.com/money/economy/fed/2004-02-23-greenspan-debt_x.htm

[250] http://content.time.com/time/specials/packages/article/0,28804,1946375_1948023_1947253-11,00.html

[251] http://financialservices.house.gov/media/pdf/109-72.pdf

[252] http://www.nbcnews.com/id/22592939/#.UtLwL9JdUQM

to cause net interest payments to balloon to nearly $800 billion, or 3.4 percent of GDP, by 2020."[253]

By 2016, the national debt was over $19 trillion—$3 trillion above CBO projections. How can you be off in your projections by $3 trillion? They were predicting $800 billion of payments for interest in 2020 on $16 trillion of debt, and that's four years from now! This prediction was after the financial crisis. They assumed a 5% interest rate to come up with the $800 billion payment on interest for the $16 trillion of debt. It is quite possible that by the time 2020 does come, the debt might be more like $25 trillion, or even higher. At a 5% rate, the interest payments on the national debt alone would be $1.25 trillion a year. That's 39% of the 2016 budget and if you add in the deficit (more debt) that Congress voted into the budget, it's 53% of the 2016 budget. I am not making this up![254]

International Monetary Fund (IMF)

"Although cycles of excess and panic have not disappeared—the subprime boom-bust being but the latest example—markets have shown that they can and do self-correct."[255]

President George W. Bush, September 20, 2007

"I say that the fundamentals of our nation's economy are strong," Bush told a White House news conference. "I would be pessimistic if I thought Congress was going to get their way and raise taxes," he added. Pressed on whether he was concerned that the nation was nearing a recession, Bush said: "You need to talk to economists. I think I got a B in Econ 101."[256]

---

[253] http://www.cbo.gov/sites/default/files/cbofiles/ftpdocs/119xx/doc11999/12-14-federaldebt.pdf
[254] http://federal-budget.insidegov.com/l/119/2016-Estimate
[255] http://www.imf.org/external/pubs/ft/scr/2007/cr07265.pdf
[256] https://news.google.com/newspapers?nid=2026&dat=20070920&id=ddsyAAAA IBAJ&sjid=PPAFAAAAIBAJ&pg=6837,2400469&

Republican 2008 presidential candidate John McCain, February 3, 2008

"The issue of economics is not something I've understood as well as I should. I've got Greenspan's book."[257]

President Barack Obama, February 2009

"I will cut the deficit we inherited in half by the end of my first term in office. I refuse to leave our children with a debt they cannot pay. That means taking responsibility right now in this administration for getting our spending under control."[258]

President Barack Obama

"Number 43 [George W.Bush] added $4 trillion by his lonesome so that we now have over $9 trillion of debt that we are going to have to pay back. That's irresponsible. It's unpatriotic." When President Obama took office the national debt was $10.6 trillion, and is over $8.4 trillion higher in 2016—north of $19 trillion.[259]

Paul Krugman - Nobel Prize-winning economist

Krugman believes that the U.S. should not practice austerity, but keep spending to get out of the hole they dug themselves. He said this about proposals for cutting the deficit in 2010: "Many economists, myself included, regard this turn to austerity as a huge mistake."[260]

This is, of course, the Keynesian philosophy he follows, which we discussed in the Economics section. Keynes himself said this spending

---

hl=en

257 https://www.youtube.com/watch?v=_1X3efvVTLA

258 http://www.youtube.com/watch?v=SaQUU2ZL6D8

259 http://nation.foxnews.com/president-obama/2011/08/24/flashback-obama-says-adding-4-trillion-national-debt-unpatriotic

260 http://www.nytimes.com/2010/06/18/opinion/18krugman.html

by government should only be a temporary thing. Adding $1 trillion to the deficit each year is hardly “temporary,” and it is clear that Obama has got Keynes wrong because of such advice from Krugman, according to Allan Meltzer, Professor of Political Economy Tepper School of Business at Carnegie Mellon.[261]

John Williams - Economist

John Williams is mostly known for running a statistics company called Shadow Government Statistics. He does a good job of showing how certain government-related numbers that come out each year utilize a changed formula for calculating certain data, to make the data appear more favorable (or governments appear to be doing a good job). For example, the CPI has changed many times over the years, and most recently, GDP is calculated differently from years past.

Each time these calculations change, they make the government economic data look better. For example, by changing the way CPI is calculated, the government can pay less to Social Security recipients who are promised a cost-of-living increase each year. These changes are what Williams keeps track of, and are not a bad way of showing what the data would be if the old way of calculating were still utilized. Of course seniors who do draw a Social Security check know that what they receive isn’t keeping pace with the higher prices, and that the CPI is flawed. In fact, the cost-of-living adjustment (COLA) for 2016 had no increase for seniors on Social Security because the Consumer Price Index (CPI-W) the government uses to pay increases—which are supposed to keep up with rising prices—showed no increase in inflation from the third quarter of 2014 to the third quarter of 2015. Everyone but our leaders knows that prices are rising (as described in the Inflation chapter, where we learn how government is behind some of the higher prices) but they hide it in plain sight.

---

261 http://archive.fortune.com/2010/02/04/news/economy/meltzer_keynes.fortune/ index.htm

But Williams has been calling for hyperinflation for years, at least since 2008 with his HYPERINFLATION SPECIAL REPORT he sends out to subscribers. Every year he comes out with his hyperinflation calls, and it's like *The Boy Who Cried Wolf*, in that the wolf (hyperinflation) never appears. In his 2011 report, he said: "I don't think you have until 2012 before this gets out of control and there's hyperinflation." But he has said the same thing in 2012, 2013, 2014 and 2015.[262] These were some very good years for the U.S. dollar, and the price of gasoline and many other items declined. Hyperinflation can only come when you lose faith in a currency,[263] but Williams uses this fear to sell a lot of subscriptions.

Hank Paulson - Former Treasury Secretary

Paulson begged Congress for a bailout in 2008, and got $700 billion in TARP funds for those entities he thought needed help in getting their balance sheets in order. He claims now that this 2007-2009 crisis was a "100-year storm."[264] I want you to simply remember this comment and judge for yourself after reading this book if this was indeed a once-in-a-lifetime storm.

Advisor Predictions

You will notice a common thread with many of the following gurus/advisors. They write a book full of wrong predictions, and then write another book (or article) making the same predictions because their timing was off in the prior book. If you continually write negative books, sooner or later you'll be right—and you have to let the world know that you predicted the crisis! You may not be familiar with some

[262] http://seekingalpha.com/article/3344695-april-call-to-wait-and-buy-gold-below-1000-still-in-effect
[263] http://seekingalpha.com/article/267292-john-williams-hyperinflation-and-double-dip-recession-ahead
[264] http://www.businessweek.com/videos/2013-09-12/hank-paulson-financial-crisis-a-100-year-storm

of these advisors, but they are well known in the industry, with many touted by CNBC.

Robert A. Wiedemer – Author of Aftershock

Wiedemer was asked the following question in 2011: "Won't the bubbles in the real estate and stock markets re-inflate?" His reply: "One of the worst things you can do right now is assume that just because something is 20% cheaper than it was a few years ago, that it has reached a bottom. Make sure you don't sit there and think that we got an up cycle. That bubbles automatically re-inflate. Protect yourself. Reduce your exposure to things like stocks, bonds and real estate." It seems like every year they come out with a "revised and updated" version of *Aftershock*, where they say, "Our timing was a bit off in the earlier edition."[265] Sooner or later, they'll be right.

Nouriel Roubini - Chairman of Roubini Global Economics, an economic consultancy firm

In May 2010, Roubini, another guru to whom CNBC constantly turns for predictions, said that stocks would tumble another 20%. "From here on I see things getting worse... Prices in both stocks and commodities are likely to take a hit, and investors may only be safe in cash and other safe havens."[266] He made the comment when the S&P was trading at 1,072. It was almost a straight line to double that by the middle of 2015.

Roubini's book, *Crisis Economics: A Crash Course in the Future of Finance*, came out in May 2010, as the stock market was in bull mode. Roubini was on CNBC in November 2009, when gold was trading at

---

[265] http://www.amazon.com/Aftershock-Protect-Yourself-Financial-Meltdown/dp/1118375629/ref=pd_sim_14_1?ie=UTF8&dpID=51Z8W-wql3L&dpSrc=sims&preST=_AC_UL160_SR108%2C160_&refRID=17TS34Z08XNG8QBK8VPT

[266] http://www.cnbc.com/id/37259541/Stocks_to_Tumble_Another_20_Cash_the_Safest_Place_Roubini

$1,000 an ounce and he called commodities expert Jim Rogers call of gold rocketing to $2,000 an ounce "utter nonsense." Gold hit $1,921 two years later.[267]

Martin Weiss - Author

Martin Weiss is the author of *The Ultimate Depression Survival Guide: Protect Your Savings, Boost Your Income, and Grow Wealthy Even in the Worst of Times*, written in June 2010. Since this "depression" didn't come to fruition, he said in May 2012: "We now face the growing danger of a new financial megashock that could strike at almost any time. It has the potential to be larger than the Lehman Brothers shock of 2008."[268]

Weiss is also the author of many other books that he has been selling since 1981, all based on fear. [269]

Dennis Gartman - Trader, newsletter writer – The Gartman Letter

Gartman readily admits he's wrong 80% of the time, as he stated at an LPL conference in Chicago I attended in 2007. Still, he is always called upon by CNBC to offer his expert opinion, appearing on shows such as *Fast Money*. For this advice, Gartman gets paid $400 per month for his newsletter.

He has flip-flopped on gold quite a bit[270] and in September 2013 did admit to CNBC that he was wrong about being bullish on gold and that it would outperform stocks.[271] He said: "Clearly I'm wrong on the gold, and there's no reason to be anything other than truthful about it."

---

267 http://buygoldandsilversafely.com/tag/cnbc/

268 http://www.moneyandmarkets.com/lehman-type-megashock-looming-49669

269 http://www.amazon.com/Martin-D.-Weiss/e/B001HD09WS/ref=ntt_athr_dp_pel_1

270 http://buygoldandsilversafely.com/gold/dennis-gartman-flip-flopping-on-gold-and-u-s-dollar/

David W. Tice - Tice Capital LLC

Tice was asked on CNBC in October 2012 what would make him change gears (about being bearish on the stock market), and his answer was "I'm not going to change positions here."[272]

Robert Kiyosaki - Author, Rich Dad, Poor Dad

Kiyosaki is a successful author known the world over. In October 2006, though, he wrote "The Last Days of the Dollar," where he said, speculating on something that seems to be a common thread among many that sell on fear, that other countries would abandon the dollar: "If the oil-producing nations stop accepting the dollar and switch to gold or the euro, things will definitely get sticky. The world might be tipped into a global recession and possibly even a depression."[273]

Again, the timing is just off, and he—like many others—were and still are not willing to look at price action and provide the same "dollar crash," "hyperinflation," etc. mantra that has flown in the face of one of the best dollar rallies in decades.

Doug Eberhardt – Author, Buy Gold and Silver Safely

I too can be criticized for my timing but I'm not one sided.

You'll read more about what I have had to say over the years in the Investment section. My first book came out just before the 2011 highs in the price of gold.[274] I wrote the book to keep investors from getting ripped off by the multitude of unscrupulous gold dealers, and even Congress was interested in what the book said—and forwarded it to

---

271 http://www.cnbc.com/id/101030561
272 http://www.businessinsider.com/david-tice-bearish-2012-10
273 http://www.richdad.com/Resources/Articles/YF---10-17-2006.aspx
274 http://www.amazon.com/Buy-Gold-Silver-Safely-Learn/dp/0982586116/ ref=tmm_pap_title_0?ie=UTF8&qid=1390268867&sr=8-1

the Santa Monica city attorney, who used my testimony to recoup over $4 million from one gold dealer for wrongdoing.[275]

While I am and have been pro gold, I recognized the bullishness of the dollar, and for the last few years had been cautioning investors that the rising dollar could put pressure on the price of gold, and to dollar-cost-average into a position, rather than go all in. The point being, when many others were writing books about the crashing dollar and advising everyone to buy gold, I was calling for a higher dollar, gold possibly going down to $900, and writing about it publicly— sticking with my conviction even with each bounce in gold that most everyone thought was the bottom.[276] I also have been adamant about deflation over these years, while anyone selling gold was warning of inflation.[277]

This book furthers my concept of helping investors understand those who make predictions, give advice or write books, and the awareness it provides helps the investor make good future investment decisions—whether they do business with us or with anyone they run across who is providing recommendations on how to and what to invest in. With this awareness, you reduce the anxiety, and fewer mistakes are made.

Some may accuse me of having a hidden agenda in writing this book, as I have other products and services that readers can purchase (which I openly revealed in the introduction). First off, after reading the book

I think you'll see that I simply am about awareness and the investor making a good decision. Second, I suggest that an investor talk to as many advisors as possible before making a decision on where to place their hard-earned dollars, or simply take control of your own wealth

---

[275] http://www.smgov.net/departments/cao/Content.aspx?id=29440
[276] http://buygoldandsilversafely.com/gold/sticking-with-stronger-dollar-and-weaker-gold-through-end-of-year/
[277] http://buygoldandsilversafely.com/gold/why-gold-and-silver-will-break-to-new-lows-and-tax-moves-to-capitalize-upon/

and invest your money yourself. I also recommend not going with one advisor, but several whom you thoroughly trust.

Lastly, I do believe in capitalism and if I am presenting good, sound, investment information, then I have earned the right to ask for some of an investor's business. Warren Buffett said: "There's something about smart people explaining ideas to an orangutan that makes their decision making better."[278]

Buffett wasn't calling investors orangutans, but rather pointing out that obtaining a little more information can make you a better investor. I hope you find that to be the case with this book, especially after reading the next section on investments.

Conclusion

Asking the right questions from the beginning helps an investor pinpoint who it is they are actually hiring to manage their investments. Since we have shown that even the most educated professional managers of mutual funds and hedge funds can't beat the market, then perhaps an investor may not need a professional advisor, as they can just invest in the indices through an asset allocation program, which will be explained further in the index funds section of chapter 27.

When you see the so-called investment gurus and economic experts on TV claiming they called the market or economy right, keep in mind they were also probably wrong at some point. Yesterday's star advisor may lose your money tomorrow.

Can an advisor or economist still claim victory when the market has moved against their call for two or more years? Sure they can and will, but not without some egg on their faces. Even the trader we spoke of, Dennis Gartman, says he is wrong 80% of the time… but he is still a personality on CNBC, which values his opinion.

---

[278] http://www.harpercollins.com/9780062031358/thoughts-of-chairman-buffett

Chapter 21 - Advisors' Hidden Agendas

Hidden Agendas of the Experts - A Case Study

Earlier it was mentioned that those who do the predicting through writing books might have an agenda. The authors of the very popular *Aftershock* series of books (over 600,000 copies sold) seem to have an agenda beyond the strategy of fear mongering.

The *Aftershock* series has become popular because the three main authors—David Wiedemer, Robert Wiedemer and Cindy Spitzer—wrote a book in 2006 that warned of a crisis coming: *America's Bubble Economy.*

It wasn't that difficult to call a bubble before their book came out. Paul Krugman wrote a *New York Times* op-ed on August 29, 2005 called "Greenspan and the Bubble," where he used the word "bubble" seven times.[279]

Stephen Roach, chief economist at Morgan Stanley, wrote an essay on April 25, 2005 called "Original Sin," and he used the word bubble 12 times when referring to the economy.[280]

Writing a book with "bubble" in the title and a little marketing went a long way for the *Aftershock* authors. But what they have done since then is lose all credibility. Simply reading the reviews on Amazon.com of all their books tells you the real story, and what their objectives are. You can see what they have done in the following table.

---

[279] http://www.nytimes.com/2005/08/29/opinion/29krugman.html?_r=0

[280] http://www.morganstanley.com/views/gef/archive/2005/20050425-Mon.html

Book Title	Month/Year Published	Top Voted Comment From Readers on Amazon.com
Aftershock 1st Edition	11/2009	"Like reading an infomercial. Does not help investors."
Aftershock 2nd Edition	8/2011	"Reads like an arrogant infomercial."
Aftershock Investor 1st Edition	9/2012	"No good specific advice."
Aftershock Investor 2nd Edition	10/2013	"Lacking credibility."
Aftershock 3rd Edition	3/2014	"Fear sells and they really milk it in this book."

The October 2013 comment that says "lacking credibility" points to the performance of their mutual funds shares they sold, which are outlined below.

All Data from Morningstar	Aftershock Strategies Fund Symbol: SHKNX	Aftershock Strategies I Fund Symbol: SHKIX
Year Started	12/31/12	12/31/12
Expense Ratio	1.55%	1.30%
Turnover	661%	661%
$10,000 investment On 12/31/12 Value	$8,972	$8,994

Today		
Benchmark Performance for Same Category	$11,514	$11,579

All Data from Morningstar	Aftershock Strategies Fund Symbol: SHKNX	Aftershock Strategies I Fund Symbol: SHKIX
Year Started	12/31/12	12/31/12
Expense Ratio	1.55%	1.30%
Turnover	661%	661%
$10,000 investment On 12/31/12 Value Today	$8,972	$8,994
Benchmark Performance for Same Category	$11,514	$11,579

Not only did the funds they promoted have high expenses (management fees for two of the authors who managed the funds—David Wiedemer and Robert A. Wiedemer), but they traded way too much and performed well below their benchmark.[281] What's worse, the fund closed down July 1, 2015 and the Aftershockpublishing.com website tab for Money Management now takes you to www.arkfinira.com, which is a non-working page. It looks as though, I guess because the fund did so poorly, that they have reinvented themselves as MacroView Investment Management LLC,[282] which lists Robert Wiedemer as managing director along with David Wiedemer, and evidently does most of its investing through Charles Schwab under the guidance of another managing director and owner, Daniel Cohen… whose SEC Form ADV lists AFTERSHOCK ADVISORS, LLC as a member but not a control person, but Robert

281 https://www.proxyonline.com/docs/aftershock.pdf
282 http://www.macroviewim.com/

and David Wiedemer as indirect owners and control persons and 50% to 75% owners.[283]

The Aftershockpublishing.com website still lists on their services page products they sell, and they would be happy to take your money and collect their $795 for 60 minutes consulting fee which is what one of the author's Cindy Spitzer charges.[284]

One-hour Private Consulting with Cindy Spitzer - $795
Please note that a limited number of consultations are provided at reduced cost for those in genuine need. Please contact us to discuss.

60 Minute Follow-up Call - $695
Additional one hour consulting call following initial consultation

30 Minute Follow-up Call - $495
Additional half hour consulting call following initial consultation

Quarterly Private Consulting - $2500
Four private consulting calls at your convenience. Includes one year of the Aftershock IRP.

Bi-Monthly Private Consulting - $4000
Six private consulting calls at your convenience. Includes one year of the Aftershock IRP.

Monthly Private Consulting - $7000
Twelve private consulting calls at your convenience. Includes one year of the Aftershock IRP.

---

[283] http://nebula.wsimg.com/0041b2ecc8cb42aba4696557e0816f4b?AccessKeyId=EFDD5F664FE55C5CF9D9&disposition=0&alloworigin=1
[284] http://www.aftershockconsultants.com/SERVICES---FEES.html

The *Aftershock* authors also sell a newsletter for anywhere from $99 to $299 a year. There is nothing wrong with subscribing to a newsletter, but just make sure you get your money's worth and get advice that makes you money, not loses it.

Full Disclosure

My company does not manage money. My goal is for you to take control of your own wealth. We do have a free newsletter, which I write five days a week under Current Thoughts at:

http://buygoldandsilversafely.com/category/current-thoughts/.

I do sell physical gold and silver bullion investments, and I do run a subscription ETF Leveraged Daily Trading Service that profits in up and down markets, and provides you with research five days a week to trade markets with your own accounts. I just want you to make money and if you do, you'll continue the service. I wrote this book because I don't think it's that difficult for you to make money but you need to take more control in doing so. More information on the ETF service can be found here; http://illusionsofwealth.com/etfservice/ This information will be discussed more in the next section on investments and for those who think I have a hidden agenda, I apologize in advance for being a capitalist. I don't think Warren Buffet would disapprove.

The Bottom Line

With some proper money management, whether you use an advisor or not, you can still keep and grow your wealth even with market downturns by implementing the strategies discussed in this book.

While no one can call the market perfectly, an advisor must look at the economy and make some educated guesses as to what will happen next, whether bullish or bearish, and not just one direction all the time (always bullish or always bearish). That's why it's important for your advisor to know a little about what the Federal Reserve and Congress are up to beyond what the stock or bond market is doing, and how their policies and decision making may affect your wealth. You now have the foundation for being a great investor laid out for you. What's next is what you have been patiently waiting for: a complete analysis of investing.

In fact, some companies like UBS are now offering what are called robo-advisors to manage portfolios based on automated advice from a computer without a human involvement. The odds of computers beating mutual and hedge fund managers may be good but index funds do the same thing. UBS thinks that using smarter data will derive better results. Let's see how this advice works during the next downturn in the market.

PART 8 – INVESTING

Chapter 22 - Start with the Basics

Understanding What You Are Doing

An informed investor is something that is lacking in this society, which is why many rely on others to manage their investments. This book—and in particular Part 8—will change all that. From now on, investors will make good choices and work with their advisors, or do it on their own without worry, stress, or fear of failure. Growing and keeping your wealth will no longer be an illusion, but something you are in control of forevermore. Whether you go it alone or have a team of qualified advisors, or both, the awareness this section brings will help you navigate the choppy waters ahead. You will be free to change course, and know why you are charting a new one. Once you take the emotion out of investing, what's left is enlightenment and profit.

A good many investors typically do the wrong thing. They see an ad on television or receive a tip from their neighbor about a certain stock, and are at first hesitant to move. Then they see that the investment keeps going higher and higher, until they finally make the move and allocate a portion of their wealth to that investment.

The problem lies in the fact that the investment they just put their funds into was overheated, and the investor quickly sees their investment go down. They think to themselves, "I'm just a lousy investor," when in reality they just didn't look at the big picture as to where that investment sector was in relation to its average or mean price. To put it bluntly, they were just lazy or, to give them some credit, didn't know to do a little research before investing. If you are lazy with your investments, you reap what you sow. We need to take the laziness out of investing.

Knowing where a sector you want to invest is in relationship to its historic mean will give you the ability to garner more profit if you are not chasing a sector higher, which again, most seem to do. Every sector has a cycle, and where you are in that cycle matters most. But our psychological makeup doesn't allow us to buy what's beaten down. We forget the golden rule of "buy low and sell high," and we just follow the masses over the cliff of market losses that always seems to come at the top of a sector in bubble territory. Always place your investment choices or current allocation into the following cycle chart and you'll have more opportunity to profit.

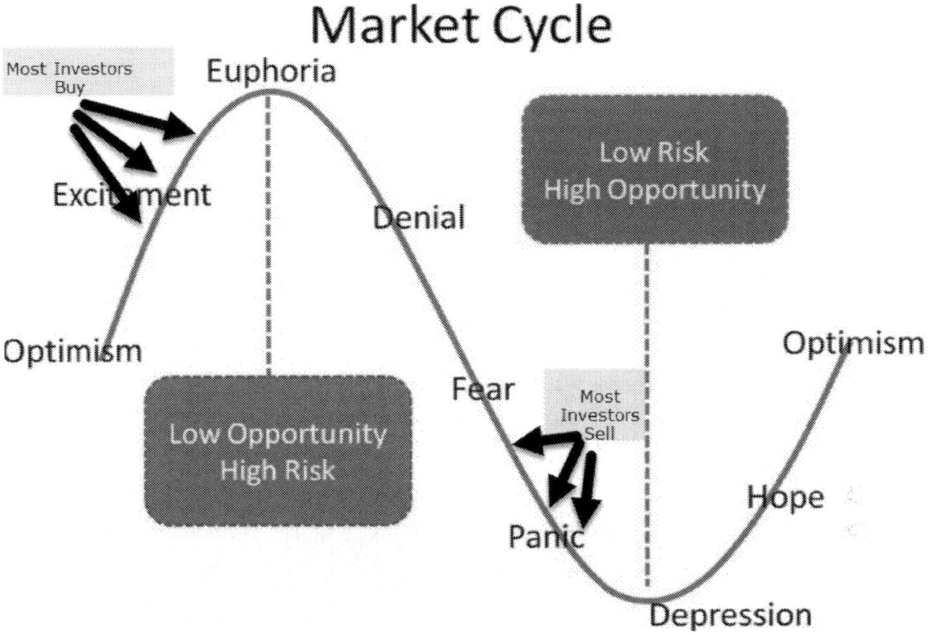

An investor can lose wealth rather quickly if they don't know what they are doing. It's like the new gambler going to Las Vegas, playing blackjack and hitting on a 13, 14, 15 or 16 when the dealer is showing 3, 4, 5, or the 6 card face up. Odds are the dealer will bust, but if you take his bust card, the rest of the players at the table aren't going to be happy with you. But with your own hard-earned money, why are you gambling without knowing what you are really doing?

When it comes to investing, the seller on the other side of your trade, the professional traders, are like the dealer in Vegas. Because they know what they are doing, they will more than likely make a better decision on what to invest in, and when to invest in certain asset classes. These traders are more than happy to take your money, as that's how *they* make money. But the deck doesn't have to be stacked against you as you can also trade with the professionals.

There are always two sides to the trade, and the world is full of novice investors who simply don't take the time to learn before they earn. You don't make money by dipping your toes in a certain strategy without practicing first. Whether it be simulators to actual trading that most brokerage houses offer, or paper trading like you are already in the investment, taking profit or keeping stops, practice trading before you subject your real money to risk.

Having a Trading Plan

But before you get into simulated trading, you have to have a trading plan. Whether you are a buy-and-hold investor, swing trader, or day trader, not all investments will go your way. Before you invest, you need a trading plan—and you trade your plan. This includes keeping stops and taking profits when handed to you. Like the old saying goes, you can't go broke taking profits. But the biggest mistake you will ever make is not keeping a stop when an investment goes against you.

Keeping a Stop

The only one who is wrong when a trade goes against you is the person you see in the mirror. The market is never wrong. All the right reasons for you to be in a trade may be there, but the market will do what it does, and if it goes the opposite of what your trade or investment is, you have to keep a stop. A stop is simply selling the investment after deciding on a pre-set amount of money you are willing to lose on one investment and keep a stop at that potential loss figure. More times than not you will see your potential small loss turn into a big loss unless you religiously keep a stop you have decided upon before even making the trade. It should be an automatic action, like stopping at a red light.

Keeping a stop is the number one rule in trading. Only you know how much you are willing to risk on one trade. The important part, and this will be a challenge to most of you, and I guarantee if you don't adhere to it (see next section on your emotional state) then trading or investing is something you need professional help with. But if you can cover this one thing, controlling losses, then you will be great at trading.

The odds are probably 90% that if you don't keep a stop and the trend is heading lower on the investment you are in, it will continue lower. Fighting the trend is not the way to make money. Yes, there are times when the charts tell you to buy the dip, but this book isn't about chart reading and trading Fibonacci retracements, stochastic or MACD indicators or even candlestick patterns. That would take an entire book to explain and only for a small select group of traders who put in the time to learn. The simple rule of trading with the trend will eliminate the need to worry about keeping a stop or having to learn how to trade like a professional. Just look at the price action and keep your trading simple, utilizing stops.

Earmark this section on stops and your emotions or make a copy or make a copy and keep it where you can see it while trading as a reminder.

Your Emotional State

But what keeps some traders from keeping a stop? The answer is "ego," most of the time. The most important aspect of trading other than keeping stops is your mental state, and knowing yourself. We simply don't want to admit we are wrong. We stay in a trade, it goes down more, and we somehow think it will come back to break-even. Then one of two things happens: It comes back to your break-even price, goes a little higher, and you think to yourself, "See? I was right! I'm profitable now!" And then what do you do? You don't sell. So the investment goes lower than before. Next you say, "I can't take the pain of losing on this investment anymore," so you sell it... and shortly thereafter, it goes on to a higher price.

To make matters worse, some investors will double down on their losing investment. In an attempt to get their losses back, they buy more shares of the losing investment. That way their break-even point will be lower, and they assume the investment will move up to that price and they will sell. Then the investment goes lower, and the losses are even greater.

Psychologically we as humans don't like to admit we're wrong. There was an episode of Happy Days years ago for those of you who remember the 70's TV show, where the main character The Fonz" couldn't say the word "wrong." According to The Fonz, he was never wrong. But in trading we have to admit we are wrong and the market is right and keep that stop.

I had a fellow trader tell me once that he needed his wife standing over him ready to stick him with a sowing needle if he didn't keep a stop. That's how powerful your emotions are to deal with.

The beauty of keeping a stop is this; 1. You protect your nest egg. 2. You can always get back in the investment you were stopped out of, hopefully at a lower price. The reason you got into the investment to begin with is probably still valid.

It seems no matter what some traders do, they can't make money when doing it themselves because they can't keep a stop and so they give up or just can't take any more losses. Don't be like The Fonz. Admit you are wrong and keep a stop.

Taking Profit

Taking profit is the second most important aspect to trading along with knowing where the investment is in its cycle and following that trend.

Because most investors are taught a buy-and-hold philosophy, when the economy sputters, advisors would have you hold your investments the entire move down in the markets. Instead of locking in those gains, financial advisors as a whole advise you to "invest for the long run." We have had several episodes where markets have crashed and wiped out years of growth. Yes, most of the time the market does recover, but as you know from reading this book, the economy is not what it used to be in allowing these recoveries to continue.

If you agree with what is written here, you may want to lock in some of the profit you have made on bonds, stocks and other assets, or at a minimum, insure any downside risk if you concur the economy shows signs of weakness.

Greed

The other problem is when an investor is up nicely on an investment. They continue to think investments always go higher; similar to what happened with real estate before the 2007–2009 crisis. Those who kept buying real estate learned a hard lesson about greed. Those in the stock market have to decide what risks they are taking based on the strategies you'll read about next, and whether or not to lock in profit.

Summarizing Your Trading Plan

Here's the way to turn your investing and trading around:

1. Keep a stop at a pre-determined dollar loss—admit you are wrong and the market is right if the trade goes against you.
2. Have a trading plan and know what your profit goals are before you invest in an asset.
3. Don't add to losing positions.
4. Take profit when handed to you. This can be done either by moving stops up as the investment goes higher or selling shares as the price move up. This is called a trailing stop. You can't go broke taking profit and you will profit by moving stops up.

5. Add to a winning position if you are at the beginning of a trend. You'll learn more about this under Asset Allocation Strategies.

You want to have more winning investments and trades than losing ones, and when you invest long enough and make the same mistakes over and over; eventually you understand the importance of having a plan and sticking with it. Sometimes pain comes first, but hopefully this book can set you straight before you attempt to go it alone against the professionals, and you adhere to stops. Believe me, they are there to take your money. That's their job. But you can beat them at their own game.

Research Before You Invest

While this book is a good source for knowing more about investing and holding on to your wealth while growing it, I spend every day looking at the headlines and reading stories from CNBC, *The Financial Times*, *The Wall Street Journal*, Seeking Alpha, MarketWatch, *USA Today*, Yahoo, CNN, and other media sources. I also read the alternative media that is always negative on the economy and predicts doom and gloom constantly, like ZeroHedge.

I like to hear from other investors around the world, so I make comments on articles to engage others and see what I might be missing. I'm always learning. The key is to not let these individuals know what you know, but ask questions to see what *they* know and if it agrees with your own interpretation of the markets. Telling them what you know doesn't make you smarter, but always be willing to help others.

Another source I like to read regularly to know what economic news is coming out for the day or week ahead is Investing.com (Economics Calendar) and the daily economic reports that can affect the investments you are in. Investing without knowing what important reports are coming out is simply gambling. How is GDP this quarter? Is it in line with expectations? Did it beat last quarter's data? Was last quarter's GDP revised higher or lower? What is the trend? The data you read about in the Economics section of this book should be tracked so you know these trends and invest accordingly.

The Fed and the Wealth Effect

What you can take from the next table is that the years 1995-1999 and 2003-2007 were followed by significant downturns for the stock market. What will even a longer period from 2009-2016 be followed by…? We had a hint with the first two weeks of 2016 being the worst ever beginning to the stock market. What occurs after that will depend on what the Fed's next move will be. After all, it seems the markets mostly move these days not by valuation or economic data, but what the Fed will do next. We've seen what quantitative easing has done for the stock market with the so-called wealth effect.

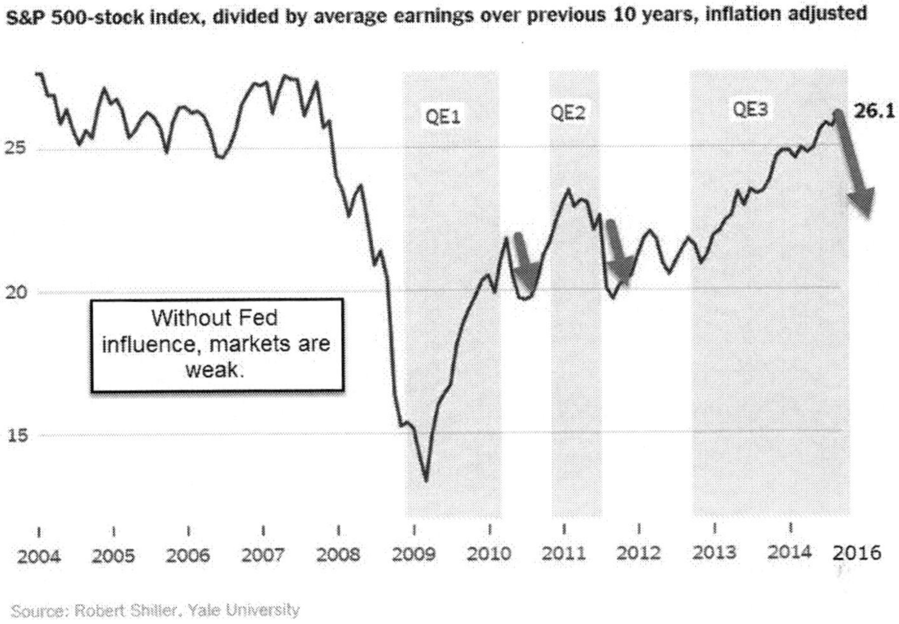

Former Fed chairman Ben Bernanke said the following in 2010, and if you track the movement of stocks, or what some call the "wealth effect," we had a nice move higher overall. But we also saw a stall in the markets shortly after the end of QE each time. This tells us the markets are built on fluff from the Fed more than valuations, as you'll see soon.

> *Easier financial conditions will promote economic growth. For example, lower mortgage rates will make housing more affordable and allow more homeowners to refinance. Lower corporate bond rates will encourage investment. And higher stock prices will boost consumer wealth and help increase confidence, which can also spur spending. Increased spending will lead to higher incomes and profits that, in a virtuous circle, will further support economic expansion.*[285]

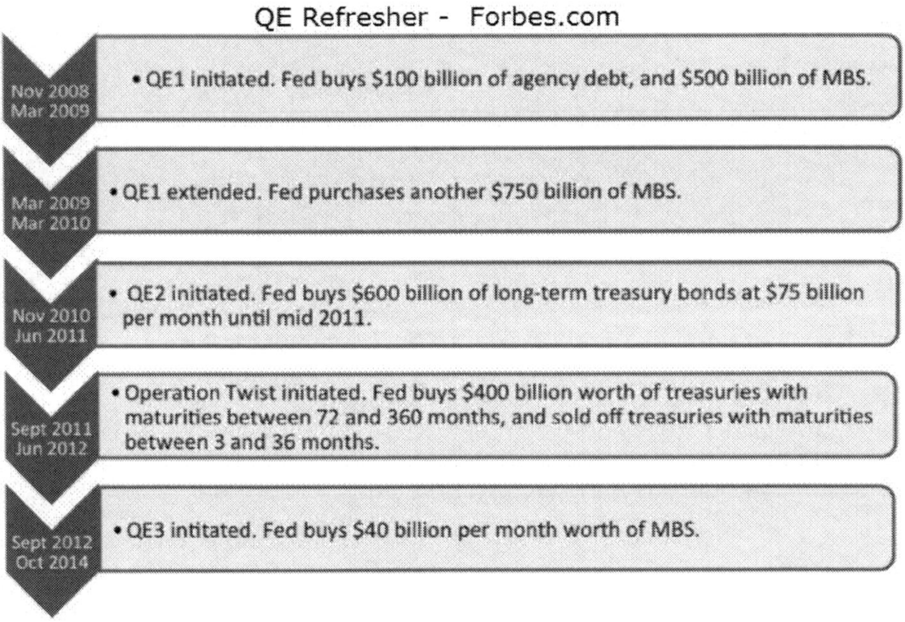

Recently former Dallas Fed president Richard Fisher had this to say on CNBC in February 2016:

---

285 http://www.washingtonpost.com/wp-dyn/content/article/2010/11/03/AR201011 0307372.html

> *What The Fed did (since the financial crisis), and I was part of it, was front-loaded an enormous rally market rally in order to create a wealth effect.*[286]

Fisher spoke, however, of the limitations of monetary policy in a speech he gave in September 2011:

> *Monetary policy is an awesome weapon. But it has limitations. We must carefully harbor its power. If we deploy it incorrectly, we might level more than interest rates and destroy that which we seek to create. And if we let it fly too far from our grasp, we may never get it back. In conducting policy going forward, we must constantly bear this in mind.*[287]

In 2014 and 2015, the market moved on speculation of whether or not the Fed would raise interest rates. Supposedly if they raised rates, then investors thought all was well with the economy. In December 2015, rates were raised—and what we saw was the worst opening for the stock market ever. By March 2016 the Fed decided not to raise rates as quickly and the market moved higher.

Sooner or later, valuations and economic data do matter, and if you know a potential market turn may be imminent, perhaps it's time to lock in some profit. The good news is there is money to be made on the way down in a market too, especially with all the inverse market ETFs that are available, which we will discuss later. Sometimes just following what the Fed does is an easy way to make money, but if the Fed pulls raises rates, you also need protection from declines.

---

286 http://www.zerohedge.com/news/2016-01-05/we-frontloaded-tremendous-market-rally-former-fed-president-admits-warns-no-ammo-lef
287 http://www.dallasfed.org/news/speeches/fisher/2011/fs110927.cfm

Risk

Before you make an investment, you want to know where it is in the big picture, and what risks are associated with it. Depending on the nature of the investment, the following potential risks need to be considered:

1. Liquidity risk - If everyone runs for the exit at the same time, you need buyers—and your price by the time you exit may be lower than you expected. Selling real estate in a declining market and selling your hedge fund position where the hedge fund managers may halt liquidation to save some of the assets in the fund from being sold at large losses are two examples.
2. Interest rate risk - When interest rates move higher, your bond funds will lose principal.
3. Inflation risk - Make sure you invest in areas that will automatically compensate for inflation when it rears its ugly head.
4. Geographic risk - Emerging markets will be a difficult area moving forward. Look for the lowest Debt to GDP countries.
5. Natural disaster risk - weather (flooding, hurricane, typhoon, drought), nuclear disaster from earthquake-prone areas (Fukushima).
6. Geopolitical risk - ISIS, al Qaeda, war or threat of war, terrorist activity hotspots, coup d'état.

Interconnectivity of Markets

It's important to remember that the world is more interconnected today than it ever has been, and we already discussed this from a banking perspective. A crisis that begins in one country can quickly spread to others.

As a reminder of how quickly things can unfold for the markets, take a look at the returns and moves for various countries that we saw in 2008, as illustrated in The Market Oracle:

> ICELAND…Bankrupt…Oct. 2008 nationalizes banks; turns to International Monetary Fund for help.
> BALTIC DRY INDEX…Down 90%… a leading indicator of shipping rates & global trade.
> JAPAN (NIKKEI) … Down 81%… from all time high of 38,957 on December 29, 1989.
> RUSSIA (RTS & MICEX) … Down 77%… exchanges shut down several days to stem panic.
> CHINA (SSE)…Down 72%… from all time high of 6,029 0n October 16, 2007.
> KOREA (KSE)…Down 68%… from high in May 2007.
> ARGENTINA (MERVAL)…Down 64%… moves to take over $30 billion in private pension funds.
> INDIA (BSE)…Down 60%… since January 2008.
> TURKEY (ISE)…Down 59%… from high in November 2007.
> HONG KONG (HANG SENG)…Down 55%… past 12 months.
> ITALY…Down 53%… past 12 months.
> BRAZIL (BOVESPA)…Down 52%… from May 2008 peak. Trading suspended five times in three weeks.
> FRANCE (CAC)…Down 50%… from June 2007.
> GERMANY (DAX)…Down 50%… year to date.
> GREAT BRITAIN (FTSE)…Down 47%… from all time high of 6,930; now "officially" in recession.
> MEXICO (IPC)…Down 47%… since June 2015.
> AUSTRALIA (ASX)…Down 45%… from all time high of 6,829 on November 1st 2007.
> U.S.A (DJIA)…Down 46%… to 8,154 on Oct. 10, 2008 from 14,198 on Oct.11, 2007. Interesting that the American market (where this crisis all began) is down less than so many others…but not surprising really with the U.S. Fed prepared to monetize as much debt as necessary to avert a Financial Armageddon.

> OIL…Down 54%… after peaking at $139 in June 2008. OPEC Nations hastily cut supply.
> COPPER…Down 50% from July 2008 high.
> NICKEL…Down 62% year to date.
> GOLD…Down 26% +… from high of $1,010 on March 17, 2008.

I'm not sure why I hold on to old things, but for some reason I kept a *Wall Street Journal* from March 19, 1992. The headline in the Money & Investing section was: "With Tokyo Off 49%, Is it a Good Time to Buy?" The Nikkei Index reached its peak in December 1989 at an intraday high of 38,957.44. It closed at 19,764 the day that *Wall Street Journal* article came out.

The article stated the Nikkei was "the cheapest major market in the world" by a portfolio manager at State Street Bank & Trust in Boston. The Nikkei fell to 7,054.98 by 2009 and it took until April 2015, 23 years after that *WSJ* article to get back to the 19,764 level—from where it fell again. Watch Japan for what's to come for many a nation, as we have seen their efforts to weaken the yen continue and how a potential deflationary scenario can wreak havoc on a buy and hold strategy with no stop in place.

One note: While gold did fall in February 2008 after breaking $1,000 an ounce for the first time, it did rebound faster than most every other asset, and hit an all-time high of $1,920 in September 2011. That's almost double in 3.5 years. We'll talk more about gold in a bit.

Bear Markets

Baby Boomers have fueled this stock market, and so far the going's been good overall since 2009. But these Boomers also have fresh in their memories the 2009 market crash, and at any sign of trouble will move out of the stock market, as they can't afford to take another hit like the last one. Consider this your early warning sign of trouble, and my recommendations would be to dollar-cost-average out of some of the stock market risk. This doesn't mean that some stocks won't be winners, but it does mean you should be cautious moving forward, and at least hedge your stock positions if you are going to hold onto them (probably after having a conversation with your longtime adviser).

The good news, though, that is there will be a time when the stock market becomes more attractive, as the following chart from Ed Easterling at Crestmont Research shows. (We'll discuss this more in the Strategies chapter, when we speak about P/E ratios.) You can also see where the danger zone is for stocks.[288]

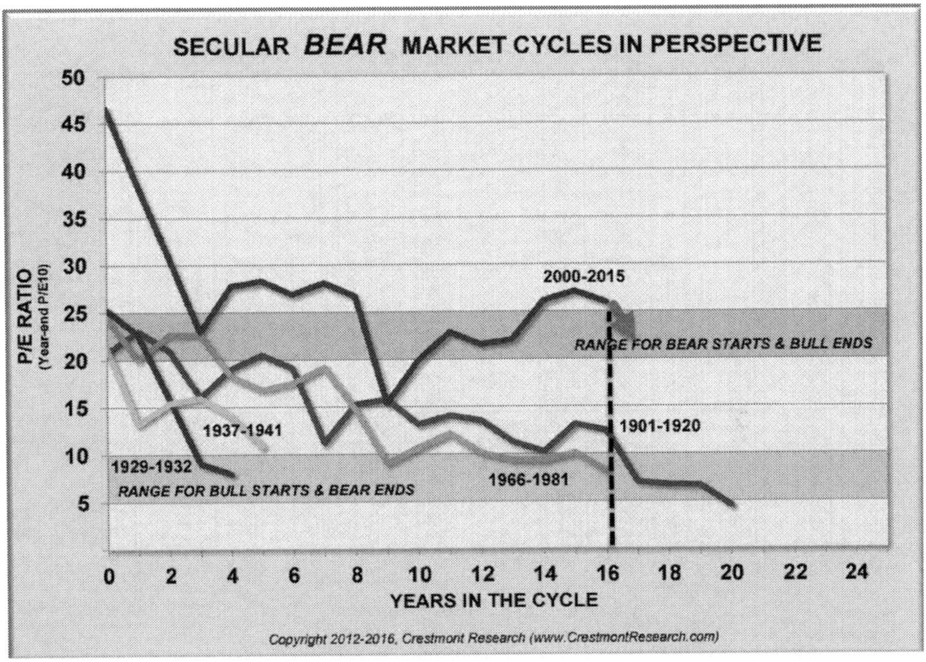

What else can cause a selloff in the markets? If we are indeed in a deflationary contraction, as I outlined earlier, then government will have to take some of the wealth invested in markets to start paying bills. Saudi Arabia hasn't been making money on oil the way they

288 http://www.crestmontresearch.com/docs/Stock-Secular-PE.pdf

used to, and neither has Denmark. The countries are invested in what are called sovereign wealth funds.

Sovereign Wealth Funds (SWFs)

Sovereign wealth funds (SWFs) are special purpose investment funds or arrangements owned by the general government. Created for macroeconomic purposes, SWFs hold, manage, or administer assets to achieve financial objectives, and employ a set of investment strategies that include investing in foreign financial assets. SWFs are closely linked to public finances (through their funding and withdrawal rules), monetary policy (liquidity conditions), and external accounts (exchange rate variations).[289]

SWFs typically get their wealth from mostly oil-related industries for the largest funds, such as UAE, Saudi Arabia, Kuwait, Qatar and Norway. China has two large SWFs that derive funding from non-commodity, but do have some exposure to Canadian resource companies.[290]

Over $7 trillion is invested in these funds, primarily in public equities, fixed income, private equity, real estate, infrastructure, and some hedge funds. We saw the first decline in them since the end of the financial crisis occur in 2015.

---

[289] https://www.imf.org/external/pubs/ft/wp/2013/wp13231.pdf
[290] http://www.reuters.com/article/us-cn-invst-new-york-idUSKBN0TX22120 151214

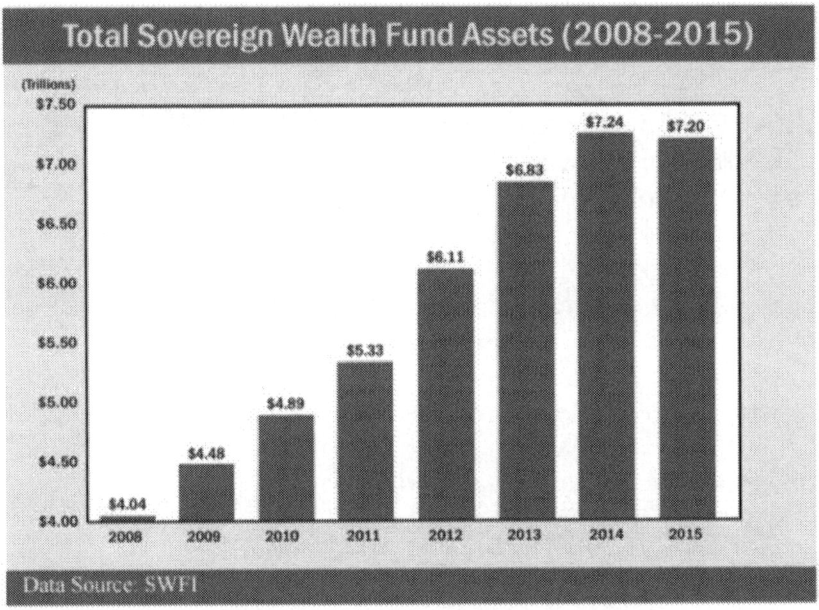

The SWFs typically have a longer-term investment horizon, but as things really deteriorate—and I think we make the case for this—will they be forced to liquidate at losses? How do these oil-producing economies get through an extended downturn in the price of oil? Let's look at one of the largest SWFs, Norway.

Norway alone has $817 billion invested. Lower oil prices are hurting their economy, and they are on the verge of a recession because oil is the engine of their economy. The fund lost $32.71 billion, or 4.9%, in July-September 2015, and entering 2016, we saw oil and the markets decline even more before a bounce higher.[291] If deflation does really continue, then oil will lead the way lower still.

During the 2007-2009 financial crisis, SWFs incurred large losses just as they are beginning to do now, but many weathered the storm of the last crisis. In fact, while some of these funds were quasi-bailed out

[291] http://www.cnbc.com/2015/10/28/norways-giant-oil-fund-sees-biggest-loss-in-4-years.html

through help from the Fed and their buying spree, one SWF, for example, was buying shares in troubled Citigroup.[292] In other words, they were a bailout source for Citigroup. When markets are crying for liquidity for the next crisis, though, will these funds that were doing well with $100 oil be able to help out these institutions when oil is 2/5 the cost? I think not. This time it truly will be different.

You have seen what the Fed's balance sheet is like today. What can they possibly do but press digital buttons to buy more problem assets out of thin air should a future crisis occur? What will be the sentiment of the markets when the Ponzi game is exposed? How are you protected?

Warning from a Billionaire Investor

Billionaire Carl Icahn has been worried about the stock market for some time, and in September 2015 put out a video revealing his concerns with the Fed keeping rates at zero too long, and now even talk of negative rates.[293]

Simulated Trading – Practice before you invest

There are some good stock market simulators out there that make sense for you to play around with—using fake money before your hard-earned money is invested. These simulators allow you to trade a stock or multiple stocks as if you were trading live with the market. If you were to practice doing this for a month, it would give you an idea of whether or not you are ready to risk your own money.

I will throw out one caution: If you practice your trading or even go to live trading in a bull market, almost any investment moves higher and you'll look brilliant with your choices. But when the market turns south, investing becomes much more difficult. What worked before

---

[292] https://www.preqin.com/docs/samples/The-2015-Preqin-Sovereign-Wealth-Fund-Review-Sample-Pages.pdf
[293] https://www.youtube.com/watch?v=ZyKIvnied-o

with a bull market may not work in a bear market. It's important to understand the trend and trade in its direction.

You can check with your current online broker if they have a stock simulator but some good ones can be found below.

thinkorswim paperMoney from TD Ameritrade https://www.thinkorswim.com/t/innovation.html
Market Watch VSE http://www.marketwatch.com/game/
Investopedia http://www.investopedia.com/simulator/
Wall Street Survivor http://www.wallstreetsurvivor.com/

One thing an online stock trading simulator won't do is allow your emotions to enter the picture. It is only through live trading, with your own money, that emotions get in the way of your trading. Some of you will learn this the hard way if you don't keep a stop as discussed earlier. Trust me on this.

Chapter 23 - If You Think You Know It All, There's More

Not everyone will think the same way as I do and invest the way I suggest in this book, but after finishing this section on investments and using what you learned in previous chapters you'll be able to jump ship should things not go your way, rather than sit through a potentially prolonged downturn that can deplete your wealth, as has happened so many times before to investors. There is plenty of opportunity to profit moving forward, and what worked in the past may not be the best path forward.

Patience

There will come a time when you have sold many of your good investments and locked in profit. Some investors may become concerned that their money is earning virtually nothing sitting in cash or a money market account. But the patient investor simply waits for the right opportunity. This can be when markets cross their 200-day moving average higher and it's time to go long or cross lower and time to buy inverse market funds or ETFs, described later in this chapter.

Good investors develop a feel for the market. They wait for the "panic" to develop in the market cycle, and they cost-average into their allocation, which we'll discuss soon. They then simply wait for the inevitable rebound in that sector. Patience is rewarded.

Diversification/Investment Pyramid

Your typical financial advisor views investing based on a pyramid of risk similar to this one:[294]

---

[294] http://srsinc.com/wp-content/uploads/PDF/Investment%20 Pyramid.pdf

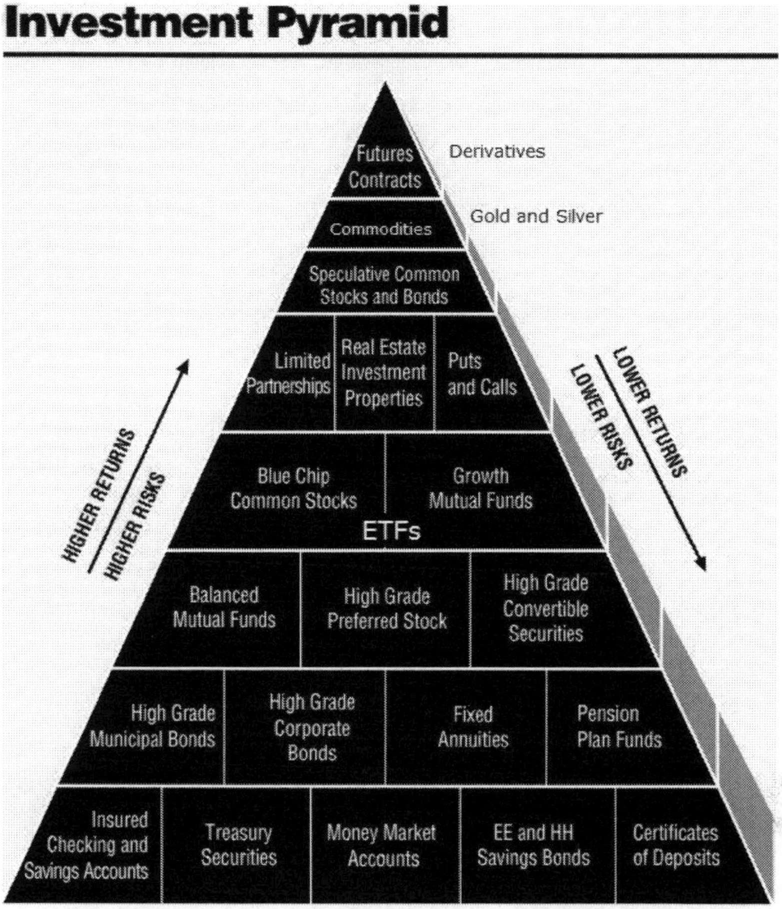

How did this pyramid hold up during the 2007–2009 financial crisis? All in all, almost every asset listed got hurt except the bottom row and some in the second to bottom row. But since that crisis we have seen most every asset rise in value except for commodities. However, I take extreme exception to this pyramid moving forward, as you'll see in the bond section later in this chapter (the last two levels of the pyramid are known as the safest) and I take particular exception with gold and silver at the top of the pyramid, known as the second riskiest investment in the pyramid used by most financial advisors. This will be explained more in Chapters 27 and 31.

The Callan Periodic Table of Investment Returns in the next table shows the annual returns from 1996–2015 of key indices ranked by performance, updated a www.callan.com/research/periodic/. Please note that in 2008, it didn't matter what you invested in for the most part, it didn't do well. But in the next crisis, I don't see the Barclays U.S. Aggregate Bond Index shooting up to the top if interest rates shoot higher like it did then. It may be a good temporary alternative during deflation, but be leery of rising rates. The next crisis should be a repeat of 2007-2009 investment returns and a sharp downturn at some point similar to 2008.

This chart gives you one of the main reasons to be cautious, but in good times it also gives a clear observation of the old investment adage of allocating from what is performing well to what is beaten down. You'll be able to take profit and lock it in when the indices rise to the top or see the indices at the bottom of the table as a "buy low" opportunity and ride them higher. This for me is a smarter, more proactive way to diversify.

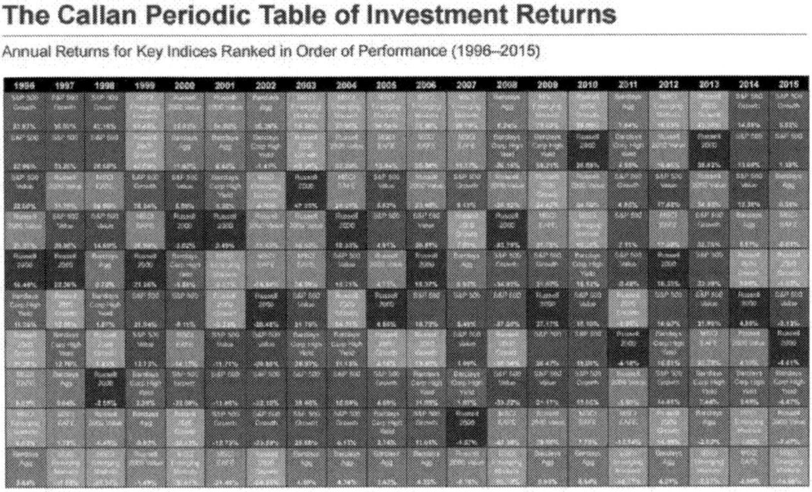

Real Returns After Inflation and Taxes

When it comes to looking at the returns of your investments, you must consider the entire picture or "real" return after expenses, taxes, and inflation have been accounted for. The following chart shows how an investment of $100 in 1983 would have an 11.34% return if invested in the S&P 500 Index, to a total of $2,510 by December 31, 2014, but once you take out expenses and taxes, and compensate for inflation, your real return is only 6.38% or $639.[295] The S&P 500 closed at 2,058.90 on December 31, 2014. By 2016 the S&P had moved lower, and it will become harder and harder to get a good return with deflation on the horizon.

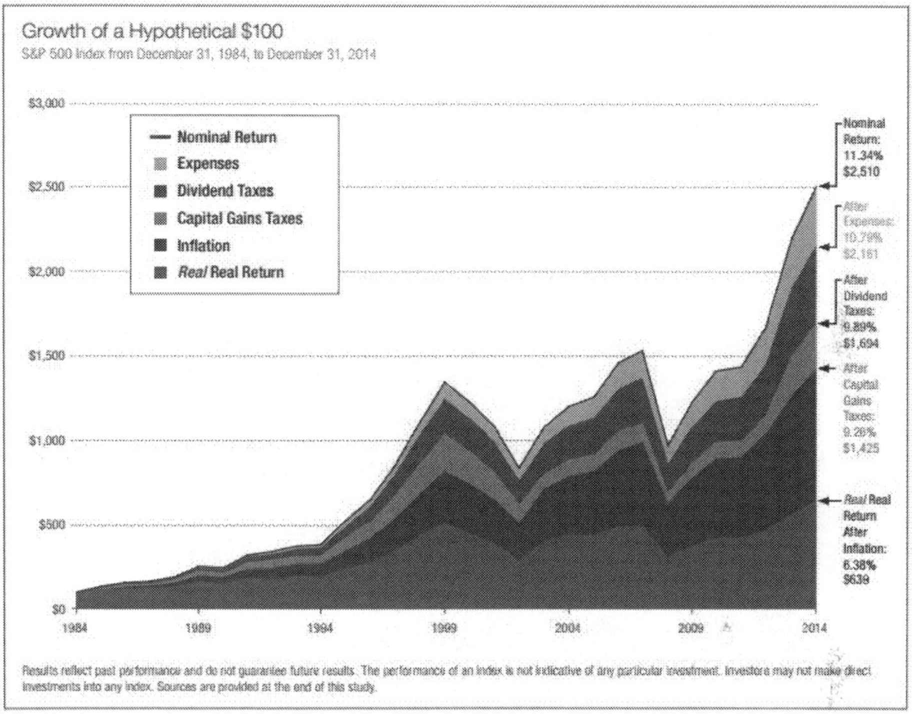

[295] **http://www.thornburg.com/pdf/TH1401_real_real_returns.pdf**

When we project that same average inflation rate of 2.82% forward, over the next 25 years, much of your investment will be eaten away by inflation. This simply means that before you even make the investment, you have to earn 2.82% to break even, and worse, taxes and expenses are added—and this *assumes* that the inflation rate will only average 2.82%. Have you seen the debt this country is in? Are expenses going to all of a sudden be reduced? Is Congress going to ever balance the budget? Not when they have a 10-year plan to increase the deficit every year but one. Yes, chances are we will experience higher inflation than 2.82% on average in the coming years.

A Picture of Inflation

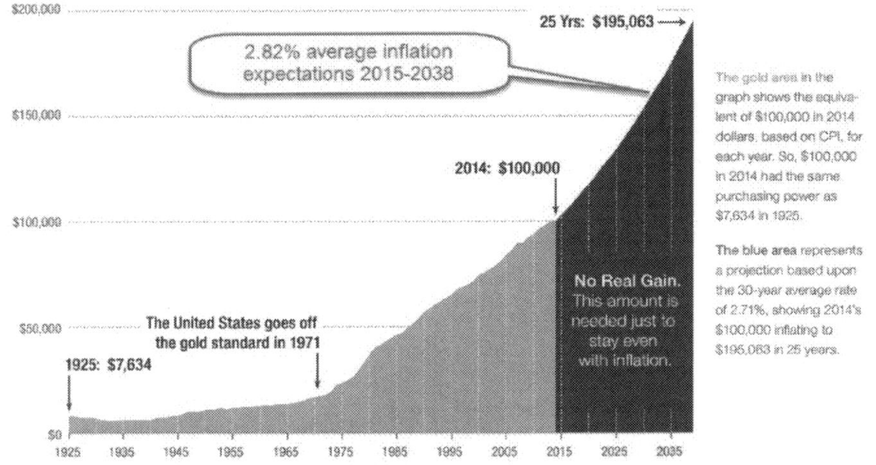

Source: Calculated by Thornburg Investment Management using data presented in the Ibbotson SBBI® 2014 Classic Yearbook, ©2014. All rights reserved. Used with permission.

Chapter 24 - Now That You Know It All – There's Still More, and We Haven't Even Gotten to Actual Investments Yet

High-Frequency Trading

Are you smarter than a computer? Can computers actually come in and trade your portfolio better than you ever could? It sure would make life easier if you could do that and be profitable. Most investors think of computer trading as the type of programmed trading done by computers by big Wall Street firms, where stocks are bought and sold en masse when certain price levels are hit. Most of us small investors aren't privy to such technology. But lately there has been a growing trend toward computerized trading that may be putting some investment advisors out of business. If you think about it, history shows that most mutual fund and hedge fund managers can't beat the market, why do we need to pay them such high fees? If we can get a computer to do it, and that keeps fees low, perhaps a computer can do a better job than the market itself. I mean, they're not bad chess players, right?

Large investment firms (including Vanguard, Charles Schwab, Blackrock and even on the insurance side, Northwestern Mutual) have entered into the automated trading arena. If big money is behind it, you know there is some validity there.

An algorithmic trading investment approach is not for everyone, but there is a niche it can fill for those who have no time, are new to investing, or don't want to pay high fees for advice.

Is this type of trading for you? One of the companies, AlgoTrades, offers a quiz to find out.[296]

---

[296] http://www.algotrades.net/wp-content/uploads/2013/10/1MinuteQuiz.pdf

Answer the statements below with a YES or NO answer. Add up the total numbers of Yes's	YES	NO
Are you an active trader?	○	○
Are you a casual investor?	○	○
Are you tired of watching your account decline during market down turns and bear markets?	○	○
Do you have a detailed investment plan to work from?	○	○
Do you currently have a financial advisor managing your money?	○	○
Do you have clear trade and investment criteria for new position and position management?	○	○
Use a protective stop on every trade to limit losses in the event of a selloff or market crash?	○	○
Do you try to manage your own investments?	○	○
Do you have trading rules but do not stick too?	○	○
Do you have a routine that gets you back on track when you're trading is off?	○	○
Do your losing investments typically out-weigh your winners?	○	○
Do you have having several winning trades, followed by larger crash and burn type of trades?	○	○
Do you experience hesitation, apprehension, uncertainty, or fear when you are about to trade?	○	○
Do you double-down after a losing streak or when you're losing to re-gain profits faster?	○	○
Have you ever experienced the "I don't care" mode and watched your money disappear?	○	○
Were you successful in another profession and find trading is affecting your confidence and ego?	○	○
Do you lose sleep over your trading and investments?	○	○
Are you exiting positions too quickly instead of waiting for its full potential?	○	○
Do you want your positions managed properly for maximum profit potential?	○	○
Are a high percentage of your trades defensive?	○	○
You logically know what to do in a trade but find you are not taking the actions you should?	○	○

If you add up the total number of "YES" answers and it is more than six, they say an automated trading system is for you, and it is "risk controlled" and "100% fully automated." AlgoTrades says their "proprietary INNER-Market Analysis method uses a number of data points including up/down volume flow, market sentiment, cycles, moving averages, volatility, momentum and price patterns which are recalculated on every tick." They utilize your own brokerage account to do the trading, but it has to be from a list of their recommended brokers. They require a minimum of $35,000 to open an account (others require less), with a $300,000 maximum. They only trade the S&P 500 index through the use of three mini futures contracts. The fees range from $1,500 to $4,000 a year, depending on what you go with. Naturally in the disclosure they say, "No representation is being made that utilizing the First Algorithmic Trading System will result in profitable trading or be free of risk of loss. Futures trading and trading exchange traded funds involve a substantial risk of loss and is not appropriate for everyone." In other words, there are no guarantees. But this something that I do recommend you check out if you are looking for a hands-off investment program where they say can profit in up or down markets.

Another Reason Stocks Have Done Well - Stock Buybacks

Stock buybacks are up, and it shows companies to have stronger earnings than they normally would have because fewer shares exist.

This has led to GAAP (Generally Accepted Accounting Principles) earnings being suspect, as the companies are selling at huge multiples.

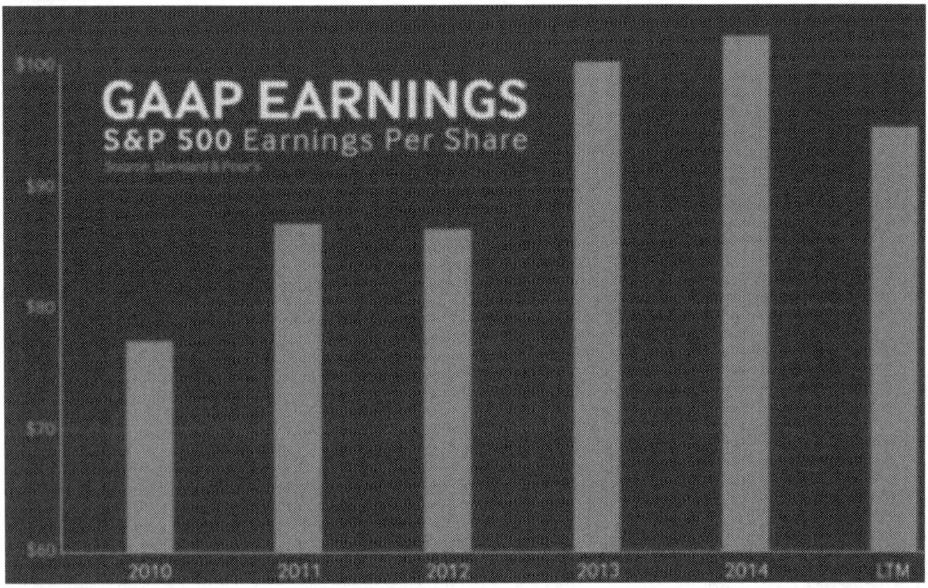

Margin Debt

Many talk about margin debt as a reason to be worried about stock market valuations, and for good reason. In 2013 we hit record highs in margin debt, and in 2015 we were near record highs still. While the stock market can be irrational longer than you can be solvent, as the saying goes, at some point that irrational behavior will reverse course and margin debt will begin to subside—and with it, stock market returns. We've seen record margin debt before, in 1999-2000 before the technology bubble, 2006-2007 before the financial crisis, and beginning in 2013 through 2015, where we have already seen a decrease of 11%. And even though the stock market pushed to highs again in late 2015, we're still at multi-year highs. Can you not see the bubble in the graph below, from Doug Short at Advisor Perspectives?[297]

---

[297] http://www.advisorperspectives.com/dshort/updates/NYSE-Margin-Debt-and-the-SPX.php

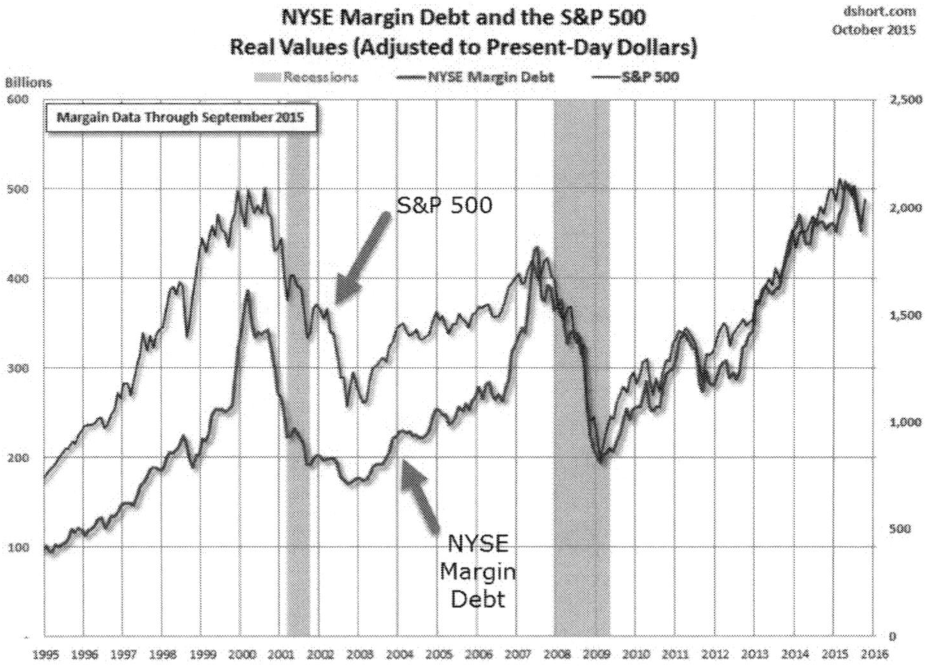

Shorting the Market

Most advisors don't recommend shorting the market because of their mantra of "buy and hold," and the assumption that stocks always go up. Also, if they are ever sued by an investor they advised to short an investment, they would more than likely lose the case and be reprimanded by the SEC for violating the Prudent Man Rule, which asks what a prudent man would do with his investments (hint: It's not "short the stock market").

It used to be that a stock had to tick higher in order to short it. If a stock was falling you couldn't just jump in and ride it down. Today, however, you can buy inverse ETFs (discussed in Chapter 28) in almost any sector, whether it be the market indices, commodities, specific countries and more, and you don't need any uptick in the stock to do this. Many do not choose to short or buy inverse ETFs because they are not familiar with the process, but the returns can be phenomenal, especially when the markets are tanking.

For example, one of the best ways to bet gold is going lower is to buy a gold ETF that goes up when the price of gold goes down. To do this, you can buy the ETF DGZ, which, according to Yahoo Finance, "seeks to replicate, net of expenses, the inverse of the daily performance of the Deutsche Bank Liquid Commodity index - Optimum Yield Gold Excess Return. The index is intended to reflect changes in the market value of certain gold futures contracts and is comprised of a single unfunded gold futures contract."[298] Naturally, if gold goes up in price, this investment will lose you money. The point being that you get to choose your investment direction or follow the trend based on your own research and observations of what's going on with any particular asset class.

The point here is to not be intimidated with all the articles that come out against shorting the market. If you know a particular company is in trouble and you can get your hands on shares from your broker to short this information, by all means do so.

Tax Planning - Taking Losses (Non-IRA/401(k)/Pension Assets)

Too often, investors hold on to losing positions in their investments without taking advantage of the tax laws that can allow them to write off that loss against any gains in the year of the loss, and potentially subsequent years. This loss can be utilized against any capital gains for that year should you sell an investment that has capital appreciation, dollar for dollar, or the loss can be taken as a deduction from income earned up to $3,000 per year until it is exhausted by any subsequent years' capital gains or earned income. Please discuss with your accountant, and take those losses! There is one thing to watch out for: The "wash rule" states that you won't be allowed to buy the same asset back for 30 days, or you lose the exemptions—30 days is not long to wait, and chances are, whatever asset you sold for a loss is probably

[298] http://finance.yahoo.com/q/pr?s=DGZ+Profile

down more. Unfortunately, you do not get this tax benefit for your IRA/401(k)/pension investments.

There is a way to sell your investments, whether real estate, stock or even precious metals without paying capital gains. It is beyond the scope of this book but it involves utilizing charitable trusts. Check with your tax advisor or contact someone at the Planned Giving Design Center for help. http://www.pgdc.com/

The Ratings Game

All you need to know about ratings is that when times are good, no one notices the ratings except those who might be close to retirement and only want highly rated investments. But when times are bad, as we saw from the movie *The Big Short* (and the book by Michael Lewis), ratings may not matter.

Part of the problem comes from conflicts of interest. Many investments are paying for the ratings and will choose (pay) the company that gives them the highest rating. Also, issuers can ask the ratings agency what rating it would give a "proposed financial instrument with certain characteristics." These companies know in advance what rating they might get and will simply go with the company that offers the highest. Lastly, and I just laugh at this one, according to the Centre for Studies in Economics and Finance, "credit rating agencies are largely immune to civil and criminal liability for malfeasance, because according to several U.S. court decisions, they are to be considered as 'journalists' and their ratings are opinions protected by the First Amendment (freedom of speech)."[299] Excuse me, but aren't most all of the talking heads at CNBC telling us what to do with our money also financial journalists?

There seems to be no accountability to investors which is why I want investors to take control of their own wealth and why I wrote this book.

---

[299] http://www.csef.it/WP/wp239.pdf

Trading the News

How would you like to know what a stock will do before the general public does? A trader back in the late 1990s used to run a trading room and charge $400 a month for his calls. I have a knack for figuring things out with the markets, so I reverse-engineered his calls and discovered how he was making such great ones. First off, I want to say that he did get in trouble with the SEC for front running the traders in his room. Meaning, he would buy shares in XYZ stock, and then tell everyone in his trading room to buy XYZ stock, and then sell into that strength as the stock popped higher.

What he didn't get in trouble for was figuring out a way of getting his information on stocks 15 minutes before the market knew because he somehow set himself up as a journalist and would receive news releases from PR Newswire and Business Wire from companies—and trade on that news.

Effective October 8, 2000, PR Newswire changed its distribution policy so the media and the general public now receive new releases at the same time.[300] Access to this data is a must if you want to get in on trades early, when some news comes out that can move a stock higher or lower. But if you really want to be top dog in getting access to news quickly through live streaming, you need the Bloomberg Terminal, but this is mostly used by professionals at a cost of $2,000 a month.

But there are now social media options for your average trader that work well too, and are free. This includes StockTwits, where you can share ideas with 230,000 other investors. This service allows you to see in real time what is going on with a certain stock or ETF, and how it is trending.

Some other sources for active traders are TradingView[301] and NextCapital,[302] which track all your investments in one place. A good

---

300 https://prnmedia.prnewswire.com/

301 https://www.tradingview.com/

302 https://nextcapital.com/#/

analysis of the various social trading networks and platforms can be found at http://socialtradingguru.com/networks/social-trading-networks

Check them out to see what fits your investment goals, objectives, and trading style. Take control of your wealth.

Chapter 25 - Investment Strategies To Consider

Philosophies on Investing

Sometimes when it comes to investing, you have to simply use your brain and ask questions. What's the hottest trend? Who makes the products related to that trend? Where are we with the Baby Boomers? What will they be doing in retirement?

Some of the industries that I see worth investing in for the coming years are those that either do well in bad times, or have an upward growth that never seems to run out of customers, meaning the demand is always there. The following list of industries should be considered for a diversified portfolio.

Food-related - Especially organic, as more people become health conscious.
Addiction/Enjoyment-related industries - Alcohol including spirits/wine/beer and coffee.
Entertainment/Hollywood - An escape mechanism.
Marijuana/Medicinal - Another escape mechanism and growth opportunity in some states and potentially national approval.
Gambling/Online Gaming – People looking for ways to get ahead that only make the casinos rich.
Vitamins - Another growth industry for a health-conscious population.
Self-Driving Cars - In its infancy stage.
Robotics - The rise of the machines is upon us.
Apple/Amazon/Google/Facebook - All powerhouses to contend with, and most any business related to the industries they are involved in can do well. But keep an eye out for the next powerhouse to emerge by seeing what new technology evolves.

Asset Allocation

An old adage says to put the percentage of your assets in stocks that correlate to your age and the rest in bonds. If you are 20, then 80% should go into stocks because you have more time to ride out the ups and downs of the stock market, and 20% into bonds. If you are 80, then 20% should go into stocks, as you have less time to recoup losses, and 80% into bonds. How did this philosophy work from 2007–2009? It didn't.

I can't really get behind this strategy, because you need stocks to provide your portfolio with some growth over time, but at age 80 you could miss out on easy profit because some silly rule tells you that your investments should be allocated a certain way—without knowing what the heck is going on in the economy. For example, you would have missed the entire bull market with 80% of your portfolio in bonds from 2009 to 2015, when stocks outperformed all other assets. The next crisis could take both stocks and bonds down with it depending on interest rates.

The best way to take the guessing game out of investing, in my opinion, is to simply diversify your investments among asset classes and continually take from what is doing well or hitting new highs and allocate more to what is beaten down. But don't just do this automatically. You still have to do some analysis.

If the asset you are invested in is hitting lower lows, that is the first sign to bail on it. If it is hitting higher highs, you want to obviously be in that investment or possibly add to it. So when do you bail on one doing well and put that money into the beaten-down asset? And just as important, when do you lock in profit, and maybe just go to cash for a bit?

To answer these questions, you must first know that you're not going to time investments perfectly. You can come close, though, to have your last buy of a beaten-down sector or your last sell out of a topping sector come to fruition. There are techniques for this.

To know when to switch from one investment class to another, or out of stocks and into cash, open your eyes to what's going on—do a little reading. But don't just listen to the always bullish CNBC or the always bearish Zerohedge.com for what's going on in the markets. Use some of your own intuition and common sense about the markets. Ask yourself the following questions:

1. What does my financial advisor say to do? (They are almost always bullish on the market.)
2. Trade with the trend, not against it, unless you are allocating to a beaten-down sector.
3. What do the charts of the Dow, S&P, and NASDAQ show compared to their 100-day moving average? If above, stay long and strong in stocks and if below possibly begin buying some insurance via short the market ETFs, explained in Chapter 28. You can also buy options to protect your portfolio, discussed later in the Investments section. Options are typically over the head of most investors, but they can be used to profit if you know what you're doing.
4. What are interest rates doing? If they are falling, be in bonds, bond funds, and stocks. If they are rising, bond mutual funds aren't the place to be, and stocks in general fell in 1994, 1999 and 2004 with each FOMC rate increase. Know where we are in the big picture historically. Right now we are at historic lows for interest rates, which means we at some point will have the propensity to move higher.
5. What is the VIX showing? The VIX shows 30-day market expectations of market volatility. Where is volatility? Are the markets calm and the VIX falling, or are the markets falling as the VIX rises?
6. What is the unemployment rate doing? If it is falling, stocks are great. If it is rising, stocks are not so great.
7. Where are we with stocks' earnings per share compared to historic norm? Right now we are above the mean based on the Shiller P/E Ratio.[303]
8. Is your neighbor telling you to buy this or that investment? Look into the opposite. As Warren Buffett has advised, be

---

[303] http://www.multpl.com/shiller-pe/

fearful when others are greedy and greedy when others are fearful.

9. What is the Fed doing? Follow them, but be aware at some point their game may fail (see Gold section).
10. Predict the future. Open your eyes. Read. Become your own guru.
11. Know what's going on with inflation. The 1960s saw the Dow drop 35% during that inflationary episode. The 1970s had a two-year drop in '73 and '74. Volcker and his preceding heads at the Fed who were tightening monetary policy in the late '70s didn't help the markets, but loosening things up finally got the roaring '80s underway. We simply don't have that luxury today, to get us out of what I see as a recession and worse on the horizon. If we were to get to super-inflation though, stocks may do very well, but possibly not even keep up with double digit inflation.

Market Valuations

One way to see whether today's stock market is undervalued or overvalued is to compare the market cap to GDP. According to Gurufocus, "The Total Market Index is at $ 21,865.2 billion, which is about 122.1% of the last reported GDP. The U.S. stock market is positioned for an average annualized return of 0%, estimated from the historical valuations of the stock market. This includes the returns from the dividends, currently yielding at 1.99%."

This is represented in the following charts, which show that we are presently overvalued and higher in valuation than at the height of the financial crisis, but under the extreme valuations after the tech bubble reached its peak in 2000.[304]

[304] http://www.gurufocus.com/stock-market-valuations.php

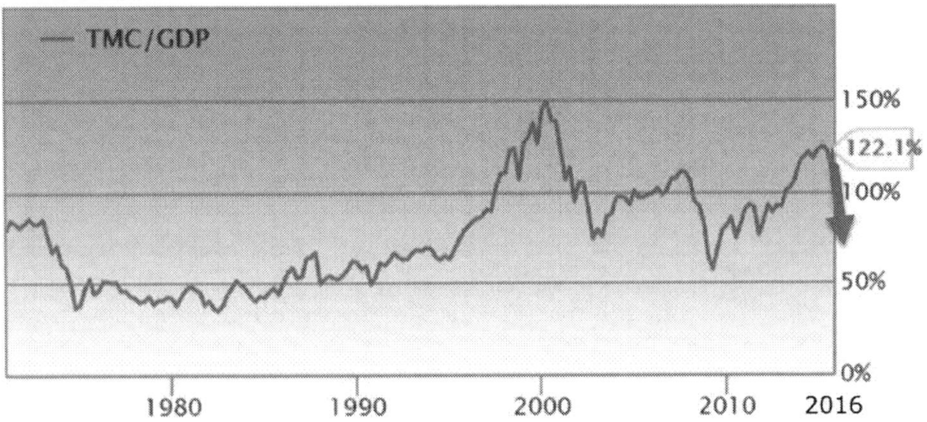

Ratio = Total Market Cap / GDP	Valuation
Ratio < 50%	Significantly Undervalued
50% < Ratio < 75%	Modestly Undervalued
75% < Ratio < 90%	Fair Valued
90% < Ratio < 115%	Modestly Overvalued
Ratio > 115%	Significantly Overvalued
Where are we today (**11/07/2015**)?	Ratio = **122.1%**, **Significantly Overvalued**

Ratio = Total Market Cap / GDP	Valuation
Ratio < 50%	Significantly Undervalued
50% < Ratio < 75%	Modestly Undervalued
75% < Ratio < 90%	Fair Valued
90% < Ratio < 115%	Modestly Overvalued
Ratio > 115%	Significantly Overvalued
Where are we today (**02/29/2016**)?	Ratio = **110%**, **Modestly Overvalued**

Jill Mislinski from Advisor Perspectives concurs with her inflation-adjusted S&P 500 index price that shows it is 80% above its long-term trend line dating back to 1871.

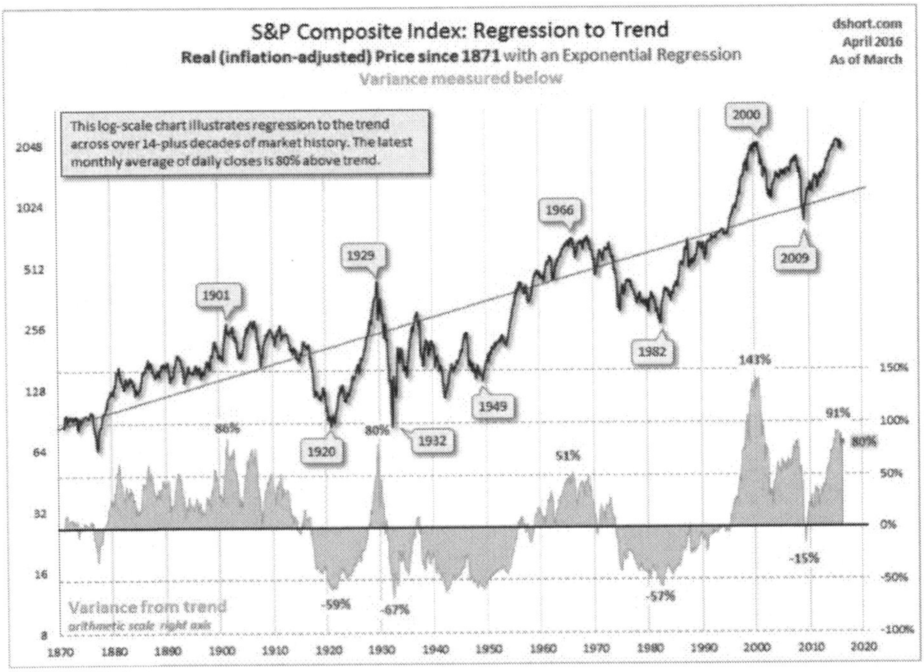

PE Ratios

The price-earnings ratio is calculated by taking the current stock price of a company and dividing it by its earnings per share. Crestmont Research also provides some good data for us to analyze through the work of Ed Easterling, who I mentioned once before.

> *Secular bear markets are periods of below-average returns. The magnitude of the annualized return (or loss) depends upon the investor's time period. Most notably, however, is that none of the scenarios provide average or above average returns. As history has shown, average or above-average returns cannot occur from levels of relatively high valuation without the multiple expansion of a rising P/E. From today's lofty levels, bubble conditions would be required...and that's not a reasonable assumption for any investor's portfolio.*[305]

The following chart is from Doug Short of Advisor Perspectives, where he uses the Crestmont P/E Ratio analysis[306] showing current P/E to be about 90% above its average (arithmetic mean).

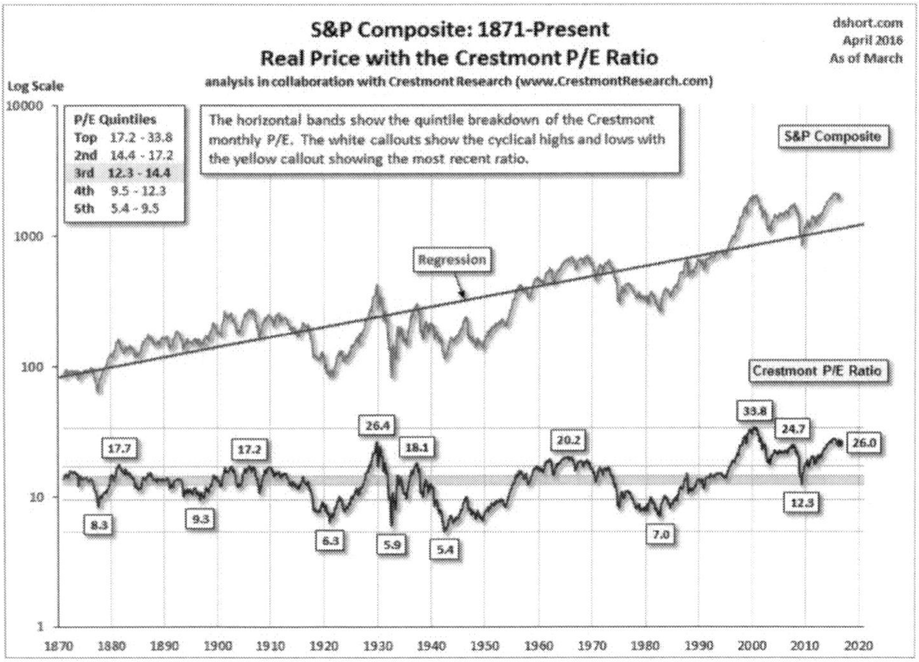

The following conclusion about P/E Ratios from Ed Easterling isn't very promising.

The current normalized P/E is 26.5—well above the levels justified by low inflation and interest rates (assuming historically-average economic growth). BUT, secular markets are driven by longer-term annual trends rather than momentary market circumstances. The secular analysis for each year relates to the average index across the

---

305 http://www.crestmontresearch.com/docs/Stock-PE-Report.pdf

306 http://www.advisorperspectives.com/dshort/updates/Crestmont-PE-Ratio

year; so for each year, the price (P) in P/E (price/earnings ratio) is the average index for all days of the year. The stock market has recovered well beyond its declines from late 2008 and early 2009; therefore, it's now fairly clear that the period in late 2008 and early 2009 was just a cyclical (short-term) bear market blip within a longer secular bear market. Of course, that makes the period since early 2009 a cyclical bull market inside a secular bear market (it has happened many times before). If the stock market does not recover further or cannot sustain the recovery gains from the past five years due to significant inflation or deflation, the normalized P/E over the next few years will likely decline below the historical average and the foundation for a secular bull market would begin to be laid.

To give you an idea of the accuracy of Easterling's work, the following chart of the Shiller PE Ratio, one of the most popular used by the financial media, shows the P/E ratio has fallen from 26.56 in November of 2015 to 25.92 in April 2016. The historic average is 16.6, which gives you an idea of whether the market is overheated or weak (a buy or sell). This charts also show you just how overvalued the markets were in the year 2000, and today we are close to where we were in 2007—before the last financial crisis hit.[307]

[307] http://www.multpl.com/shiller-pe/

Shiller PE Ratio for the S&P 500

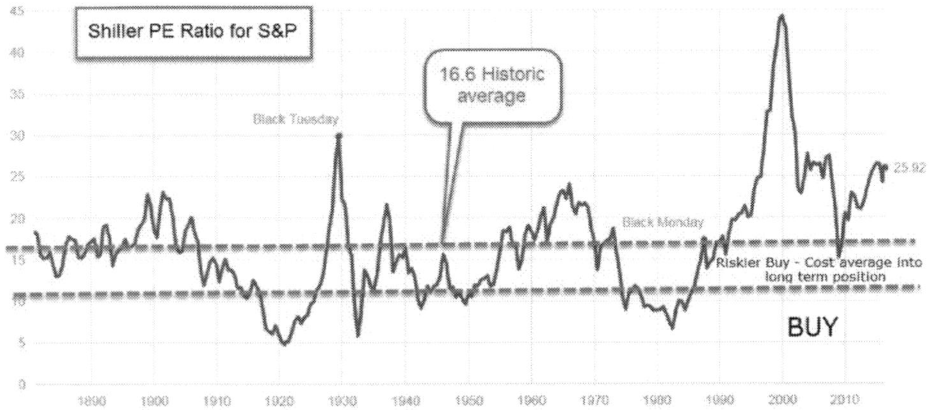

Accounting Ratios Give You the Truth about Which Companies To Invest In

When analyzing the sustainability and growth potential of a company, it is important to analyze the financial data first and foremost. The key financial data and ratios analyzed for each company you are contemplating investing in can be found through analysis of the last 10 years of annual returns and the latest 10Qs (quarterly reports) to verify whether the data continues to add up to a winning stock.

The most important are the following. Compare these with past performance and the data of competitors.

1. Net Profit Margin – Divide net profit before tax by net sales to see if net profit is good. (higher is better)
2. Asset Turnover – The amount of sales or revenues generated per dollar of assets (higher is better).
3. Financial Leverage – The use of debt to acquire additional assets (lower is better).
4. Return on Total Assets – Profit compared to assets (higher is better).

5. Return on Equity – Profit compared to equity (higher is better).
6. Current Ratio – Current assets divided by current liabilities. Measures ability to pay short-term liabilities. You want a ratio that shows more assets than liabilities (generally higher is better).

Moving forward, it is of the utmost importance to know that the company you invest in has its debt under control and enough cash to weather financial and economic downturns or slowdowns. If you know of an asset class you want to invest in, apply these ratios to the companies that are in that asset sector, and you'll be able to see which companies comes out on top. If you only do one thing in analyzing whether a company is worthy of your investment dollars, applying these six ratios and analyzing the results while comparing to the competition is it. The best of the best is what you are looking for, and you'll see throughout the investment section that I continually refer to this section to do your analysis on the companies either mentioned or researched in this book. Please earmark this page for future reference as I will mention it several times when we talk about researching individual companies in the next chapters.

Elliott Wave Theory (EWT)

Elliott Wave Theory (EWT) is a useful technique in deciphering market direction by waves, as described by Avi Gilburt from Elliotwavetrader.net a trading service I highly recommend:

> *Elliott Wave theory understands that public sentiment and mass psychology moves in 5 waves within a primary trend, and 3 waves in a counter-trend. Once a 5 wave move in public sentiment is completed, then it is time for the subconscious sentiment of the public to shift in the opposite direction, which is simply a natural cause of events in the human psyche and not the operative effect from some form of "news."*[308]

[308] https://www.elliottwavetrader.net/elliottwavetheory/

There are, of course, some things such as natural disasters, territorial disputes, wars or black swan events that no investment theory can predict. We can look at cycle theory and speculate that eventually somewhere there will be a future natural disaster or war. Unfortunately, it is inevitable.

Chapter 26 - Investment Categories to Consider (How to Think Outside the Box)

Where Do Your Tax Dollars Go?

There are certain industries that benefit from how the government spends your tax dollars. It makes sense, then, as part of your investment philosophy, to invest in these industries. Why? Because you know they will be funded by the government. Sometimes it's even mandated that they be funded.

In 2015 there were $428,950,903,231 in federal outlays to more than 3.6 million companies. There was also $614,050,292,215 in grants handed out. That's over $1 trillion of your tax dollars that you can follow to the recipient—and possibly profit from, with a little bit of digging.

The largest benefactors of this government spending, making up 49% of the outlay, are the defense and healthcare industries, as outlined in the next graphic.[309]

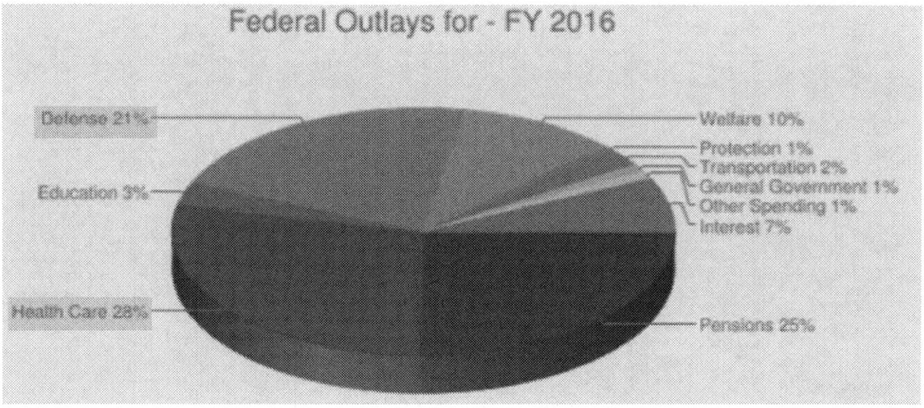

[309] http://www.usgovernmentspending.com/federal_budget

Defense Spending

If the government is warmongering around the world, like sending ships to China or troops on the ground in Syria, as these activities increase, it can benefit the military industrial complex and companies like Lockheed Martin, Boeing, BAE Systems, General Dynamics, and Raytheon.

You can see this graphically by looking at the outflow of money spent by the United States Department of Defense, and the rise of contract spending on military maneuvers in late 2015.[310] It is important to keep an eye on the announcements of these contracts, but when you have a willing buyer for your product, the U.S. government, the companies in the military industrial complex are an easy addition to your portfolio. If conflicts abroad continue to escalate, those receiving contracts from the government should outperform the overall market.

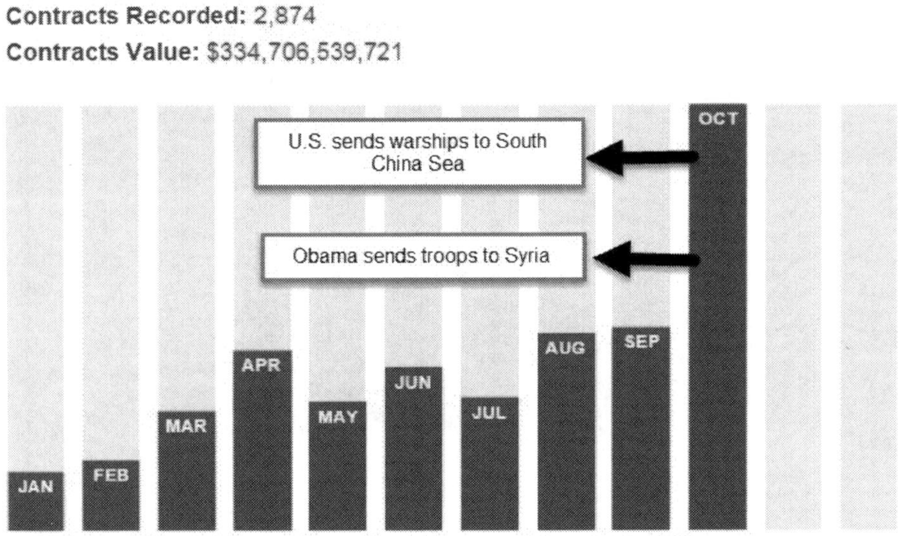

[310] http://www.militaryindustrialcomplex.com/2015-totals.asp

How does this spending by the government help the defense industry? Below you can see how Lockheed Martin, with all its government contracts, has easily beat the returns of the S&P 500 Index. Please also note that the industry in general has outperformed the S&P 500 Index.

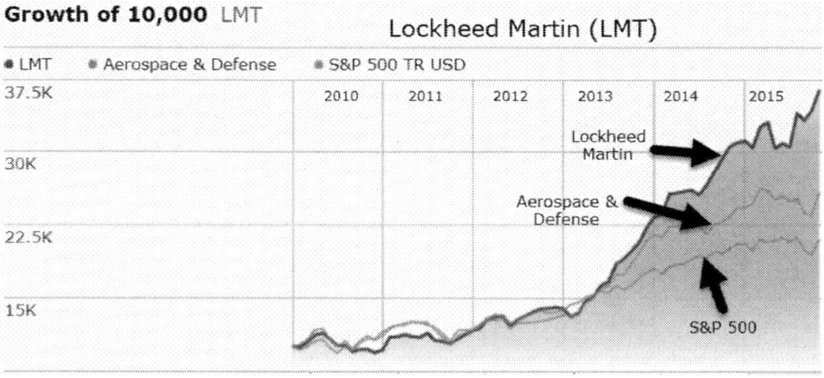

You can view the $7 million worth of contracts awarded to the U.S. Department of Defense each day at the defense.gov website, and use this information to invest accordingly.[311]

Healthcare Spending

Drug and health insurance companies were two of the biggest vendors receiving contracts from the government in 2014, an increase over 2013 of nearly 7%.[312]

[311] http://www.defense.gov/News/Contracts
[312] http://www.healthcarefinancenews.com/news/hhs-spends-215-billion-healthcare-contracts-2014-report-says

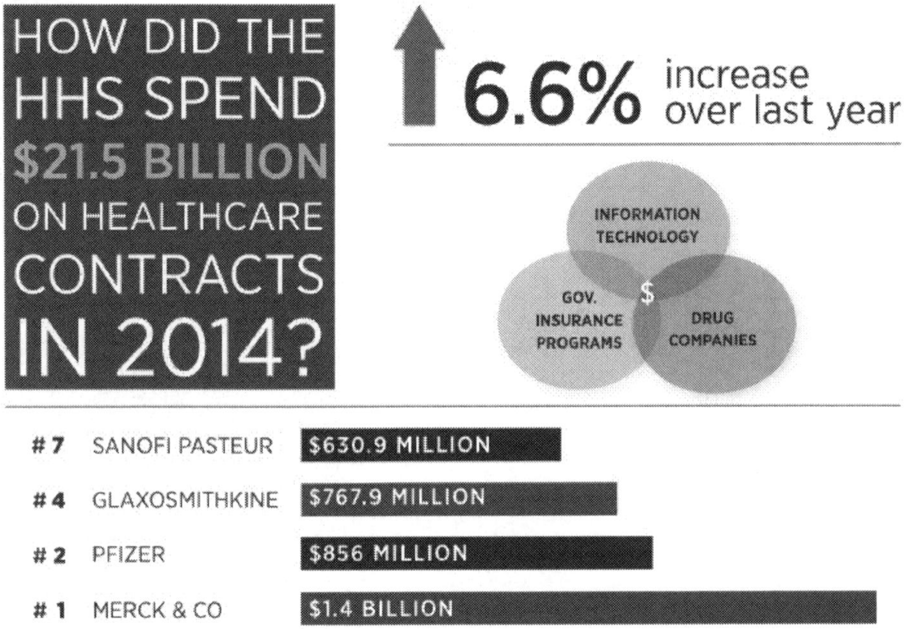

Merck and Pfizer were the top two recipients of these government contracts, and since 2010 we have seen their stocks perform quite well, with Pfizer readily beating the S&P 500. Merck has had problems with a product recall and inquiries, while GlaxoSmithKline's stock crashed in 2013 after allegations of bribery, and is just now beginning to recover.[313]

In 2015 there were 83,069 government contracts, for a total of $19,189,840,555 in government spending. Of these contracts, 672 companies received between $5 million and $500 million, totaling $11,771,259,777, the majority of the expenditures. This information can be found on the USASpending.gov transparency spending map, broken down by company and amount received.[314]

---

313 http://www.wsj.com/articles/SB10001424127887324798904578529413574312372

314 https://www.usaspending.gov/transparency/Pages/Spending

On the insurance provider side, where they were given the Republican influence on Obamacare, mandating purchase of their insurance company products, and where prices in only but a few states are allowed to keep going up, their stocks have done nothing but move higher.

Aetna Inc. (AET) just since 2012 has tripled in value. The same is true of Anthem Inc. (ANTM), Cigna Corporation, (CI) and Health Net, Inc. (HNT), which are considered to be the highest-rated and best-managed healthcare companies according to TheStreet.com.[315] United Health Group, (UNH) decided to pull out of Obamacare because of large losses, so do keep an eye on those accounting ratios and keep your stops.

Energy Spending

Investments in the green revolution and the drive toward clean energy sprouted in 2004, and grew with the election of President Barack Obama. This phenomenon briefly spiked in 2011 before immediately

Map.aspx
[315] http://www.thestreet.com/topic/25901/top-rated-equity-healthcare-providers.html

dropping back down to 2007 and 2008 levels, but is still an industry that receives billions from the government.[316] One could have easily rode that wave higher (and naturally I'm not trying to play Monday morning quarterback here, but say; follow the money incentives based on government policy.

FIGURE 3. GLOBAL TRENDS IN RENEWABLE ENERGY INVESTMENT 2013 DATA TABLE, $BN

Category (Year / Unit)	2004 $bn	2005 $bn	2006 $bn	2007 $bn	2008 $bn	2009 $bn	2010 $bn	2011 $bn	2012 $bn	2013 $bn	2012-13 Growth %	2004-13 CAGR %
4 New Investment by Sector												
4.1 Wind	14.5	25.1	32.1	56.8	69.3	73.0	94.8	85.9	80.9	80.1	-1%	21%
4.2 Solar	12.1	18.3	21.7	38.7	59.5	62.9	100.3	157.8	142.9	113.7	-20%	28%
4.3 Biofuels	3.7	9.2	27.6	29.3	19.2	10.4	8.9	9.4	6.6	4.9	-26%	3%
4.4 Biomass & w-t-e	6.2	8.0	10.6	13.2	14.1	13.6	14.2	15.5	11.1	8.0	-28%	3%
4.5 Small hydro	1.7	4.9	5.4	5.5	7.2	5.4	4.8	6.8	6.0	5.1	-16%	13%
4.6 Geothermal	1.3	1.0	1.4	1.9	1.5	2.7	3.5	3.7	1.8	2.5	38%	8%
4.7 Marine	0.0	0.1	0.9	0.7	0.2	0.3	0.2	0.3	0.2	0.1	-41%	11%
Total	[illegible]	[illegible]	[illegible]	[illegible]	[illegible]	[illegible]	[illegible]	[illegible]	[illegible]	214.4	[illegible]	[illegible]
5 New Investment by Geography												
5.1 United States	5.5	11.7	28.2	33.6	35.9	23.5	34.7	53.4	39.7	35.8	-10%	23%
5.2 Brazil	0.6	2.6	4.8	11.0	12.2	7.8	7.7	9.7	6.8	3.1	-54%	21%
5.3 AMER (excl. US & Brazil)	1.4	3.3	3.2	4.9	5.8	6.1	11.5	8.7	9.9	12.4	26%	27%
5.4 Europe	19.7	29.4	39.1	61.8	73.4	75.3	102.4	114.8	86.4	48.4	-44%	10%
5.5 Middle East & Africa	0.5	0.5	0.9	1.8	2.3	1.4	4.3	3.2	10.4	9.0	-14%	37%
5.6 China	2.4	5.8	10.1	15.8	24.9	37.1	36.7	51.9	59.6	56.3	-6%	42%
5.7 India	2.5	2.9	4.4	6.3	5.4	4.2	8.7	12.6	7.2	6.1	-15%	10%
5.8 ASOC (excl. China & India)	6.8	8.2	9.0	10.9	11.4	12.9	20.7	25.3	29.5	43.3	47%	23%
Total	[illegible]	[illegible]	[illegible]	[illegible]	[illegible]	[illegible]	[illegible]	[illegible]	[illegible]	[illegible]	[illegible]	[illegible]

In 2015, there were 12,784 government contracts worth $25,081,758,621, and just 506 of these companies represented $19,419,804,352 in expenditures.[317] Solar company stocks, for example, did great after these contracts were handed out. This doesn't even include the tax advantages U.S. homeowners who bought green technology received, a financial incentive that drove them to many of these companies to buy solar.

I remember writing a paper in college 30 years ago for a Business Law class, where I had to break down and analyze a company and submit it for my final exam. I chose Archer Daniels Midland (ADM), as my father worked for the investment side of the company. Dwayne Andreas was CEO at the time, and I noticed he did something that didn't really make sense to me then: he gave money to both the Democratic and Republican political parties.

Why would anyone give money to both parties, I thought. Typically, you are affiliated with one party or the other, not both. It was my first

---

[316] http://www.unep.org/pdf/Green_energy_2013-Key_findings.pdf

[317] https://www.usaspending.gov/transparency/Pages/SpendingMap.aspx

lesson in political workings and the relationship of politicians with corporate America. The reason Andreas gave to both parties was to get ethanol subsidies passed so his company, ADM, could benefit, as they produced ethanol from corn and were its largest producer. His political bribes led to the subsequent Clean Air Act, and an eventual move by then-president Clinton to mandate ethanol at the nation's gasoline pumps. To this day, ADM still benefits from these subsidies.[318]

ADM's stock price was $2.50 back then, had multiple stock splits, continually beat the S&P 500 (especially since 2004), and has continually paid an increasing dividend, presently yielding 2.90%, much higher than what one would get on any CD at a bank.[319]

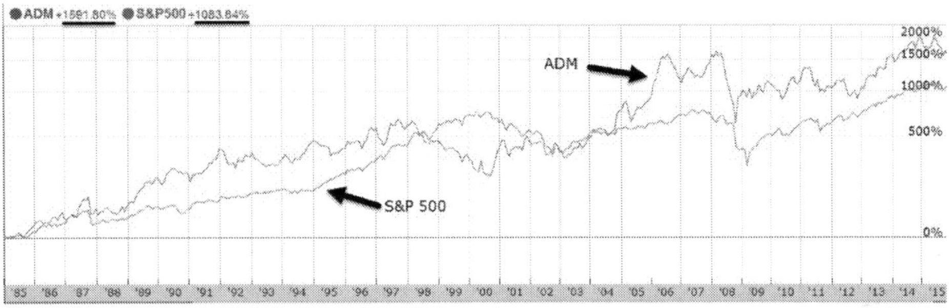

Defense spending, healthcare and energy are the areas to watch for future profit potential, as the government funds those industries, and these companies have easily performed better than the S&P 500. But like any industry, issues can develop that hurt the company stock, or the subsidies once provided by government can be taken away.

Other government stimulus plans when announced can be profited from as well, including past programs like Cash for Clunkers,[320] the

---

318 http://www.cato.org/pubs/pas/pa-241.html

319 http://www.adm.com/en-US/investors/stock_info/_layouts/StockDSHistory.aspx

320 http://www.brookings.edu/~/media/research/files/papers/2013/10/cash-for-clunkers-evaluation-gayer/cash_for_clunkers_evaluation_paper_gayer.pdf

$7,500 first-time homebuyer credit (subsequently increased to $8,000 in 2009 for homes closed by Sept. 2010),[321] and the government program that gave you rebates up to $250 for buying over 56 different new energy-efficient appliances.[322] All of these government handouts benefited particular industries, and you could have profited from the right investments if you'd simply followed the government flow of money.

Bottom line: Know what benefits your government is handing out to help certain industries, as it can enhance your ability to profit. Apply the accounting ratios discussed in the last chapter to the companies receiving the biggest contracts, and invest in the top companies that pass the balance sheet tests. Naturally there will also be some smaller companies benefiting from contracts, and with the right analysis they should outperform the larger companies. Just apply the ratios and compare with their peers. Once you have one contract as a corporation, chances are you'll get more in the future. That is, as long as the government is still functioning naturally.

Consumer Spending - Where Do Consumers Spend Money?

Another investment opportunity that offers investors a way to profit is learning where consumers spend their wealth. The government releases the consumer expenditures report once a year and the next table shows the top categories of consumer spending by year.[323] It's also important to know whether that expenditure is rising or falling, based on current economic conditions. The latest release is from 9/3/2015, as they are very slow with their data, but it is still valuable to see where money flows.[324]

---

[321] https://www.irs.gov/uac/First-Time-Homebuyer-Credit-1
[322] http://abcnews.go.com/Technology/JustOneThing/story?id=8401046
[323] http://www.bls.gov/news.release/pdf/cesan.pdf
[324] http://www.bls.gov/cex/

Item	2012	2013	2014	Percent change 2012-2013	Percent change 2013-2014
Average income before taxes	$65,596	$63,784	$66,877	-2.8	4.8
Average annual expenditures	$51,442	$51,100	$53,495	-0.7	4.7
Food	6,599	6,602	6,759	0.0	2.4
Food at home	3,921	3,977	3,971	1.4	-0.2
Food away from home	2,678	2,625	2,787	-2.0	6.2
Housing	16,887	17,148	17,798	1.5	3.8
Shelter	9,891	10,080	10,491	1.9	4.1
Owned dwellings	6,056	6,108	6,149	0.9	0.7
Rented dwellings	3,186	3,324	3,631	4.3	9.2
Apparel and services	1,736	1,604	1,786	-7.6	11.3
Transportation	8,998	9,004	9,073	0.1	0.8
Gasoline and motor oil	2,756	2,611	2,468	-5.3	-5.5
Vehicle insurance	1,018	1,013	1,112	-0.5	9.8
Healthcare	3,556	3,631	4,290	2.1	n/a
Health insurance	2,061	2,229	2,868	8.2	n/a
Entertainment	2,605	2,482	2,728	-4.7	9.9
Cash contributions	1,913	1,834	1,788	-4.1	-2.5
Personal insurance and pensions	5,591	5,528	5,726	-1.1	3.6
All other expenditures	3,557	3,267	3,548	-8.2	8.6

n/a - Because of the questionnaire change for health insurance, the 2013-14 percent change is not strictly comparable to prior years.

In good times, eating away from home, apparel and services, entertainment, and vehicle insurance are industries that do well. But in bad times, these industries will more than likely suffer the most. Is this a difficult thing to do… adjust your portfolio accordingly? Can you ask your local restaurants how business is, or just observe for yourself how many tables are filled at dinnertime? One of the first signs of a weakening economy is that discretionary spending is reduced.

The following chart shows where money was mostly spent in 2015.[325]

[325] http://www.zerohedge.com/news/2016-03-25/thanks-obamacare-what-americans-spent-most-money-2015

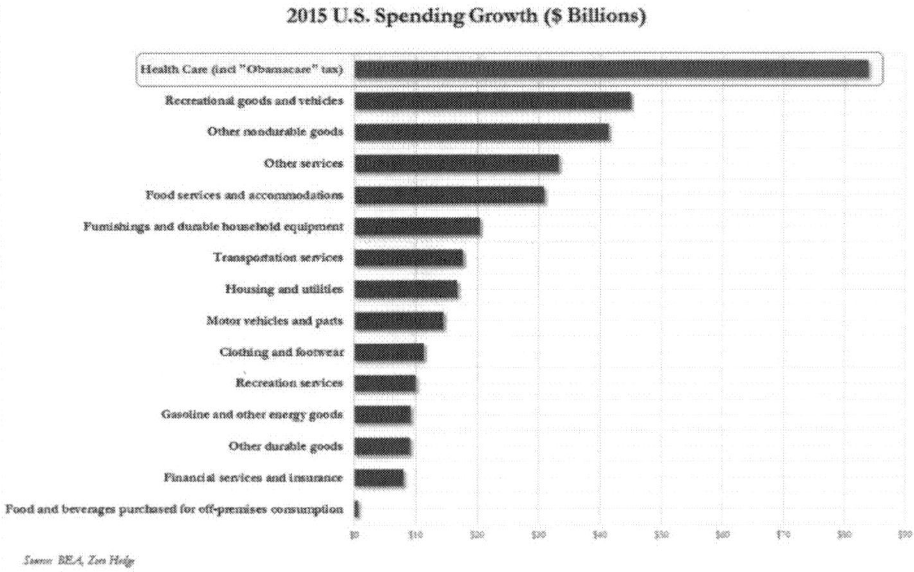

The United States Is Number One

There is more wealth in the United States than anywhere in the world.[326] One thing an investor has to consider is where this wealth flows, as collectively it will move markets up or down. When the markets are moving higher, almost any stock investment will do fine, as will real estate.

The 30 Largest Countries by Net National Wealth (in billions USD)

Rank	Country	2000	Country	2005	Country	2010	Country	2015
	World	117,225	*World*	171,577	*World*	216,374	*World*	250,145
1	United States	42,941	United States	59,664	United States	57,114	United States	85,901
2	Japan	19,316	Japan	18,143	Japan	23,474	China	22,817
3	United Kingdom	7,184	United Kingdom	11,026	China	17,505	Japan	19,837
4	Germany	5,800	France	9,537	France	13,441	United Kingdom	15,601
5	Italy	5,497	Italy	9,054	Germany	12,303	France	12,697
6	China	4,664	Germany	8,970	United Kingdom	11,827	Germany	11,939
7	France	4,566	China	8,674	Italy	11,619	Italy	10,025

326 https://en.wikipedia.org/wiki/National_wealth

But at this point in time, you must also consider that these billionaires and millionaires may decide to remove wealth from certain asset classes. What effect would this have on those investments? Let's take a look at a few places where money will flow to in the future.

China – On the Cusp

One area is China, but they have a few problems to fix in their shadow banking system before I would get too excited. Few realize that China has overtaken the U.S. in the number of billionaires. Is this really a surprise, since all of our U.S.-domiciled corporations operations went overseas to take advantage of the cheap labor and lack of regulation?[327]

Because the U.S. has sided with being more concerned about the safety of products and the environment, many industries went to where there was a lack of regulation, like China, which has amassed an unbelievable amount of wealth, but also has air pollution issues. While I do see the Chinese banking system causing a future crisis similar to the 2009 beat down in the U.S., once this occurs, and with a little more implementation of corporate citizenship, this would be a golden opportunity to buy some beaten-down, dividend-paying Chinese stocks.

On that list would be:

CHL: China Mobile
CHU: China Unicom
SNP: China Petroleum & Chemical
CEO: CNOOC Offshore Oil and Natural Gas
DSWL: Deswell Industries
PTR: PetroChina

China's merger and acquisition activity is exploding at present. Some may call this a bubble in the making and we'll have to wait and see,

---

[327] http://www.thefiscaltimes.com/2015/10/18/US-No-Longer-Leads-World-Billionaires

but many are getting wealthy in the meantime. Industries benefiting from this growth can be found in the chart below.[328]

But I must warn again that the credit expansion in China seems to be reaching a top, according to Rachel Morajee from Reuters. To summarize her thoughts from March 29, 2016, there was $540 billion in new loans for January and February 2016 and it's not reaching nimbler private companies, which represent 80% of the jobs in China's cities and 60% of GDP. In other words, yes, the wealthy are reaping the benefits and the small-fry companies will be hit the hardest when everything implodes.[329]

Other countries worth looking into for investment growth potential are listed in the next table.[330] The most important data to me is the quarterly

---

[328] http://www.wsj.com/articles/china-is-on-an-overseas-buying-spree-1458042732

[329] http://www.breakingviews.com/chinas-credit-hose-leaves-many-firms-parched/ 21240894.article

growth and low debt-to-GDP ratio. A government whose budget is under control is attractive. Quarterly growth improving month over month is a good sign. Growth greater than 4% is a better sign.

COUNTRIES ▼	GDP	GDP YoY	GDP QoQ	Interest rate	Inflation rate	Jobless rate	Gov. Budget	Debt/GDP
India	2067	7.00%	1.60%	6.75%	4.41%	4.90%	-4.50%	66.10%
China	10360	6.90%	1.80%	4.35%	1.60%	4.05%	-2.10%	41.06%
Ireland	246	6.70%	1.90%	0.05%	-0.30%	9.30%	-4.10%	109.70%
Philippines	285	5.60%	1.80%	4.00%	0.40%	6.50%	-0.60%	45.40%
Malaysia	327	4.90%	1.10%	3.25%	2.60%	3.20%	-3.50%	52.80%
Indonesia	889	4.73%	3.21%	7.50%	6.25%	5.81%	-2.25%	25.02%
United Arab Emirate	402	4.60%	4.60%	1.00%	4.30%	4.20%	5.00%	15.68%
Pakistan	247	4.14%	4.14%	6.00%	1.61%	6.00%	-5.00%	64.30%
Turkey	800	3.80%	1.30%	7.50%	7.58%	9.80%	-1.30%	33.00%
Saudi Arabia	746	3.80%	3.80%	2.00%	2.30%	5.70%	-2.30%	1.60%
Spain	1404	3.40%	0.80%	0.05%	-0.70%	21.18%	-5.80%	97.70%
Sweden	571	3.30%	1.10%	-0.35%	0.10%	6.70%	-1.90%	43.90%
Poland	548	3.30%	0.90%	1.50%	-0.80%	9.60%	-3.20%	50.10%
Colombia	378	3.00%	0.60%	5.25%	5.89%	9.00%	-2.40%	38.00%
Egypt	287	3.00%	4.30%	8.75%	9.20%	12.70%	-11.50%	90.50%
Thailand	374	2.80%	0.40%	1.50%	-0.77%	0.80%	-2.50%	45.70%
Hong Kong	291	2.80%	0.40%	0.50%	2.00%	3.30%	2.80%	32.00%
South Korea	1410	2.60%	1.20%	1.50%	0.90%	3.50%	-1.80%	35.98%
Mexico	1283	2.40%	0.60%	3.00%	2.52%	4.50%	-4.00%	30.70%
Nigeria	569	2.35%	2.57%	13.00%	9.40%	8.20%	0.10%	10.50%
United Kingdom	2942	2.30%	0.50%	0.50%	-0.10%	5.40%	-5.70%	89.40%
Argentina	540	2.30%	0.50%	21.00%	14.50%	6.60%	-2.50%	43.00%
Norway	500	2.20%	-0.10%	0.75%	2.10%	4.60%	9.10%	28.40%
Israel	304	2.14%	0.07%	0.10%	-0.50%	5.10%	-2.80%	67.50%
United States	17419	2.00%	1.50%	0.25%	0.00%	5.00%	-2.50%	102.98%

Countries to Avoid

If these countries weren't performing well during the good years, more than likely they will underperform in the down years that are forthcoming, especially if they have a high Debt to GDP ratio or have some sort of political strife. Also, keep an eye on their jobless rate and inflation rate.

---

330 http://www.tradingeconomics.com/

COUNTRIES	GDP	GDP YoY	GDP QoQ	Interest rate	Inflation rate	Jobless rate	Gov. Budget	Debt/GDP
Russia	1861	-4.30%	-2.01%	11.00%	15.60%	5.20%	-0.50%	17.92%
Venezuela	510	-4.00%	6.80%	20.89%	[illegible]	7.90%	-11.50%	49.80%
Brazil	2346	-2.60%	-1.90%	14.25%	9.93%	7.60%	-0.60%	58.91%
Iraq	221	-2.40%		6.00%	2.10%	16.00%	-2.69%	37.02%
Taiwan	489	-1.01%	0.05%	1.75%	0.31%	3.79%	-2.10%	36.50%
Finland	271	0.10%	0.20%	0.05%	-0.60%	8.40%	-3.30%	59.30%
Iran	415	0.60%		21.00%	11.17%	10.80%	-2.58%	16.36%
Italy	2144	0.70%	0.30%	0.05%	0.30%	11.80%	-3.00%	132.30%
Japan	4601	0.80%	-0.30%	0.00%	0.00%	3.40%	-7.70%	230.00%
Canada	1787	1.00%	-0.10%	0.50%	1.00%	7.00%	-0.30%	86.51%
Austria	436	1.00%	0.30%	0.05%	0.70%	8.70%	-2.40%	84.50%
France	2829	1.08%	0.00%	0.05%	0.00%	10.30%	-4.00%	95.00%
Switzerland	685	1.20%	0.20%	-0.75%	-1.40%	3.20%	-0.10%	34.20%
South Africa	350	1.20%	-1.30%	6.00%	4.60%	25.50%	-3.80%	39.00%
Belgium	533	1.30%	0.20%	0.05%	1.28%	8.70%	-3.20%	106.50%
Singapore	308	1.40%	0.10%	0.21%	-0.60%	2.00%	-0.13%	99.30%
Euro Area	13403	1.50%	0.40%	0.05%	0.00%	10.80%	-2.40%	91.90%
Portugal	230	1.50%	0.40%	0.05%	0.90%	11.90%	-7.20%	130.20%
Germany	3853	1.60%	0.40%	0.05%	0.30%	4.50%	0.70%	74.70%
Greece	238	1.70%	0.90%	0.05%	-1.70%	24.99%	-3.50%	177.10%

If we do enter a worldwide recession, however, cash will be king, and you'll just have to be patient for the right buying opportunity.

Chapter 27 - Most Popular Investment Alternatives

Index Funds

I'm listing index funds before mutual funds, which are more popular with investors, because as we discussed in Chapter 19, they are a better choice than managed mutual funds and hedge funds. This is partly because of lower fees and for the simple fact that fund managers have proven time and again that they are not good at beating the market indices.

We pointed out that in 2015, 75% of large-cap core mutual funds lagged the benchmark index. Investors are waking up to this fact, and increasingly shifting their assets to index funds, as the next chart shows.

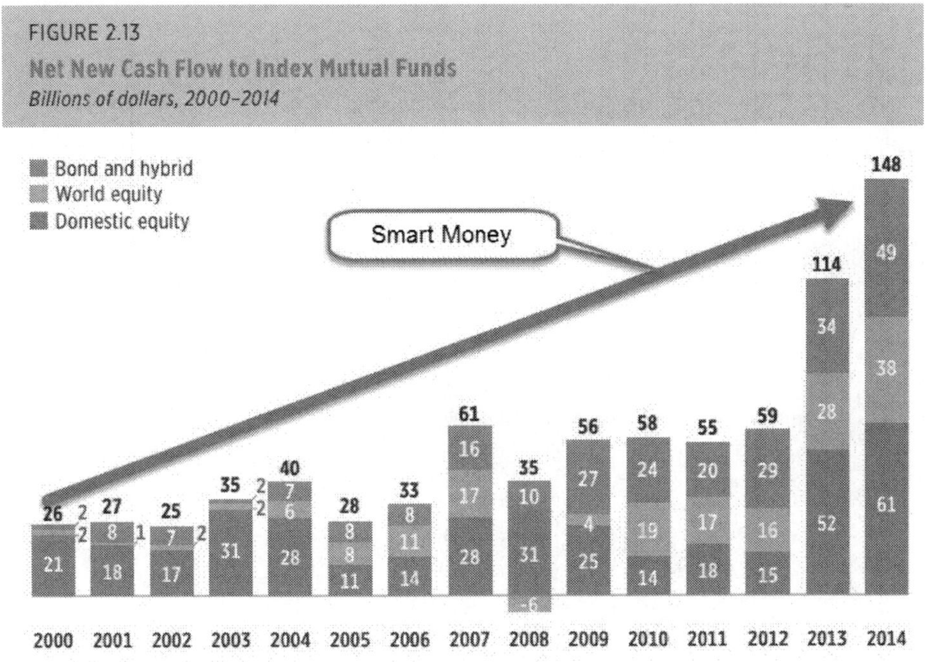

You can see that the small number of billions invested in index funds pales in comparison to the entire $16 trillion in all mutual funds. This is mostly because mutual funds are sold by financial advisors who collect a nice commission, as they receive trips and other perks from the mutual fund companies that sell these funds. How do I know? Because I went on trips to Ireland and cruises to Alaska, and stayed at 5-star resorts domestically back when I used to sell their products. I was wined and dined and entertained at broker conferences by mutual fund sales executives who had virtually unlimited expense accounts to induce you to sell their products over other fund managers' products. The more you sold their products, the higher the value of the perks. This still goes on today.

The fees are higher for these equity funds for a reason: It's all part of the plan in getting a broker to recommend their mutual fund. It's a little game that brokers play to win trips, and now you are aware of it and can call them out by asking the right questions as outlined in Chapter 18. Tell your broker you want a no-load index fund. They probably won't like it.

Expense ratios are simply much less on index equity and bond funds than actively managed funds. That's more money in your pocket, as discussed in Chapter 19.

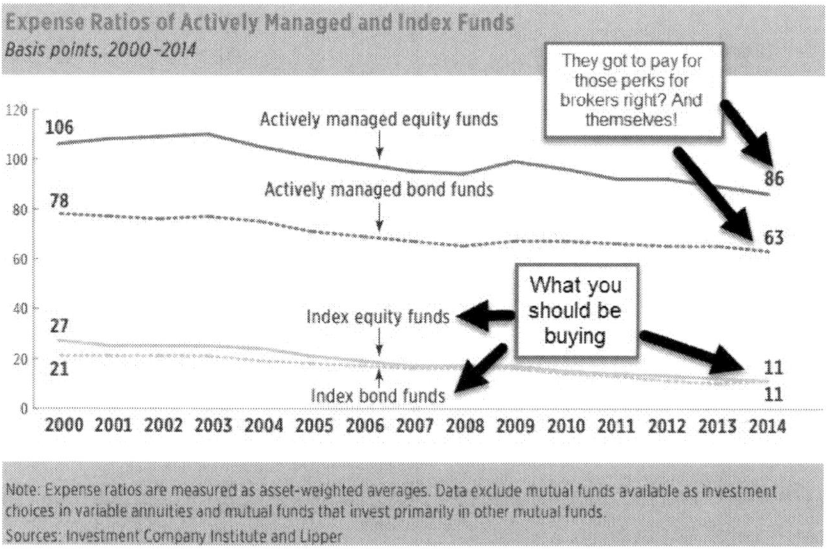

Investing Like Warren Buffett

In 2012, *Time* magazine named Warren Buffett one of the most influential people in the world.[331] He is referenced often to this day on CNBC as an expert on investing, and is well respected in the financial services industry. Granted, his performance before 2011 was unrivaled, but the same can't be said for the time since. The Vanguard S&P 500 Index Fund (VXINX) has outperformed Buffett's Berkshire Hathaway Inc. (BRK-A) since January of 2011, some of the best years for the stock market.

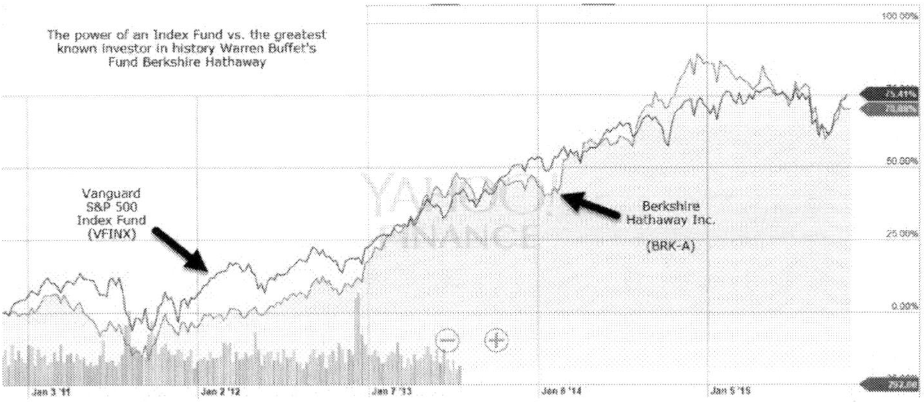

It should be noted here that even Warren Buffett's fund lost big from Dec. 2007 to February 2009, just like most other assets—hence this book, to buoy your portfolio should we see any future problems with the markets, which I believe I have shown the potential to occur.

Dividend-Paying Stocks

One sign of a healthy company is when they are paying dividends to the investor. Dividends used to represent 60% of the total return for stock investments. We have heard for decades that stock returns average 10% over time, and while this was true. That 10% was divided

---

331 http://content.time.com/time/specials/packages/article/0,28804, 2111975_2111 976_21 1 2 005,00 .html

as follows: 4% growth and 6% dividend = 10% total. Today we have an average 2.31% dividend, and that means if we were to average 10% total return we would have to get 7.69% of that return from growth. That's just not happening, nor will it happen anytime soon.

There are still some companies out there that continue to pay a good dividend. There may be an opportunity for some of these dividend-paying companies to pay you an income that can keep pace with inflation. Yes, the Net Asset Value (NAV) value may get hit on a market downturn, but income will be a difficult thing to come by in the years ahead, as you'll be limited to many asset classes that will be hurt by a market downturn (stocks and bonds alike) or lag real rates like CDs and annuities will do.

This has been tracked since 1979 by Credit Suisse, and is illustrated in the following graph and commentary from Thornburg Securities.[332] Deciles 8 and 9 were higher yielding.

> *Credit Suisse produces a report annually that demonstrates the performance impact of companies based on dividend yields. For the 35 years ended December 2014, figure 2 shows that when the S&P 500 Index is divided into deciles based on dividend yield, the highest yielding deciles outperformed the index, and the lowest yielding deciles underperformed. Chasing the highest yield is not a good strategy—notice how deciles 8 and 9 are the sweet spot for savvy investors.*

[332] http://www.thornburg.com/pdf/TH2059_MoreToDividends.pdf

Figure 2 | Longer-Term, Higher-Yield Stocks Have Significantly Outperformed
S&P 500 Index Stocks Ranked by Yield (Equal-Weighted Decile Performance)
Returns from a Hypothetical $100 Invested on 12/31/79

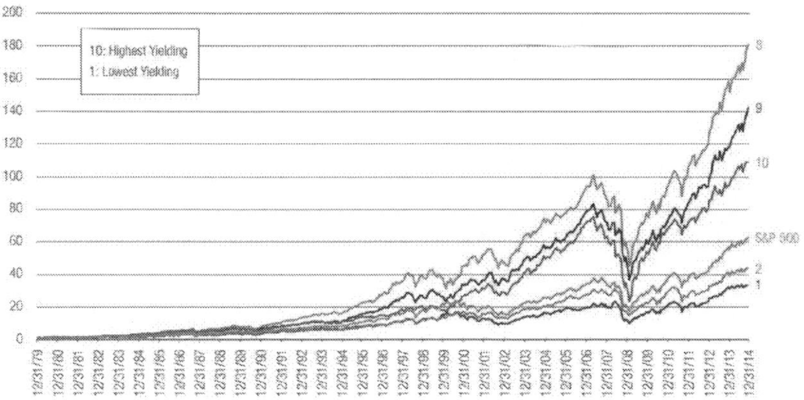

Source: Credit Suisse

Mutual Funds

There were almost $16 trillion invested in mutual funds in the U.S. as of the end of 2014. By the end of 2015, and into 2016 it's about the same.

Total Net Assets Mutual Fund Industry	Long-term funds							
		Equity			Bond		Money market funds	
Year	Total	Domestic	World	Hybrid	Taxable	Municipal	Taxable	Tax-exempt
2014	15,852.34	6,234.99	2,079.33	1,351.84	2,894.45	566.48	2,464.47	260.79

We've already shown that most mutual fund managers can't beat the indices, and yet these funds are pushed on investors by financial advisors who make commissions or fees. The key to investing in mutual funds, outside of the index funds is to find managers who have been with the fund longer than three years and have a good track record of outperforming other funds in the same sector. Morningstar.com is a good source to compare funds, and your financial advisor should be able to provide you with data sheets to analyze.

There are many different types of mutual funds that represent all aspects of the market, from large-cap to mid-cap to small-cap stocks, all the way down to the most risky pink-sheet stocks—which I don't recommend investors waste their money on unless they really know what they are doing and can weather the illiquidity. No matter what diversification a hybrid mutual fund may offer, you are still most likely better off simply finding an index of that asset class and holding it, rather than going with an actively managed fund. There are rare exceptions, and again, Morningstar is a good guide to identifying them. But take a closer look at what that fund invests in, use your accounting ratios, and make a decision on whether or not you can create your own mutual fund of stocks that can outperform those funds. I think you can, with a little research.

Inverse Funds

I do want to mention some funds I like, based upon the research you have seen in this book that shows signs of trouble ahead. There are inverse funds that will move higher if the markets move lower. These funds have been dogs from the 2009 crisis through 2015, but can pick up steam. Since I do lean more bearish, look at ProFunds short NASDAQ-100 Inv Fund (SOPIX) or the Rydex Inverse S&P 500 2X Inverse Strategy A Fund (RYTMX).

These bear market funds can short certain asset classes or even countries. For example, if you wanted to short China, you could put some money in ProFunds UltraShort China Inv (UHPIX). From December 2015 through February 2016, it returned 14.75%. The ProFunds UltraShort Japan Inv (UKPSX) returned 30.96% in that same timeframe.

You can find a list of many more bear market funds and compare their holdings with what you have learned in this book by going to this link from Morningstar.com: http://news.morningstar.com/fund-category-returns/bear-market/$FOCA$BM.aspx

Bonds

Bonds represent $3.46 trillion of total mutual fund assets, and these funds are subject to interest rate risk. When interest rates begin to move higher, these mutual funds' NAV will decline, whether by market loss or withdrawal, as investors rush to exit.

Holders of individual bonds have a specified coupon rate and will fulfill that bond payment until maturity, while mutual fund managers do not have the luxury of fulfillment when investors are pulling their money out all at the same time. Bonds will have to be sold at a loss. Naturally holders of individual bonds who need to raise cash prior to maturity in a rising interest rate market will incur losses too. There really isn't much of a bright side to bonds when interest rates take off higher.

Story after story came out in 2013 about the slaughter of bonds. Billions were lost in a short amount of time with just the threat of tapering the Fed's quantitative easing program by then-Fed chairman Ben Bernanke. Interest rates did, however, continue to fall after markets normalized. But what do you think will happen with these bonds, especially the high-yield bonds, which are now in 2016 in even more of a bubble?

The chart below represents the effective yield of the Bank of America Merrill Lynch U.S. High-Yield Master II Index,[333] which tracks the performance of U.S. dollar-denominated, below-investment-grade-rated corporate debt publicly issued in the U.S. domestic market. Many of you own this debt without being aware of it.

---

[333] https://research.stlouisfed.org/fred2/series/BAMLHYH0A0HYM2TRIV

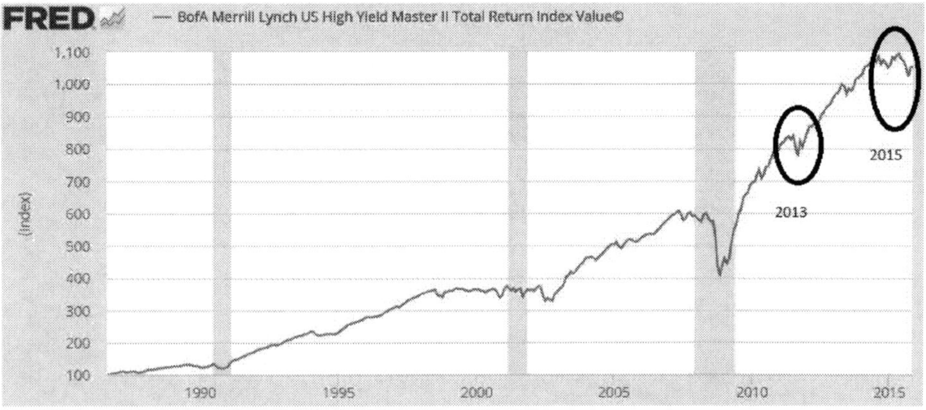

In December 2015, we saw just the tip of the iceberg when Third Avenue Management closed its $789 million Third Avenue Focused Credit Fund and told shareholders they were freezing redemptions to prevent forced liquidation of current holdings at a loss.[334]

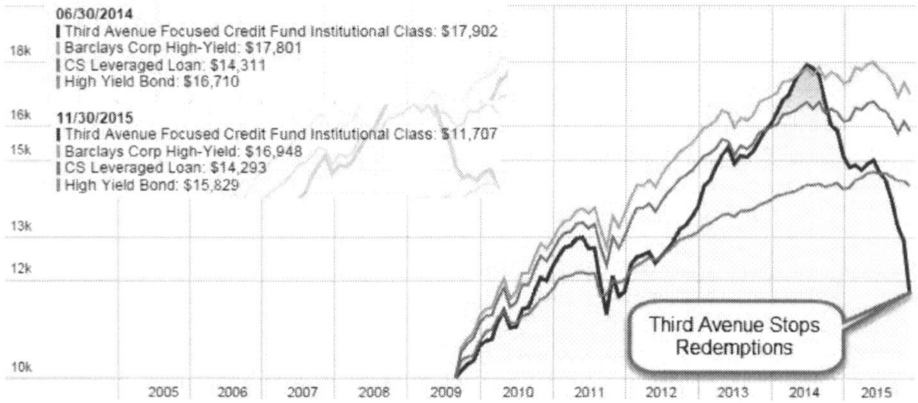

How liquid are the investments in the funds you hold? Have you asked your broker? Are you clear on what a mass exit of your funds would do to your returns? Early investors redeeming shares can get their money back, but sooner or later the fund manager will have to dip into

334 https://fundresearch.fidelity.com/mutual-funds/performance-and-risk/884116708

bonds that are illiquid or have to be sold at big losses. To "protect" the investor, the fund closes down and liquidates the fund incrementally over time to try and keep losses at a minimum.[335]

The Municipal Bond Insurance Association (MBIA), which rates municipal bonds, seems to still be on the hook for future problems after a disastrous 2005, when it had to restate seven years of earnings and defend its relationship with bond issuers (and what those issuers pay MBIA for the ratings they receive). By 2008, MBIA had its own rating decreased by Fitch, Moody's and S&P, and in 2015 this is what Moody's had to say about MBIA:[336]

> *The B2 IFS rating of MBIA Corp., with negative outlook, reflects the company's weak capitalization relative to its remaining insured exposures, and its modest liquidity position.*

I know many seniors like municipal bond funds and some city bonds that are rated highly by MBIA, because of their tax-free nature. But if MBIA itself is under pressure financially, it may cut corners to get more funds (payments for its services) from those it rates. These seniors will be in for a surprise either way if they hold their money in even the AAA-rated funds.

As an example, Fidelity's Intermediate Municipal Income Fund (FLTMX), with Bernanke's threat of taper and higher interest rates in May 2013, lost 4.49% in just four months. Would it make sense to go to cash with the first uptick you see in interest rates, rather than lose principal just for the benefit of tax-free income that you receive? Remember, we are at historic lows for interest rates.

---

335 http://thirdave.com/wp-content/uploads/2015/12/FCF-Shareholder-Letter-12-2015.pdf

336 https://www.moodys.com/research/Moodys-affirms-B2-IFS-rating-of-MBIA-Insurance-Corporation-changes--PR_319760

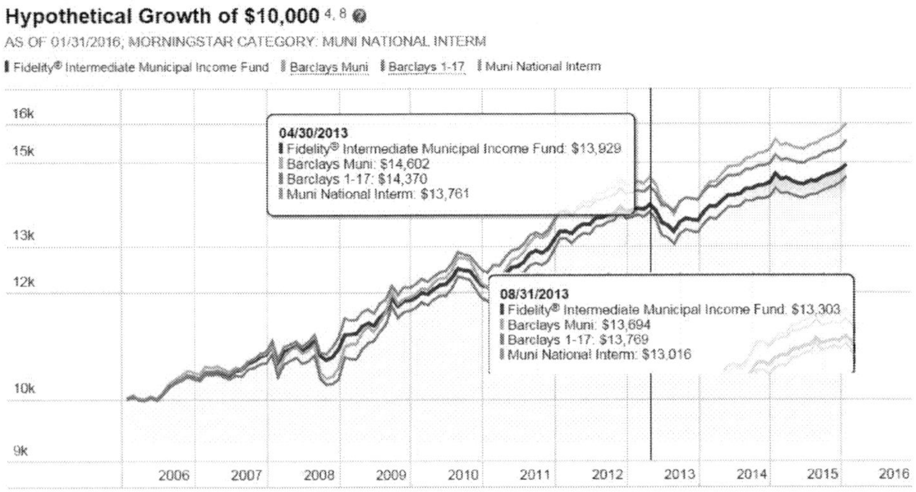

When rates rise, bond mutual funds lose principal. One of the largest bond funds, Pimco Total Return Fund, saw an outflow of $18.4 billion in 2013, when interest rates were heading higher in May, June and July. It was the biggest three-month outflow since Morningstar began tracking the fund in 1993.[337]

Imagine for a moment that interest rates were double what they were today. What effect would this rise in rates have on the economy and markets? It wouldn't be pretty. We've come a long way from the 1970s' high-interest-rate era to the record low rates today. Moving forward, the extra income you get from higher interest paid on the bond won't be enough to make up for the decline in your NAV (principal).

Certificates of Deposit (CDs) and Money Market Funds

CDs and money market funds are places to keep liquid cash and for now don't pay much interest. The rate of return will increase as rates rise with no real downside risk, although with money market funds

[337] http://www.reuters.com/article/us-investing-fundflows-pimco-idUSBRE9710WS20130802

there is always the threat of negative interest rates, where the value of the fund could fall below $1. Bankrate.com has a listing of the nation's top-paying CDs and money market funds.[338] For bank CDs, you can also use the site to compare the ratings of each financial institution and pick one you are comfortable with.[339]

[338] http://www.bankrate.com/

[339] http://www.bankrate.com/funnel/savings/savings-results.aspx

Chapter 28 - Exchange-Traded Funds (ETFs) and Exchange-Traded Notes (ETNs)

ETFs and ETNs have become one of the most popular ways to invest, similar to index funds, because of their low fees and liquidity. But not all ETFs and ETNs are built the same, and not all have the liquidity you would want in an investment. Many actually deteriorate over time, so be careful in choosing ETFs for long-term holds. They do, however, work great for day trading and swing trading, especially the leveraged ETFs that can give you 2 to 3 times the normal return.

For simplicity in my analysis below, I will use "ETF" to also include ETNs so I don't have to say "ETFs and ETNs" every time I mention them.

ETFs and ETNs Defined[340]

ETF: Security that tracks an underlying asset, like commodities, indices (including country-specific indices) or bonds.

ETN: Senior unsecured debt obligation: open-ended securities that track exactly the performance of their underlying market benchmark, whether it be commodities or indexes.

Typically when you buy an ETF, you get to invest in either the bullish side of the underlying asset or the bearish side, similar to the inverse funds we just discussed. For either investment, you want the value of the ETF to move higher. Unlike shorting a stock and hoping the value falls, when investing in an inverse ETF, you will see it move higher as the underlying assets go lower in price.

All in all, ETFs provide a good way to diversify and manage your own portfolio at a low cost. For some, though, an index fund would be more apropos on the long side and an inverse fund on the short side, but having the ability to buy an inverse ETF when the market is

---

[340] https://www.nyse.com/products/etp-funds-etn

tanking is a simple, inexpensive and potentially profitable way to hedge your long portfolio. In other words, there are no big fees paid to advisors, just a small fee.

But buying an ETF is not the same as buying the physical asset. For example, when you purchase the ETF iShares Silver Trust (SLV), you are not buying actual silver that you can take delivery of. You are buying a paper proxy, or shares that say you have ownership of the silver. The custodian of SLV is the only one who can redeem shares to authorized dealers, and the silver you think you own is not even insured. Also, anything run by banks as custodians—in this case, JPMorgan Chase—I suggest a little caution when buying.[341]

Rules for Trading ETFs

The first rule for buying ETFs is to make sure there is plenty of liquidity. Typically you want the average volume to be 1 million shares or greater. It's ok to trade smaller volume ETFs but just know that if you were to keep a position overnight while swing trading it, which is typically a few day trade, and some news comes out the pre and post market may not have the volume you want to exit the trade at a competitive price.

It's easy to get caught in these ETFs and see that they are hitting 52 week lows and speculate the bottom is in because the price is so low, only to have the ETF do a reverse split. Most stocks split when they have been doing well and the price is going higher and higher. The split causes the stock to lower the price and make it more affordable to investors. The reverse split is the opposite. Since these ETFs can't go to zero, they simply exchange 1 share at say $2 and make it $20 by doing a 1:10 reverse split. Your investment amount in the ETF hasn't changed, just the amount of shares you own. If you had 1000 shares before at $2 a share or $2,000 with a 1:10 reverse split you would have 100 shares of a $20 ETF worth $2,000, The reverse split is typically a

[341] https://www.ishares.com/us/literature/prospectus/p-ishares-silver-trust-prospectus-12-31.pdf

sign of weakness which means the opposite of that ETF is probably doing quite well (the trend) and what you should be trading long.

For leveraged ETFs there is time decay and sometimes contagion to worry about and you need to keep the trades for shorter timeframes. Leveraged ETFs also have extreme volatility and are not for new or even for some seasoned traders. It does make sense to paper trade these and get used to them before doing any actually investing with your own money. Also for leveraged ETFs you don't want to double down on your losses. It's investment suicide and you will lose most of your money if you do. You'll read more about leveraged ETFs shortly.

Diversified and Professionally Managed ETF Portfolios

For the portion of your portfolio where you wish to take advantage of up and down markets and investing in various market sectors, other countries, and certain commodities, some specialists take a fee-only approach. This type of advisor might be able to proactively help you manage your portfolio to take advantage of market conditions in other countries, or by riding the trend of certain sectors, such as commodities.

My Favorite ETF Portfolio Moving Forward

An allocation into a basket of non-leveraged commodity sector ETFs would look something like this, with an equal allocation of GLD, SLV, GDX, USO and UNG (pricing and percentages as of November 5, 2015). As you can see, they are all commodities that have been beaten down and have the propensity to move higher once the velocity of money comes into play.

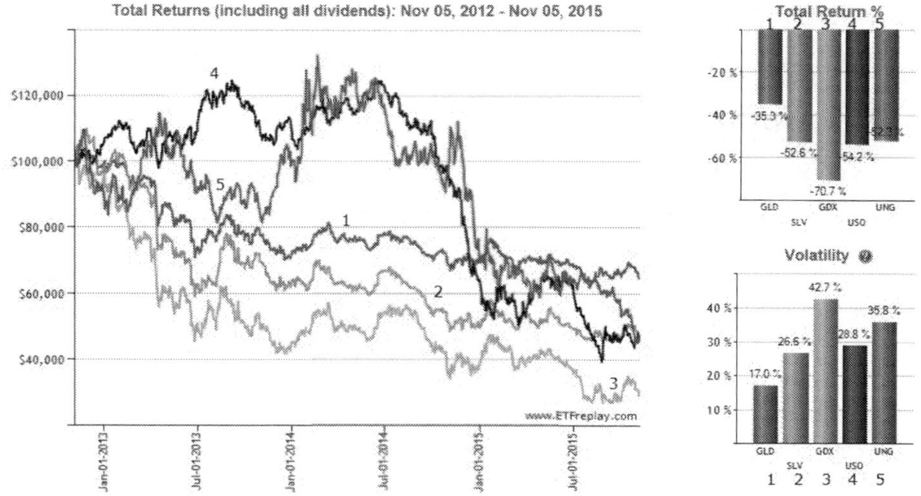

Leveraged ETFs and ETNs

Because of the way these trading vehicles are created, they do not represent the complete opposite of each other, however. In fact, over time, both ETFs can possibly lose you money, like the Direxion Daily Junior Gold Miners Index Bull 3x Shares (JNUG) and the Direxion Daily Junior Gold Miners Index Bear 3X Shares (JDST) seen in the graphic below.[342] One shows a loss of 79.73% (bull case) and opposite you would think should be up by that percentage, but was actually down 79.07%. This is why for leveraged ETFs and because of the deterioration over time I only recommend you day or swing trade these for a short period of time moving stops up.

---

342 http://www.nasdaq.com/etfs/etf-comparison.aspx

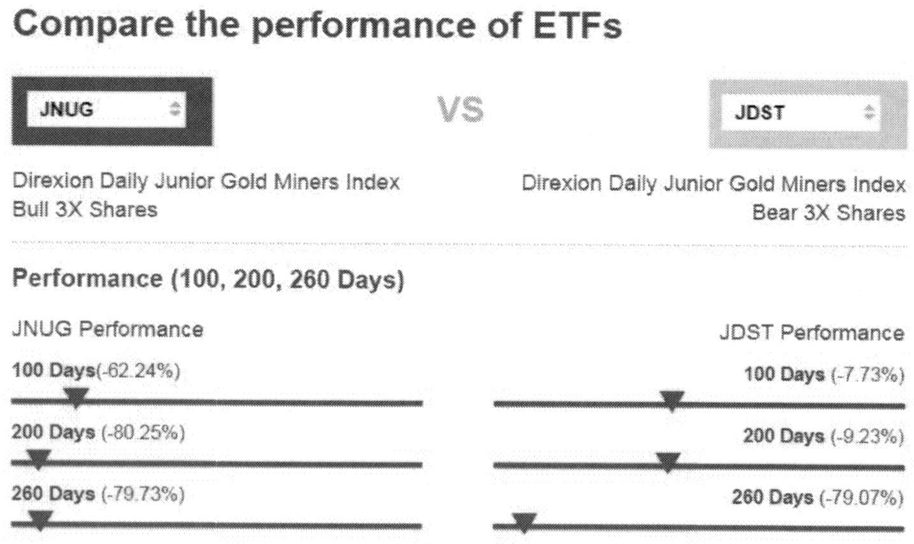

A Way to Make Money Regardless of What the Market is Doing.
rg78501•Jan 24 8:02 PM

I consider myself one of the few experts out there on trading leveraged ETFs, and because I wanted to share my expertise with other investors, I started my own ETF Leveraged Trading Service. You can read more about it at www.illusionsofwealth.com/etfservice.

The service is geared to swing traders who will hold the trade for a few days, weeks or months. I consider this the new type of trading for those who want more control of their wealth and look to profit in a shorter timeframe. Investors can do this one day if they choose where the returns at times are 10% to 30%. I do have subscribers who do this full time, and the results have been very good, as these reviews of the service show.[343]

[343] http://seekingalpha.com/author/doug-eberhardt/research/reviews

Very Strong!

gherring•Nov 08 9:51 AM

Doug provides a very strong service and I would highly recommend it for the niche that it is designed to fill. He is very much on top of the changes in these fast moving ETFs and is very quick to respond to client questions. A winner on all counts!

Financially Rewarding Service

Kenlorne•Dec 07 8:52 AM

I began using Doug Eberhardt's ETF Research Trading Analysis service in April of this year before he brought the service over to Seeking Alpha. Up until a couple of years ago, I was a buy and hold investor, but the loss of bond earnings took away my ability to balance my portfolio. Most of my trades have been less than $20,000, but none have exceeded $30,000 in total funds traded at any one time. During that time, I have earned almost $23,000 net of commissions and stop losses. Most of that has been in the last couple of months.

Solid and Honest Advice

augeor•Jan 12 8:54 AM

Doug provides expert analysis in this irrational market. Doug helps his clients capitalize on trends while also reducing risk. His wit and sense of humor also help make this service fun for me. The trading rules are requiring me to change a number of bad behaviors I've had in investing and old habits do die hard, but the more I follow them, the greater my success is. This is a great service for anyone that has the self-discipline to follow Doug's rules. My recommendation is to follow a few pairs of contrasting ETFs (e.g., DWTI/UWTI, DGAZ/UGAZ, JNUG/JDST) and get good at these. Find some pairs you like and their success can lead to broadening the ones you want should you choose to.

Prescience approaching clairvoyance

Musiclover59•Jan 23 9:32 PM

This service assumes the subscriber possesses a certain knowledge of trading mechanics and financial markets, as well as emotional control. Given these, the subscriber can make consistent, large profits regardless of whether the market is up or down by following Doug's trading rules and making the swing trades he recommends. He provides astute analysis of the markets from both a micro and macro point of view. Of course, as a human being, he occasionally makes mistakes. To his credit, he doesn't marry any one point of view or trade, but adjusts fire quickly in the event that the price action proves his thesis wrong. Bottom line: Highly recommended, but you must follow his trading rules and pay close attention to his daily comments.

Doug gives prices to look for and information that can determine which way the ETFs could go. He lets us know what happened overnight that could change the day's trades. When I first joined (at the end of this week, I will be in his service for two months), my goal was to make a modest $800 to $1,000 each month. My hope was to make the $1,000 and come out of the year ahead by $12,000. With still one week to go to complete my first two months, I have profited more than $3,263. I have exceeded my highest hopes.

With this type of trading, we don't care if the market is going up or down, we only care about what is moving—and profiting from it. This type of trading sounds simple enough, but you must know the ins and outs because there are risks involved, and trading rules to be followed.

You'll find stories out there that talk about the underperformance of ETFs, but this is primarily related to those who buy and hold the leveraged ETFs,—which, again, I do not recommend to hold long term.

For more on ETFs, I suggest you go to the NASDAQ site, and read through the list of FAQs.[344]

---

[344] http://www.nasdaq.com/etfs/etf-faqs.aspx#/

Chapter 29 - Alternative Investments

International Stock and Bond Investments

Whether it is through mutual funds, bonds or ETFs, you can invest in almost any country you wish. Emerging markets at times offer fantastic opportunities to profit, while at the same time to bet against them. You can go long on Vietnam, or short Russia. With oil prices crashing and sanctions in effect, Russia is in deep trouble when their Central Bank runs out of money as some like William Browder of Hermitage Capital is saying.[345] If a crisis develops somewhere then jump on that trend with an inverse ETF.

When markets trend, you simply trade with that trend and take profit from it. If the trend begins to reverse, you can sell or just use money management techniques like selling half after a nice run higher and letting the rest ride with the trend, selling shares incrementally and locking in more profit as the price increases. Your goal would be to sell the last shares just as the trend is peaking, but don't expect perfection. Coming close to the top is good enough. Then you simply look for the next trend. There is always a trend happening somewhere—often many at a time. This is the beauty of active trading and taking control of your wealth.

Foreign Currencies

Most people in the U.S. keep their money at a U.S. bank, where it is subject to the risk of dollar depreciation. But there is another U.S. bank that is FDIC insured, and allows you to invest in foreign currencies.

Everbank.com offers you the opportunity to hold your cash in one of many currencies, such as the Canadian dollar, Chinese renminbi or the

---

[345] http://www.cnbc.com/2016/01/21/when-russias-money-runs-out-the-real-trouble-starts.html?__source=yahoo%7Cfinance%7Cheadline %7Cheadline %7Cstory&par=yahoo&doc=103319326&ref=yfp

Swiss franc. You can buy these foreign currencies through a CD that is FDIC insured.[346]

There is volatility in these currencies, but there is also opportunity. From 2011 to 2014, the Chinese renminbi moved higher against the dollar, but since has fallen, as seen in the following chart.

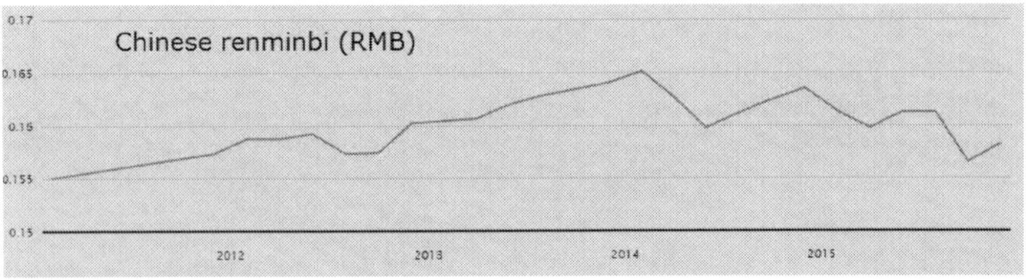

Everbank has a $5,000 minimum investment for a U.S. dollar account, and you can use your ATM card at any bank you want—and the fees will be refunded.[347] Why can't all banks be that way?

Real Estate Investment Trust (REIT)

When real estate is in a bull market, REITs are a great way to invest and get a good income return at the same time. What is nice about some of the REITs is that you can dive into the assets they hold, and make a judgment call as to whether that asset is poised to weather any downturn in the markets or a rise in rates.

For example, let's say the REIT had as one of its assets a prison in Texas with 100% occupancy. You can probably speculate that the prison will be self-sufficient and all bills paid no matter what the economy does. You can look at the long-term leases of buildings that the REITs own to see how long of an income stream your REIT will

346 https://www.everbank.com/currencies
347 https://www.everbank.com/banking/atm-freedom?cm_sp=account enhancer-_-atm-_-freedom

provide. The longer a lease is, the better the consistency of the REIT's return, especially if the tenants are companies that have been around awhile.

A Word of Caution on REITs

Fed chairman Bernanke's comments in May 2013 led to a sharp selloff of Real Estate Investment Trusts (REITs) and some other asset classes, such as emerging market equities that were reliant on "easy money" from the Fed.

The Dow Jones U.S. Select REIT Index dropped 15.8% from its peak on May 21, 2013 (the day preceding the Fed comments), to its 2013 low on June 22. However, as markets calmed, the index recovered most of its losses by mid-July, and reached new highs in 2014.[348]

Real Estate Investment Trusts are great investments in good times, but there is some caution warranted to be sure. REITs are typically illiquid and you can lose principal. In 2013, the last episode of rising interest rates, REITs, along with corporate and junk bonds, got hammered. The interest they generate can make up for some of the losses, but there is a good chance you will lose principal as rates rise.

[348] http://us.spindices.com/documents/research/the-impact-of-rising-interest-rates-on-reits.pdf?force_download=true

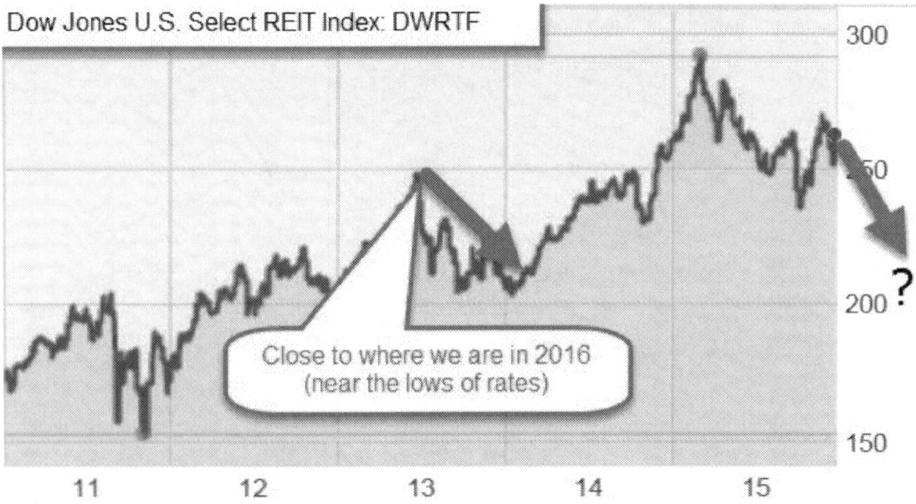

Ultimately, whether interest rates are rising or falling does not seem to be the key driver of REIT performance over medium- and long-term periods. Rather, the more important dynamics to address are the underlying factors that drive rates higher. If interest rates are rising due to strength in the underlying economy and inflationary activity, stronger REIT fundamentals may very well outweigh any negative impact caused by rising rates.

There are some of these REITs and Income Strategy ETNs that are currently yielding 8%-10% or more, but again, you have to know your risk. Check out the following links to analyze what UBS has to offer that might fit your income needs, or talk with your broker about the pros and cons of a REIT investment. It just may be that a future rate increase that can hurt bonds may not hurt REITs if you choose wisely.

http://etracs.ubs.com/product/list/index/assetClass/reits
http://etracs.ubs.com/product/list/index/strategy/income
http://etracs.ubs.com/product/list/index/assetClass/mlps

Treasury Inflation-Protected Securities (TIPS) and I Bonds

When you have an interest rate environment where there will be a mad rush to exit bonds and bond funds, there is still a need for a conservative investment that pays interest. You may need to purchase Treasury Inflation-Protected Securities (TIPS) or I Bonds.

TIPS

TIPS are expected to counter the inflation risk of your return and are guaranteed by the U.S. government. They are both liquid and exempt from state and local income taxes, but federal income taxes are paid the same year interest is received.[349] But even TIPS got slammed with higher rates in 2013, as they lost 8.5% that year.[350]

I Bonds

I Bonds are guaranteed to never lose value, and track the CPI-U inflation rate. They have to be held for a minimum of one year and are illiquid during that time. They are subject to a 3 three-month interest penalty if redeemed within the first five years. The I Bond rate for Nov. 2015 – April 2016 was 1.64%.[351]

The major difference between TIPS and I Bonds is that inflation indexing is monthly for TIPS, and semiannually for I Bonds. Also, TIPS are bought and sold in the secondary securities market, while I Bonds cannot be.[352]

---

349 http://www.investopedia.com/articles/bonds/07/tips.asp

350 http://performance.morningstar.com/funds/etf/total-returns.action?t=TIP

351 https://www.treasurydirect.gov/indiv/products/prod_ibonds_glance.htm.

352 http://www.ibonds.info/About-I-Bonds/Compare-I-Bonds.aspx

myRA - The Government to the Rescue for Conservative Investors?

The United States Treasury has designed a new retirement savings option with no minimums, fees or risky investments. It's called myRA (my Retirement Account) and is a type of Roth IRA.[353] The myRA has the backing of the U.S. Treasury and a maximum allowed account value of $15,000. Contributions are limited to $5,500 per year, or $6,500 per year for individuals 50 years of age or older at the end of the year, but the downside is that these limits apply to all IRAs—meaning that if you max out your IRA for one year, you can't contribute any additional amount to the myRA. The myRA is available for individuals directly or through employers.

At first glance, the benefits look good.[354]

1. Withdraw the money you put into your account at any time without paying tax and penalty.
2. Withdraw interest you earn without paying tax and penalty (if under 59 ½ or buying first home).
3. myRA will not go down in value.
4. You pay no fees for maintenance of the account.
5. Investment is backed by the United States Treasury.

The negatives of myRA:

1. Limited to those earning less than $131,000 (single) and $193,000 (married couple filing jointly).
2. The return is the same as the investments in the government securities fund available to federal employees - Thrift Savings Plan G Fund, which listed its only risk: "The G Fund is subject to inflation risk, or the possibility that your G Fund investment will not grow enough to offset the reduction in purchasing

---

[353] https://myra.gov/

[354] https://myra.gov/individuals/#benefits

power that results from inflation." That rate of return is just a hair over 2%.[355]

3. Under present law, this fund can be suspended if the statutory debt limit is reached, but the principal and interest are still guaranteed.

Energy-Related Investments

Energy is an area that I really like for the years ahead, but if Nikola Tesla's free energy were to ever come into play, it would put these companies out of business. Naturally I am not suggesting this would happen, but rather speculating that you shouldn't put all your eggs in this basket, but diversify into several industries.

Solar companies, utility companies that can raise rates anytime they want, and even nuclear energy-related companies are all a good place to park funds. The same is true for natural gas-related investments. Nations always will have a need for energy.

I had a client many years ago who received a $50,000 gift from her father when she was a child. She took his recommendation to invest in utility companies because they pay a dividend. That $50,000 gift she never touched and it had grown to over $3 million over her lifetime.

A couple of good utility plays would be Duke Energy (DUK) or the Vanguard Utilities ETF (VPU). You can also see which companies the majority of mutual funds invest in, and apply those accounting ratios to each company. Go to Morningstar.com and look for the Utility sector mutual funds. Once there, click on each of the top 5 funds based on the last year and three-month returns, and take a look at their top holdings. It's one of the easiest ways to see which utilities are most popular, but armed with our knowledge of the accounting ratios and acquiring the annual reports and 10Qs, you can use that detective work to find out who has the best balance sheet.[356]

---

[355] https://www.tsp.gov/InvestmentFunds/FundOptions/fundPerformance_G.html

Some industries, like solar, get added incentives from government tax breaks that make them more attractive, as we discussed earlier. Just know where they are in the cycle and make sure the government doesn't take away the tax incentives because they are running out of money.

There is one particular energy investment that needs singling out, and that is oil.

Oil and other Commodities

The price of oil falling to the lows hit in 2016 is a gift to investors. I really would like to see oil in the teens for the perfect price entry into the ETF (USO), which tracks the oil price, or any good oil company stocks in the U.S. like Exxon Mobil (XOM), that has good income and cash flow.

While most investors will buy the large producers like Exxon, there are some smaller companies where using the accounting ratios I spoke of earlier can possibly get you higher returns, while shedding off some good income. A good site to find them is dividend.com and for oil companies in particular, use this link: http://www.dividend.com/dividend-stocks/basic-materials/oil-and-gas-drilling-and-exploration/

It seems to me that OPEC is in no hurry to push prices higher, even though some countries like Venezuela are struggling with their finances due to the lower prices. Banks are already worried about the loans they have been providing to many of these new U.S. companies at an assumed higher price for oil.

We have already seen the Federal Reserve step in and change the rules for these banks, as discussed in the banking section, by giving them the ability to not count the hundreds of millions in loans as losses on their books. According to the Fed, there have been massive layoffs

[356] http://news.morningstar.com/fund-category-returns/utilities/$FOCA$SU.aspx

with over 70,000 employees in the oil and gas industry, and over 300 rigs were dropped in 2015. It's been nothing short of a disaster.[357]

But now 80% of companies are spending within their cash flow, and those that are can become more attractive investments as the oil price bottoms and begins to finally rise. These companies have also become more efficient as the following graph shows.[358]

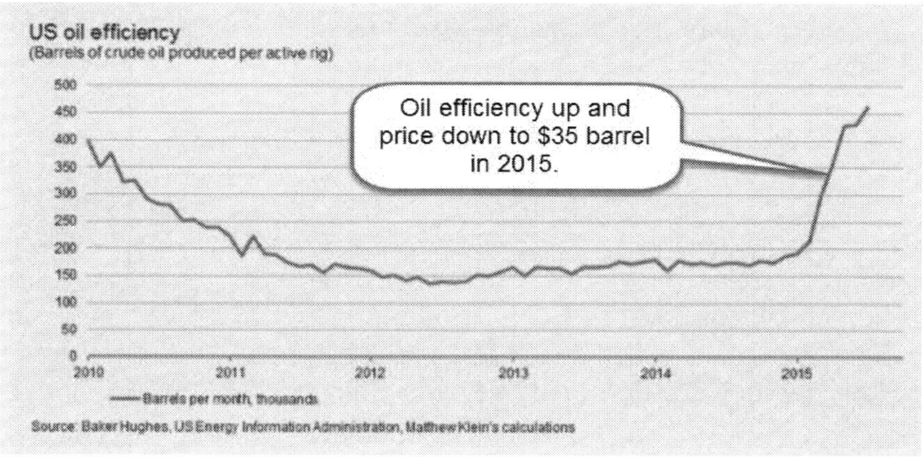

OPEC can wait a decade if they have to, and keep prices low and bankrupt as many of these companies as they can but I imagine war will breakout somewhere (the Europeans seem to want inflation that way if you recall) that in and of itself makes oil an attractive investment for years to come.

Other Commodities

Commodities such as copper, steel, iron ore and aluminum (we'll deal with silver separately) or what we call industrial metals, rely on a

357 http://fuelfix.com/blog/2016/01/05/sapped-u-s-shale-budgets-to-come-in-lower-than-1980s-bust/#36696101=0
358 http://ftalphaville.ft.com/2015/10/12/2142058/saudi-arabias-gambit-for-market-share-meets-yankee-ingenuity/

healthy economy to move higher. China and other emerging markets need continued growth for these metals to move higher, but if the world is contracting because of a deflationary episode, they will be hard pressed to move higher. However, at some point they will bottom and become fantastic investments. Not everything moves down in a straight line. Timing is what an investor needs to consider.

The old saying that the market can stay irrelevant longer than you can stay solvent has taught many an investor who has been long commodities since 2011 a lesson. But no investor has suffered through a real deflationary contraction, and your goal just may be to hold on to your wealth rather than grow it. Patience will be rewarded.

If we do get a continued downturn in commodities, then the exchanges where metals are traded will become the story as Glencore PLC was recently, before they started selling assets and a rebound in commodities commenced in the beginning of 2016. If you invest in commodities, you need to keep an eye on the liquidity that caused of Moody's to downgrade Glencore's rating to Baa3.[359]

In fact, if China doesn't continue to rebound and goes into a deeper slump as the price of copper declines to new lows, Glencore's credit default swaps may reach multi-year highs quickly and wreak havoc if counterparties default.[360]

---

[359] https://www.moodys.com/research/Moodys-downgrades-Glencores-ratings-to-Baa3-stable-outlook--PR_339642

[360] http://www.bloomberg.com/news/articles/2016-01-11/glencore-debt-swaps-jump-to-six-year-high-as-copper-price-slides

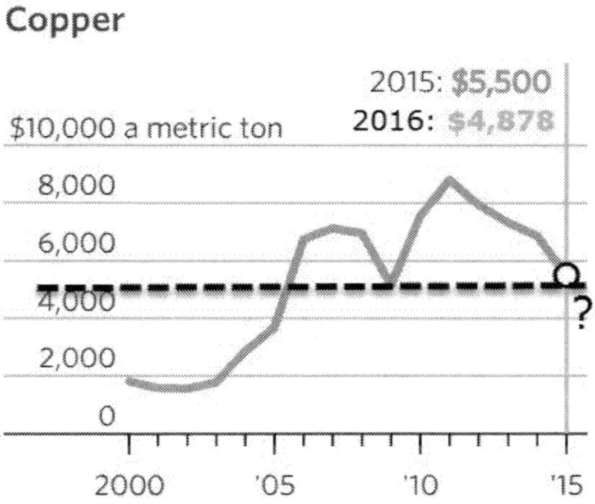

The question becomes, are commodity trading firms too big to fail themselves? While there have been examples of firms failing by making bad bets, like Enron in the energy sector, this price decline can spill over and affect your investments in commodities for a time. But it can also be an opportunity of a lifetime to snatch up some beaten-down assets.

Infrastructure

Our cities are falling apart, so you'll see more and more invested in infrastructures. Look for local companies, which always seem to win the bids for city contracts. It will take some digging, but all of this is a matter of public record.

Go to your state's official website (your state, followed by ".gov") and search for "contracts" or "bid," and you'll find a list of who is doing business with the state. You can also do a Google search for "bids and contracts" and the name of your city. Which companies are winning bids consistently because of their connections with the decision makers? Some of these companies will be listed and you can buy them. Others will be private and not available to invest in.

For example, if you go to Michigan.gov and do a search for "contracts," you get the result "Contract Connect." When you click on that link, you come to a page where you can choose "Vendor Gateway." This page shows a link to www.Buy4Michigan.com. Click on "Active Contracts" and see who the city is doing business with. The first contract on the list is for Mental Health and Substance Abuse Insurance, with the vendor Magellan Behavioral Health Inc. A search for that company shows it is a listed company with the stock symbol MGLN. The contract date was February 1, 2014 and became public record that day. The stock could have been bought the first day of trading after that approval by the state of Michigan for $59.55 a share. By April 1, 2015 the stock hit $71, a 19% return. I would have sold that day, as the quarterly report showed a sharp decrease in gross profit and net income.

This is how doing a little homework can help your profit, and also shows how important it is to stay on top of the companies you are invested in, by applying the accounting ratios to their quarterly reports.

Robotics

Many of you who are avid watchers of the TV game show *Jeopardy* were impressed by the winning streak of contestant Ken Jennings—74 games in a row and over $3.1 million over a 182-day span.[361] Jennings and another contestant, Brad Rutter, who defeated Jennings in two *Jeopardy* championship tournaments, were pitted against IBM's "Watson" computer, named after the company's first CEO, industrialist Thomas J. Watson. The computer was programmed to answer questions with only its four terabytes of disk storage and no connection to the internet. Watson handily defeated the two former champions, for a $1 million prize.

This is indeed the rise of the machines I spoke about earlier, and an age where computers are taking over the jobs of more and more working Americans. But beyond auto manufacturing, computers like

[361] https://en.wikipedia.org/wiki/Ken_Jennings

Watson have evolved to taking on bigger tasks like utilization management decisions in lung cancer treatment at Memorial Sloan Kettering Cancer Center, in conjunction with health insurance company WellPoint.[362] This technology is the wave of the future, and a must for your portfolio.

The market for robot systems is growing at a good clip and is expected to continue to grow, as shown in the following chart (naturally this is not a good sign for the manufacturing sector and furthermore contributes to deflation of jobs along with lower prices as a result).

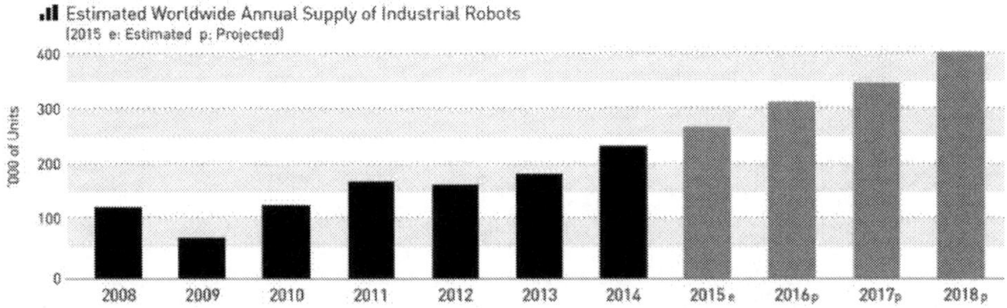

There is a website that lists the top 50 robotics companies—some listed, some private—and you can apply the accounting ratios to these, but understand this is a newer field and you will have to do research to learn more about it before investing. The *Robotics Business Review* provides you with the *RBR*50, and considers these to be the most influential public and private companies in the global robotics industry.

http://www.roboticsbusinessreview.com/rbr50

3D Printing

3D technology has arrived to revolutionize many industries, from car makers to aerospace and defense, as well as oil and gas. There is even

362 https://en.wikipedia.org/wiki/Watson_(computer)

use of 3D technology for creating organs and tissues. Some in Congress don't like that you can make your own guns with this discovery, but I don't think there is much they can do about it. 3D technology is here to stay, and is a future growth industry.[363]

Some of the companies to keep an eye on are ExOne Company (XONE), 3D Systems Corp. (DDD), Stratasys Ltd. (SSYS) and Voxeljet AG (VJET). Apply the accounting ratios to see which offers the most value.

One of the companies to watch regarding an IPO is Carbon3D, which boasts Google as one of its investors for its 3D printing technology. Their CLIP (Continuous Liquid Interface Production) technology is faster than standard 3D printing methods, printing in a fraction of the time.[364]

Options, Covered Calls, Buying Puts

Options are basically bets on what an underlying asset is going to do in the future. Buying a call option at a higher price means you think the underlying asset is going to move up. Buying a put option at a lower price means you think the underlying asset is going to move down. The further out the option is from current price, the cheaper it becomes. In volatile, quickly falling or rising markets, you'll find options can be more expensive.

---

[363] http://finance.yahoo.com/news/3d-printing-stocks-near-52-200808555.html

[364] http://www.forbes.com/sites/aarontilley/2015/11/04/how-carbon3d-plans-to-transform-manufacturing/

There is some validity to options, but for most investors it is too complicated to explain without writing a separate book. I prefer to leave this analysis for those who wish to do further research as experienced investors, or to discuss with your financial advisor—who may have experience with these investments.

Because trading options can be quite technical in nature, it makes sense to paper trade what you would do in advance of trading, keeping an eye on whether the bid and ask liquidity is there for you. A book I recommend for learning more about trading options is *Understanding Options*, by Michael Sincere.[365]

Hedge Funds

I see no validity in investing in hedge funds, as they seem more of a way to make fund managers rich, not you. There are exceptions, but why can't you do what they do, using what you have learned in this book? Just like with mutual funds, I'd suggest confirming a proven three-year track record of outperforming the indices before investing in a hedge fund, otherwise I'd pass.[366]

---

[365] http://www.amazon.com/Understanding-Options-2E-Michael-Sincere/dp/0071817840/ref=zg_bs_2672_2
[366] http://www.businessinsider.com/hedge-funds-returns-in-2015-2015-10

Chapter 30 - Gold and Silver

When I use the word "gold" in this section, I am including silver, but for simplicity in explaining how gold and silver fit into a diversified portfolio, I'll use just one word for both. I'll explain later how gold and silver differ as investments, but historically they have moved up and down in price together, with silver being more volatile in the price swings.

You've read the sections where I talked about the economy, Fed, debt and even a history that explained how gold and silver were circulated as money—and at one time backed Federal Reserve Notes in one way or another until 1971.

Gold is an asset typically hated by anyone at the Federal Reserve, CNBC, advisors who are compensated by a pro-stock or bond agenda, and even Warren Buffett. I'll get to all that soon enough. But first, why buy gold and silver?

Why Gold and Silver?

There are times to own gold, and there are times when it doesn't make sense to. Knowing where we are in the cycle dictates whether or not you should own gold. Gold of late has been beaten to a pulp, but I think it will be bouncing back soon enough.

Gold typically works inverse to the dollar. If the dollar goes down, gold goes up, as it did from 1971–1980 and 2000–2011. And when the dollar goes up, gold tends to go lower, as from 1980–1999 and 2011–2016.

Since 1971, the exception to this would be the 1985–1987 timeframe, when the central banks of the world colluded to crash the dollar. This culminated in the 1987 stock market crash, and an era of dollar strength until the year 2000, when the dot.com bust happened and gold entered its bull phase through 2011. Note: Crashes occur for many reasons that can be traced to intervention in free markets. We have seen unconventional moves by the Federal Reserve, setting up the next crash. It's just a matter of time. Most who sell gold continually try to sell on fear and a dollar crash. From 2011 – 2015 the dollar shooting higher and higher and gold going lower and lower didn't change their thinking.

I was dollar bullish beginning in 2012, as I became very negative on the yen and euro, which make up 71.3% of the dollar index. If I was right about the yen and euro getting weaker, I said it could put pressure on the price of the metals—and it did, until 2016. I believe I was one of the only people in the U.S. who sold gold investments, yet warned about the dollar's strength and advised others to be cautious with gold.

Unlike Other Investments, Gold Is Unique

Gold has no counterparty risk. There are no bondholders, stockholders, government regulators, Federal Reserve members or politicians who can cause your investment in gold to go to zero. It is an investment that gives you the insurance you need in case something goes wrong in the system or government economists and central banks don't see the next crisis or another black swan event.

Gold is a security blanket you can wrap yourself up in and have the peace of mind that no matter what happens, you have some real wealth that is tangible, fully liquid, and can be converted into the scrip of the day to buy whatever you need. It doesn't hurt that over time it also maintains its purchasing power.

But I do think there will come a time when you will sell your gold and buy beaten-down stocks or real estate. That's what asset allocation is all about. How severe of a shakedown we get from our government's sins is the only unanswered question, but I believe I have laid the foundation in your mind that it could happen, and gold is just one of the options available for your portfolio diversification.

Central Banks, CNBC and Warren Buffett Hate Gold

Central banks hate gold because it is competition for their currency scheme, yet they all own many tonnes of it. More on them in a bit.

CNBC and Gold

CNBC hates gold because it is against their "always bullish on stocks" point of view. They bashed gold all the way from the year 2000 to its high in 2011, and were confused by it the entire time it was moving higher. I have video of former CNBC hosts Erin Burnett and Mark Haines discussing the higher price in gold, and Burnett actually wondering why humans have a need for valuing something. Doesn't our entire economy work on valuing something, pricing that something in dollars, and figuring out if it is expensive or cheap?

Gold doesn't change. If you'd buried it in your backyard 10 years ago and dug it up today, it is the same gold. Only what it is *priced in* changes. And if it's priced in U.S. dollars, over time it takes a lot more dollars to buy gold—and pretty much everything else. It's not a human need to value gold, as Burnett assumes, but rather a misunderstanding of what gold and money represent and an ignorance of the history of what gold and money once were. Remember, as I pointed out in Part 1, our current experiment with the monetary system not having a relationship to gold is only 45 years young.

I will say that FOX Business Channel talked more about gold when Glenn Beck was on the network, and every other commercial is about buying gold because gold buyers are mostly conservatives, it seems. Chapter 8 of my first book Buy Gold and Silver Safely goes into detail in Chapter 8 on these gold dealers who advertise there, pushing investors to the wrong type of gold with extremely high commissions.

Warren Buffett and Gold

Warren Buffett hates gold because he says it's a non-productive asset. Yet his fund Berkshire Hathaway owned 129,710,000 ounces of silver in 1997 and 1998 that he bought at approximately $4.60 an ounce, because of this reasoning: "Widely-published reports have shown that bullion inventories have fallen very materially, because of an excess of user demand over mine production and reclamation. Therefore, last summer Mr. Buffett and Mr. Munger, Vice Chairman of Berkshire, concluded that equilibrium between supply and demand was only likely to be established by a somewhat higher price."[367]

Buffett's fund actually took delivery of the physical metal, and quickly made a 50% profit. By February of 1998, silver was trading at over $7 an ounce and his investment was up 60%.

From Berkshire Hathaway's 1997 letter to shareholders: "Our second non-traditional commitment is in silver. Last year, we purchased 111.2 million ounces. Marked to market, that position produced a pre-tax gain of $97.4 million for us in 1997. In a way, this is a return to the past for me: Thirty years ago, I bought silver because I anticipated its

[367] http://www.berkshirehathaway.com/news/feb03981.html

demonetization by the U.S. government. Ever since, I have followed the metal's fundamentals but not owned it. In recent years, bullion inventories have fallen materially, and last summer Charlie and I concluded that a higher price would be needed to establish equilibrium between supply and demand. Inflation expectations, it should be noted, play no part in our calculation of silver's value."[368]

The only reason anyone knew Buffett had any silver to begin with, it seems, was because regulators were on him about the investment. In 1998, he had this to say in his letter to shareholders listed in the annual report:

> *Last year I deviated from my standard practice of not disclosing our investments (other than those we are legally required to report) and told you about three unconventional investments we had made. There were several reasons behind that disclosure. First, questions about our silver position that we had received from regulatory authorities led us to believe that they wished us to publicly acknowledge this investment.*[369]

Buffett didn't acknowledge selling the silver until a 2006 Q&A during the shareholders annual meeting, where he and his partner Munger said about the silver purchase:

> *Munger: We've demonstrated how little we know about commodities by our activities in silver.*
>
> *Buffett: I bought [silver] early and sold early. Silver was my fault. [Speculation] is wildest at the end.*[370]

In acknowledging that at first Buffett and Munger knew nothing about commodities, it's important to note that their claim of selling early was true. The average price of silver in 2006, when they revealed they sold

---

368 http://www.berkshirehathaway.com/1997ar/1997.html
369 http://www.berkshirehathaway.com/1998ar/1998ar.pdf
370 http://www.jvbruni.com/Berkshire2006annualmeeting.pdf

(we don't know really when it was sold) and the years following the price of silver rose steadily:

Year	Average Price of Silver	% Increase (Decrease) in Silver	Average Price of Gold	% Increase (Decrease) in Gold
2000	$4.95	----	$279.11	----
2001	4.37	(11.72)	271.04	(2.89)
2002	4.60	5.26	309.73	14.27
2003	4.85	5.43	363.38	17.32
2004	6.66	37.32	409.72	12.75
2005	7.31	9.76	444.74	8.55
2006	11.54	57.87	603.46	35.69
2007	13.38	15.94	695.39	15.23
2008	14.98	11.96	871.96	25.39
2009	14.67 (financial crisis)	(2.07)	972.35	11.51
2010	20.19	37.62	1224.53	25.94
2011	35.11	73.89	1571.52	28.34

Why do I spend so much time analyzing what Warren Buffett did? Because everyone looks to him as the go-to guy when it comes to investing, but we already showed that this has changed, with Buffett's

Berkshire Hathaway performing the same as an S&P 500 index fund would have, for several years now.

Buffett came out and criticized gold in 2011 during a CNBC interview. This was at a time when gold had reached new highs, and naturally on CNBC he can't say anything that goes against the investment philosophy of Berkshire Hathaway, which primarily invests in stocks of companies. But he did reveal some wisdom for holding gold at certain times, before mocking it.

He said: "Basically gold is a way of going along on fear, and it's been a pretty good way of going along on fear from time to time. But you really have to hope people become more afraid in a year or two years than they are now. And if they become more afraid, you make money; if they become less afraid, you lose money. But the gold itself doesn't produce anything."[371]

Based on what you have read in this book, I don't think we need to use the word "hope," but I do think we will begin to see more of the "fear" in the years ahead that Buffett speaks of. While gold doesn't produce anything, neither do many, many stocks. Heck, what interest rates are you even getting on your savings at the bank? But how many stocks that produce something do well during a real recession or financial crisis?

Buffett goes on to say that all the gold in the world would fit into a 67-cubic-foot cube, as if this means something. Most central banks have many cubic feet of gold just sitting there. Why is that? To give the illusion that gold backs currency. Why else would they hold on to it if gold doesn't produce anything?

Gold was trading at $1,434 the day Buffett made those comments on CNBC in March 2011, and went on to a high of $1,921.50 by September before the dollar bottomed and started its current run higher. That was a 34% gain for gold in 7 months. The Dow lost 8.9%

---

[371] http://www.cnbc.com/id/41867379

during that time. I guess there was a little more fear left in the market back then.

Buffett makes the mistake of comparing gold to stocks. One should not compare a commodity such as gold to a stock. They complement each other in a diversified portfolio, and when fear enters the picture, which Buffett acknowledges is a reason to own gold, act inversely to each other. Gold actually comes from the ground, is dug up, and sold on the open market by companies listed on the stock market, and started 2016 as the best-performing sector. Some of these companies pay dividends too, Mr. Buffett. And if you want a sector that is poised to go much higher in the years to come—because gold is going to go much higher—look no further than this mining sector.

Lastly, Buffett's father Howard, a U.S. congressman, strongly supported the gold standard because he believed it would limit the ability of government to inflate the money supply and spend beyond its means. This sounds like something a wise person might say today, when you analyze government spending. Here is what Warren's father Howard said in 1948, before U.S. citizens were allowed to own gold again.

> *Unless you are willing to surrender your children and your country to galloping inflation, war and slavery, then this cause demands your support. For if human liberty is to survive in America, we must win the battle to restore honest money. There is no more important challenge facing us than this issue -- the restoration of your freedom to secure gold in exchange for the fruits of your labors.*—Human Freedom Rests on Gold Redeemable Money, *by Hon. Howard Buffett, U.S. congressman from Nebraska.* The Commercial and Financial Chronicle *May 6, 1948.*[372]

---

[372] http://www.math.snu.ac.kr/~hichoi/finmath/Human%20freedom%20rests%20on%20gold%20redeemable%20money%20(Howard%20Buffett).pdf

Gold has survived every fiat currency in the history of mankind. Younger generations may mock gold because they don't understand its history, but I'll listen to the elder Buffett over Warren, as I think he and our forefathers knew how important sound money is to the survival of a nation.

With all the debt and spending that back the dollar today, the national debt elephant in the room grows larger every day. When we have to pay higher interest payments on that debt, investors of all ages may want to acquire some insurance that represents the real wealth found in gold, as it has been known as money since the time of Jesus.

> *With thy wisdom and with thine understanding thou hast gotten thee riches, and hast gotten gold and silver into thy treasures.*—Ezekiel 28:4

Central Banks and Gold - Why Do They Hold It?

Virtually all central banks own gold, to give the illusion that it backs their various currencies. But there is no connection between gold and the fiat money printed by these central banks. In fact, there have been agreements to sell gold by many of them in the last 15 years.[373]

Central Bank Agreements to Sell Gold

We have already discussed the. To show you how smart they are, the entire decade that gold was moving up in price, there were two central bank agreements to sell gold that were five years in length. Certain central banks were required to sell gold (get it off the balance sheet) but not the Fed. This began in 1999, and continues to this day.[374]

---

[373] http://www.gold.org/reserve-asset-management/central-bank-gold-agreements

[374] http://www.gold.org/news-and-events/press-releases/central-bank-gold-agreement-renewal-demonstrates-continued-commitment

Beginning with the 2009 agreement, central banks could have sold up to 2,000 tonnes at much higher prices per the agreement, but instead only sold 25 tonnes. In other words, central banks sold gold for the nine years that the price of gold went up, and the entire five years gold went down, they didn't sell—and suffered losses. Most of the gold sold as the price moved higher was held by the Swiss, and you can bet their citizens weren't too happy with their central banks being forced to sell their gold. It was because the Swiss franc was too strong. But guess what? The Swiss franc is still strong.

According to the World Gold Council, the following changes have occurred since 2003 for the world official gold holdings of central banks. Notice the decrease for many European countries, especially the Swiss, and increases for China and Russia.[375]

Country (2014 Ranking High to Low)	2003 Tonnes	2016 Tonnes (February 2016)	Increase/(Decrease)
United States	8135.4	8133.5	(1.9)
Germany	3439.50	3381	(58.50)
IMF	3217	2814	(403)
Italy	2451.80	2451.80	Unchanged
France 3024.80	3024.80	2435.60	(589.20)
China	600.30	1762.30	1,162
Russia	388.20	1,392.70	1004.50
Switzerland	1,722.80	1040	(682.80)

[375] http://www.gold.org/research/latest-world-official-gold-reserves

Japan	765.20	765.20	Unchanged
Netherlands	842.50	612.50	(230)
India	357.70	557.70	200
ECB	766.90	504.80	(262.10)
BIS	193.70	108	(85.7)

If central banks were again called upon to sell gold as the price once more moves higher, it would be a sign of perceived weakness, not strength. Use it as a reason to buy all the gold you can if you hear about it. It is confidence in the currencies they will be fighting, not confidence in gold.

It should be noted that Germany did ask the U.S. for some of their gold back—which they had been storing at the Federal Reserve Bank in New York. The U.S. agreed, but of the first 50 tonnes expected in December 2013, only 5 tonnes came from the New York Fed, with a promise of 300 tonnes by 2020. By January 19, 2014, though, 85 tonnes had been sent to Frankfurt and an additional 99–100 tonnes in 2015.[376]

[376] http://www.zerohedge.com/news/2016-01-27/germany-has-repatriated-over-366-tonnes-gold-new-york-and-paris

	From Paris in tonnes	From New York in tonnes	Total in tonnes	Share as a percentage
To be transferred by 2020	373.7t	300.0t	673.7t	100%
Transferred in 2013	31.6t	5.0t	36.6t	5.4%
Transferred in 2014	35.2t	84.5t	119.7t	17.8%
Transferred in 2015	110.5t	99.5t	210.0t	31.2%
Transferred to date	177.3t	189.0t	366.3t	54.4%
Still to be transferred	196.4t	111.0t	307.4t	45.6%

The problem that the media fails to address is what Peter Boehringer, initiator of the German campaign to repatriate its gold,[377] brings up: The Bundesbank has failed to deliver a gold bar number list. These bars were originally numbered, but they are not receiving the same gold that was originally deposited at the Fed. This is an unfinished story, and we may never get straight answers, but it does show how all is not what it seems. The gold changed hands, but wasn't actually stored.[378]

More countries are asking to repatriate their gold, as referenda are forcing central banks to disclose where the gold is held, and whether or not it has been leased out.

---

[377] http://www.bloomberg.com/news/features/2015-02-05/germany-s-gold-repatriation-activist-peter-boehringer-gets-results
[378] https://www.bullionstar.com/blogs/koos-jansen/guest-post-47-years-after-1968-bundesbank-still-fails-to-deliver-a-gold-bar-number-list/

What Do Central Bank Heads Really Think of Gold?

If you want a peek into the mind of a central banker, look no further than the two Fed chairmen before Janet Yellen: Alan Greenspan and Ben Bernanke.

Greenspan:

> *In the absence of the gold standard, there is no way to protect savings from confiscation through inflation. There is no safe store of value. If there were, the government would have to make its holding illegal, as was done in the case of gold. This is the shabby secret of the welfare statists' tirades against gold. Deficit spending is simply a scheme for the confiscation of wealth. Gold stands in the way of this insidious process. It stands as a protector of property rights. If one grasps this, one has no difficulty in understanding the statists' antagonism toward the gold standard.*[379]

Bernanke:

> *The conclusion that deflation is always reversible under a fiat money system follows from basic economic reasoning. A little parable may prove useful: Today an ounce of gold sells for $300, more or less. Now suppose that a modern alchemist solves his subject's oldest problem by finding a way to produce unlimited amounts of new gold at essentially no cost. Moreover, his invention is widely publicized and scientifically verified, and he announces his intention to begin massive production of gold within days. What would happen to the price of gold? Presumably, the potentially unlimited supply of cheap gold would cause the market price of gold to plummet. Indeed, if the market for gold is to any degree efficient, the price of gold would collapse immediately after the*

---

[379] http://www.constitution.org/mon/greenspan_gold.htm

announcement of the invention, before the alchemist had produced and marketed a single ounce of yellow metal.[380]

Why would I highlight Bernanke's quote, which is somewhat negative for gold, if such a technology existed to enable an alchemist to create gold? Because he beautifully described our monetary system as it stands today, without the limitations that the gold standard Greenspan described puts on it. The alchemist is the creator of the printing machine that shoots out unlimited quantities of Federal Reserve Notes, "a scheme for the confiscation of wealth." Bernanke was trying to mock gold. Substitute the word "dollars" for "gold" in what Bernanke said, and we get this:

> *Now suppose that a modern alchemist solves his subject's oldest problem by finding a way to produce unlimited amounts of new dollars at essentially no cost. What would happen to the price (value) of dollars? Presumably, the potentially unlimited supply of dollars would cause the market price of dollars to plummet.*

But I don't even have to substitute "dollars" for "gold." Bernanke does it for us.

> *What has this got to do with monetary policy? Like gold, U.S. dollars have value only to the extent that they are strictly limited in supply. But the U.S. government has a technology, called a printing press (or, today, its electronic equivalent), that allows it to produce as many U.S. dollars as it wishes at essentially no cost. By increasing the number of U.S. dollars in circulation, or even by credibly threatening to do so, the U.S. government can also reduce the value of a dollar in terms of goods and services, which is equivalent to raising the prices in dollars of those goods and services. We conclude that, under a*

---

380 http://www.federalreserve.gov/boarddocs/Speeches/2002/20021121/default.htm

> *paper-money system, a determined government can always generate higher spending and hence positive inflation.*
>
> *Sustained deflation can be highly destructive to a modern economy and should be strongly resisted. Fortunately, for the foreseeable future, the chances of a serious deflation in the United States appear remote indeed, in large part because of our economy's underlying strengths but also because of the determination of the Federal Reserve and other U.S. policymakers to act preemptively against deflationary pressures. Moreover, as I have discussed today, a variety of policy responses are available should deflation appear to be taking hold. Because some of these alternative policy tools are relatively less familiar, they may raise practical problems of implementation and of calibration of their likely economic effects. For this reason, as I have emphasized, prevention of deflation is preferable to cure.*

And this, dear readers, is why deflation will only last for a limited time, as the Fed and other central banks will resort to whatever means necessary to "prevent" deflation. This is also why you need to have an allocation in gold.

The Fed has been fighting deflation, and so are central banks around the world with their quantitative easing programs to try and stimulate the economy. In a sense, all it is doing is kicking the can down the road and making matters worse if the economy doesn't pick up steam and increase GDP. Their solution is and always will be, per Bernanke, to add more stimulus, whether it be quantitative easing or the printing press or dropping money from helicopters, which Bernanke also mentioned in his "making sure deflation doesn't happen here" speech.

When the stock market crashed, gold fell hard at first too. But gold finished the year higher and proceeded to go up for three more years after 2008 to its all-time high, as fear was still fresh in the minds of investors.

Year	Price of Gold (End of Year)	Price of Silver (End of Year)
2000	$274.45	$4.57
2001	276.50	4.52
2002	347.20	4.66
2003	416.25	5.96
2004	435.60	6.81
2005	513.00	8.83
2006	632.00	12.90
2007	833.75	14.76
2008	869.75	10.79
2009	1087.50	16.99
2010	1405.50	30.63
2011	1531.00	28.18
2012	1657.50	29.95
2013	1204.50	19.50
2014	1206.00	15.97
2015	1060.00	13.82
2016	????	????

Gold and the National Debt

All nations have issues with growing debt that continually eats into their GDP growth. As this debt grows, it eventually becomes unsustainable. A country has a choice of defaulting or receiving stimulus from their central bank, a loan from the International Monetary Fund like during the Asian financial crisis we discussed, or a direct investment by other countries like Germany did with Greece in 2014–2015.

Receiving a loan or stimulus is only a temporary solution. You must instead resolve the underlying problems. The U.S. government has projected deficits for 10 years and has seen debt grow exponentially since the time of Reagan. Yes, spending did stimulate and lead to one of the greatest and most productive times in our country's history, but what happens when stimulus stops? Can the printing and glory days continue forever? We are soon going to discover that no, they can't. Events will occur most likely in other countries like Europe with the PIIGS, China or Japan who has the world's largest debt-to-GDP and you'll see a mass exit of assets that will make the 2007-2009 financial crisis seem like an undercard to the main event.

Our economy, and that of most nations, is built on a house of sand (debt). Unfortunately many don't have an asset like gold that can counteract the debt issue when money velocity, interest rates and inflation start to tick up. This debt will eat away at your purchasing power, and gold will be a must for your portfolio to counteract it.

Remember, pricing currencies in each other is part of the greatest illusions of all time. It is the purchasing power of your wealth that matters, not valuing your weak currency versus other weak currencies. The world's currency ship is sinking, and the lifeboats are made of gold.

In looking at the chart below, though, one has to wonder what's really going on with gold. How can gold, year after year, trade higher with debt now over $19 trillion, but all of a sudden have a separation as shown in the chart?

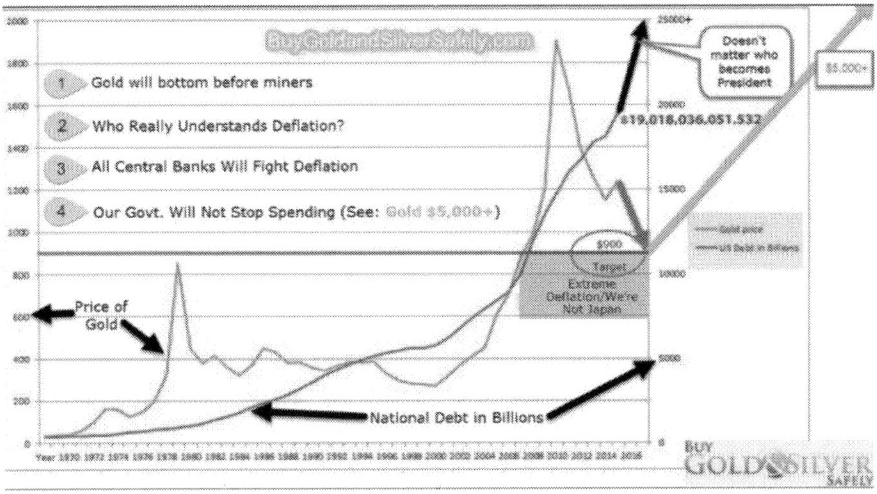

The only real answer we can speculate on is the data pulled straight from the Office of the Comptroller of the Currency Quarterly Report on Bank Derivatives Activities (it's those banks again).[381]

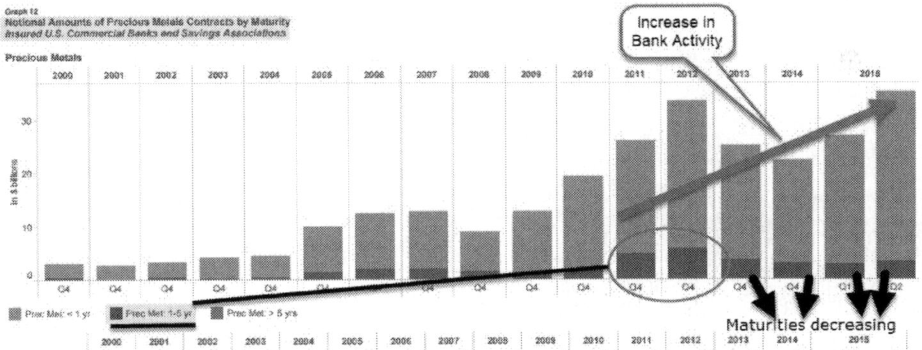

	2000	2001	2002	2003	2004	2005	2006	2007	2008	2009	2010	2011	2012	2013	2014	2015	
	Q4	Q4	Q4	Q4	Q4	Q4	Q4	Q4	Q4	Q4	Q4	Q4	Q4	Q4	Q4	Q1	Q2
Prec Met: < 1 yr	2.51	2.44	2.72	3.87	4.04	8.59	10.35	10.72	7.56	11.56	17.47	21.12	27.68	21.41	19.29	23.08	31.80
Prec Met: 1-5 yr	0.26	0.23	0.46	0.33	0.51	1.29	1.75	2.10	1.51	1.24	1.89	4.74	5.82	3.80	2.84	2.98	3.43
Prec Met: > 5 yrs	0.16	0.00	0.00	0.00	0.00	0.06	0.33	0.01	0.00	0.06	0.03	0.10	0.03	0.00	0.29	0.00	0.02

---

[381] http://www.occ.gov/topics/capital-markets/financial-markets/trading/derivatives/ derivatives-quarterly-report.html

With banks' derivatives activity having been taken away, their ability to trade gold derivatives was maintained. Banks salivate over Gold—being a very small market along with precious metals in general (mainly silver)—as an easy moneymaker. You can see by the chart the increase in bank activity from 2011 when gold peaked to 2015.

Banks, knowing they have a nice control of a market like gold, took out some long-term contracts of one to five years when gold was at its high, and beginning in 2015, have been collecting on those bets. But they are not betting long term on anything right now. They technically don't want the price of gold to go higher, as it competes with their currency, the U.S. dollar. They don't want their currency exposed as weak. If they were smart, they would see the writing on the wall like all the buyers of physical gold and silver right now, and make bets on the price of metals moving higher over the next five years.

While I have said there are times to hold gold and times not to, inflation expectations still drive the price higher. From 2011 to 2016 there was no expectation of inflation. Soon there will be, but we must finish out this deflationary credit contraction cycle first.

The real issue investors need to be concerned with is whether or not their wealth maintains its purchasing power over time. This is where metals since 1971—when Nixon took us off the gold standard—have maintained their purchasing power quite well as we showed in Chapter 2 with the purchasing power of the 1964 silver coins that contained 90% silver versus 1965 coins the government minted that contained no silver.

If you think Congress has their act together, then you don't need to buy gold. If you think they will continue the same plan no matter who is president because that is their history, and expect another crisis at some point in the future, you buy gold as insurance.

COMEX Gold - Where's the Gold?

If you really want to see the price of gold skyrocket, it's quite simple to accomplish. Instead of buying an Exchange Traded Fund like GLD or SLV—which don't even insure your gold/silver and have as their custodian banks like JPMorgan Chase (see banking section) and HSBC—buy the physical metal. The more the supply of the metals is depleted from the market, the more the price has to move higher to pry supply out of everyone's hands.

But the paper gold market is something to behold. Not only do you have the alleged gold and silver held by the various ETFs, but you also have the contracts bought and sold in large quantities over at the COMEX (commodity exchange), owned and operated by the Chicago Mercantile Exchange (CME).[382]

As you might recall from the movie *Trading Places*, commodities can be exchanged in open pits (or on computers), where one trader is buying and the other is selling. While trading is pretty much computerized nowadays, in the movie they were trading orange juice futures and betting on whether the price would be higher or lower after the report on orange crops came in. If you bet the wrong way, you lose and the right way you make money. But no one ever takes delivery of truckloads of orange juice. The same is true for coffee, barrels of oil, and anything else traded at the CME.

Gold and silver are bought and sold by traders at the CME, but they don't take delivery of the bets they make on the price of the metals, either. The amount of gold and silver these traders exchange each day are multiple times the actual physical metal available for delivery. They just trade these contracts as a form of legalized gambling, but the amount traded on the exchange is said to be 298 times the actual gold stored at the warehouses.[383]

---

[382] http://www.24hgold.com/english/interactive_chart.aspx?etfcode=COMEX% 20WAREHOUSES%20REGISTERED&etfcodecom=gold
[383] http://jessescrossroadscafe.blogspot.com/2015/11/ratio-of-

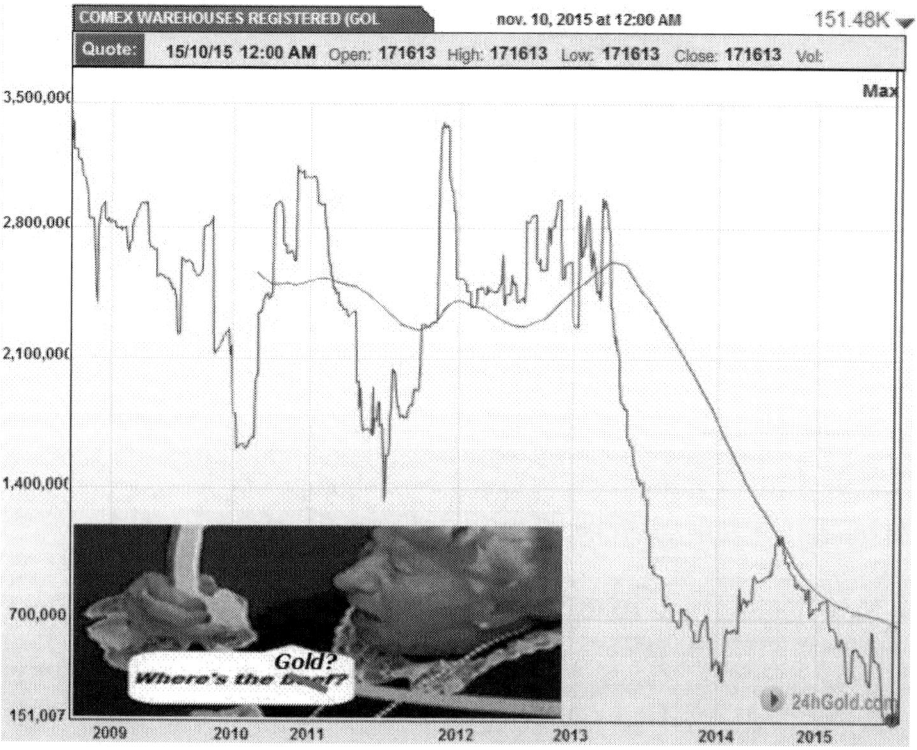

If some of these traders actually took delivery of the metal, it could spark a run on gold. In fact, much of the metal these past few years has been transferred over to the Shanghai exchange, where there are now more billionaires than in the U.S. Gold is popular with the Chinese and Indian, and this trend should continue.

---

registered-deliverable-gold-to.html

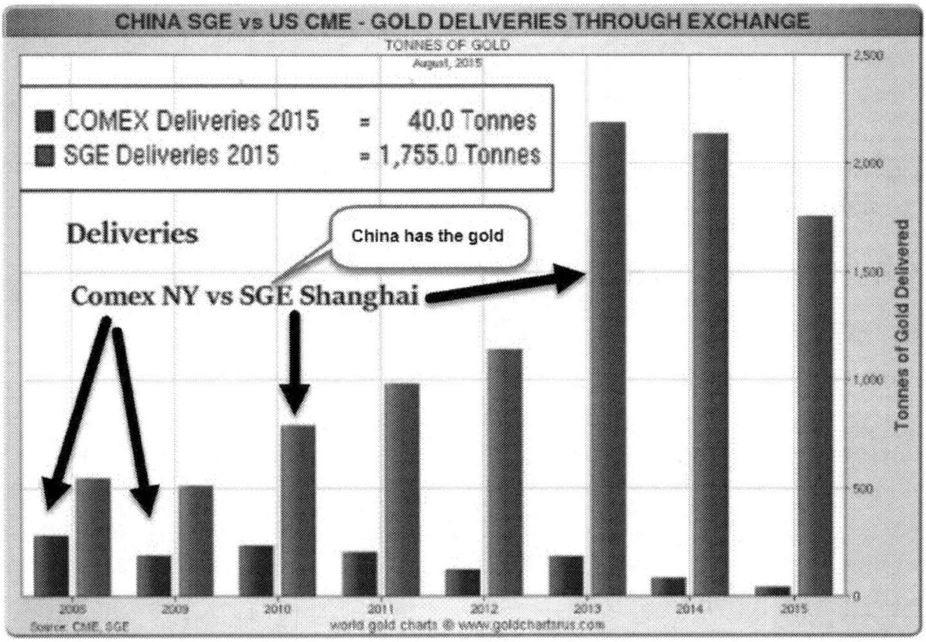

Something's Gotta Give

The Hunt brothers cornered the market in silver leading up to the 1980 high of $50 an ounce, when they accumulated 100 million ounces. Prices fell, and the brothers lost billions and had many lawsuits against them.[384] Of course Warren Buffett does it with more ounces of silver than the Hunt brothers years later… the price of silver rose 40%–50% rather quickly, but nothing came of it. But he did feel enough pressure make a point of mention his holdings in a letter to shareholders.

The point is that this type of hoarding by investors and COMEX traders can easily move markets higher. We've even seen mysterious large sell orders come out of Asia in the middle of the night, driving the price of the metals lower. Who in their right mind dumps a large order in an illiquid market in the middle of the night?

---

384 https://en.wikipedia.org/wiki/Silver_Thursday

I don't use the word "manipulation," and have shown how banks are involved big time in the gold and silver derivatives market, but this is the key for prices to move higher: The supply will dry up with the trillions of currencies floating around the world, losing purchasing power and looking to find a home in what little metal there is available.

What Is the Fair Value of Gold?

Because gold is a commodity, it doesn't pay interest. Some challenge the value of gold because it's difficult to determine, yet they ignore its history as money and ignore that it's difficult to determine the value of *any* commodity, yet the market does so every day. The real issue here is not the commodity, but what the commodity is priced in: dollars, yen, euros, etc. The commodity doesn't change. Gold will be priced higher or lower based on supply, demand, government policy, government debt, deflation, inflation, wars, interest rates, etc. One way to value gold, then, is to price other assets in gold and see where they stand historically with their mean.

If you price other things in gold, you see where that asset is versus its historical norm. But you also see that if prices of that asset were higher in the past, gold was also higher. Let's take a look at two of those assets priced in gold: oil[385] and the Dow[386]. With this analysis, you are comparing one asset versus the other as to which would be better to buy.

[385] http://pricedingold.com/crude-oil/
[386] http://pricedingold.com/dow-jones-industrials/

Oil Priced in Gold

DOW Priced in Gold (DJIA)

As you can see from the chart, the Dow is getting close to its resistance area priced in gold, leading us to speculate that gold may soon be the better-performing asset of the two until the chart reverses.

Gold and Silver Coins and Bars to Buy

There's only one type of gold and silver to buy: the lowest cost to spot.

For silver, it is the 1-ounce rounds and 1- and 10-ounce bars, and for IRA purchases, the 100-and 1,000-ounce bars. Silver American Eagles are the most popular, but not the lowest cost per ounce. Stay away from the 1.5 ounce Canadian coins like the polar bear. These are very high commissioned silver coins pushed on the public by greedy gold dealers.

For gold, it is 1-ounce bars and 10-ounce bars first, then higher premium Canadian Maple Leaf, and American Eagle coins (because these are the two most popular coins). I personally think it makes sense to pay as little as possible for your gold and silver.

What are the most popular coins in the U.S.? The American Eagle Silver and Gold coins, and are highly liquid, mostly because investors like the fact the U.S. Mint creates them. Ironically, if you went to the U.S. Mint to try and buy them though, the premiums are much higher.

Demand for Gold and Silver Coins

When supply becomes tight because of fast drops in prices, gold and silver do not act like a stock no one wants. They actually attract buyers and the premiums move higher. Every month the suppliers to gold dealers have to order from various mints to satisfy what they believe will be future demand. They pay the current price when they purchase from the mints. If the prices fall quickly, the suppliers are not going to take a loss, so they raise the premiums to dealers—who then have to charge more to investors.

Because of this high demand, suppliers have also run out of silver from time to time, and delay the delivery of the metals, sometimes for up to three months. The creators of the metal during these gold and silver rushes simply can't produce the product fast enough. Remember, this is at a time when prices are falling. Demand will be 10 times this in the future, when more and more discover that their purchasing power is being cut by owning a depreciating currency.

Gold and silver, over time, have held up quite well with their purchasing power. And as I said, there are times when currency is more valuable to possess, and times when gold and silver are better. But as time marches on, there is nothing our government is doing to solve their spending habits and reduce debt. It just gets worse and worse. It is this perception people have of the government that could eventually pour over onto the dollar (as it does with any other currency where the debt-to-GDP is out of control). When citizens start to lose faith in currency, gold and silver are what they turn to.

Gold in Your IRA/Roth IRA/401(k)/Transfer/Rollover

Many are not aware that they can buy physical gold and silver through a self-directed IRA or 401(k). This can be done through a transfer or rollover. The benefit of doing so allows an investor to withdraw metals from their IRA and take possession of them. Normal IRA withdrawal rules apply, with income taxes to be paid or a 10% penalty for any withdrawals before age 59 ½ (not recommended). Precious metals can also be bought for a Roth IRA.

There are only a handful of companies that handle self-directed plans, including The Entrust Group, New Direction IRA Inc. and GoldStar Trust Company. The process works like this: You choose which self-directed IRA company you wish to use. It's important to ask about fees before choosing. An application is completed along with a transfer/rollover form, which is sent to the company you choose. They will contact your current custodian and send the requested funds to the new company. Once the funds arrive, you will need to contact a gold dealer, who will provide you with the metals you wish to hold in your

IRA. Only certain metals qualify. Some gold dealers will push proof American Eagle coins or other high-commission products (that's how they make their money) and you should stay away from them and any gold dealer who tries to sell them to you. Your goal is to pay as close as possible to the spot price of gold or silver.

The trade for the metals you want is made, and the price is secured. The self-directed IRA company sends the funds to the gold dealer to pay for the trade. The gold dealer takes his commission and sends the funds to the supplier, who then ships the metals to a storage facility of the IRA holder's choice. This can be a company that specializes in holding IRA metals, like Delaware Depository. A company like Brinks, with a strong track record, will also do. Either way, you can have your metals sent to you at any point in time upon your request and taxes will have to be paid.

Companies are now setting up the purchase of physical metals for their employees as an option along with stocks and bonds in their 401(k). Check with your plan administrator how this works or contact your gold dealer. But also keep in mind that most plan administrators don't even know that you can own physical gold in your 401(k).

What really irks me, though, is the fact that most 401(k)s today don't give you the freedom to choose your own investments, as if you can't make a decision on your own. Typically a large investment company provides you with a limited number of options to invest in, usually mutual funds, and almost never an option for gold or gold mining stocks, let alone other assets you would love to be in if given the opportunity—like inverse ETFs or mutual funds to take advantage of falling markets.

Counterfeiting Gold and Silver

I was in the Philippines a few years back and saw some old silver U.S. coins while walking the Chinese district. They looked real, and for $1 each I decided to buy 10 of them. I brought them back to the U.S., handed them to a numismatist, and he said they looked authentic, too.

He held one in his hand, checking the weight, and without a scale could tell they were fake. The weight wasn't there, he said, and mentioned the Chinese were making a lot of fake coins.

It is very difficult for the average person to detect fake gold coins or bars. Sometimes lead is used as a heavy weight, and then covered with gold or silver plate with the appropriate design to look real. But tungsten is most often used, because its weight is similar to that of gold.

The following is from Regina R. Monaco, Ph.D. of Theoretical Chemistry at the University of Texas at Austin.

Density is the mass of the substance per volume (D = m/V).

The density of gold = 19.30 g·cm−3

The density of tungsten = 19.25 g·cm−3

(For reference: one troy ounce of gold = 31.1034768 grams, 1 cubic centimeter of pure gold weighs 19.32 grams.)

You can see these densities differ by only 0.05 grams per cubic centimeter, which is a very small amount. For a 10-oz bar (which is 283.5 grams and 16.131 cubic centimeters) - the weight would be light by only .08 grams, which cannot be reliably detected on an electronic scale sensitive to 1 or 2 decimal places.

Tungsten velocity of sound = 5174 meters/second

Gold velocity of sound = 3240 meters/second)

The excellent news, however, is that ultrasound testing can distinguish gold from tungsten because sounds travels through tungsten approximately 2 times faster than it does though gold.

A handheld ultrasound tester can be purchased on Amazon for between $100-$300 dollars but they mostly work on bars compared to coins because it's difficult to get a good coupling between the coin and the transducer.

For testing of coins there are acid test you can do but I recommend using a product called The Fisch, along with The Ringer, which you can find at https://www.thefisch.com/.

More on Hyperinflation

For hyperinflation to occur there has to be a loss of confidence in the currency. The U.S. is not the Weimar Republic after WWI (1921–1924). It is not Zimbabwe, which had no economy to speak of and 40% unemployment. These two cases of hyperinflation happened because no one would buy their debt. When no one buys your debt, you have to print money to pay for things, and the value of that printed money decreases as it multiplies.

The U.S. is the leader of the free world, and as long as our military is the strongest, its currency can survive. However, this currency will be stretched in the years to come, because our leaders can't do simple math. I always joke that there is a reason our kids' calculators don't allow numbers to be computed into the trillions. If they knew the truth about what we have done to their future, they would just give up hope.

My next book *We the Serfs!* goes into detail about what can be done to right this sinking ship our government is responsible for. We are still a young nation, and we have made several mistakes in our 240+ years of existence. But we must deal with our out-of-control spending, and my next book will have solutions that can keep us from sinking into the black hole of debt. In reality, if government would listen to what I have to say in that book, it would put my gold and silver company out of business. But I'll keep my day job for now, because the government takes 10 years to just balance a budget, and won't take the steps necessary quickly enough to allow our children and grandchildren the chance of a good life—like we have all enjoyed with the credit expansion since 1980.

I have covered in detail subject matter that I don't need to repeat here, because much of it overlaps with my first book, *Buy Gold and Silver Safely*. This includes things like supply and demand, storage, ratio analysis, and questions to ask gold dealers so you know you won't get ripped off.

Conclusion on Gold and Silver

If you look at the graphic of an up-to-date version of Exter's pyramid posted earlier, you see a good chance of the economy imploding should governments not be able to get a handle on their spending and continue to apply the wrong medicine: more spending, more quantitative easing or the like. The graphic shows that money flows from risky investments or "illusions of wealth" to the perceived wealth, first in Treasuries and dollars, and eventually into metals.

I do see a time when gold and the dollar can move up together, because I believe things will implode internationally first where the debt-to-GDP ratios are much worse than in the U.S., and money will flow to the U.S. as a perceived bastion of safety, a stable government and monetary system—and of course the world's largest military.

With this demand for safety, Treasury yields could possibly go negative as investors look for quality. Because world currencies would then be collapsing, it will drive the price of gold higher also, but in local currencies first.

What do you think the price of gold will do if there is such a small amount available and trillions from the currencies of the world are chasing it, trying to maintain their purchasing power as most every other asset falls in price? You must have some insurance with an allocation to physical gold in your portfolio, just as you have insurance on your car, home and health in case something goes wrong. Should the price of gold go higher, though, your insurance becomes more expensive.

Because I do sell gold and silver for a living, some may accuse me of pushing the precious metals as an investment. Anyone can read the last few years' worth of articles and Current Thoughts I have written five days a week, and grasp that I call it like I see it. You'll note that I have been negative on gold, calling it lower in price as the dollar moved higher from 2011 to 2015.

I set out with this company and my first book, *Buy Gold and Silver Safely*, to do two things: 1. Educate investors on what gold and silver to buy, so they make themselves rich instead of the broker, and 2. Offer the right type of metals, only at lower prices than anyone else. That first book answers more questions about gold than this section can possibly detail, and I will be updating it soon, but the message is the same today as it was then.

I do think I have made here a strong case for the future rise in the price of gold, and do feel it is important for a diversified portfolio. I write books to make investors aware. You can buy gold from whomever you want, and that's fine by me. Just insure yourself, please.

Chapter 31 - Real Estate

Real estate has always been a good investment for the long term, but like any investment, it has its cycles. However, it isn't the dream investment it once was. Shows about flipping houses has led to a new way of earning a living in America, but despite our government's goal of everyone owning a home, I don't view it as being the "American Dream" it once was.

A house is an expense, a depreciating asset, and the bank takes years of interest from you—which is about triple the original price of the home. The house and property have to be maintained and insured, and the sales commissions and fees to buy or possibly sell in the future—it all adds up. Your hope is that you get out of it, at some point, the appreciation in price of the land you own, or if you rent it out, more income than the expense involved in owning. A lot of that has to do with timing, which this chapter will address. I'm not addressing flippers—those people on TV shows who buy foreclosed homes at auctions, fix them up quickly, and dump them—in this section.

The Positives of Owning Real Estate

There are many reasons to own real estate, from the appreciation potential, income it can provide if you rent it out or have rooms you can rent, tax deductions for your mortgage, and even a lesser-known reason: the stepped-up basis you receive if it is owned by a living trust upon the first spouse's death, or upon the death of the final owner if you set up the estate properly (I could add an entire section on estate planning, inheritance planning and the like but my simple recommendation is speak to a board certified estate planning attorney as well as a tax attorney/CPA if you own a large amount of assets including IRAs).

You can even do well with real estate in this low-interest-rate environment if your mortgage payment is less than the rental income you receive. In this case, as long as you don't need to sell the property, you really don't have to worry about its value going lower. Your income versus expenses is what's important. Looking at the following chart from CNBC[387] shows how rents have shot up since the 2007-2009 financial crisis where many lost their homes and were forced to rent as banks tightened lending policies.

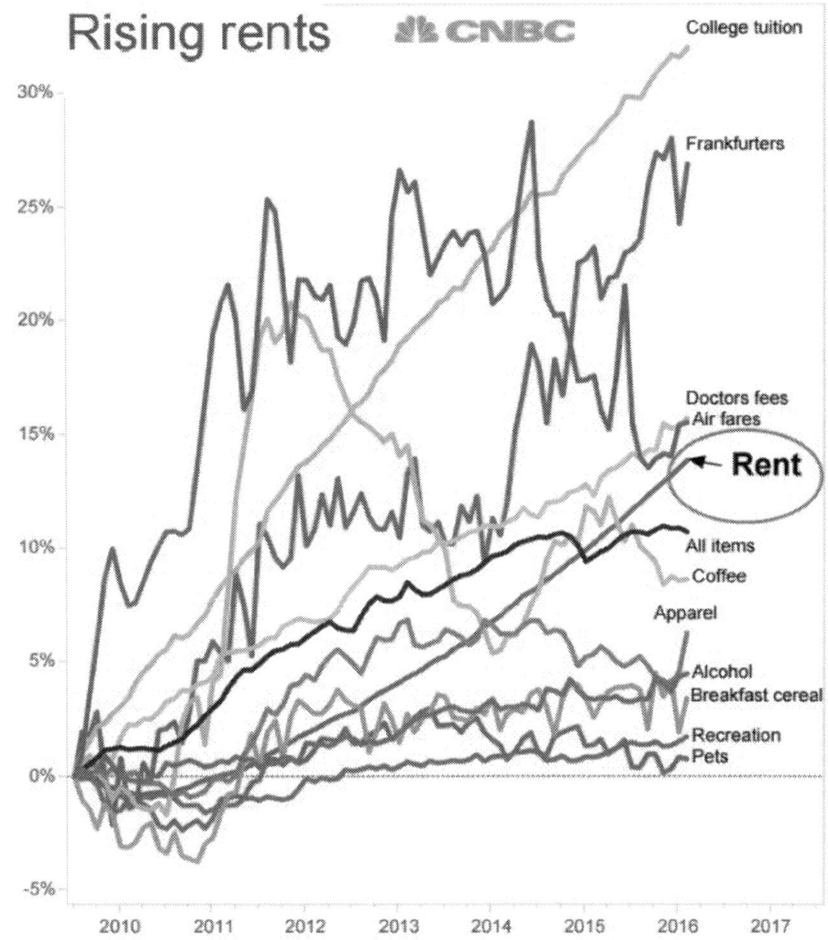

387 http://www.cnbc.com/2016/03/30/tired-of-rising-rent-maybe-you-should-consider-becoming-a-landlord.html

Here are some more positives for owning real estate:

- Can always rent out rooms to help with mortgage payment.
- Family members can move in if times get worse, and they could help pay the mortgage.
- Can have property with land to grow food (recommended to have some land for this).
- Can make home self-sustainable with solar, reclaimed water, and other improvements to save money that you can't do with a rental property.
- Don't have to worry about rent increases.

What Real Estate to Buy

Land and single-family homes are the worst investments to buy, as it is difficult to get any income from them. Buying in areas with a history of maintaining growth, or desirable retirement areas with moderate weather can keep prices buoyed despite an overall decline. Buy apartment complexes that are not too old (higher maintenance expenses) instead of shopping centers, as shopping centers will be the first to go as the economy declines. You can always raise rents as long as the demand is there, which it should be, as more are forced out of their homes again with the next economic downturn. Buy rental property in the right location near colleges, senior centers and where the cultural activity is good.

The Problems with Owning Real Estate

Below is a list of what can go against your real estate investment.

- Property taxes can always go higher.
- Variable rate loan costs move higher with rise in rates.
- Cost of insurance goes higher.
- Maintenance costs (heating, cooling, foundational, water damage and nature related (landscape maintained, snow removal).
- Association dues and potential future assessments.

- Illiquid. If you need to raise capital and can't qualify for a loan, and your home is the only place to obtain the capital, it may have to be sold at a discounted price to find a buyer who will take it on short notice.
- Even if you don't have to sell quickly, when the time comes, you still need a buyer at the price you want. The timing may or may not be in your favor, depending on the market in the future. If everyone is selling, you won't get the best price.
- Real estate commissions upon sale take from profit.
- Rates move higher, fewer will qualify to buy your home and prices will fall.
- Those who took out adjustable rate mortgages may not be able to afford higher payments, adding more inventory to the market and driving prices lower.
- Poor job growth in the future and lower wages means fewer people buy, and demand could fall.
- Real estate or land is never truly yours, as you can always lose it to the tax collector.
- Tighter mortgage rules make it more difficult to enter the market, thus hurting demand (but this is good for those who shouldn't be buying to begin with).
- Buying condos in new complexes at the top of the market can leave you holding the bag for upkeep should not all condos from the project get sold.

Benefits of Renting

No headaches of ownership listed above. If the rent is increased to where you can't afford it, you can always move somewhere more affordable. You can even move to another country to save money—and use some of the savings to fly in your loved ones for a visit. You may just find your quality of life improving a bit.

Housing Bubbles

When the Fed lowers interest rates, their intent is to get the markets moving with a trickle-down effect. A housing market that is appreciating creates the demand for more housing-related goods, and subsequently Home Depot, Lowe's, and other companies are benefiting, so the local economy improves. But if you interfere with the free market rate to manipulate the real estate market to increase demand, there is typically a whipsaw effect, and that's what we saw with the 2006 housing bubble. We saw the Fed keep rates low, stimulating the housing bubble, and then increasing rates killed the housing market (granted, there were other reasons, such as subprime lending and derivatives repackaging of these loans, which enhanced the crisis).

We had a nice bounce in real estate since the crisis, but it was fueled by quantitative easing and artificially lowered rates by the Fed, as they want to keep rates low to stimulate the economy. The fact of the matter, though, is that the economy did not grow, and the Fed can't even get 2% inflation out of it. Money velocity, as we learned in the Economic section, is going nowhere. The Fed has failed once again, but who gets hurt during the latter part of a bubble? It is those investors who think what CNBC says on TV is gospel; that all is well in the economy, and the Fed should raise rates. These investors believe this nonsense, trust in the Fed, and assume housing doesn't have a cycle where prices can move lower. They wrongly think rates will be low forever, and they can sell down the road and profit. Instead, the bubble bursts and we experience deja vu. The wealthy, meanwhile, have already locked in their profit and are moving on to the next asset they can buy low.

Watch for bubbles to burst first in Florida and Nevada should we see trouble ahead.

The American Dream?

Many may not feel like the home they bought is the American Dream as our government makes it out to be with all their programs to help people buy a home. Since the financial crisis, the homeownership rate hasn't even come close to where we once were. Do these charts look healthy to you?[388] [389]

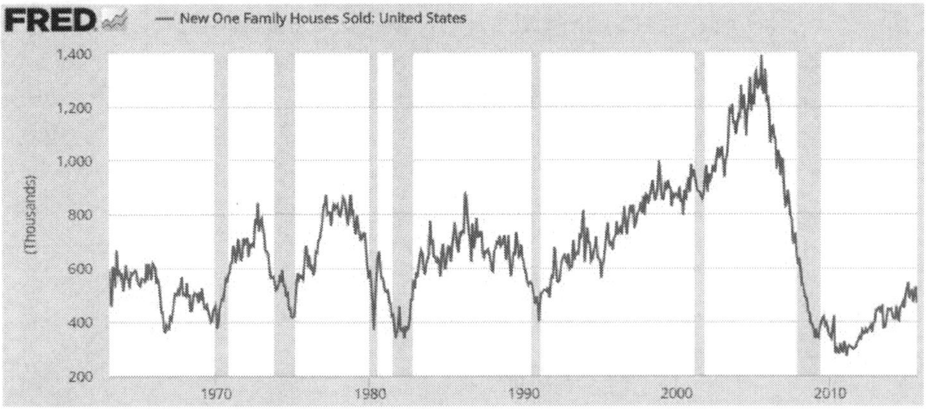

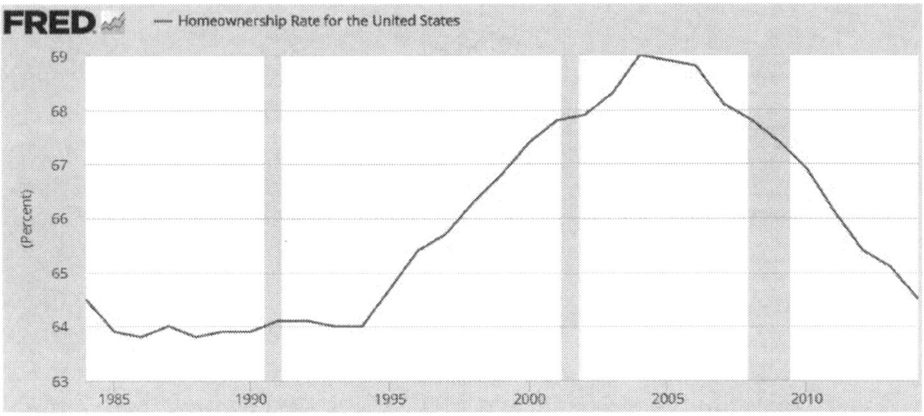

So that raises the question: When should you buy real estate?

---

388 https://research.stlouisfed.org/fred2/series/HSN1F
389 https://research.stlouisfed.org/fred2/series/USHOWN

When to Buy Real Estate?

The simple answer is to buy real estate when the market is dead and no one wants to buy. If you see the demand for electrical hookups increasing, that is a sign real estate is turning the corner higher. It's difficult to trust the data that comes from the real estate companies, so it pays to do your own digging and ask those in the trenches. You'll also never hear a realtor tell you, "This is not a good time to buy."

When to buy:

1. Buy during the recovery phase: This is when you don't see cranes around high rises or new construction going on.
2. Buy where there is a restricted supply: California only has so much space, but many people want to live there because of the weather. Age 65+ communities need housing care facilities, including hospice care.
3. Buy where there is plenty of water or access to water.
4. If buying an investment property, be sure it gives you a decent 6% to 10% cash return above your costs.
5. Ask a realtor friend how business is (I say "friend," because it's more likely they'll be honest with you).
6. Check the foreclosure listings for a trend. If the number is rising, the market is weak.[390]
7. One other consideration is will you ever be able to afford a home when rates move higher again. While there will be downward pressure on prices at first as the demand for homes will decrease because less can afford to pay the higher costs, we'll also have issues with falling wages and higher unemployment. But those who do manage to have larger down payments or somehow pay cash for their home might be able to bottom scrape some good buys.

---

[390] http://www.realtytrac.com/news/foreclosure-trends/midyear-2015-foreclosure-market-report/

When to Sell Real Estate?

When the market is booming and everyone wants to buy, sell. When there is oversupply and a strong amount of construction going on, sell. Also sell, when you begin to see median prices of homes fall (this would have to be after the big run-up).

2015 YTD	2014	2013	2012	2011	2010	2009	2008	2007	2006	2005
Sept.	INDEX LEVELS									
5.83%	4.35%	13.38%	6.94%	-4.07%	-2.40%	-3.08%	-18.61%	-9.03%	0.67%	15.52%
Threat of higher rates	BENCHMARK* INDEX LEVELS									
5.47%	4.17%	13.54%	6.03%	-4.14%	-1.34%	-2.42%	-19.23%	-9.77%	0.22%	15.93%

* The index benchmark is the S&P/Case-Shiller 10-City Composite Home Price Index

Of course you can also judge the real economy for what it is, and make that decision before the decline becomes apparent. Watch consumer debt levels to see if people are taking on too much debt. Watch mortgage application trends for drops—they fell recently by 3.2%. Watch for higher interest rates, which will put a damper on lending.[391]

Don't listen to the experts. Fed chairman Alan Greenspan said this in 2005:

> *Although we certainly cannot rule out home price declines, especially in some local markets, these declines, were they to occur, likely would not have substantial macroeconomic implications. In conclusion..., despite some of the risks that I have highlighted, the U.S. economy seems to be on a reasonably firm footing.*[392]

Farmland - Always a Need for Food and a Good Source of Income

There is only so much land available to grow food and raise livestock. Every acre of land can earn you income, whether you rent it out for

---

[391] http://www.cnbc.com/2015/11/25/mortgage-applications.html

[392] http://www.federalreserve.gov/boarddocs/Testimony/2005/200506092/default.htm

money or do the farming yourself. And for those of you who believe Armageddon is coming, and I know you're out there, you can always use it to "live off the land." I know my mother told me that she and my father would never sell the farmland we own, just in case we need to live off it someday. I do remember my mother's garden and how much food it provided, and you've never tasted such good sweet corn as my father would bring from the field for dinner. I still like eating raw green beans to this day, because it reminds me of the "good ol' days" on the farm.

But now decades have passed, and my parents are in their 80s. They taught us the meaning of cash rent, and while they have seen the value of their acreage increase over the years, they have also seen their income increase. Farmland is a good way to invest, as it gives you the potential of appreciation, but also an income that keeps pace with inflation. Whether you'd need to go live on the farm, grow your own food and raise livestock is unknown, but it's hard not to like this type of investment.

Reverse Mortgage

Reverse Mortgages may make sense for some individuals but one has to beware of the pitfalls and get family involved as they may lose out on inheritance. What's most important is the ability to have a nice quality of life of the home owner and sometimes though, that can trump any inheritance.

A Reverse Mortgage is for those homeowners who have no loans on the property or very small loans to receive an income for life as long as you stay in the home or until you can no longer meet the obligations of the mortgage. This type of program is primarily for those who cannot afford to pay bills from their current income and may want to get a boost in income without doing anything but tapping some of the home equity they have accumulated over the years.

The amount of income will be based on the person or person's age, current interest rate and value of the property. There is a maximum that can be paid so there may be better options if your home is worth more than $625,000.

One must read over the questions answered on the US Department of Housing and Urban Development website as well as a requirement for counseling from a HUD-approved agency before proceeding with a Reverse Mortgage.[393] There are also different payment plans based on whether you go with an adjustable rate mortgage or a fixed rate mortgage. With a low interest rate environment your costs will go up with an adjustable rate mortgage and these costs will eat away at what is paid you at exactly the wrong time, when items become more expensive.

The fixed rate option has the problem of giving you a lump sum where you may spend the money too quickly and not offering a monthly income option. One could receive a monthly annuity described in the next section and be able to receive that income, possibly for the rest of their life. Or, they could go it alone and invest according to what they have learned in this book.

There are good alternative to Reverse Mortgages through some good charities that will provide many more tax advantages and income choices, but there are downsides to these as well. You can contact your favorite charity directly or learn more about what options you have through an advisor who specializes in this area through the Planned Giving Design Center which has the world's largest community of planned giving professionals.[394] I at one time was a Certified Specialist in Planned Giving (CSPG) and it would take an entire book to give you all the various options available for charitable planning.[395]

---

[393] http://portal.hud.gov/hudportal/HUD?src=/program_offices/housing/sfh/hecm/rmtopten

[394] http://www.pgdc.com/

[395] http://www.plannedgivingedu.com/subs/certified.shtml

Chapter 32 - Life Insurance and Annuities

I happen to understand the life insurance business quite well, as I was a part of it for more than a decade and have kept tabs on it since. The industry itself is all about commissions, as that is how their agents get paid.

I remember decades ago, most of us were taught to sell cash-value life insurance and an upstart company called A.L. Williams came along with a multi-level marketing approach whose mantra was "buy term and invest the difference." It cut at the heart of the insurance industry, as investors got out of their cash-value policies and bought the cheaper term products. But the A.L. Williams agent took the saved money and sold them the lousiest mutual funds on Earth at the maximum commission allowed (8%), and their philosophy was short-lived. A.L. Williams eventually became Primerica, and has done a pretty good job since originally shocking the industry.

I personally believe in the "buy term and invest the difference" philosophy but there is one aspect to using these new hybrid insurance policies, such as variable life, that allows you many different investment options within your policy if you fund it at the maximum under Section 7702 of the Internal Revenue Code. In other words, you put as much money as possible into the life insurance policy without it becoming a taxable event. At some point in the future, you can withdraw the funds tax free to pay for children's education, take a trip, buy a car, or put a down payment on an investment property. In a sense, you become your own bank, and don't have to sell investments and pay taxes on the capital gain. There is a small loan fee, but the loan can be paid off at your leisure.

Eventually this same policy can be used to supplement your retirement through a series of loans calculated to last your lifetime—and you never have to pay it back, as it is paid off as a reduction of the death benefit upon your passing. The only caveat is you can't let these policies lapse by taking out too big a loan before you die because taxes will have to be paid on any gain over your cost basis. These are insurance policies, so if you do pass away before mortality tables say you should, your heirs receive a death benefit free of income tax. This type of policy would be included in your estate for estate tax purposes.[396]

On what other investment can you get market returns and use the money tax free? The cost of insurance does grow every year, but the benefits far outweigh the future insurance costs (basically term costs). Worst-case scenario, you pay some taxes on the policy if it lapses. Accept those risks, and a maximum-funded life insurance policy that gives you many investment options makes sense if you're looking for some tax advantages throughout your life.

The downside is that you may be limited in investment options. For example, switching to an inverse fund if the market is falling may not be an option, but there are fixed-return options available. Not all policies are the same, so look at several and their fees before diving in. Insurance agents make a hefty commission on this for a reason, but this is calculated into the plan.

One thing insurance companies have on their side that most other businesses don't is that they can always raise rates, costs or fees if things don't go their way. Try to stick with a company that has a history of sound financial progress and low fees.

If you are buying a cash-value policy and not maximum funding it, then I don't think it is a good buy. Stick with the low-cost term insurance and get rid of the policy when the need for insurance is no longer there.

Annuities

Insurance agents are also known to push annuities on their clients. I say "push" because these products are sold to, not bought by, consumers. Investors don't rush out and tell their financial advisor, "I want to buy an annuity." They are sold by mostly insurance agents, but

---

[396] https://www.law.cornell.edu/uscode/text/26/7702

also financial advisors. Many who sell them will "push" the higher-commission products with longer penalty fees associated with them. You may not see the commission come off your first-year and subsequent-year illustration the agent shows you, but it's there. Assume that whatever the first-year cost of cashing in the policy, your agent is making 50% to 100% of that dollar figure—sometimes amounting to an 8% to 15% commission or more. The way to figure this out is to ask your agent if you bought this annuity today and sold it tomorrow, how much would you get for it? Your agent won't like answering that question.

Annuities, whether fixed or variable, are ways for you to have your after-tax money grow tax deferred in an account that pays you a flat rate (fixed) each year or a variable rate based on the investments you choose, similar to the variable life insurance policy described above. The fixed annuity may or may not have an inflation protection aspect, but if it is an option, take it.

Fixed annuities were a good product to own in years past because they had a high minimum guarantee of 3% to 4%, and those who bought those policies are very happy with them today, as interest rates are lower than that. Fixed annuities also were unaffected by the recent financial crisis, and that was a benefit of ownership. However, as interest rates rise, those who have a fixed annuity will find that their rate may not keep up with the market, and they could have what's called a Market Value Adjustment (MVA) that can hurt their return if ever cashed in.

With a MVA for an annuity, if you surrender your policy or take out more than 10%, there may be an adjustment—higher or lower, depending on what interest rates are doing. It works similar to owning a bond and selling it. If interest rates have fallen since you bought the annuity—which is the case with most annuities as of 2016, if you bought in the last 10 years—and you have an MVA policy, you may want to convert it now to a non-MVA annuity via a 1035 tax-free exchange so as to not pay any income taxes on it. You'll receive a bonus that you may not know is there waiting for you.

But if you hold on to your MVA annuity and eventually surrender it or take out more than 10%, the annuity holder may owe the insurance company money, which will be subtracted from the surrender value.

It is for this reason I am not a fan of any MVA annuity now, as I think we will be moving higher in rates soon enough, and I'm not even a fan of fixed annuities because I don't think they will keep pace with interest rates moving higher. Just like with TIPS described earlier, fixed annuities that have an inflation adjustment incorporated into them probably won't keep pace with the real inflation rate. Variable annuities may not give you all of the options you need to grow wealth but during a crash you can go to the fixed-rate option to ride the financial storm out. Then after the crash occurs, switch back to beaten-down stocks. I do like this flexibility.

The tax deferral benefit is good, but you'll eventually have to pay taxes yourself on withdrawals of that money as ordinary income taxes, at a possibly higher tax rate than today if our government can't get a handle on their finances. Your heirs would also have to pay taxes on any income received if you don't tap into the annuity in your lifetime and leave it to them.

Lastly, annuities are not good for IRAs because you want growth assets in your IRA, and your fees would be greater. The only benefit of purchasing an annuity with your IRA is the lifetime income you may want to take down the road. There are no benefits other than that, because the entire annuity is taxed at ordinary income rates.

Immediate Annuities

You'll see many commercials pop up on CNBC and other financial networks trying to get you to receive a lifetime income from your money: an income you cannot outlive. It sounds attractive, as it takes away the worry of how you will receive income in the future, but there are a few problems to be aware of.

Most immediate annuities will not keep pace with inflation. If the inflation rate goes higher and things cost more, your income will stay the same. You don't want this kind of investment today. Even those that have an inflation clause will probably not keep up with real inflation, like the fixed annuity we discussed earlier, but it's better than nothing. The other problem is if you die, your heirs receive nothing, unless you choose to take a lower payout and provide an income for a spouse for life or a specified time.

Another thing that makes it seem like immediate annuities are attractive is the income they pay you. It will be higher than any Treasury or bond you can get in the open market on a fixed basis. Why is this? Because the immediate annuity pays you back some of your principal, too. This is what makes them look so attractive. It is the combination of a low interest rate plus your principal, calculated on how long the insurance company says you will live based on mortality tables, that dictate how much you will receive.

One good thing about annuities is that if you are going to leave your children a lot of money and they are not good at handling it, leave them the stream of income only an annuity can provide upon your passing. It's an income they can't outlive, and it keeps them afloat. No matter how bad they are with finances, a check will always come every month. It's better than them squandering it, which unfortunately many do.

You only have to look at the multi-million-dollar lottery winners and many professional athletes to understand how bad many of us are at managing large sums of money. I personally believe the first thing every professional athlete should do with some of their windfall is buy an annuity that will pay them an income for life. A 20-year-old will receive a payment of $53,303 a year for 57 years, their life expectancy. I bet many former athletes today wish they would have done that.[397]

Insurance Company Ratings

If you are going to be paying money into a life insurance policy for many years, or taking out an annuity where you want the money to be there when you need it now or in the future, you want to make sure the company you are doing business with is financially sound.

There are several agencies that rate insurers in various categories. A.M. Best is the most popular rater of insurers, but you can also get ratings analysis from Fitch, Moody's, Standard & Poor's and Weiss Ratings. Stick with the highest-rated companies with a sound balance sheet.[398] But take it one step further and see what their portfolio of investments consists of. Also, are they life only, or are they subject to high claims by covering areas that are subject to natural disasters like hurricanes—that if large enough, can do significant damage to an insurance company's balance sheet. Look at their bond portfolio average weighting. Those with shorter bond maturities should be able to keep pace with upcoming higher rates. Those with longer-term maturities may be playing catch-up, and take more risk to maintain their profitability and pay their policyholders. Of course they can always just pay the policyholder a lower payout. Insurers make all the rules.

Conclusion for Investing

Many advisors and the industry in general tell you to invest according to your years away from retirement, and that once in retirement, to get more conservative. They say to "buy and hold" through any downturns and tomorrow will take care of itself. I believe you can do better.

If you are at or near retirement today, and got more conservative investing in bond funds, I can tell you flat out that as interest rates rise,

---

[397] https://www.dinkytown.net/java/ImmediateAnnuity.html
[398] http://www.insurance.wa.gov/find-companies-and-agents/financial-rating-services/

your bond fund will lose money, and that's not a conservative investment.

I can say with a higher degree of probability of success that a diversified portfolio moving forward that includes index funds (domestic and international), dividend-paying stocks, commodities, defense, healthcare and energy (government funded industries) related stocks, and an allocation to a well-managed basket of ETFs that can counter any stock market pullback, and a little gold insurance should provide you with the ability to maintain and grow your wealth in the years to come.

You simply need to take a little more "hands on" approach to your investing and follow the advice given in this book to take control of your wealth. Ask the right questions of your advisor and keep tabs on what our government is saying and what the economy is doing. Lastly, open up your statements each month rather than see an advisor once a year for a review. A lot can happen in a month, and if your portfolio is dropping in value, you need to take action to prevent further losses or adjust your portfolio to what is moving higher. There is always an asset class that is moving higher, so don't be afraid to lock in some of that profit when you see that your portfolio has a certain sector that has earned a much higher than normal return.

Stay involved with your investments, and profit is always within reach

PART 9 – RETIREMENT

Chapter 33 - Social Security

Many who have contributed to the Social Security system calculate what they have paid into it over the years, and compare what Social Security says they will receive to what they could have earned if they had done the investing themselves. But one thing is typically missing from this calculation. The employer also contributed to the pot an equal amount on their behalf. That amount is 6.2%, matching what you put in, or 12.4% total.[399] Wouldn't you have rather received that extra 12.4%, invested it yourself, and had control of your investments so you could leave that wealth to your heirs if you didn't spend it all?

Many reading this might say that Social Security is there for those who need it most—the people who live off this income as their only means of support. I understand this, and don't deny it is an issue—a very big issue too many. The government does, however take care of those who struggle with making ends meet with other programs, like the Supplemental Nutrition Assistance Program[400] (SNAP)—formerly called food stamps—and government-assisted housing via HUD's Public Housing Program. This includes programs for low-income, elderly, and rental assistance.[401] The entire budget for HUD in 2015 was $48.3 billion,[402] a drop in the bucket compared to the $581 billion spent on the military.[403] We know that many want to keep America safe, but there are many who struggle every day because of government fraud and abuse and our system is broken to say the least.

---

399 http://www.irs.gov/taxtopics/tc751.html

400 http://www.fns.usda.gov/snap/supplemental-nutrition-assistance-program-snap

401 http://portal.hud.gov/hudportal/HUD?src=/topics/rental_assistance/phprog

402 https://en.wikipedia.org/wiki/United_States_Department_of_Housing_and_Urban_Development

403 https://en.wikipedia.org/wiki/List_of_countries_by_military_expenditures

My point in bringing up taking control of your own investments, a central theme of this book, is that you can do a better job of investing than the government can. My next book, *We the Serfs!*, will go into detail on how to take care of those in need, but what we really have in our present Social Security system is a Ponzi scheme of the largest scale.

If you take from investors and rely on future investors to keep the income payments going, what happens when the funds aren't coming in fast enough to cover the income paid out? The question that needs to be answered for many is will there be funds available to keep paying recipients in the future? I don't say this as fear mongering, but just a matter of simple math, and some understanding of investments.

The problem with Social Security is that the Trust fund invests in such a manner that the return is just a little bit better than you would be getting from a CD at a bank. Since June 2010, just after the financial crisis, the fund has not returned more than 3% in any year.[404] The following were the fund's averages since that time. For comparison, I have included the return of the S&P 500.[405]

Year	Return for SS Trust Fund	S&P 500 Return
2010	2.76%	12.78%
2011	2.42%	0.00%
2012	1.46%	13.41%
2013	1.88%	29.60%
2014	2.27%	11.39%
2015	2.02%	-0.73%

404 http://www.ssa.gov/oact/progdata/newIssueRates.html
405 http://1stock1.com/1stock1_141.htm

Granted, this is a narrow period of time, but it doesn't matter. You can pick almost any period of 10 years and stock returns have beaten what the Social Security funds are earning. The problem is, and this should scare many of you, the Trust fund's investments, with their paltry return, has an average year-to-maturity of 7.5 years. My bet is that interest rates will rise in those 7 years and the fund naturally won't keep pace with inflation. Even if we had a few more years of low interest rates, as we see the effect of deflation take force before the inflation arrives, picking maturity dates at this point in time so far out is dangerous.

The government also borrows from the Trust fund from time to time, but no one knows what has been borrowed or what is owed. While this is supposed to be an untouchable "lockbox" asset, it isn't. When the government has a fiscal gap, they know where to get the money. As the old saying goes, "He, who has the gold, makes the rules," and Washington is the best at it.

Speaking of inflation, those who are living off Social Security know full well their cost of living increases aren't keeping pace with what grocery stores are charging. This is because of another illusion the government keeps changing on seniors, and that is the way they calculate the inflation increase to payments each year.[406] The government keeps changing the way this increase is calculated. They did so in 1983, 1987, 1988, and 1999.[407]

Could I Get Some Good News on Social Security, Please?

There may be some. In 2014, there were some proposed changes made to how the Trust fund can invest,[408] to possibly be phased in before 2019.[409] The first thought that comes to my mind: Congress finally

[406] http://www.nber.org/papers/w7759.pdf
[407] http://www.bls.gov/opub/btn/volume-2/owners-equivalent-rent-and-the-consumer-price-index-30-years-and-counting.htm
[408] http://ssa.gov/oact/solvency/provisions/index.html
[409] http://ssa.gov/oact/solvency/provisions/investequities.html

gets it! The second: Who will manage these funds, and how is the timing of investing these funds when we are at the highs of the stock market? Where was Congress in 2010?

What do you think will be the result of how well these funds will be managed, as you near the end of this book? If you are like me, you have doubts to their success. For reference see: Medicare, Medicaid, War on Drugs, Immigration, Fannie Mae and Freddie Mac, among others.

And finally, the government hasn't done you any favors the last few years. They have raised the age to qualify to start receiving Social Security benefits, and if you were a good investor over your working years, and have an income over a certain government-imposed threshold, then you get the privilege of having 85% of your Social Security benefits taxed.

The bottom line is that if you think you will receive your full benefits the rest of your life, think again. Just like with the defined benefit plans mentioned in the Retirement section, where retirees thought they would get a fixed payment the rest of their lives but received notices those benefits would be cut drastically, expect the same thing to happen with Social Security payments in the future. The money just won't be there. Perhaps some of it will be there, and perhaps they will raise the retirement age to 100 (I'm joking). Leaving your future in the government's hands is not one of the pillars America was founded upon. Social Security will always be there for you, but alas, what will the purchasing power of those benefits be?

As with all Ponzi schemes, the first out reap the benefits, and the last in discover that the promises made to them were just an illusion.

Chapter 34 - The Illusion of Retiring at 65

Many of us have been told that you work your entire life, save up enough money, and then retire at age 65. With a Social Security supplement and your company pension plan, your retirement will be "golden."

According to the Investment Company Institute, there are $18.2 trillion invested in mutual funds and exchange-traded funds. Of this amount, 58% is invested in defined contribution plans like 401(k)s and IRAs. The following graph, which includes defined benefit plans from employers (which we will discuss shortly), shows a nice upward trend in retirement funds for retirees.[410]

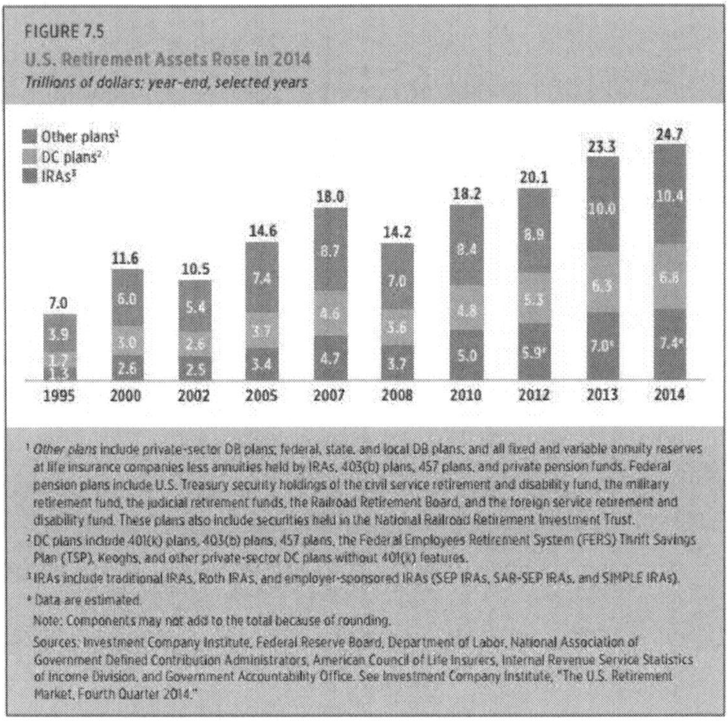

---

410 https://www.ici.org/pdf/2015_factbook.pdf

Is it still the case today, with 2016 opening with the worst start to a stock market ever? The S&P 500 returned a little less than 1% in 2015, and most Americans are probably wondering if they will make it to or through retirement. They may be wondering if their money will last as long as they thought it would.

A recent Nielsen survey showed that 69% of global respondents will achieve financial goals, but only 28% think current planning efforts will be sufficient.[411] Americans in particular believe in the fairytale that you work hard and invest your money, by the time retirement comes, they will be set for life. But there are a few things that have changed since the days when the man brought home the bacon and the women stayed home with the kids.

Spending Too Much and Saving Too Little

Part of the problem is that Americans are spending too much, and saving far too little.[412]

One thing everyone saving for retirement has to do is lose their "keep up with the Joneses" mentality. Your future retirement nest egg is more important than a new car to keep up with your neighbor—who is also probably a long way from retirement. Managing credit card debt is probably what most are dealing with, and they have to get that under control, too. The best thing to do is simply cut up the credit cards and only use your debit cards, and deal with your spending habits head on. No one else is going to provide for your retirement. It's up to you to work hard, earn an income, and invest wisely what you do manage to save.

One of the reasons for not saving enough is that people simply are not earning what they used to and for many; taxes are higher than they have been in the past. If you are just trying to make ends meet, how can you get ahead of the game and put money towards retirement?

---

[411] http://www.nielsen.com/us/en/press-room/2014/nielsen-survey-69-of-global-respondents-believe-they-will-achieve-financial-goals.html
[412] https://www.ici.org/pdf/2015_factbook.pdf

FIGURE 7.7

Many U.S. Households Have Tax-Advantaged Retirement Savings

Percentage of U.S. households, mid-2014

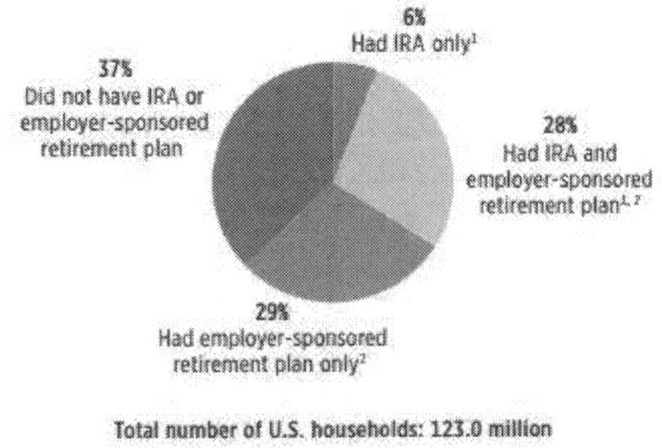

[1] IRAs include traditional IRAs, Roth IRAs, and employer-sponsored IRAs (SEP IRAs, SAR-SEP IRAs, and SIMPLE IRAs).

[2] Employer-sponsored retirement plans include DC and DB retirement plans.

Sources: Investment Company Institute and U.S. Census Bureau. See *ICI Research Perspective*, "The Role of IRAs in U.S. Households' Saving for Retirement, 2014."

Younger generations are living at their parent's home longer, as it is difficult to afford living on their own. This puts even more burden on the parents, who are trying to save for retirement—31% of those known as millennials who make up the 18-to-31 age bracket live with their parents.

Owning a home used to be the American dream, as we discussed, but today, that dream needs to shift to having enough money to retire. A home may or may not get you there, but a home doesn't produce income for you in retirement unless you rent some rooms out. A home is an expense, and if you have a mortgage that isn't paid off by the time you retire, it is an expense that takes away what should be your the golden years.

A recent Department of Labor and Statistics study on retirement states that U.S. workers retiring in the 2050s will have saved enough in their 401(k) accounts to replace an average of 22% of their pre-retirement income, and 37% have no savings at all.[413]

Retirement Plan Not Available Or Limited To 401(k) with High Fees and No Options To Counter Declining Market But Cash

One reason retirement is an Illusion for many is the ending of the defined benefit pension plans of the past, wherein the company you worked for promised you (and your spouse) an income that you can't outlive. This is what many retirees are living off today but Baby Boomers don't have this same options their parents had—37% of the elderly in the U.S. collect pensions, but only 10% of Baby Boomers do.[414]

Roughly 20 million boomers are already entering retirement with a net worth of $50,000 or less, according to the Employee Benefit Research Institute (EBRI). Social Security is all they have for income.[415]

When you add in the recession that killed the lifeblood of savings in stocks that Boomers had at that time, many simply have to delay retirement.

Boomers are forced to put money into a company's 401(k) plan and hope that the options they have are sufficient to meet their needs come retirement. Then, after retiring, hope that they manage their funds to where they can afford to withdraw the percentage of their working years' income they need to maintain a comfortable retirement. This didn't work so well in 2007–2009, when we saw many employees' 401(k)s lose a good percentage of their value. Who is to say this won't happen again? How are investors prepared?

Even those who invest in 401(k)s aren't aware of all the fees involved when they look at the monthly statement (if they look at all). Many investment houses have gotten rich off the 401(k) investor, and if your

---

413 https://www.census.gov/hhes/www/laborfor/Working-Beyond-Retirement-Age.pdf
414 http://finance.yahoo.com/news/baby-boomers--poorer-in-old-age-than-their-parents-162653066.html
415 https://www.ebri.org/

company is still only providing you with a choice of high-fee mutual funds, then employees need to demand change. Last year alone, Wall Street bagged $17 billion in fees that went to advisors.[416]

The investment choices for the 401(k)s employees have at work are also limited in options and typically have none of the inverse funds we discussed in Part 8 on Investing. How can an employee with limited funds grow his wealth in a down market? Why can't the employees demand alternative asset classes from their employers? The fact is, they can and should meet with the human resources department, speak with the plan administrator, and demand change.

What's worse is Boomers who are retiring today stay invested in 60% stocks and 40% bonds—what happens if stocks crash again, and interest rates rise, causing investors to lose their principal of their bond investments? Is just putting your money into the index funds really the way to manage your money if indeed we see future stock and bond market crashes? What insurance does your portfolio have against this potential scenario?

And finally, the government is proposing to reduce the tax incentives for employers to offer retirement plans to their employees, just as millions of Americans need to start saving more.[417]

Which Is Better, a 401(k) or a Roth IRA?

You should get a Roth IRA while you can, if you are in a high tax bracket… as they won't last. Roth IRAs allow you to put after-tax funds into an account that grows tax deferred, and you can take out your investment tax free. Taxes will be higher in the future with all of our debt and future obligations, so Roth IRAs are great investment

---

[416] https://action.aarp.org/site/Advocacy;jsessionid=F1E44E8318B 09DBC0E63 C314DC544834.app262b?cmd=display&page=UserAction &id=4935&autologin =true&CMP=EMC-SNG-ADV-CON-041815

[417] http://www.cnbc.com/2014/03/18/obamas-budget-bad-for-401(k)-savers.html

vehicles and you should max out your contributions each year. There are eligibility requirements, so check with your advisor or research more at www.rothira.com/what-is-a-Roth-IRA

If your company matches your 401(k) contributions, take advantage of it to the maximum they allow. If they match with their company stock, it depends on the faith you have in your company as to whether it makes sense to participate. The dot.com bust saw many a plan like this wipe out the wealth of employees when their companies' stock crashed.

The tax deductions you get from your 401(k) are great, as long as you can invest the money the way you want to and not be limited in your choices. I believe that many of you, if given more choices and control, can take your after-tax income, invest it, pay capital gains taxes when buying and selling, and come out much further ahead. To do so, you have to be pretty smart at investing. Hopefully this book has given you some ideas on how to take more control of your wealth.

Investing for retirement with unlimited choices may trump getting the tax deduction today, and letting the government control how your money is taxed later. They will clearly be looking for money somewhere in the future, and the best way for them to get it will be by taxing your retirement funds even more.

If you can control your retirement income by taking income from the Roth IRA in high tax years, and from taxable plans in low tax years, then it makes sense to have both. I don't put too much hope in low tax years moving forward, though. I like the fact though that with the Roth IRA, you get control of where to invest, including inverse funds, ETFs or physical gold, that most 401(k)s don't allow because of the giant financial industries that control the pension industry.

Chapter 35 - Problems for Those in Retirement

Those in Retirement Have Other Potential Issues as Well

What about those already in retirement and receiving pensions from their employers? Many of them have seen their benefits reduced and even pension cuts, like those in Detroit had. In 2013, defined benefit plans were cut in Detroit, giving retirees less than what they were promised at retirement.[418]

Many unions across the nation are now up in arms because Congress approved a plan to allow pension cuts. This is supposed to keep around 150 pension funds from running out of money.[419]

They are making these cuts naturally, to preserve the plans for both retirees and current workers. But after having the stock and bond markets provide phenomenal returns since 2009, the fact that so many pension plans are in trouble now is alarming. Being that in 2015 the stock market started to decline, and with 2016 being the worst start for the stock market ever, what good news can there be for pension plans moving forward?

Unfortunately it's worse than many retirees think. They work hard their entire lives, are living a comfortable retirement, and all of a sudden one day they receive a notice in the mail telling them they will be receiving a 30% or more reduction in payments each month. How outraged would they be? But we will see this more and more, especially during this next downturn in the markets.

In 2005, State Pensions funding gap was $260 billion. Over 1,100 companies needed some sort of assistance from the Pension Benefit Guaranty Association (PBGC).[420]

---

[418] http://money.cnn.com/2013/06/14/news/economy/detroit-debt-payments/
[419] http://money.cnn.com/2014/12/22/retirement/pension-cut/index.html

Back in 2005, the government agency had $39 billion in assets, and liabilities of $62 billion. We crashed in 2009 and have since recovered, but the projections of PBGC's insolvency are a 75% chance by 2023.[421] What if we get another crash before then? I'd say the odds are pretty darn good of that occurring. I'm not trying to make you fearful, but I am suggesting you have alternative plans in case things like this do happen.

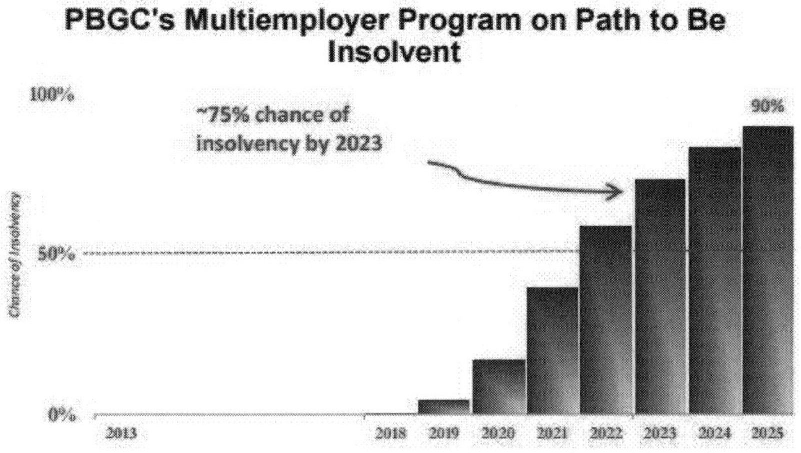

Another issue is how most public pensions record their book assets. Do they account for unfunded liabilities? How do you know? Unfunded liabilities are what is owed to retirees in the future. Most pension funds will record 6+ years of increasing unfunded liabilities. This is taxpayer money. Illinois, for example, only funds 43.4% of its pensions and has an unfunded liability of $82.9 billion, or 20.7% going unfunded for each person.[422] CNBC says that 85% of public pensions across the U.S. could fail in the next 30 years.[423] This, unfortunately,

---

[420] http://www.pbgc.gov/about/faq/pg/general-faqs-about-pbgc.html
[421] http://www.pbgc.gov/documents/Projections-report-2013.pdf
[422] http://www.americanthinker.com/articles/2015/04/which_states_have_the_most_underfunded_pensions_.html
[423] http://www.cnbc.com/2014/04/15/controversial-bridgewater-report-

fits well with the Illusion of Wealth concept, and why I implore you to take more control of your wealth today.

I am not trying to be an alarmist, but I can see how some may think otherwise. I am trying to bring awareness to the public how little control they have over their pension. For some, it may be wise to retire from their current job and roll over their pension to where they have control of it. If companies can allow someone to retire and then hire them back the next day, they would be doing their employees a service like no other, but don't expect employers to agree to this.

Solutions for Taking Control of Your Retirement

This book isn't written to explain all the various pension plans available. Meet with your financial advisor and ask how you can reduce current income taxes by contributing to these plans, and whether they fit your particular situation. I would have to write a 500-page book to include everything there is to know about retiring, including multiple tax strategies, estate planning, charitable planning, and much more, but many seniors wouldn't want to lift a book that size.

One important issue I will address: If you are still working or just retiring, you can roll over (once a year) or transfer (more than once a year) funds from your 401(k) or other retirement accounts from your employer upon retirement. There might even be options for you after age 59 ½ while still working, to move money out of the 401(k) (see your tax planner and plan administrator, especially if you are limited with your investments with your current plan).

Alternatives to Retirement – Living Comfortably Off What You Have Saved

Other solutions for your golden years are to keep working by doing something you enjoy—preferably your own business that gives you

---

says-most-pensions-could-fail.html

many write-offs against your income, and something that makes you happy. Then it's not really considered work and it may just keep your brain and body healthy.

Another idea I will explore in more detail in the *We the Serfs!* book is to simply pack up your things and move to Costa Rica, Ecuador, the Philippines, Europe, or anywhere you can live like a king/queen off your savings or Social Security, or whatever small amount of income you might be receiving. In my travels to some of these countries, some of the happiest people I've met have been expats from the U.S. They let it be known that they have extra income to enjoy what life offers, even though they would be falling short of that personal fulfillment if still in the States.

There are states you can move to that might not charge you state taxes, giving your retirement a boost. Some states may try to chase you down, however. All states will be hungry for your tax dollars.

Getting to Retirement

You must sacrifice some of the good times now and start saving early for retirement. Parents need to teach their children at a young age about investing and taking control of their future, because our school system has totally missed the boat on this subject. They need to discuss investing and get used to the language of investing. Get them involved in learning how to invest and give them books so they can become aware of how investing can be fun and lucrative. Start with this book! Grandparents, you can do the same thing, especially if you are doing any gifting to children and grandchildren. Get them involved with understanding investments, don't just give them money.

If you don't make this effort to help your children, who will? Most young people won't go out and buy a book on investing, or even have a clue about the economy. There is much missing from our "Common Core" education system, and at the top of that list is teaching our youth about money.

Conclusions for Illusions of Wealth

With this book, I have tried to incorporate three decades of information, from all the trial and error and discoveries. But this path has led me to bringing this awareness to you, the investor.

I started this book with a discussion of our monetary system, which included a history of money and how it has evolved over time, what it is, what backs it, and the illusion of what a dollar really is. We then introduced some alternative currencies, such as Bitcoin.

The next topic of interest was maybe the most difficult for most to follow: the different economic theories, such as the Keynesian and Austrian points of view. We moved on to understanding the economic data and the importance of GDP, as well as how government spending consisting of annual budget deficits along with future obligations, to what government has promised us in retirement over the years—the makings of the largest Ponzi scheme in history.

We went into a deeper discussion on how the U.S. and world are deflating, and how through an analysis of Exter's Pyramid you can see how money will flow from riskier assets to safer assets. We spoke about the different types of inflation being government driven or demand driven, government projections on inflation being non-realistic, and the potential of super-inflation if we don't curtail spending, as faith in the currency has to be maintained above all else.

No analysis can be complete without a history and scrutiny of the banks that led to the last financial crisis and the moral hazard they enjoy. This included a synopsis of the foreign banks, which are interconnected to U.S. banks.

We broke down the Federal Reserve from the beginning to today, how things have changed over time with the Fed's unconventional policy, and how the balance sheet of the Fed and other central banks of the world are becoming skewed.

Then, with the necessary foundation and understanding of our monetary, economic, banking and Federal Reserve systems we finally progressed to the main reason most bought this book: discussing ways to keep and grow your wealth.

The first part of this discussion centered on asking the right questions of those looking to manage your money, because the answers have to match your goals for protecting and growing your wealth, not theirs for making commissions. We discussed the performance of those who manage mutual funds and hedge funds, and asked whether you could do better investing your money yourself. We then critiqued some of those economic forecasters and financial advisors as to what they recommend and why, discovering that they all seem to be one sided with their analysis and don't change with the times. We also uncovered some of the hidden agendas some of these advisors may have.

We discussed philosophies of investing, ideas of what to look for when investing, and various thoughts on following the money flow of government to know what industries are subsidized where you can earn more profits. We discussed investment strategies, and analyzing companies yourself with various accounting ratios that tell you whether the company is worth investing in. We discussed how index funds can beat the pros and how you can make money in down markets with inverse funds and ETFs. We discussed the importance of gold in a portfolio and alternative asset classes that can perform well moving forward. We undertook a thorough analysis of real estate options, including when to buy and sell. We discussed the life insurance industry and annuities.

Lastly, we put it all together for those at or near retirement to know what to look out for with your pension plans. While much of the information seemed like doom and gloom, we provided advice for those who may not be able to retire when they want, while also presenting ideas to pursue other avenues that can allow you a better quality of life. This area will be expanded upon more in my forthcoming book, *We the Serfs!* which will also be out at some point after this one. Our entire political system needs to be overhauled or many of us will simply become serfs. I have worked 10 years on this book and I really do think it can make a difference for all of us in America moving forward. Whether you are from the left or the right, it does not matter to your investments, and I want to open this discussion to bring America together for the better, too.

For those who do want to continue to follow what I have to say, I offer many ways to do this:

1. I write my Current Thoughts on the precious metals market and the economy 5 days a week at http://buygoldandsilversafely.com/category/current-thoughts/
2. I write a nightly report 5 days a week on investing, which includes an analysis of 46 leveraged ETFs where our philosophy is simple: you can profit in up and down markets. http://illusionsofwealth.com/etfservice/
3. My company Buy Gold and Silver Safely offers precious metals like gold and silver coins and bars at the lowest cost in the nation, guaranteed.
4. Call us at 888-604-6534 or 619-500-8181 or go to the website, where you can sign up for the free Newsletter and purchase metals online: http://buygoldandsilversafely.com/gold-and-silver-prices/
5. You can sign up for the announcement of the release of my next book *We the Serfs!* at http://wetheserfs.com/book
6. An updated version of Buy Gold and Silver Safely will be out later this year. The current version is found on Amazon.com here: http://bit.ly/Buy-gold-and-silver-safely
7. For those who have enjoyed this Illusions of Wealth book, please consider a review on Amazon.com

Thank you for reading and I wish you investing success and more control of your wealth!

Index

C

G

H

J

M

N

O

P

T

Y

Z

[Created with **TExtract** / www.Texyz.com]

66569484R00245

Made in the USA
Middletown, DE
07 September 2019